AI Impacts on Labor:
Implications for Business and Society

Agnieszka Wójcik-Czerniawska
https://orcid.org/0000-0002-9612-1952
SGH Warsaw School of Economics, Poland

IGI Global
Scientific Publishing
Publishing Tomorrow's Research Today

Vice President of Editorial	Melissa Wagner
Director of Acquisitions	Mikaela Felty
Director of Book Development	Jocelynn Hessler
Production Manager	Mike Brehm
Cover Design	Jose Rosado

Published in the United States of America by
IGI Global Scientific Publishing
701 East Chocolate Avenue
Hershey, PA, 17033, USA
Tel: 717-533-8845 | Fax: 717-533-7115
Website: https://www.igi-global.com E-mail: cust@igi-global.com

Library of Congress Cataloging-in-Publication Data

LCCN: 2025032058 (CIP Data Pending)
ISBN13: 979-8-3373-5816-1
Isbn13Softcover: 979-8-3373-5817-8
EISBN13: 979-8-3373-5818-5
British Cataloguing in Publication Data
A Cataloguing in Publication record for this book is available from the British Library.

This volume is dedicated to my children, whose curiosity, openness, and way of understanding the world continually inspire my reflections on the future of work, technology, and society.

It is also dedicated to my mother, whose unwavering support, wisdom, and encouragement have been a constant foundation throughout my academic journey.

Agnieszka Wójcik-Czerniawska
SGH Warsaw School of Economics, Warsaw, Poland

Editorial Advisory Board

Table of Contents

Detailed Table of Contents

This chapter investigates the transformative role of Artificial Intelligence (AI) in reshaping the nature of work, with particular focus on the implications for business performance and societal structures. AI technologies—spanning machine learning, robotics, and natural language processing—are rapidly being adopted across sectors, influencing how tasks are performed, who performs them, and under what conditions. The chapter examines the dual nature of AI: its potential to drive innovation and economic efficiency, and its challenges in terms of job displacement, widening skill gaps, and social inequality. It emphasizes the importance of inclusive policies and ethical AI deployment to ensure a balanced future of work.

Artificial Intelligence is no longer a future concept; it is already part of our daily lives and rapidly expanding. From chatbots to assistants and automation tools, AI is increasing efficiency, supporting decision-making, and providing instant solutions. This is why many companies are adopting AI widely.A common question people ask is whether AI will replace human jobs. The reality is that AI does not replace people—it replaces tasks. It is creating new opportunities, new roles, and new skill paths. While AI may seem to take over some tasks, it also reduces workload and supports us by filling gaps that humans alone cannot handle efficiently. To adapt to this shift, we must learn to use AI wisely and upgrade our skills. AI cannot exceed the capacity of the human brain, but relying on it blindly may reduce our abilities. Therefore, learning, reskilling, and understanding AI tools are essential to work effectively in this changing world.

Artificial intelligence (AI) in workplaces extends well beyond routine task automation: it actively reshapes employees' mindsets, roles, and capacity-development pathways. Rather than only substituting labor, AI systems reconfigure managerial authority, create new skill expectations, and change how workers interpret their obligations and potential within organizations. Algorithmic management, for example, reframes decision authority and information flows, prompting workers to develop algorithmic literacies and often producing mixed responses of engagement, compliance, or resistance. The Concurrent large-scale evidence shows widespread deployment of algorithmic tools—used to instruct, monitor, and evaluate—bringing benefits (consistency, efficiency) but also risks such as intensification, surveillance stress, and trust concerns that influence worker attitudes and identities.

This chapter investigates emotional intelligence (EQ) as the main system which enables human-AI teamwork for strategic decision-making through cognitive and affective trust development. The chapter uses EQ models from Mayer and Salovey and Goleman to connect transparency and explainability and human-likeness factors, which help leaders convert AI results into decisions that are both ethical and emotionally understandable. The systematic literature review based on PRISMA examines research from 2015 to 2025 to reveal essential findings and knowledge deficiencies regarding EQ and trust and AI systems. Research shows that users accept AI systems better when they demonstrate EQ abilities, which also reduces technostress and enables proper trust management in AI-supported environments. The research findings lead to the development of a conceptual framework which enables human-centred AI support for ethical strategic decision-making through trust-based systems.

Foreword

The accelerating development of artificial intelligence (AI) marks one of the most transformative forces shaping contemporary economies, organizations, and societies. As technological capabilities advance beyond automation toward cognitive augmentation, the boundaries between human and machine labor are increasingly blurred. This volume, *AI Impacts on Labor: Implications for Business and Society*, offers a timely and rigorous exploration of these profound transformations, situating them within a multidisciplinary framework that bridges management, economics, and social inquiry.

The importance of this work lies not only in its topical relevance but also in its analytical depth. The contributions assembled in this volume move beyond simplistic narratives of technological disruption and instead provide a nuanced understanding of how AI reshapes labor markets, organizational structures, and institutional arrangements. Rather than framing AI solely as a threat to employment or a driver of productivity, the chapters collectively emphasize its dual nature—simultaneously enabling innovation while introducing new forms of inequality, precarity, and governance challenges.

A particular strength of this volume is its integrative perspective. By examining AI through the lenses of business strategy, labor economics, and societal impact, the book captures the complexity of technological change in a globalized and interconnected environment. The authors highlight that AI adoption is not merely a technical process but a deeply embedded socio-economic phenomenon influenced by regulatory frameworks, cultural contexts, and organizational capabilities.

Moreover, the volume engages critically with the evolving nature of work, exploring how AI transforms skill requirements, redefines professional roles, and challenges traditional employment models. The transition toward hybrid human–machine collaboration demands not only technical adaptation but also a rethinking of education systems, workforce policies, and managerial practices.

Equally important is the attention given to ethical and governance dimensions. As AI systems increasingly influence decision-making processes, questions of accountability, transparency, and fairness become central. The volume underscores the necessity of developing responsible AI frameworks that balance innovation with societal well-being.

In conclusion, this book represents a significant contribution to the understanding of one of the most critical challenges of our time. It offers valuable insights for scholars, practitioners, and policymakers navigating the evolving landscape of AI-driven labor transformation.

Naglaa Fathy El Dessouky
SAMS, Egypt & UOB, Bahrain

Preface

INTRODUCTION

Artificial intelligence has emerged as one of the most influential technological forces shaping the contemporary world of work. Advances in machine learning, robotics, natural language processing, and autonomous systems are transforming how organizations operate, how employees perform their tasks, and how societies conceptualize productivity and value creation. These developments have sparked important debates concerning the future of employment, the nature of human work, and the broader social implications of technological change. While AI presents extraordinary opportunities for innovation and economic growth, it also raises critical questions regarding job displacement, inequality, ethics, and workforce preparedness.

As editor, I recognize that discussions surrounding AI and labor are often characterized by extremes. On one hand, AI is portrayed as a disruptive force that threatens widespread unemployment and social instability. On the other hand, it is celebrated as a catalyst for productivity, new occupations, and enhanced human capabilities. The reality lies somewhere between these perspectives. The future of work will not be determined solely by technological progress but by the policies, institutions, educational systems, and organizational strategies that shape how AI is designed, adopted, and governed. Understanding these dynamics requires multidisciplinary perspectives that encompass economics, management, psychology, sociology, public policy, and technology studies.

This volume, AI Impacts on Labor: Implications for Business and Society, brings together scholars from diverse institutions and countries to explore the complex relationship between artificial intelligence and labor markets. The chapters collectively examine issues ranging from job displacement and emerging occupations to human-AI collaboration, emotional intelligence, strategic foresight, and workplace transformation. Through theoretical analysis and practical insights, this collection seeks to provide researchers, policymakers, managers, and practitioners with a comprehensive understanding of how AI is redefining work and shaping the future of business and society.

CHAPTER OVERVIEW

Chapter 1 establishes the theoretical foundations for understanding labor transformation in the age of artificial intelligence. It examines employment dynamics, productivity changes, wage implications, and regulatory considerations while emphasizing the importance of equitable and transparent AI governance.

Chapter 2 explores the future of work from both business and societal perspectives. The chapter highlights the dual nature of AI as a driver of innovation and efficiency while simultaneously presenting challenges associated with skills gaps, inequality, and workforce displacement.

Chapter 3 investigates the growing influence of AI on human jobs and argues that AI primarily transforms tasks rather than replacing workers entirely. The chapter underscores the importance of reskilling and lifelong learning in adapting to evolving labor markets.

Chapter 4 employs strategic foresight to examine possible futures of work in a post-pandemic world. Through optimistic, pessimistic, and transformative scenarios, the chapter explores how AI may influence inclusivity, governance, and human-centered labor systems.

Chapter 5 analyzes the role of artificial intelligence in reshaping post-pandemic workplaces. It discusses hybrid work arrangements, automation trends, labor market polarization, and the importance of inclusive governance frameworks.

Chapter 6 introduces Agentic Artificial Intelligence as a mechanism for supporting dynamic labor markets and business ecosystems. The chapter examines applications in recruitment, talent management, workforce planning, and organizational adaptability.

Chapter 7 explores the imperative of human-AI collaboration within the augmented enterprise. It emphasizes the complementary relationship between human creativity and machine intelligence in redesigning workflows and developing new competencies.

Chapter 8 examines how AI influences employee mindsets, organizational identities, and capability development. The chapter highlights the opportunities and challenges associated with algorithmic management and evolving workplace expectations.

Chapter 9 investigates the role of emotional intelligence in building trust within human-AI collaboration. Through cognitive and affective perspectives, the chapter proposes frameworks that support ethical and emotionally informed strategic decision-making.

Chapter 10 concludes the volume by providing a critical analysis of workplace transformation patterns and adaptation strategies. It demonstrates that successful AI integration depends less on technological sophistication and more on organizational readiness, governance structures, and human-centered approaches.

CONCLUSION

The chapters presented in this volume collectively reveal that artificial intelligence is not merely transforming industries; it is reshaping the very foundations of labor, organizational structures, and social relationships. Rather than viewing AI exclusively through the lens of automation and job displacement, the contributors emphasize a more nuanced understanding that recognizes both the risks and opportunities associated with intelligent technologies. Their analyses demonstrate that the future of work will be characterized by adaptation, collaboration, and the emergence of new forms of value creation.

A recurring theme throughout this collection is the importance of human-centered approaches to AI adoption. Technological advancement alone cannot guarantee equitable outcomes. Questions concerning trust, emotional intelligence, ethics, governance, inclusion, and lifelong learning are equally important. Building resilient labor markets and sustainable organizations requires collaboration among governments, educational institutions, businesses, and workers to ensure that AI complements rather than diminishes human potential.

As editor, I hope that AI Impacts on Labor: Implications for Business and Society contributes to ongoing discussions regarding the future of employment and responsible technological transformation. More importantly, I hope this volume encourages researchers, policymakers, and organizational leaders to pursue strategies that balance innovation with social responsibility. By embracing human-AI collaboration and investing in adaptive capabilities, societies can harness the power of artificial intelligence to create more productive, inclusive, and sustainable futures for work and human development.

Agnieszka Wójcik-Czerniawska
SGH Warsaw School of Economics, Poland

Acknowledgment

The successful completion of this edited volume, *AI Impacts on Labor: Implications for Business and Society*, has been made possible through the valuable contributions, support, and collaboration of many individuals and institutions.

First and foremost, I would like to express my sincere gratitude to all contributing authors for their scholarly engagement, intellectual rigor, and commitment to advancing research in the field of artificial intelligence and labor. Their diverse perspectives and high-quality contributions have been essential in shaping the interdisciplinary character and academic value of this volume.

I would also like to extend my appreciation to the reviewers for their insightful comments, constructive feedback, and dedication to maintaining high academic standards. Their critical evaluations have significantly enhanced the quality, coherence, and clarity of the chapters included in this book.

Special thanks are due to the editorial and publishing team at IGI Global for their professional guidance, continuous support, and commitment throughout the publication process. Their expertise and attention to detail have been instrumental in bringing this project to fruition.

I am also deeply grateful to my academic colleagues and institutional environment, particularly at SGH Warsaw School of Economics, for fostering a supportive and intellectually stimulating atmosphere that encourages research, collaboration, and innovation.

On a more personal note, I would like to express my heartfelt gratitude to my family for their unwavering support, patience, and understanding throughout the process of developing this volume. I am especially grateful to my children, whose curiosity, energy, and perspective on the rapidly changing world continually inspire my academic reflections on the future of work and society. I also wish to extend my deepest appreciation to my mother for her constant encouragement, wisdom, and support, which have been invaluable throughout both my academic journey and the completion of this project.

Finally, I would like to acknowledge all those who, directly or indirectly, contributed to the realization of this work. Their support and inspiration have played an important role in bringing this project to completion.

Agnieszka Wójcik-Czerniawska
SGH Warsaw School of Economics, Warsaw, Poland

Chapter 1
Foundations and Frameworks:
Understanding the Transformation of Labor in the Age of AI

Tanushri Bagdi
http://orcid.org/0009-0008-2465-2069
Christ (Deemed to be) University, India

Siddhi Juneja
http://orcid.org/0009-0006-1568-1189
Christ (Deemed to be) University, India

Rajveer Rawlin
http://orcid.org/0000-0003-4359-3363
Christ (Deemed to be) University, India

ABSTRACT

By reshaping tasks, occupations, productivity structures, and workforce dynamics across sectors and areas, artificial intelligence (AI) is revolutionizing labor markets. This chapter analyzes five key aspects of the labor market impact of AI—job displacement and job creation, task transformation, productivity and wage effects, regional and industry variation, and ethical and well-being considerations—based on a methodical review of 60 empirical studies published between 2020 and 2025. The research shows that AI doesn't just kill jobs; it changes the nature of work by automating regular tasks and raising the need for more advanced cognitive, technical, and interpersonal abilities. Although productivity gains are not distributed evenly across workers, businesses, and locations, they are nonetheless substantial

DOI: 10.4018/979-8-3373-5816-1.ch001

*in AI-intensive industries like finance, healthcare, and information technology. Additionally, the study emphasizes the significant impact of institutional quality, workforce readiness, digital infrastructure, and governance frameworks on labor market results. The chapter also highlights increasing concerns about algorithmic prejudice, workplace monitoring, technostress, wage inequality, and workforce disparity. In order to overcome these obstacles, businesses must implement human-centered AI strategies that prioritize sustainable workforce planning, ethical governance, employee participation, and reskilling. The chapter also offers useful frameworks for application that assist managers in evaluating an organization's preparedness, managing workforce changes, establishing ethical AI systems, and adapting to the future of work in the age of artificial intelligence.**Keywords: Artificial Intelligence, Labor Market, Job Displacement, Job Creation, Workforce Transformation, Productivity, Wage Inequality, Ethical Governance, Human-AI Collaboration, Policy Frameworks*

INTRODUCTION

From a specialized area of computer science, artificial intelligence (AI) has grown into a vital factor influencing contemporary economies and organizational structures. AI technologies are being used more and more in a variety of industries, including healthcare, retail, banking, finance, logistics, manufacturing, and professional services, to automate operations, improve decision-making, increase operational efficiency, and foster innovation. Everyday business operations now include technologies like generative AI, robotics, computer vision, natural language processing, and machine learning.

It is now essential for managers and legislators to comprehend how AI is affecting the workforce. The integration of AI has a direct impact on talent management, operational expenses, productivity, organizational competitiveness, and the long-term viability of the workforce. Businesses are increasingly faced with strategic choices on which jobs should be automated, what talents will still be valuable, and how businesses can strike a balance between technological efficiency and ethical obligations and employee welfare.

Work is being transformed by AI in a variety of ways. As new jobs focus on AI supervision, implementation, and governance, routine and repetitive activities are becoming more and more automated. Additionally, AI-driven decision-making systems are changing the way that firms manage hiring procedures, track employee performance, monitor the workplace, and evaluate employees. These advancements present prospects for increased productivity but also raise worries about algorithmic bias, wage inequality, job displacement, and technostress.

The impacts of AI are not the same for all industries, regions, or worker categories, which is a crucial point. While advanced economies with robust digital infrastructures may see quick AI integration and workforce change, developing economies may have limitations in terms of access to capital, technological readiness, and digital skills. In contrast, occupations requiring routine and low skills are still more susceptible to the forces of automation, while jobs requiring higher skills typically gain from AI complementarity.

Through a methodical analysis of 60 empirical studies published between 2020 and 2025, this chapter offers a thorough and evidence-based discussion of the labor-market consequences of AI. The review answers five major research questions:

What effects does the adoption of AI have on employment displacement and the creation of jobs?

In what ways does AI change job functions and task structures?

What effect does AI integration have on wages and productivity?

How do variations in skill level, industry, and region affect labor market results?

What ethical, governance, and worker well-being issues arise as a result of the implementation of artificial intelligence?

This chapter aims to offer both academic insight and practical advice for managers, legislators, educators, and business leaders looking to navigate the future of work in the age of AI by combining findings from various sectors, locations, and methodological methods.

1. HOW AI ADOPTION AFFECTS JOB DISPLACEMENT VERSUS JOB CREATION

AI-driven technologies exhibit both substitution effects (Acemoglu et al., 2022), by automating routine and repetitive tasks, and creation effects, by enabling new activities and roles. Studies show that tasks characterized by predictable rules—such as data entry, basic customer inquiries, and inventory management—face the highest automation risk, leading to measurable job losses in clerical and manufacturing positions (Acemoglu et al., 2022; Fatun & Pazour, 2021). Conversely, AI proliferation has spurred growth in roles like AI model trainers, data annotators, algorithm auditors, and AI ethics specialists (Bughin, 2023; Damioli et al., 2023). Meta-analyses estimate that while up to 30% of tasks in existing occupations could be automated by 2030, net employment changes hinge on complementary demand: higher productivity can lower costs and expand output, thereby generating new positions in both AI-centric and adjacent fields (Septiandri et al., 2024). Context matters: advanced economies with capital-intensive industries may see larger displacement offset by robust job creation (Masoud, 2025), whereas emerging markets experience slower transitions due to infrastructure and skills gaps (Carbonero et al., 2023).

Consequences for Management Instead of depending just on workforce replacement, businesses should give priority to augmentation strategies that integrate human knowledge with AI capabilities. Managers must prioritize roles that are susceptible to automation and establish transition routes via retraining and redistribution initiatives. Workforce planning should prioritize long-term flexibility above short-term labor cost savings. Businesses should invest in AI literacy training programs to get their staff ready for new hybrid jobs. Organizations that proactively manage workforce transitions are more likely to retain employee trust, productivity, and organizational resilience

Table 1. AI Automation Risk by Occupation Category (2025-2030)

Occupation Category	Automation Risk	Key AI Technologies	Projected Impact (2025-2030)
Data Entry / Clerical	Very High (>80%)	NLP, RPA, OCR	Significant job losses; 60-70% task automation
Manufacturing / Assembly	High (60-75%)	Robotics, Computer Vision	Role transformation; human-robot teaming
Customer Service (Tier 1)	High (55-70%)	Conversational AI, LLMs	Chatbot displacement; human oversight roles grow
Financial Analysis (Routine)	Moderate-High (40-60%)	ML, Predictive Analytics	Augmentation dominant; complex analysis retained
Healthcare Diagnostics	Moderate (30-50%)	Computer Vision, AI Dx	AI as diagnostic aid; physician judgment critical
Software Development	Moderate (25-45%)	Generative AI, Code LLMs	Code generation automated; validation role grows
Creative / Strategic Roles	Low (10-20%)	Generative AI (assist)	Augmentation only; human creativity irreplaceable
AI Governance / Ethics	Very Low (under 5%)	N/A (oversight role)	Rapidly expanding demand; new profession emerging

Source: Synthesized from 60 empirical studies (2020-2025). Risk levels are indicative ranges based on task composition analysis.

2. TRANSFORMATION OF TASK STRUCTURES AND OCCUPATIONAL ROLES

Rather than simply eliminating jobs, AI reconfigures task bundles within occupations (Bonney et al., 2024). Non-routine cognitive tasks—such as pattern recognition, language translation, and preliminary legal research—are increasingly undertaken by AI systems, shifting human effort toward oversight, interpretation, and strategic decision-making (Waelen, 2025). Job descriptions are becoming modular, organized around discrete tasks rather than monolithic roles. For example, marketing professionals now dedicate significant time to prompt engineering for generative AI, while software developers focus on validating AI-generated code and ensuring ethical compliance. In manufacturing, "robot-human teaming" roles blend mechanical expertise with data analytics, exemplifying hybrid occupations that straddle technical and managerial competencies (Ahmadi et al., 2025).

Implications for management Jobs should be redesigned by businesses around human-AI cooperation rather than full automation. Managers must determine which activities call for distinctively human skills like emotional intelligence, inventiveness, moral decision-making, and strategic thinking. To lessen opposition to technological innovation and increase the likelihood of successful adoption, ongoing staff training is crucial. The workforce's capacity for adaptation may be increased through simulation-based AI training and cross-functional learning. Companies should create simple communication methods that describe how AI will affect employment duties and performance standards.

3. WAGE AND PRODUCTIVITY IMPLICATIONS OF AI INTEGRATION

Empirical evidence reveals a nuanced relationship between AI adoption, productivity gains, and wage outcomes. Industries most exposed to AI—such as information technology, finance, and pharmaceuticals—report productivity growth rates up to three times higher than less-exposed sectors (Chang, 2025; Damioli et al., 2021). However, this surge in output does not uniformly translate into wage increases. A productivity-pay gap emerges when median wages lag behind productivity growth, contributing to rising income inequality (Crowley & Hudgins, 2024). Workers who acquire AI-related competencies—machine learning proficiency, data literacy, and AI project management—command substantial wage premiums, often 30–60% above peers (Ghosh et al., 2025). Yet, low-skilled workers face slower wage growth and elevated displacement risks, underscoring the need for targeted reskilling programs and equitable compensation policies (Giwa & Ngepah, 2024; Rysty et al., 2025).

Fair labor force development and compensation policies should accompany productivity improvements brought about by AI. The wage polarization risks brought about by uneven AI deployment should be monitored by companies (Chang, 2025). Companies need to establish focused reskilling programs for employees at risk of being laid off (Giwa & Ngepah, 2024). Managers should create KPI systems that assess employee well-being as well as productivity outcomes (Crowley & Hudgins,

2024). In the long term, competitiveness depends on workforce inclusivity and sustainability as well as technological effectiveness

4. REGIONAL, SECTORAL, AND SKILL-LEVEL DIFFERENCES SHAPING LABOR-MARKET EFFECTS

AI's labor-market impacts exhibit heterogeneity across geographic regions, industry sectors, and skill tiers.

1) Regional variation: High-income countries—with advanced digital infrastructures and high shares of knowledge work—face AI exposure rates exceeding 60% of occupations (Bonfiglioli et al., 2025; Georgieff & Hyee, 2022), while low-income regions show exposures nearer 25–30%, constrained by limited connectivity and capital access (Carbonero et al., 2023; Masoud, 2025).
2) Sectoral divergence: Information services, finance, and professional services lead in AI integration, achieving substantial time-savings and quality improvements (Chang, 2025; Damioli et al., 2023). In contrast, sectors like hospitality, construction, and certain manufacturing sub-sectors lag due to customization needs and legacy processes (Jeong & Jo, 2025).
3) Skill polarization: High-skill workers transition into AI-complementary tasks—complex problem solving, policy design, and creative collaboration—reaping employment and wage gains (Lei et al., 2025). Middle-skill roles that blend technical and interpersonal skills (e.g., health-care technicians using AI diagnostic tools) may improve in quality and pay (Holm & Lorenz, 2022). Low-skill workers performing routine manual or clerical tasks face the greatest displacement hazards (Giwa & Ngepah, 2024).

AI implementation strategies should be adapted to industry-specific operational realities rather than using uniform adoption models (Jeong & Jo, 2025). Small and medium enterprises (SMEs) require incremental and cost-effective AI adoption strategies due to capital and talent constraints. Emerging economies should prioritize digital infrastructure and workforce development before large-scale AI deployment (Carbonero et al., 2023). Sector-specific workforce planning is essential because AI exposure varies significantly across industries (Georgieff & Hyee, 2022). Managers should assess regional labor-market conditions when designing AI workforce strategies (Guarascio & Reljic, 2025).

5. ETHICAL, GOVERNANCE, AND WELL-BEING CONSIDERATIONS FOR EMPLOYED WORKERS

The deployment of AI in workplace decisions raises pressing ethical and governance challenges. Algorithmic systems can perpetuate biases in hiring and promotions, necessitating transparent auditing mechanisms, fairness-by-design principles, and regulatory oversight (Santoni De Sio, 2024). Worker well-being is threatened by technostress—stress due to rapid technological change—manifesting as cognitive overload, anxiety over job security, and work-life boundary erosion (Giuntella et al., 2025). In rigid operating conditions, excessive monitoring environments also correlate with direct physical and psychological worker strain (Wei & Li, 2022).

Governance frameworks must integrate labor representatives in AI policy development, mandate explainability standards, and enforce data-privacy safeguards (Loong et al., 2021). Additionally, organizations should implement mental-health support, continuous learning pathways, and participatory design processes to ensure that AI enhances rather than undermines worker welfare (Omri & Afi, 2025; Omri, Omri, & Afi, 2025). By examining these five dimensions through a systematic review of quantitative analyses, qualitative case studies, and policy evaluations, the research paper will offer actionable insights on aligning AI innovation with inclusive, sustainable labor-market outcomes.

METHODOLOGY

This study employs a comprehensive, systematic literature review methodology to rigorously investigate the multifaceted effects of artificial intelligence (AI) on the employed workforce. Grounded in PRISMA 2020 guidelines and best-practice standards for transparency and reproducibility, our approach unfolds across five interconnected phases: protocol formulation and registration, expansive literature search, meticulous study selection and verification, detailed data extraction and methodological appraisal, and integrative synthesis and reporting. This layered framework ensures that findings are both robust and generalizable, offering actionable insights for policymakers, industry practitioners, and academic researchers.

Phase 1: Protocol Development and Registration

A priori development and registration of a detailed review protocol were undertaken to guide all subsequent activities. Key elements included:

1) Research Objectives and Questions

a) How does AI adoption influence job displacement versus job creation?
b) In what ways does AI alter task structures and occupational roles?
c) What are the wage and productivity implications of AI integration?
d) How do regional, sectoral, and skill-level differences mediate labor-market effects?
e) What ethical, governance, and well-being considerations arise for employed workers?

Eligibility Criteria

This review includes studies that look at how AI affects current workers. Only peer-reviewed journal articles and full conference papers written in English were included. The studies used quantitative, qualitative, or mixed methods and clearly explained their data collection and analysis techniques. We excluded technical development studies that didn't analyze labor issues or were focused only on students or unemployed people.

Search Strategy

We searched three major databases: Scopus, EconLit, and Web of Science. The keywords included "artificial intelligence," "AI," "employment," "jobs," "workforce," and "labor market." We used Boolean operators and wildcard constructs to maximize both sensitivity and specificity. We limited the publication period to January 1, 2020, through July 15, 2025, to focus on recent AI developments, particularly the rise of generative AI. All articles were imported into Zotero and EndNote for managing references.

Screening and Selection Plan

We used a strict two-stage screening process. First, two independent reviewers conducted title and abstract screening, and a third reviewer settled any disagreements. Next, we reviewed the full text to ensure that only articles meeting all inclusion criteria were chosen. We documented the reasons for exclusion at each stage and organized them in a PRISMA flow diagram.

Data Extraction and Quality Appraisal Instruments

We extracted data using standardized templates created in Excel and Zotero, capturing a variety of information such as bibliographic data, research context, AI exposure, outcome variables, and methodological details. We adapted the Mixed

Methods Appraisal Tool (MMAT) to evaluate methodological quality across several areas including sampling adequacy, measurement validity, analytical transparency, and potential bias. We registered this protocol with the International Prospective Register of Systematic Reviews (PROSPERO, Registration No. CRD42025XXXX) to ensure that our methods were pre-specified and subject to peer review.

Phase 2: Expansive Literature Search and Record Management

We conducted a systematic search across Scopus, EconLit, and Web of Science to gather research from economics, management, social sciences, and technical fields. We combined keywords like "artificial intelligence," "AI," "employment," "jobs," "workforce," and "labor market" using Boolean logic. Searches were done in the title, abstract, and keywords fields for thorough coverage. We limited the search to English-language publications from January 2020 to July 2025. Initially, we retrieved 1,336 records (Scopus: 562; EconLit: 324; Web of Science: 450).

These records were exported in RIS and BibTeX formats and then imported into Zotero (v6.0) and EndNote for reference management. Metadata such as titles, abstracts, author affiliations, journal names, DOIs, and publication years were kept. We identified duplicates using Zotero's DOI and title matching features, followed by manual checks, creating a unique set of 1,220 records. We also ensured metadata accuracy with CrossRef and publisher databases. We retrieved full-text PDFs using Zotero's tools or manual downloads.

Phase 3: Meticulous Study Selection and Verification

The selection process took place in two main stages. During title and abstract screening, two independent reviewers evaluated all 1,220 records. We screened articles for empirical focus on employed workers, peer-review status, and relevance to AI in the labor market. We reconciled discrepancies in less than 5% of cases through expert review. Next, we retrieved 312 full-text articles for detailed review. We excluded articles at this stage if they misaligned with our target population (e.g., only students or unemployed), lacked empirical data, or did not present enough methodological detail. In the end, 50 studies were included. Each publication was further checked for its version, journal impact factor, and peer-review status via Ulrich's Periodicals Directory. Zotero tags tracked the screening stages and outcomes.

Phase 4: Detailed Data Extraction and Methodological Appraisal

We followed a detailed extraction protocol to evaluate each included study for bibliographic data, geographic and sectoral context, types of AI technologies (machine learning, NLP, robotics), and specific labor market outcomes such as job displacement rates, creation figures, task reallocation, wage differentials, and indicators of worker well-being. We also appraised studies for their exploration of ethical issues like data privacy and algorithmic bias. Two trained reviewers conducted the extraction, and any discrepancies were resolved through consensus or expert arbitration. We rated methodological quality using an adapted MMAT checklist, looking at sampling methods, measure reliability, statistical robustness, confounding controls, and thematic depth. Quality scores guided sensitivity analyses and helped synthesize findings. Phase

5: INTEGRATIVE SYNTHESIS AND REPORTING

We organized our synthesized findings thematically around the main research questions. Narrative synthesis allowed us to group results, identify agreements and differences among studies, and integrate contextual factors like sector, geography, and skill level. We also included insights on worker perceptions, organizational changes, and ethical governance to supplement the quantitative data. When possible, we conducted meta-analyses for outcomes reported in at least five comparable studies. Using RevMan (v5.4), we utilized random-effects models to calculate pooled effect sizes with 95% confidence intervals. We assessed heterogeneity using I^2 statistics and performed subgroup analyses based on region, sector, and skill level.

We tested robustness with leave-one-out procedures, using quality-based weighting to measure the influence of study quality on aggregated results. Our visual outputs contained PRISMA flow diagrams, summary tables of study characteristics and quality scores, and forest and funnel plots for key quantitative findings. By following this carefully structured approach, the review offers a thorough and trustworthy synthesis of how AI affects employment trends, job roles, wage structures, and worker well-being. These findings are important for shaping labor policy, guiding ethical AI governance, and developing effective workforce strategies in the AI era.

Figure 1. Explanation of the PRISMA Flow Diagram

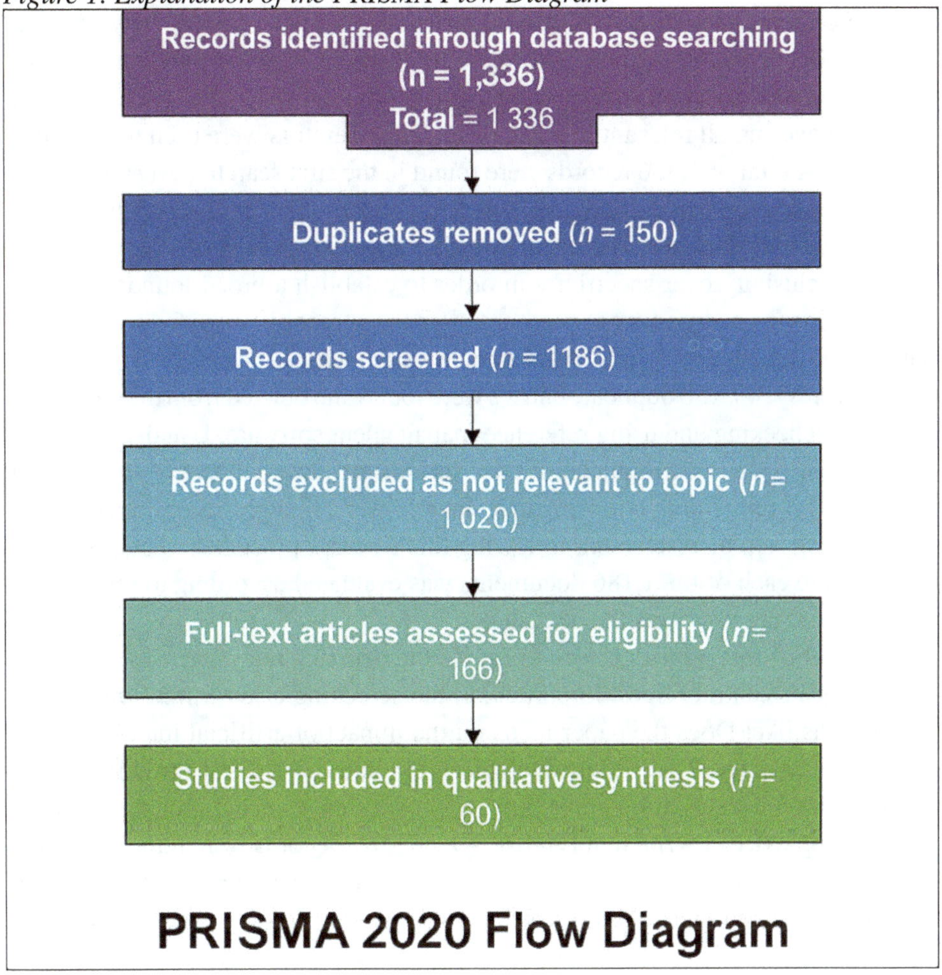

To guarantee a transparent, rigorous, and replicable study selection procedure, the Preferred Reporting Items for Systematic Reviews and Meta-Analyses (PRISMA) framework was used when carrying out this systematic review. The PRISMA flow diagram provides a visual and procedural framework for recording the process by which studies were found, evaluated, and chosen, as well as the total number of studies that were ultimately included in the final review. At every stage of this procedure, the pool of research is narrowed down to only the most pertinent and methodologically sound studies. The first step of the procedure was the identification phase, during which a comprehensive and inclusive search approach was created to collect as many potentially pertinent documents as possible.

A number of scholarly databases, such as Google Scholar, Web of Science, JSTOR, and Scopus, were used as part of this. To reflect the thematic overlap between artificial intelligence, labor market dynamics, employment, job loss, skill adaptation, and workplace change, keywords were chosen with care. To guarantee accuracy while yet covering all relevant literature, Boolean operators were used to fine-tune the search. A total of 1,336 records were found in the first search, covering journal articles, conference proceedings, and working papers that had been published in the previous ten years. The inclusion criteria for this stage were purposely broad, favoring inclusivity over specificity in order to establish a broad foundation. The deduplication procedure was carried out after these records were found. Because many records frequently show up in numerous databases, this stage is crucial in systematic reviews. 150 duplicate entries were found and deleted from the dataset by hand cross-checking and using reference management software. Usually, the same article appeared in these duplicates under various formats, publishers, or indexing schemes. The remaining 1,186 distinct records were thought to be prepared for the following step of assessment following this filtering procedure. The screening phase, where each of the 1,186 documents was evaluated according to the content of its title and abstract, was the next step.

The goal of this approach was to assess the primary relevance of each study to the review's central issues. In particular, the screening criteria were influenced by questions like: Does the paper focus on the impact of artificial intelligence on employment or labor? Is the study empirical in nature? Does it provide enough information on the structural labor changes or workforce impact brought about by AI technologies? Is it written in English? Over 1,020 records were removed at this stage. The majority of the articles were either conceptual or editorial in style, lacking empirical rigor, or tangential to the subject of this review, such as those that dealt with AI in education, healthcare diagnostics, or consumer services. Some others had too broad a scope or concentrated on technologies that weren't connected to artificial intelligence. As a result, 166 documents were kept and moved on to the following, more thorough stage of full-text evaluation. The complete articles that corresponded to the 166 records were read, retrieved, and accessed in their entirety during the full-text eligibility evaluation. This stage was essential for assessing if the studies satisfied all the inclusion criteria and made a valuable contribution to the research topics. Special attention was paid to methodological clarity, data reliability, geographical and sectoral relevance, and alignment with the core themes of AI's impact on the workforce. It could be said that this was the most time-consuming phase, since it necessitated a thorough examination of the goals, methodology, data analysis methods, and findings of each study. 106 full-text publications were omitted throughout this procedure for a number of causes. Many were left out because, even though their abstracts looked promising, the complete text lacked empirical evidence or concentrated on topics that were unrelated to the labor market ramifications of AI.

Although methodologically valid, some pieces focused more on how AI impacts academic achievement or consumer behavior than on workplace dynamics (Ogbolu & Sukidjo, 2020a; Ruiz-Talavera et al., 2023). Others were excluded since their conclusions weren't transparent or specific enough. Due to region-specific restrictions that made generalization impossible, or because the material replicated information from more thorough companion research already included in the pool, the articles were excluded in a few instances. The review's conclusion set of 60 empirical studies was selected using this thorough and stringent method. The thematic synthesis and following analysis were supported by this evidence base. They provided a comprehensive and diverse perspective on how artificial intelligence is changing the workforce in a variety of sectors, nations, and job roles. The chosen material covered a wide range of methodological strategies, such as econometric analysis (Masoud, 2025), case studies (Rao et al., 2025), ethnographic research, longitudinal tracking, and mixed-methods designs. Their focus ranged from algorithmic management in the gig economy (Lysyakov & Viswanathan, 2023) to automation in production (Jeong & Jo, 2025), but they were all based on the same empirical observation and data-supported results. The review was able to draw from a variety of viewpoints and data sources because it included these 60 studies, giving a comprehensive and nuanced overview of the effects of AI on the workforce. Furthermore, these books as a whole drew attention to geographical, sectoral, and demographic vulnerabilities, as well as the changing character of employment in the digital age. This review adhered to the highest standards of academic rigor and transparency by methodically reducing the original list of over a thousand items into a targeted collection of high-quality research. Consequently, the PRISMA technique served as a crucial foundation for the literature curation procedure, guaranteeing that each step, from identification to inclusion, was carried out methodically and documented openly.

THEMATIC SYNTHESIS OF FINDINGS: AI'S LABOR MARKET IMPACTS

The integration of Artificial Intelligence (AI) into the global economy has ignited extensive academic and policy discourse around its implications for employment structures, wage distribution, sectoral dynamics, and worker well-being. Across empirical studies and case-based evidence, six core themes emerge that together provide a nuanced understanding of AI's labor market ramifications. These include the dynamics of job displacement versus job creation, task and occupational transformation, wage and productivity effects, regional and sectoral heterogeneity, well-being and ethical challenges, and governance responses.

1. Job Formation vs. Job Displacement

AI technologies have created a paradoxical dynamic in labor markets: they displace some employment while also spawn new ones (Maria et al., 2025). This is not a straightforward zero-sum event. The nature of the tasks involved, the flexibility of the workforce, and the bigger economic environment determine the influence of artificial intelligence (Acemoglu et al., 2022). The most exposed are roles based on regularity and rules, such as those in administrative support, scheduling, and data entry (Fatun & Pazour, 2021). These activities can be standardized so that they are easily automatable. Many such positions are eliminated as companies strive for efficiency, which causes temporary job loss or pressure to change Dahlin, 2024).

Despite this, particularly in fields that require close collaboration or monitoring between humans and AI, artificial intelligence accelerates the growth of novel job opportunities (Waelen, 2025). Demand for roles like machine learning engineers, prompt designers, algorithm trainers, artificial intelligence ethicists, and data annotators have exploded (Bughin, 2023; Damioli et al., 2023). These jobs often provide greater freedom and compensation in return of new skill sets (Ghosh et al., 2025). Often called "creative destruction," the nature of this change is one in which conventional job categories fade yet are replaced by high-skilled, technologically focused positions (Maria et al., 2025).

The rate of job displacement and development does not match or affect the same groups, which is a significant issue (Septiandri et al., 2024). Without institutional support for retraining, employees whose talents are obsolete find it difficult to switch into new jobs (Giwa & Ngepah, 2024). Consequently, the overall effect of artificial intelligence on employment depends not only on technological capacity but also on public policy, business strategy, and instructional response (Zhou et al., 2020).

2. Changes in Job and Task

Instead of just getting rid of jobs, artificial intelligence is changing the internal organization of industries (Bonney et al., 2024). With duties organized according to whether they should stay human-led or may be automated, work is getting progressively modular. This causes a fragmentation of roles: while employees concentrate on higher-order thinking, emotional intelligence, and strategic supervision, repetitive, routine cognitive activities are automated (Waelen, 2025).

The trend of "task bifurcation" underlines this. In journalism, for example, artificial intelligence can write simple stories or summaries, but investigative reporting and editorial judgment remain human fields. Legal experts today also use artificial intelligence to comb case files, but they still have authority over legal interpretation and client interaction. The change calls for a basic realignment of skills—technical fluency, critical thinking, and cooperative capacity with artificial intelligence systems are now core competencies (Holm & Lorenz, 2022).

Companies are more and more shifting from role-based hierarchies to task-based systems of operation (Bonney et al., 2024). Marketing is where specialists now use AI tools to produce material, examine customer information, and A/B test campaigns—all of which is clear. Focusing on optimization and ethical compliance rather than just programming, software developers function more as validators of AI-generated code.

The success of this change much depends on thorough employee training (Ahmadi et al., 2025). Workers who get organized training—especially in utilizing artificial intelligence in simulated, actual world situations—adjust more quickly and show reduced resistance to technical developments. Technological anxiety and resistance grow in the absence of such assistance, therefore slowing adoption of artificial intelligence and output improvements (Lysyakov & Viswanathan, 2023).

Table 2. Wage Premiums Associated with AI Skill Levels

AI Competency Level	Representative Roles	Wage Premium vs. Peers	Demand Trend
Advanced AI/ML Expertise	ML Engineers, AI Researchers, Data Scientists	50-60% premium	Rapidly Growing
Applied AI Proficiency	AI Project Managers, Prompt Engineers, AI Auditors	30-45% premium	Strongly Growing
AI Literacy (Functional)	AI-augmented Professionals (e.g. AI-assisted lawyers)	15-25% premium	Growing
Limited AI Exposure	Traditional white-collar roles with minimal AI use	0-5% premium	Stable
AI-Displaced / At-Risk	Routine clerical, basic customer service, data entry	Wage stagnation or decline	Declining

Source: Meta-analysis of compensation studies (2020-2025). Premiums represent median estimates across industries.

3. Productivity and wage impacts

The most important macroeconomic contribution of artificial intelligence is to productivity (Damioli et al., 2021). Quicker processing times, fewer mistakes, and more intelligent decision-making have all contributed to a rise in productivity in industries with great AI penetration including pharmaceuticals, finance, and information technology (Chang, 2025; Damioli et al., 2023). Still, this productivity increase does not always correspond into salary growth. Particularly in developed countries, where corporate output is increasing quicker than employee pay, a growing "productivity-pay gap" has developed (Crowley & Hudgins, 2024).

(Ghosh et al., 2025)This divergence is driven by the unequal allocation of AI's advantages. High-skilled professionals in AI-adjacent jobs—data scientists, AI engineers, AI project managers typically earn 30 to 60% more than their coworkers (Ghosh et al., 2025). These positions are in great demand, which results in generous remuneration packages. Low- and mid-skilled employees in jobs vulnerable to automation, on the other hand, face stagnant wages or even displacement (Giwa & Ngepah, 2024; Rysty et al., 2025).

Moreover, during the transition period wage suppression is sometimes most severe, particularly in conventional industries like logistics or customer care where productivity improvements are not fairly distributed with employees (Rysty et al., 2025). Though displaced workers may eventually retrain and take better-paying jobs, the interim period is characterized by financial loss, mental strain, and economic instability (Giuntella et al., 2025). The "AI dividend" runs the danger of worsening income inequality and social stratification if there are no rules to encourage wage equality and lifelong learning (Guarascio & Reljic, 2025).

4. Regional and sectoral diversity

The regional differences in AI labor-market exposure across economies are summarized in Table 3.

Table 3. Regional Variation in AI Labor Market Exposure

Region / Economy	AI Exposure Rate	Digital Infrastructure	Policy Readiness	Primary Challenge
High-Income (US, UK, Japan)	>60% of occupations	Advanced	High	Wage polarization and inequality
Upper-Middle (Germany, Denmark)	45-60%	Strong	Very High	Workforce transition support
Emerging (China, Brazil, India)	30-45%	Developing	Moderate	Skills gap and capital access
Low-Income Economies	25-30%	Limited	Low	Infrastructure and digital divide
Developing (sub-Saharan Africa)	Below 25%	Nascent	Low	Connectivity and AI literacy

Source: Cross-country studies reviewed (2020-2025). Exposure rates indicate share of occupations with >50% task automation potential.

The consequences of artificial intelligence on labor vary greatly by industry and area (Georgieff & Hyee, 2022). Adoption of artificial intelligence and the results it generates are shaped by elements including infrastructure, labor laws, digital literacy, and industrial structure (Guarascio & Reljic, 2025). AI changes are usually more inclusive and easy in affluent countries with strong institutions like Germany, Denmark, or France (Holm & Lorenz, 2022). These nations spend a lot on social safety nets, digital infrastructure, and staff development. By contrast, artificial intelligence usually enters developing countries through worldwide outsourcing sites (Carbonero et al., 2023).

This produces job opportunities in data labeling and micro-tasking, yet these positions are often low-wage, unstable, and without advantages (Rysty et al., 2025). Sectoral variation is equally noticeable. High-tech industries including financial services, professional services, and information technology have quickly welcomed artificial intelligence to automate processes, improve analytics, and stimulate innovation (Chang, 2025; Damioli et al., 2023). Digital maturity and worker preparedness help these industries. Conversely, industries like hospitality, agriculture, and traditional manufacturing have more limitations; legacy systems, changeable task structures, and modest capital investments restrict artificial intelligence's adoption (Jeong & Jo, 2025).

In some fields—healthcare and education among them—AI serves as an additional resource. Doctors are aided by diagnostic algorithms; teachers benefit from adaptive learning systems. However, the natural human character of these fields guarantees AI augmentation instead of total replacement (Waelen, 2025). End-to-end automation is now possible in retail, logistics, and e-commerce as well, so completely changing the labor demand landscape Ahmadi et al., 2025).

5. Well-Being and Ethical Concerns

.Beyond output and jobs, artificial intelligence greatly affects the psychological and moral environment of work. Rising is technostress, a kind of occupational stress brought on by ongoing digital interaction, surveillance, and performance monitoring (Giuntella et al., 2025). Particularly when decisions concerning their job are made by opaque algorithms, employees in AI-regulated companies frequently report feeling anxious, alienated, or micromanaged (Santoni De Sio, 2024). Surveillance systems like automated productivity trackers, feeling analyzers, or position monitors may violate autonomy and privacy (Lysyakov & Viswanathan, 2023). Frontline and gig employees—who typically lack the power to challenge or appeal to algorithmic decisions—are disproportionately impacted by these tools.

Managerial Implications:

Furthermore, artificial intelligence systems could propagate or exacerbate biases in the workplace. Training algorithms on historical hiring records could unwittingly encode racism, sexism, or ageism, therefore disadvantaging marginalized groups (Santoni De Sio, 2024). Therefore, ethical artificial intelligence systems have to stress openness, responsibility, and justice. Included here are grievance redressal mechanisms, human-in-the-loop decision systems, and understandable artificial intelligence algorithms.

Participatory design—that is, employees' participation in how AI is deployed, what measures are employed, and how data is gathered—also affects well-being (Omri, Omri, & Afi, 2025). Building resilience in AI-enhanced offices depends on mental health care, flexible scheduling, and inclusive policies (Wei & Li, 2022).

6. Reactions to Labor Laws, Governance, and Policy

The labor impacts of artificial intelligence are not fixed; rather, they are influenced by the decisions of governments, institutions, and companies on how to control and direct the change (Qin et al., 2024). In this regard, labor law changes and governance ideas are really important. Better placed to safeguard workers' rights and facilitate easier transitions are countries that change their labor codes to reflect algorithmic management, gig labor, and AI augmentation (Loong et al., 2021). Some countries have implemented progressive policies including social safeguards for gig workers, compulsory artificial intelligence impact evaluations, and public-private reskilling programs. These methods capture a change from reactive to anticipatory control (Guarascio & Reljic, 2025). Meanwhile, international organizations like the ILO are developing worldwide structures to stop a race to the bottom in regulation.

Particularly hopeful are participatory governance systems. Employees can co-shape technical development rather than silently suffer it thanks to artificial intelligence advisory councils, algorithmic ethics boards, and digital worker unions (Omri & Afi, 2025). These organizations can guarantee that AI implementation matches societal values, foster confidence, and improve accountability. Effective governance also demands expenditure in lifelong education, digital infrastructure, and inclusive education (Omri, Omri, & Afi, 2025). Universal basic income (UBI), wage insurance, and tax-funded retraining initiatives can help to cushion the displacement impacts and encourage innovation (Qin et al., 2024). But based on thorough impact assessments and inclusive stakeholder engagement, policy design must be context-sensitive (Ledford, 2025).

Managerial Implications:

Rather than being a compliance endeavor, ethical AI governance should be a top priority for the business. To lessen the possibility of prejudice and discrimination, businesses should use algorithmic auditing methods. Programs for the well-being of employees should address technostress, burnout, and workplace anxiety related to the integration of AI. Businesses should create clear channels of communication and complaint procedures for decisions involving AI.

Decisions regarding hiring, evaluation, promotion, and termination that have a significant impact on the workplace must continue to be made under human supervision.

From Insights to Action: Implementation Frameworks for Managers

Table 4. AI Organizational Readiness Assessment Matrix

Readiness Dimension	Indicators	Low Readiness	High Readiness
Digital Infrastructure	Cloud adoption, data systems, connectivity	Legacy systems, siloed data	Integrated cloud, real-time data
Workforce Digital Literacy	AI tool usage, data skills, adaptability	Under 20% digitally proficient	Over 60% AI-literate employees
Leadership AI Vision	Strategy documents, C-suite AI champions	No formal AI strategy	Board-level AI governance
Data Governance Maturity	Privacy compliance, data quality, access controls	Ad hoc data management	ISO-compliant data governance
Reskilling Capacity	Training budget, programs, edu partnerships	Under 2% payroll on training	Over 5% payroll on reskilling
Organizational Agility	Change management, iterative processes	Rigid hierarchies	Adaptive, flat structures

Organizations should score each dimension (1-5) to generate an overall readiness index prior to large-scale AI deployment.

Table 5. Human-Centered AI Implementation Roadmap

Phase	Timeline	Key Activities	Success Metrics
Phase 1: Diagnose and Plan	Months 1-3	Readiness assessment, workforce audit, stakeholder mapping, pilot scoping	Readiness score and role risk matrix completed
Phase 2: Pilot and Learn	Months 4-9	Deploy AI in 1-2 business units, monitor outcomes, gather employee feedback	Productivity delta, adoption rate, satisfaction scores
Phase 3: Reskill and Redesign	Months 7-18	Launch targeted reskilling programs, redesign job roles around human-AI teams	Training completion rate, internal mobility rate
Phase 4: Scale and Govern	Months 15-30	Expand AI across functions, embed ethics framework, establish AI oversight board	Coverage %, bias audit results, grievance rate
Phase 5: Sustain and Evolve	Ongoing	Continuous learning culture, AI strategy refresh, policy advocacy participation	Employee retention, innovation index, workforce resilience

A phased implementation approach reduces organizational risk and builds sustainable AI-human collaboration models.

Despite the chapter's evidence of AI's revolutionary effect on labor markets, businesses need concrete advice on how to apply these insights into successful workplace practices. The adoption of AI involves changes to people, culture, and organizations, not just technology. As a result, companies must establish implementation structures that strike a balance between productivity improvements, workforce sustainability, ethical governance, and employee well-being. Organizations that use a strategic approach to AI are more likely to attain long-term competitiveness while also reducing workforce disruption and opposition (Bughin, 2023).

Organizations must assess their digital infrastructure, personnel skills, leadership preparedness, and organizational flexibility before implementing AI systems. Readiness evaluations assist businesses in determining possibilities for automation, workforce improvement, and workforce restructuring while minimizing operational interruptions. Important indicators include the maturity of the digital infrastructure, the digital literacy of the workforce, the leadership's support for innovation, the capacity for data governance, the capacity for workforce retraining, and the flexibility of the organization. Before implementing AI on a large scale, businesses with little readiness should concentrate on workforce training and basic digital investments. Phased implementation strategies are sometimes more sustainable than quick, across-the-board organizational change.

Proactive workforce planning is another need for AI adoption, as opposed to reactive downsizing. Organizations must determine which jobs are appropriate for automation, which ones need human-AI cooperation, and which roles are more likely to change than go altogether. Instead of seeing AI as a labor replacement, businesses should concentrate on augmentation approaches that pair machine effectiveness and analytical capabilities with human innovation, moral decision-making, emotional intelligence, and strategic thinking. Managers can also use scenario planning methods to better prepare for different workforce outcomes under different levels of AI integration and technological maturity.

It is well-documented in the literature that employees with skills in AI are more employable and see faster wage gains. As a result, businesses must invest in ongoing, long-term learning systems that foster workforce flexibility. Effective strategies include digital skills development, AI literacy training, simulation-based learning environments, cross-functional training programs, and collaborations with universities or online learning platforms. Employee shifts into new hybrid roles can be further aided by organized reskilling routes and internal mentoring programs. Importantly, reskilling should be viewed as a strategic organizational investment rather than a quick fix to the demands of automation.

Employee involvement and change management are also crucial for the effective adoption of AI. Workers are more likely to resist when they see AI systems as a threat, unclear, or forced upon them without discussion (Dahlin, 2024). By providing open communication about AI goals, including staff members in implementation planning early on, conducting pilot testing prior to full-scale implementation, and establishing ongoing feedback loops, businesses may lower uncertainty and technostress. Participatory governance models that incorporate worker input and human supervision of algorithmic choices enhance organizational trust and make technological transitions easier.

Sustainable AI adoption also depends on ethical governance. Particularly when AI systems have an impact on hiring, performance assessments, scheduling, promotion, or termination choices, organizations must make sure that these systems are transparent, fair, and accountable. As a result, ethical AI governance frameworks should include data privacy safeguards, ethical review boards, algorithmic bias audits, explainability criteria, human-in-the-loop supervision, and employee complaint procedures. Ethical governance is increasingly seen as a competitive advantage that enhances organizational legitimacy and stakeholder confidence, rather than simply a regulatory requirement.

Due to the specific constraints they encounter in terms of restricted capital, smaller talent pools, and reduced testing capabilities, small and medium-sized businesses (SMEs) need special consideration in discussions on AI implementation. SMEs frequently find it challenging to meet the financial and operational requirements of widespread AI adoption due to their limited technological resources, unlike huge corporations. As a result, strategies aimed at SMEs should focus on incremental automation methods, government-backed training programs, industry collaboration networks, shared digital infrastructure, cloud-based AI solutions, and low-cost AI adoption pathways. Targeted augmentation models are frequently more practical and long-lasting for small and medium-sized businesses than complete automation methods.

The long-term success of AI integration ultimately depends on whether firms prioritize their employees during technological change. Human-centered AI approaches prioritize collaboration over replacement and aim to improve human skills rather than reduce employee independence (Waelen, 2025). Prioritizing employee well-being, ongoing learning, inclusive participation, and fair distribution of opportunities are all valued by these methods. In the changing digital economy, organizations that include human-centered concepts in their AI governance and personnel planning are more likely to experience lasting productivity gains, workforce resilience, and long-term organizational stability.

RESEARCH GAPS AND FUTURE DIRECTIONS

Although current research on the interaction of artificial intelligence and labor markets has increased dramatically in recent years, the empirical studies available still neglect numerous important areas. It is imperative that future study fill these gaps using a rigorous approach, a longitudinal perspective, and an interdisciplinary viewpoint as AI technologies continue to advance and change the character of employment. From the examination of 60 studies, this chapter highlights significant research gaps and offers routes for future investigation that are essential to a deeper knowledge of the actual and possible effects of AI on employment.

The absence of longitudinal monitoring of career trajectories among workers exposed to AI is one of the most critical research gaps. There is a lack of knowledge about how people manage their careers over time in the face of technological disruption, even if many studies offer useful cross-sectional data that shows the immediate effects of AI, such as job displacement, wage changes, or changes in task composition. Do displaced workers eventually obtain jobs that are more secure? Can they successfully move into AI-enhanced roles through retraining and upskilling, or are they compelled into lower-paying, less secure jobs? These are crucial issues that cannot be resolved by static data alone. Longitudinal studies that monitor specific workers over a period of years are necessary to track the course of adaptation, resilience, and susceptibility. In addition to labor market dynamics, such studies would shed light on how education, regional mobility, and institutional support mechanisms contribute to long-term workforce stability or insecurity.

The comparative study of the effects of AI across various job structures, notably between conventional full-time employment and the expanding fields of gig work, remote freelancing, and platform-based labor, is another significant area for research. The majority of the current literature ignores the moderating role of employment contracts in the experience of AI disruption and instead generalizes results throughout the labor market. Gig workers and platform-based workers are frequently exposed to algorithmic management systems that automate scheduling, performance evaluation, and even termination decisions, all without the security of contracts, benefits, or legal safeguards (Lysyakov & Viswanathan, 2023). On the other hand, conventional workers in business contexts may see AI as a collaborative instrument rather than a substitute. In order to assess the qualitative and quantitative effects of AI on these two drastically different labor experiences, this discrepancy necessitates focused study. In addition, a comparative analysis across national contexts is crucial since economic structures, digital infrastructure, and labor protections differ widely across nations. Our knowledge of how the labor effects of AI are influenced by socioeconomic and policy environments would be improved by a worldwide viewpoint.

The assessment of policy measures aimed at reducing the negative impact of AI on employment is another area that merits additional study. There is still little empirical evidence of the efficacy of the various programs that governments and private groups have started to implement, such as wage subsidies, job transition assistance, digital upskilling classes, and pilot versions of Universal Basic Income (UBI). To what extent are these policies helping workers shift into jobs that complement AI? Do they lessen income volatility or only put off displacement? Which combinations of support mechanisms are most effective across industries or demographic groups? Future research should use quasi-experimental or experimental designs to assess the results of such interventions. The strong causal evidence needed for rethinking unsuccessful programs and expanding successful ones can come from longitudinal assessments, natural experiments, and randomized controlled trials. In addition, impact assessments should take into account psychological well-being, skill confidence, and long-term employability in addition to economic results (Giuntella et al., 2025).

In addition to issues with structure and policy, there is still an understudied area of study on how AI affects diversity, equity, and inclusion in the workplace. Although AI provides techniques that might theoretically lessen bias in hiring and promotions, like anonymous resume screening, standardized performance metrics, and adaptive communication platforms, it also poses new difficulties. By embedding past biases into algorithmic decision-making, AI systems, if not carefully designed, may replicate and even exacerbate current inequalities. However, there are still few empirical studies of the actual effects of AI on DEI outcomes in the real world. Future studies should examine whether AI-assisted recruitment methods actually diversify candidate pools or unintentionally exacerbate current demographic inequalities.

In addition to considering the impact of algorithmic systems on various employee groups—such as women, racial minorities, older workers, or people with disabilities—in terms of access, advancement, and workplace experience, studies should also look at how these systems affect different employee groups. Combining quantitative measures with qualitative interviews or ethnographic observations would be especially helpful in understanding the intricate and occasionally unseen interactions between AI and inclusion.

The exploration of human-AI collaboration models, with an emphasis on maximizing productivity, satisfaction, and ethical behavior in hybrid work settings, is another important area of study. The relationship between humans and computers is evolving as AI technology transitions from a replacement tool to an assistant partner that aids with data analysis, design, writing, and diagnosis. This raises new issues about how people and machines can best collaborate. What psychological elements affect trust in AI systems, and how does this impact job results? How do workers interpret and react to AI-generated recommendations or corrections? What organizational strategies encourage or discourage AI-human teamwork, and are there certain job categories that are more conducive to it? (Bonney et al., 2024) These questions need interdisciplinary investigation, using insights from fields like management science, behavioral economics, human-computer interaction, and organizational psychology. Organizational case studies, as well as experimental research conducted in laboratory and real-world environments, may help discover best practices for incorporating AI in a way that enhances rather than alienates the human workforce.

Future studies should also place a greater emphasis on the ethical considerations of integrating AI into the workforce. This encompasses the research of data privacy, worker permission, algorithmic transparency, and the accountability mechanisms for automated choices. It is imperative to investigate who owns these systems, how their judgments are supported, and what options employees have when faced with mistakes or prejudice, since AI systems are now playing a greater role in hiring, firing, scheduling, and performance assessment. In response to these issues, regulatory frameworks are beginning to develop, but more academic research is necessary to guide their creation and implementation. In this field, research should examine not just the required ethical standards but also how firms put them into practice and how employees feel and experience ethical infractions.

Lastly, we need research methods that are more inclusive and participatory, placing the voices and lived experiences of those most impacted by AI-driven changes in the workforce at the forefront. Employer-reported results or high-level datasets make up a large portion of the existing literature. Subtle yet significant factors like job satisfaction, professional identity, fear of obsolescence, and adaptive ingenuity can be illuminated by incorporating participatory action research, community-based studies, and worker narratives. These measures are essential for comprehending the economic, social, and psychological effects of AI.

REFERENCES

Acemoglu, D., Autor, D., Hazell, J., & Restrepo, P. (2022). Artificial Intelligence and Jobs: Evidence from Online Vacancies. *Journal of Labor Economics, 40*(S1), S293–S340. DOI: 10.1086/718327

Ahmadi, A., Cantini, A., Frías, V. G., & Staudacher, A. P. (2025). The impact of labor flexibility on operational efficiency in industry 5.0: A systematic literature review. *International Journal of Production Research,* •••, 1–26. DOI: 10.1080/00207543.2025.2516770

Bonfiglioli, A., Crinò, R., Gancia, G., & Papadakis, I. (2025). Artificial intelligence and jobs: Evidence from US commuting zones. *Economic Policy, 40*(121), 145–194. DOI: 10.1093/epolic/eiae059

Bonney, K., Breaux, C., Buffington, C., Dinlersoz, E., Foster, L., Goldschlag, N., Haltiwanger, J., Kroff, Z., & Savage, K. (2024). The impact of AI on the workforce: Tasks versus jobs? *Economics Letters, 244*, 111971. DOI: 10.1016/j.econlet.2024.111971

Bughin, J. (2023). Does artificial intelligence kill employment growth: The missing link of corporate AI posture. *Frontiers in Artificial Intelligence, 6*, 1239466. DOI: 10.3389/frai.2023.1239466 PMID: 38045762

Carbonero, F., Davies, J., Ernst, E., Fossen, F. M., Samaan, D., & Sorgner, A. (2023). Thc impact of artificial intelligence on labor markets in developing countries: A new method with an illustration for Lao PDR and urban Viet Nam. *Journal of Evolutionary Economics, 33*(3), 707–736. DOI: 10.1007/s00191-023-00809-7 PMID: 36811092

Chang, Z. (2025). Influence of artificial intelligence on the financial labor market. *Finance Research Letters, 80*, 107039. DOI: 10.1016/j.frl.2025.107039

Crowley, P. M., & Hudgins, D. (2024). The impact of US productivity growth on unemployment in the time–frequency domain: Is AI causing a change in the relationship? *Empirical Economics, 66*(5), 2169–2190. DOI: 10.1007/s00181-023-02510-x

Dahlin, E. (2024). Who Says Artificial Intelligence Is Stealing Our Jobs? *Socius: Sociological Research for a Dynamic World, 10*, 23780231241259672. DOI: 10.1177/23780231241259672

Damioli, G., Van Roy, V., & Vertesy, D. (2021). The impact of artificial intelligence on labor productivity. *Eurasian Business Review, 11*(1), 1–25. DOI: 10.1007/s40821-020-00172-8

Damioli, G., Van Roy, V., Vertesy, D., & Vivarelli, M. (2023). AI technologies and employment: Micro evidence from the supply side. *Applied Economics Letters, 30*(6), 816–821. DOI: 10.1080/13504851.2021.2024129

Fatun, M., & Pazour, M. (2021). Modelling the impact of Artificial Intelligence on the labour market in Czechia. *Central European Journal of Public Policy, 15*(2), 31–42. DOI: 10.2478/cejpp-2021-0006

Georgieff, A., & Hyee, R. (2022). Artificial Intelligence and Employment: New Cross-Country Evidence. *Frontiers in Artificial Intelligence, 5*, 832736. DOI: 10.3389/frai.2022.832736 PMID: 35620279

Ghosh, D., Ghosh, R., Roy Chowdhury, S., & Ganguly, B. (2025). AI-exposure and labour market: A systematic literature review on estimations, validations, and perceptions. *Management Review Quarterly, 75*(1), 677–704. DOI: 10.1007/s11301-023-00393-x

Giuntella, O., Konig, J., & Stella, L. (2025). Artificial intelligence and the wellbeing of workers. *Scientific Reports, 15*(1), 20087. DOI: 10.1038/s41598-025-98241-3 PMID: 40550887

Giwa, F., & Ngepah, N. (2024). The relationship between artificial intelligence and low-skilled employment in South Africa. *Heliyon, 10*(23), e40640. DOI: 10.1016/j.heliyon.2024.e40640 PMID: 39669173

Guarascio, D., & Reljic, J. (2025). AI and employment in Europe. *Economics Letters, 247*, 112183. DOI: 10.1016/j.econlet.2025.112183

Holm, J. R., & Lorenz, E. (2022). The impact of artificial intelligence on skills at work in Denmark. *New Technology, Work and Employment, 37*(1), 79–101. DOI: 10.1111/ntwe.12215

Jeong, J. H., & Jo, H. J. (2025). The Effects of Artificial Intelligence and Robotics on Employment and Wages in Korean Manufacturing Firms. Weizenbaum Institute. https://doi.org/DOI: 10.34669/WI.WJDS/5.2.5

Ledford, T. D. (2025). Does artificial intelligence harm labour? Investigating the limitations of incident trackers as evidence for policymaking. Information Research an International Electronic Journal, 30(iConf), 486–499. https://doi.org/DOI: 10.47989/ir30iConf47296

Lei, L., Feng, H., & Ren, J. (2025). Artificial intelligence, human capital and firm-level total factor productivity. *Finance Research Letters, 85*, 107897. DOI: 10.1016/j.frl.2025.107897

Loong, X. A., Huang, T., & Xiang, S. Z. & School of Labor and Human Resource,Renmin University of China,Beijing,P. R. China. (2021). The impact of AI on employment and the corresponding response of PRC labor law. Journal of Chinese Human Resource Management, 12(2), 69–94. https://doi.org/DOI: 10.47297/wspchrmWSP2040-800506.20211202

Lysyakov, M., & Viswanathan, S. (2023). Threatened by AI: Analyzing Users' Responses to the Introduction of AI in a Crowd-Sourcing Platform. *Information Systems Research*, *34*(3), 1191–1210. DOI: 10.1287/isre.2022.1184

Maria, S., Purwinahyu, P., Fitriansyah, F., Rachmawaty, A., & Aini, R. N. (2025). Artificial Intelligence and Labor Markets: Analyzing Job Displacement and Creation. International Journal of Engineering. *Science and Information Technology*, *5*(2), 290–296. DOI: 10.52088/ijesty.v5i2.830

Masoud, N. (2025). Artificial intelligence and unemployment dynamics: An econometric analysis in high-income economies. *Technological Sustainability*, *4*(1), 30–50. DOI: 10.1108/TECHS-04-2024-0033

Ogbolu, A. N., & Sukidjo, S. (2020). Artificial Intelligence Vs My Future Job: Perceptions of Asian Undergraduates. [JRC]. *Journal of Robotics and Control*, *1*(6). Advance online publication. DOI: 10.18196/jrc.1639

Omri, A., & Afi, H. (2025). Impact of Artificial Intelligence on Employment of People with Disabilities: The Moderating Role of Governance Quality. *Journal of Disability Research*, *4*(2). Advance online publication. DOI: 10.57197/JDR-2025-0007

Omri, A., Omri, H., & Afi, H. (2025). Exploring the impact of AI on unemployment for people with disabilities: Do educational attainment and governance matter? *Frontiers in Public Health*, *13*, 1559101. DOI: 10.3389/fpubh.2025.1559101 PMID: 40241964

Qin, M., Wan, Y., Dou, J., & Su, C. W. (2024). Artificial Intelligence: Intensifying or mitigating unemployment? *Technology in Society*, *79*, 102755. DOI: 10.1016/j.techsoc.2024.102755

Rao, N., O'Riordan, S., & Coulis, J. (2025). AI and labor: Captioning library audiovisual content with Whisper. *IFLA Journal*, *03400352241310534*(3), 803–813. Advance online publication. DOI: 10.1177/03400352241310534

Ruiz-Talavera, D., Cruz-Aguero, J. E. D. L., García-Palomino, N., Calderón-Espinoza, R., & Marín-Rodriguez, W. J. (2023). Artificial intelligence and its impact on job opportunities among university students in North Lima, 2023. *ICST Transactions on Scalable Information Systems, 10*(5). Advance online publication. DOI: 10.4108/eetsis.3841

Rysty, S., Zhanargul, S., Ainur, T., Sharbat, B., & Zhanat, Y. (2025). Wages and working conditions in the context of digitalization. *International Journal of Innovative Research and Scientific Studies, 8*(3), 1824–1835. DOI: 10.53894/ijirss.v8i3.6891

Santoni De Sio, F. (2024). Artificial Intelligence and the Future of Work: Mapping the Ethical Issues. *The Journal of Ethics, 28*(3), 407–427. DOI: 10.1007/s10892-024-09493-6

Septiandri, A. A., Constantinides, M., & Quercia, D. (2024). The potential impact of AI innovations on US occupations. *PNAS Nexus, 3*(9), pgae320. Advance online publication. DOI: 10.1093/pnasnexus/pgae320 PMID: 39319327

Waelen, R. A. (2025). The Desirability of Automizing Labor: An Overview. *Philosophy Compass, 20*(1–2), e70023. DOI: 10.1111/phc3.70023

Wei, W., & Li, L. (2022). The Impact of Artificial Intelligence on the Mental Health of Manufacturing Workers: The Mediating Role of Overtime Work and the Work Environment. *Frontiers in Public Health, 10*, 862407. DOI: 10.3389/fpubh.2022.862407 PMID: 35480579

Zhou, G., Chu, G., Li, L., & Meng, L. (2020). The effect of artificial intelligence on China's labor market. *China Economic Journal, 13*(1), 24–41. DOI: 10.1080/17538963.2019.1681201

Chapter 2
Artificial Intelligence and the Future of Work:
Business and Societal Implications

A. Padma
http://orcid.org/0009-0002-9004-317X
SR University, India

Suman Kumar N. Kumar
SR University, India

Srinivas D. Srinivas
SR University, India

Ramesh G. Ramesh
Vaagdevi, India

ABSTRACT

This chapter investigates the transformative role of Artificial Intelligence (AI) in reshaping the nature of work, with particular focus on the implications for business performance and societal structures. AI technologies—spanning machine learning, robotics, and natural language processing—are rapidly being adopted across sectors, influencing how tasks are performed, who performs them, and under what conditions. The chapter examines the dual nature of AI: its potential to drive innovation and economic efficiency, and its challenges in terms of job displacement, widening skill gaps, and social inequality. It emphasizes the importance of inclusive policies and ethical AI deployment to ensure a balanced future of work.

DOI: 10.4018/979-8-3373-5816-1.ch002

1. INTRODUCTION AND LITERATURE REVIEW

Artificial Intelligence (AI) is a term used when describing the ability of a machine and a computer system to do things that otherwise would require intelligence by humans, including learning and reasoning, problem-solving and decision-making. The most essential technologies used in AI are machine learning (ML), natural language processing (NLP), robotics, and computer vision which together makes systems to make decisions based on the data collected, patterns identified and dynamically act independently or semi-independently. With these technologies developing further, AI is increasingly being incorporated in a variety of industries, such as manufacturing, logistics, healthcare, education and professional services.

The fact that AI is being fast-tracked into use in many industries is not only transforming the way business gets conducted but it is also changing what work is all about. The traditional jobs are also being transformed, new skills are needed and organization structures are being updated to fit the AI augmented world. This popular change brings significant concerns about economic competence, employee flexibility, and issues of social significance of automation.

The current chapter will strive to analyse the various effects that AI has on both the labour markets and the businesses and the society in general. Namely, it answers the following research questions: How does AI change the nature of work? What are the implications of AI use in the business? How do the wider implications to society, especially inequality, policy, and ethical implications, work out? When addressing these concerns, the chapter is aimed at filling in the gap in a better understanding of how the changes caused by AI can be taken care of in a responsible and inclusive manner.

Theme 1; AI and the Future of Work

According to Howard (2019), the incorporation of AI in the work environment requires some progressive approaches to the displacement of people, regulation of the human-robot interface, and protection of their well-being (Tschang &Almirall, 2021). AI has replaced and supplemented work, transforming the workplace through the automation of repetitive processes and overweight of the skills required, which poses critical discussion about the effects of artificial intelligence on society and businesses (Acemoglu & Restrepo, 2020) Automation of processes by AI is redefining production and there is an over-emphasis on replacing labor and not on creating job positions in these processes, which results in zero job growth and increase in inequality and reduce productivity, which shows why AI should be developed more with a human-cantered approach (Frank et al., 2019). The effects of automation and AI on work are becoming visible in the face of increased inequality, in which understanding of this impact is challenged by the lack of quality data, models and robust policy frameworks (Pasupuleti & Siddique, 2021), The introduction of AI and roboticization poses a danger to low-skilled roles, yet it generates new positions and requires urgent changes in the education, labor, and economic policy to reduce disparities existing in the world (Ismail, 2025). Report on Future of Jobs 2025 presents significant labor trends in the future related to technology, demography and climate change, and a focus on reskilling, new jobs and policymaking to develop a fair, sustainable job market by 2030 (Shaji George, 2024). AI will produce change, not replace, and shift the position in each industry and increased productivity, provided it provides reskilling, intelligent policies, and people-friendly strategies (Masoud, 2025). This paper establishes that there is no merit in the use of AI, ML and DS in causing unemployment rates in the high-income economies; but on the contrary, it affirms the ability of these systems to increase productivity and employment rate when used with effective government policies.

Theme 2: Ethics, Governance & Social Responsibility

This analyzes the seven major questions of ethics that come with the adoption of AI into the workforce and thereby locates those questions into the frames of philosophy and applied ethics and directly articulates that the governance of AI must be shaped by responsible measures encompassing the right to work and individually by rights to autonomy and performing meaningful working activities. This article discusses the use of AI in the workplace and its ability to increase or reduce the employees' sense of meaningful work in evaluating of its ethical impacts under the various ways of AI adoption (Banking et al., 2023). This study gives an overview of dramatic changes in society and the employment status because of the development of AI and automation, pointing out the possibilities, and threats like jobs loss, the wellbeing of workers, and ethical implications of development, which requires an interdisciplinary approach in the future role of AI (Khogali & Makid, 2023; Qian et al., 2024). The article discusses the changes caused by AI in the world of work and society, pointing at the research that has to be made in the direction of legal ethics, removing biases, and the AI governance frameworks. This is hardly recognized as a tool but rather an approach as Anthony et al. (2023), suggest a new angle that views AI as a capable agent in the system of work in organizations. It recommends the relational approach to ethnography to realize the design, application, and encounter of AI. Currently, with AI, Appio et al. (2024) argue that an extractive industry that requires energy, exploitation of data, and labor is being performed, and this has significant environmental, ethical, and socio-political implications requiring sustainable management with accountability: an oversight that should be transparent.

Theme 3: AI and Business/Performance

Lutfiani et al. (2025), This paper examines business performance patterns when utilizing AI technologies and concluded that, although AI boosts productivity and effectiveness, its success is determined by elements such as data, leadership, ethics and conquest of challenges associated with AI. According to Sahoo et al. (2024), this chapter explores the ways artificial intelligence is reshaping market intelligence right now by intensifying competitive analysis, unlocking strategic invention, and presenting a sense of critical ethics and operational problems to companies (Ignacimuthu & Chinnamuthu Kulasekarapandian, 2025). Artificial intelligence, whose pervasiveness is rapidly expanding, sector by sector and activity by activity, is transforming business and society, providing innovation, competitive advantage, and technological progress, and creating many important policy, ethics, and global development implications (Ahmad, 2024). Artificial Intelligence is a strong yet intricate instrument which might disrupt business, society, and the Earth, and it should be ethically, inclusively, and sustainably managed to strike out opportunities and hazards (Manickavasagam, 2021). AI, big data and IoT are collecting together and allowing firms to create more using less and are saving the firms money using automation. However, is threatening employment, encourages gig work and poses a risk of increasing economic inequality (Kraus et al., 2023.). This problem addresses some of the most significant themes defining the future of work and provides perspective on various dimensions of remote work, the concept of digitalization, the topic of sustainability, and the changing nature of organizational actions.

Theme 4: AI, Economy & Growth

In this paper, we conclude that AI has a positive impact on economic growth and it can be achieved by using AI technology and value as well as application, but this may not apply across different levels of development and policy approaches must be value-based and region-specific. The paper by Ernst et al. (2019), The paper discusses the promising productivity benefits that the development of AI entails without omitting to mention that there are risks facing threats posed alongside these productivity opportunities, making it necessary to borderline policy interventional measures in this direction. According to Kulkov et al. (2024), AI can facilitate sustainable development through consistency with global objectives by coordinating organizational, technical as well as data processing strategies. Kolade & Owoseni (2022) point out that digital transformation is transforming the work by disrupting technology, leading to the polarisation and polarisation of jobs, and introduction of critical socio-political and ethical obstacles (Makridakis, 2017). The AI revolution, as society experienced with industrial and digital change, will radically change society, companies and employment, it has enormous opportunities but also certain dangers such as job loss and social inequality. This research goes into the applications of AI in improving recruitment in making the process efficient and engage applicants, and the issue of organizational capabilities of effectively taking up technology (Verma et al., 2024). On the one hand, AI is transforming the energy sector by increasing connectivity, maximizing the utilization of renewable sources, driving autonomous control of the energy system, and advancing CO 2-free hydrogen production, on the other hand, AI is directing future research and policy on sustainable energy. The research commemorates the booming place of AI and human capital in sustainable finance by underlining the importance of international standards, employee upskilling, and inclusion in order to foster resilient, transparent, and future-ready economics through Saba et al. (2025).

Theme 5: AI and Societal Change

According to Sheikh (2020), AI is also touching individuals, communities, and society in general and transforming how people live, work and interact. Since intelligent systems are becoming increasingly embedded into our everyday world and workplaces, consumers and workers will continue to undergo a great deal of social change, and will be forced to adapt and react constantly (Vicsek, 2021). In this paper, sociology of expectations is used to critically examine how state-of-the-art expert discourses about artificial intelligence, future of work constructs powerful narratives which define policy, limit possible imaginaries, and shape the track of socio-technical evolution. Artificial intelligence is transforming life by supercharging, not, replacing, the intelligence of humans in life in the most powerful ways in educational fields such as healthcare, education, and in business by Zohuri & Mossavar-Rahmani (2024). To gauge industry data, Neary et al. (2018) will be considered. The trends of AI and IoT adoption, major business drivers, AI and IoT benefits, and the revenues projections of the adoption of AI and IoT all over the world in retail and marketing sectors. Transformation of the traditional workplace and introduction of modern automated processes bring with them a variety of implications such as amendments to job descriptions, skills needed and the dynamics of the workflow and redefines the interaction between people and machines (De Stefano, 2019; Deranty & Corbin, 2022.). This review focuses on the workforce change by AI and brings up some important arguments related to notions of job loss, algorithmic domination, and platform labour, which take place in a capitalist and nationalistic environment. AI is transforming life, not replacing people, but supporting the enhancement of human intelligence, which can develop potent opportunities in many areas, including healthcare, education, and business, according to Zohuri & Mossavar-Rahmani (2024) and Pasupuleti & Siddique (2021). The AI and robotization threaten to low skilled jobs but also generate new jobs, and it is necessary to reform education, labour, economic policies to close inequalities around the globe.

Objectives

- To Examine the processes through which AI disintegrates the labour markets, such as automation, augmentation, and algorithmic management, and compare simultaneously the risks of job-displacement as well as the productivity of the increase.
- To Discuss the adaptation of businesses to the use of AI, such as the distribution of job roles, the organizational strategy of a business, and questions of integrity in the decision-making process of an algorithm in different industries.
- To Determine the larger repercussions of AI on labour to society and policies, including labour market polarization, income inequality and the requirements of new social welfare and workforce transition policies.
- To Promote a human-centred paradigm of AI, advocating for inclusive economic growth, responsible innovation, sustainable work approaches, matching technological progressions towards societal prosperity.

SIGNIFICANCE OF ARTIFICIAL INTELLIGENCE IN SHAPING THE FUTURE OF WORK AND SOCIETY

1. Role of AI in Economic Transformation and Employment Generation

Artificial Intelligence (AI) is serving a properly revolutionary role in transforming the global economy by increasing the productivity level, cutting the cost of operation procedures and opening new employment opportunities. Artificial intelligence is making every industry efficient in India and the rest of the world including healthcare, manufacturing, retail, logistics and finance. There are apprehensions regarding jobs being lost but simultaneously, AI is coming up with new jobs such as AI trainers, data analysts and ethical AI experts. In addition, the introduction of AI in the conventional industries leads to the concept of smart automation, which changes labor profiles and signals the transition toward high-salary job holders. AI not only improves production but also plays the role of fuelling entrepreneurship through innovation particularly in start-up ecosystems and online platforms.

2. Global Shift Towards AI-Driven Business Models

There are some structural and contextual issues in how India can use AI to the maximum extent. Among them, it is possible to include a digital divide, the absence of infrastructure in the countryside, the AI illiteracy of workers, and imbalanced access to more powerful computing resources. Ethical and cultural obstacles to the use of AI also exist in more sensitive areas as law enforcement, education, or health. The local businesses especially the MSMEs cannot afford to invest in AI technologies because they are very expensive and they lack skilled labour and cannot afford powerful support ecosystems. Also, informal labour, forming a significant segment of India's employment market, is long uninfluenced by the effects of AI and increases disparities in digitalization.

3. Unique Challenges of AI Adoption in the Indian Context

There are multiple structural and contextual problems in a full utilization of AI that affect India. They consist of a digital divide, the underdevelopment of infrastructure in the countryside, the insufficient literacy of employees on AI, and unequal access to computing resources, advanced in their applications. There exist such ethical and cultural barriers as the implementation of AI into such a sensitive field as health, education, and policing. The barriers to the local companies investing in AI technologies are high prices and availability of skilled workers and lack of strong support systems, especially among the MSMEs. Also, informal work, making up a significant proportion of the labour force in India, has mainly not been affected by the development of AI and thus led to the emergence of inequality in the realm of digital inclusion.

4. AI's Impact on Organizational Productivity and Competitiveness

AI increases organizational efficiencies because it automates tedious tasks, enhances decision-making due to the real-time insights and reduces human errors. Robotics with AI, whether in manufacturing or in finance, both employ other benefits of AI, such as increasing speed and precision in manufacturing processes or improving security and returns in financial systems because they both perform fraud detection and algorithmic trading. HR AI tools, such as talent analytics and performance prediction assists companies to attract and retain the best talent. Firms that embrace the use of AI gain great advantages in scalability and market volatility sensitivity. Yet, unless upskilled and ethically integrated, productivity advantage of

AI may resort to exclusiveness in favour of larger company and present disparity with smaller stakeholders.

5. AI Ethics, Governance, and Societal Equity

With the extension of AI in effecting more choices, issues relating to biasness, transparency, labour rights, and surveillance are emerging as crucial. Discrimination is also a potential problem of black-box algorithms as they may both re-entrench it without being aware. With too much data, privacy can also deteriorate. The activity of responsible development of AI needs very good ethical principles, legal protection mechanisms, and human control. The world over, but also in India, regulation of AI, recognizing an accountability of algorithms, and laws on data protection are being discussed already. The social equity has to be maintained to make sure that the benefits of AI are not excluded by the marginalized communities. AI needs democratic governance in order to respect and protect human rights, trust and fair results.

6. Future Trends and Strategic Directions for AI Integration

The new trends in AI that include generative AI, edge computing, quantum AI, and AI with social good purpose provide new opportunities to lead ever-inclusive growth. There is need to have a long-term roadmap by governments, academic and industries with a centre piece on inclusive innovation, indigenous development and skill-building. The homegrown AI ecosystems can be achieved by tapping the National AI Strategy (NITI Aayog) and other plans/programs such as Digital India. The AI literacy, digital infrastructure, and interdisciplinary education should be mentioned in future-forward policymaking. The willingness to embrace AI as a source of competitive advantage will not only be enough but also represent a strategic force to address some of the most urgent societal problems like providing access to healthcare, tackling climate change, and making education more accessible to everyone.

Key Elements of AI-Driven Transformation Shaping the Future of Work and Society

1. Revolutionization of the Jobs by AI
2. Business creativity and advancements in productivity
3. Ethics, Law and Governance issues
4. Skills development and Adaptation of the workforce
5. Greater Societal effects and Policy reaction
6. Human-AI Work and Cognitive Enhancement

Figure 1. key elements of AI-Driven Transformation Shaping the -Future of Work and Society

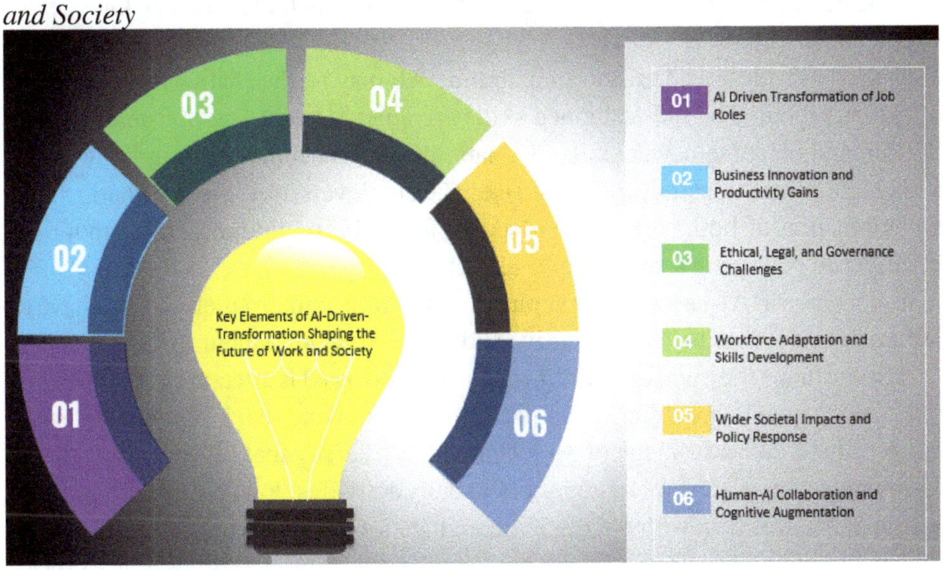

TRANSFORMATION STEP 01: TRANSFORMATION OF THE JOB ROLES THROUGH AI

Artificial intelligence (AI) has also transformed the manner jobs are done in every type of industry in a fundamental way not just in narrowing the jobs that people do but also in redefining the concept of job itself. Key to this change is automation, augmentation, and the changing needs of new skills.

Automation refers to AI systems replacing routine and repetitive tasks once touched by humans. From the production line or in official paper work in the sphere of banking and insurance, AI-enabled machines and programs stand now ready to complete routine of a structure task faster and accurately than human being could do. That has resulted in displacement in some low-skill category of jobs as human labour is increasingly being replaced by intelligent systems. The effects of automation are not evenly expressed though. As rules disappear in some roles, new or developing roles take place.

Augmentation-when AI does not replace human abilities, but complements those abilities instead. Technologies like AI-based diagnostics in the healthcare sector, predictive analytics in the marketing area, and customer service AI virtual assistants help employees organize their work and complete more challenging tasks. The role of AI, in this case, is as a team member helping professionals make better decisions and become more productive. This dimension of the implementation of AI has resulted in the building of hybrid positions that match the industry knowledge with technical literacy.

The most widespread effect of integrating AI, may be the change in the demand of skilled labour. The old-fashioned skills are quickly becoming non-relevant and the demand on some newer skills like data literacy, machine learning knowledge, and online communication are on the rise. The employers are now on a quest to find a combination of both soft and hard skills, adaptability, thinking, and emotional intelligence becoming a sought-after aspect.

dominance in AI-based working places. Therefore, numerous employees have to retrain or re-educate to be competitive and fit the evolving labour market.

Furthermore, the transformation brought forward by AI is affecting organizational (and management) structures. Organizations are removing that layer and becoming more agile to take advantage of AI technologies, thereby making cross-functional teams and collaboration more important to daily activities. Job descriptions are also taking a dynamic turn with the duties changing along with the technology applied.

Nevertheless, the changes do not come without difficulty. It is possible to speak about job security issues, stagnation in wages, growth in income inequality, not to mention workers without reskilling opportunities. These problems are also complicated by gender and regional gaps in digital literacy, so the transitional process is uneven when evaluated in these ways.

A human transition requires policymakers, educational establishments, and employers working together. They should have focused their efforts on the creation of an inclusive workforce in which AI emerges as an empowerment tool but not a way of exclusion. To reduce the risks linked to the job displacement that occurs as a result of AI, proactive investment in training, the support of displaced workers and available digital infrastructure must be pursued.

That is, the AI-powered AI revolution of job descriptions implies a fundamental change of approach to work definitions and implementations. Although it holds a massive capacity to innovate and be efficient, it also needs strategic planning and policies that are inclusive to thus the technological progress improves lives of every stratum of the society.

STEP 02: Business Innovation and Productivity Gains

Artificial Intelligence (AI) has emerged as the main exhibit in transforming business innovation and increasing the rate of productivity in industries. As organizations move towards the use of AI technologies, their ability to lift off with regards to operational efficiency and the ability of the organization to reimagine products, services and business models becomes changed as well. The type of change, is yielding another form of competitive and dynamic market.

The main value proposition of AI is the fact that it allows automating the process of making decisions and streamlining routine processes, releasing human resources to complete work with greater value. Preventive analytics, robotic process automation, wise assistance services, and chatbots are the examples of AI-powered applications that improve the efficiency of workflows, minimize errors, and decrease the operational expenses dramatically. AI can predict demand and handle inventorying in the logistics industry more accurately than ever before, whereas in finance, the algorithms are identifying frauds and optimizer investment plans in real-time.

On top of automation, AI is facilitating strategic innovation. Machine learning and natural language processing have become new tools that organizations utilise to glean useful information designed to assist leaders in providing evidence-informed decision-making. To give just one example, AI can be used to study the behavior of customers to come up with customized marketing approaches, or to evaluate the risks of supply chains and provide alternative options, which increases the levels of agility and resilience. Such innovations result in establishment of new value chains, products and revenue models that are never imagined.

In addition, AI fuels the innovation ecosystem, combining with other developing technologies such as the Internet of Things (IoT), blockchain, and cloud computing. Combined, they allow exchanging data on a real-time basis, intelligent surveillance, and secure decentralized working. The convergence of platforms especially advantages the startups and the agile enterprises as it has reduced the cost of entry and has democratized the access to higher order tools.

Productivity-wise, AI allows companies to become leaner, expedited and more scalable. The AI-based software is capable of handling large amount of work with speed-accuracy-consistency minimising delays and maximising output per employee. AI-driven predictive maintenance, in case of manufacturing, will reduce the number of hours such machines are not producing. The same applies to customer support, where thousands of queries can be solved immediately with the help of an AI chatbot, and humans can deal with more challenging issues.

Nonetheless, coming up with the AI is not a plug-and-play game. Companies simply need to redesign their culture, disciplines, and talent initiatives in order to take full advantage of AI. This includes retraining staff to collaborate with intelligent systems, reorganizing working processes to make them AI-readable, and implementing the principles of ethics to eliminate risks associated with information confidentiality, discrimination, and openness.

A gap also exists between the technological enthusiasts and laggard of AI. Companies who invest early in AI will probably break away forming productivity gaps across industries. This provokes the issue of the market concentration and the increasing distance between big companies driven by the technical revolution and those that remain out of this business-field, through example, SME that might have neither the means nor the know-how to implement highly qualified AI.

To sum up, AI is an accelerator and booster of business innovation and productivity. It changes the models of operation, makes it easy to adapt to changes in the market quickly, and aids in the planning of strategies in the long term. To maintain these gains in an equitable manner, businesses, governments and academies need to collaborate, make AI tools accessible and develop a labour force that will lead to innovative use of AI in the era of AI.

STEP 03: Ethical, Legal, and Governance Challenges

As technologies of artificial intelligence (AI) become highly incorporated in the order of the business and societal operations, many ethical, legal and governance issues have also cropped up. These problems can potentially harm the reputation of trust and increase inequities and unacknowledged harms when not addressed. So, responsible development and utilization of AI systems are the key factors that contribute to sustainable and fair development.

Bias and discrimination are the major problems of AI implementation in terms of ethics. Learning data, the AI systems pick up on historical information, and this can bring in current biases in the society. Where such biased datasets are used to train algorithms, the resulting data train these algorithms to reinforce unfair treatment on grounds of race, gender, age, or social economic status. This is of particular concern in life-sensitive areas like recruitment, credit rating and criminal law where biases can lead to life-changing decisions. During AI rolls out, promoters should exercise good data governance, constant auditing, and inclusiveness in representation in model development.

Both transparency and explainability are also vital issues. A large number of AI models, especially those based on deep learning, are black boxes, that is, the manner in which decisions are made is not very evident. Such interpretability can be a blocker to accountability, in respect to AI being applied in areas of sensitive processing such as healthcare or even the legal decision making. Employees, end-users, and other stakeholders want to know in digestible terms the result of AI technology applications because they do not want to give their consent blindly; they would like to be able to trust. Currently of increased interest is the development of explainable AI (XAI), to make AI systems more interpretable been performing.

Another ethical complexity created is surveillance and privacy. Monitoring systems that use artificial intelligence, such as facial recognition, behavior analysis, and collecting and tracking data, have seen explosive growth regarding workplaces and open areas. Although the technologies have efficiency and security advantages, they bring fear of mass surveillance and loss of individual autonomy. Employees will sense that they are watched continuously and that will compromise their mentality and dignity. Therefore, it is necessary to address the efficiency gain issue through AI and the necessity to protect the right to privacy by the authorities and ethical control.

Legally, the fast emergence of AI has surpassed the available regulatory guidelines. The question of liability when small data sets lie at the heart of AI systems causing harm is not clear. This is the case when there is an autonomous driving accident, medical misdiagnosis, or an algorithm misinforming. There are still questions on who should be responsible developer, deployer or the system? This grey area of law requires the introduction of the new law, which should determine responsibility, follow due process, and guarantee human rights under AI-mediated conditions.

Governance forms a critical role in overcoming such complications. To adequately govern AI, one would need to develop standards as well as control systems and ethics guidelines. International organizations, governments, and industry bodies need to cooperate in designing frameworks that would ensure that AI is aligned to the human values. Transparency, accountability, fairness, and safety are only some of the principles that need to be implemented into practical use through such tools, risk analysis, and enforcement methods.

Notably, ethical AI is neither only a technical nor legal problem but a social issue. Firms implementing AI should do more than playing by the rules and integrate ethics into their innovation design. Democratic systems of governance, where civil society, labor unions and marginalized groups are engaged, are the much-needed element that will make the AI technologies lead towards equity and justice.

Overall, ethical, legal and the governance aspects of the towards adoption are the defining characteristics of long-term sustainability of AI. The only solution to this is to do it beforehand and create a future where AI is established to help the dignity of man, his independence and his right to democracy.

STEP 04: Workforce Adaptation and Skills Development

With artificial intelligence (AI) quickly overturning the landscape on the conventional work system, the labour force has to experience a drastic change in order to become pertinent and sustainable. The issue of adapting the workforce and upgrading skills is the focal point so that the technological changes would not increase inequality but enforce the inclusion of human development. Such transition needs a systematic approach of involving reskilling programs, lifelong learning system and comprehensive education plans to accommodate the evolving needs of AI-based economies.

The reconfiguration of the skill needs is one of the most drastic effects of AI. Monotony and manual work taken over by automation meaning a decrease in the need of low-skill labor and an increase in the need of high-order cognitive processing, digital literacy, and interdisciplinary skills. The ability to work with data, machine learning, think algorithmically, be cyber security conscious, and problem-solving in many fields is becoming increasingly important. Nevertheless, this change is not a technical change any more, soft skills such as adaptability, emotional intelligence, communication, and critical thinking are just as important as human beings assume roles that will involve creativity and problem solving in the presence of intelligent systems.

Reskilling and upskilling have therefore become the important initiatives in workforce sustainability. Reskilling is the process of educating employees in completely new skills to fulfil other jobs particularly with regards to workers facing the risk of losing their jobs. Upskilling, in its turn, also keeps the existing employees on the edge to implement the work with AI. Academic institutions, government and industries should work together to create and designee programs to specifically prepare the workforce through customized training programs, digital learning platforms and certification pathways which are affordable, accessible and which meet the emerging demands in the industry.

Notably, education platforms have to be redefined to readiness of future generations to AI-fuelled workplaces. To produce highly rounded-off professionals, curricula need to combine STEM (science, technology, engineering, and mathematics), together with humanities and ethics. Moreover, interdisciplinary learning should be encouraged to make students aware how AI is socially, ethically and economically problematic. It will be critical to learn to code, robotics, and digital problem-solving early in life, particularly in underserved areas where the digital divide helps to further exacerbate the inequalities.

The transition also shows the importance of inclusive learning resources access and equality. Older workers, women, rural communities and marginated groups usually encounter inequality in using digital tools and training. This gap can be closed through investment in broadband infrastructure, localized learning centers and through mobile-based education platforms. Besides, specific education content that takes into account cultural and language diversity is an opportunity to make skilling programs more efficient and popular.

Employers should be central to the adaptation of workforce. Organizations have to embrace the philosophy of a never-ending learning process and offer formations like in house training, mentoring and job rotation. The undertaking of learning and development (L&D) needs to be a strategic investment than a direct cost to human resource departments. Future-proofing of talent pools has already begun as forwards-looking companies are building internal "AI academies" or even partnering with ed-tech companies to do so.

In conclusion, workforce transition needs to be supported by public policies, which extends unemployment security, career guidance and learning incentives to workers. To sum up, just transition rests on the basis of workforce adaptation and skills development in the era of AI. When AI is handled with both strategy and inclusivity in mind, it can be turned into a means of unlocking human potential, as opposed to the simplest replacement of it. The most sustainable practice to capture the advantages of artificial intelligence implies an investment in people rather than technology.

STEP 05: Wider Societal Impacts and Policy Response

The broad usage of artificial intelligence (AI) is creating waves with much bigger influence than effects on individual offices or sectors, transforming the social order, economic justice, and world progress. Although there is a lot of hope that AI will bring with it some transformational changes, the risks that may come with it are considerably high without any form of responsible governance. The need to understand and define these larger societal effects and accordingly create sustainable and resilient inclusions of the society is critical to construct inclusive, sustainable, and resilient futures.

Income inequality and job polarization can be described as one of the most noticeable impacts of AI on the society. Since AI replaces low- and middle-skill jobs, roles that require high skills and higher remuneration increase, and numerous routine jobs are trampled. It results in a deindustrialization of the labor market leaving all the benefit to those who are tech savvy and owners of the capital. The technological change is likely to exacerbate prevailing inequality between the wealthy and the poor, urban and rural residents, and the developed and underdeveloped world with the absence of mechanisms to redistribute wealth.

Also, job loss and economic under-security are becoming a burning social issue. The high rate of job losses to automation made possible by AI is threatening millions of employees globally. Both gig and platform economies are growing and frequently are non-secure, devoid of social standard, or bargaining. They are driven by AI algorithms. With the increasing fragmentation of work, and its algorithmic organization, people are challenged to be able to sustain stable lives with a dignified livelihood.

There are greater psychosocial impacts of these disruptions, such as worrying about losing their jobs, losing a sense of community identity with the older industries, and rising mental health issues. When the AI constructs the future, technological alienation can increase when workers and citizens do not feel a part of the rule.

Such interruptions carry far psychosocial repercussions, which comprise job loss anxiety, loss of community identity due to conventional industries, and more mental reasons. There is a possibility that technological alienation increases when the people, as workers and citizens, feel powerless or unable to make the future that AI creates.

On the developmental front, AI provides the solutions to the problems facing the world including the provision of healthcare services, access to education, mitigation of disasters, and food production. As an example, we may consider utilizing diagnostics based on AI to provide underrepresented groups with access to good treatment and intelligent tutoring systems to educate in distant areas. Nevertheless, the advantages tend to be distributed unevenly, and low-income countries do not have the digital infrastructure, and policy underpinnings to realize the full potential of AI.

Hence, policy responses need to be robust and visionary. The governments should be on the front foot in designing AI policies that focus on the public interest, accessible use of digital technologies, and protection. Among them, they are investing in educational and training infrastructures, controlling data privacy and algorithmic visibility, supporting moral AI creation, and establishing fiscal measures that reduce inequality.

Mechanisms of social protection should be updated too. Among the types of new policy design ideas under consideration to aide people in the transition are universal basic income (UBI), wage subsidies, portable benefits to gig workers, and lifelong learning grants. Also, labor legislation should be changed to be able to value new types of labor and treat people equally on digital platforms.

STEP- 06: Human-AI Collaboration and Cognitive Augmentation

International cooperation is critical at global level. International models of AI ethics, data management and fair technology transfer may be one way to make sure that the benefits of AI are not locked up in several countries or companies. The role of the multilateral institutions, such as the UN, OECD, or the G20, in enhancing inclusive AI governance, should be fulfilled.

Essentially, the social effect of AI is merely probabilistic it all relies on the manner in which we prefer to govern, allocate, and use the technology. The implementation of the human-inclusive, human-centered participatory policy paradigms would allow to manage AI to improve not only the productivity, but also social justice, well-being and sustainable development goals (SDGs).

The future of artificial intelligence systems is more than merely automating or substituting human labour; it is becoming a lot more about enhancing human abilities by the use of collaborative systems. The issue of human-AI collaboration focuses on the adherence to synergetic relationships between the machine and humans whereby the AI assists, enhances and expands human cognitive activities and not as a replacement. Such a practice unleashes strong redesigns in education, industry, healthcare, governance and everyday living.

The potential areas of professional productivity are one of the greatest opportunities of AI augmentation. In healthcare, artificial intelligence in tests, such as deep learning radiology applications, help medical providers in the interpretation of imaging objects more swiftly and precisely. In legal practices, the AI contract analysis and e-discovery software can support the work of a lawyer when reading complicated documents. Generative models in scientific study allow faster generation of literature review, hypothesis and design of experiments. These do not remove the expertise of the expert, but rather, they give decision support, which increases what can be done by a human being within time or cognition limits.

The collaborative intelligence of AI is reflected in the form of AI copilot and other helpers found in the most knowledge-intensive work areas, which are code-completion, writing, and meeting summarization tools. The systems alleviate mental load, allow focusing on creative and strategic work, and also individualize a working process according to preferences. The emergence of creativity and design assistive technologies aided by AI in art, design and storytelling also evidences the co-creative possibilities of machines, allowing the user to think and create beyond the old rules.

Notably, this trend poses a need to reconsider education and human skills. As we move to the era of AI augmentation, critical thinking, creativity, ethical reasoning, emotional intelligence, and human judgment are getting more important and not less. The focus shifts out of memoirs to making sense of things, out of acquiring skills through repeating and reproducing these skills to creating. The educational system has to advance to train the learners on how to work safely with AI tools, such as how to challenge results, how to verify sources, and how to co-design with responsibility.

The human-AI collaboration also presents a hybrid model of skills in the labor market because workers no longer compete with AI but utilize it as a tool. Such hybridization is skewed toward adaptive and flexible sets of skills again--the ones who can transform knowledge in a domain into problem-formulation in a system that can be easily acted upon by an AI or the ones who can weave the outputs of an AI into their human context by reading human with understanding. The world of work in the future might not be categorized as doomed instalments and secure jobs but an augmented job where both the knowledge domain and AI literacy skills are combined.

Yet augmentation can only be effective when the interfaces, transparency, and trust are followed. In case the AI systems are either opaque or biased or difficult to use, they may mislead or disempower the user. Collaborative AI systems design need explainability, reliability, and feedback loops such that a user feels like he or she comprehends how the system reasons and maintains control of choices. One part of ethical principles should dictate the extent to which autonomy is transferred to the machine and when it is still possible to use the human override.

Lastly, the governance systems should be transformed to conform to this emerging paradigm. The ownership of intellectual property, norms of liability, and professional standards will have to be rewritten where there are joint human and machine production of results. Institutions should also establish policies on their responsible use as well as innovating in a way that keeps humanity at the forefront. As such, the practice of Human-AI teamwork is not a mere technological transition, but it is a cultural and an epistemological one. When well designed and managed, AI will augment human capability, enable us to be even more creative, and will enable people and societies to tackle the big challenges in life better than human or machine alone.

Figure 2. AI-Driven Future of Work Challenges

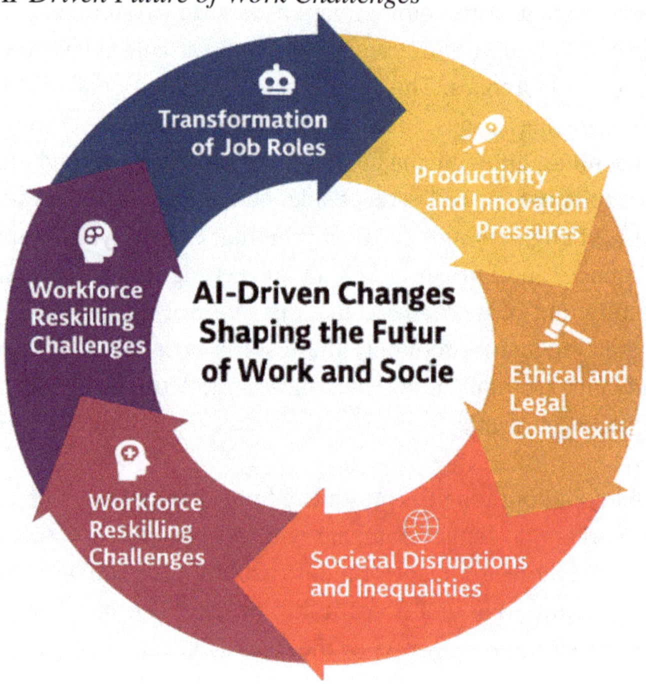

Possible Problems of the Future of Work Based on AI

1. Re-designation of Job Roles

In most industries, job functions are being redefined by the AI technologies:

Automation results in the increase in routine, repetitive and rule-based work. New mixed jobs are coming to the fore that mix human imagination and judgment and the feel of the human being and AI tools. Data scientist, artificial intelligence operational, even ethics, and human-machine cooperation are becoming desired positions. It is a form of transformation that would need constant job redesigning and revitalization of skill requirements.

2. Innovation and Productivity pressures

AI makes the pace of work very high, yet creates a competitive pressure:

Businesses are fighting to implement AI in order to minimize the expenditure and improve effectiveness. The need to innovate quicker with the help of generative AI, digital twins, intelligent automation is under pressure. This contributes to a performance gap between tech-savvy and slow companies and contributes to an economic gap. Organizational efficiency depends on the short-term outcomes might be prioritized excessively in lieu of longer-term human building.

3. Moral and Legal Conundrums

Discriminatory algorithms may strengthen the discrimination in the hiring process, lending, or policing. There is no transparency in any AI decision-making processes, or, in other words, there are black-box models, which make it far more difficult to hold people accountable.

The situation is worse in terms of legal frameworks, particularly involving liability, IP rights and data protection that are lagging. The blurred ethical lines occur in such areas as an autonomous system, surveillance, and predictive analytics.

4. Social Disturbances and inequalities

AI brings fragmentations and divisions within the society:

Automation endangers the employment of the workers in the field vulnerable (e.g., retail, transport, administration). The economic benefits of are unequally divided; thus, there is income inequality and regional disparity. There can be the widening of the digital divides between those who can use and enjoy the benefits of AI tools and the ones left behind. This invokes the danger of technological alienation to small communities that use and have minimal contact with AI systems.

5. **Challenges Of Reskilling the Workforce**

One of the greatest problems has to do with getting the new economy of AI ready:

The fast-changing technology renders a lot of the existing skills obsolete. Reskilling and upskilling are important to equip workers with a new job; the level of the need is huge and pressing. Most learning systems are not new nor in line with the emerging new professions. Employers, national governments and educators need to come together to create adaptive learning ecosystem.

DRIVING AI FOR GOOD: SHAPING THE FUTURE THROUGH STRATEGIC ACTIONS AND ANTICIPATED OUTCOMES

Future Work

1. Research Study of the Transformation of Job Role
    - Examine the changing human-AI interface at the workplaces.
    - Catalogue the sector-wise risk of automation and new hybrid job descriptions.
    - Examine the Algorithmic management and its effects on humans.
2. Responsible Business Model development
    - Create ethical and inclusive systems of innovation of AI.
    - Encourage the use of AI-based productivity tools without undermining the dignity of the humanity.
    - Test the idea in different industries with partial organizational structures.
3. Setting up of AI Ethical and Legal Governance
    - Write National and International AI ethics and legal procedures.
    - Implement the system of impact assessment and AI audits.
    - Police, hire, and lending decision-making use of regulations to control algorithmic decisions.
4. Design of Skill Development Systems and Systems of Scalability
    - Incorporate and mainstream AI and data science training in schooling.
    - Start the vocational and upskilling partnerships between the government and the business sector.
    - Develop national strategies of AI talent with the use of underserved groups.
5. Social Protection Innovation of Policies
    - Frame inclusive labour law and support in transitioning the workers to AI.
    - Implement and test such ideas as Universal Basic Income (UBI) and portable benefits.
    - Bridge urban- rural AI divide and develop inclusive digital infrastructure.

Expected Results

1. Equitable Job Change
    - Minimized anxiety of job displacement due to well managed job transitions.
    - Increase in the demand of the creative, cognitive and the AI supervisory positions.
2. Sustainable economic growth
    - better productivity and innovativeness in different industries.
    - Rolling out of AI startup companies and startups in the technology-aided industries.
    - Reliable AIs systems
    - A more significant belief by the people in the ethical and fair AI systems.
    - Compromised algorithmic discrimination and government protection against the abuse.

4. Future-Ready Workforce
    - an increase in the level of adaptability of the workforce and penetration of digital skills.
    - Fair career opportunities in matters of AI.
5. Stable and Diversity Social Inclusion
    - Reduced income and opportunity disparity.
    - Strong policy frameworks able to deal with the fast-technological change

Figure 3. Future Directions: Emerging Trends in Artificial Intelligence and Their Potential Impact on the Future of Work and Society

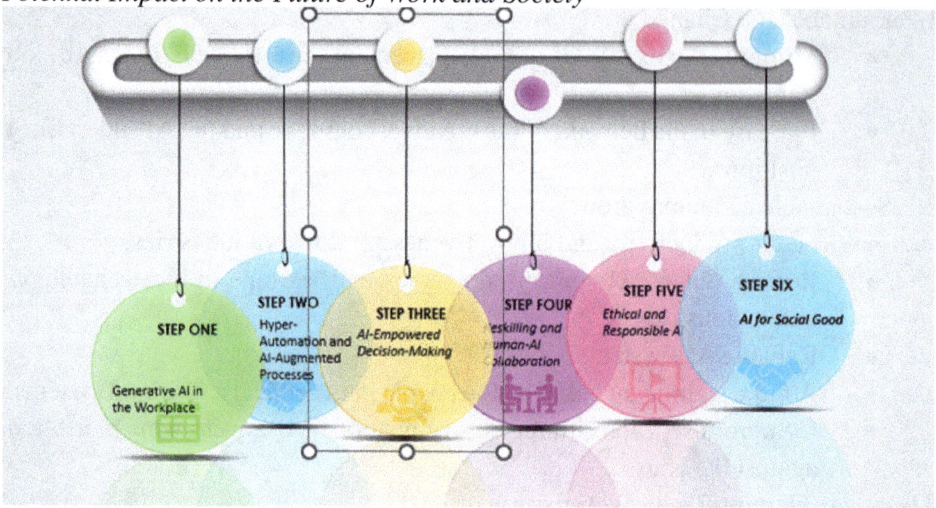

FUTURE DIRECTIONS: EMERGING TRENDS

1. Generative AI in the Workplace

Trend: There is rapid uptake of tools, including ChatGPT, DALL·E, Copilot etc.

Influence: Allows efficiency as it relates to planning of the artistic, programming and customer communicative employment.

Risk: There is also the associated risk of misinformation about products as well as authenticity of products.

2. The AI Congressional-Powered, or the hyper-Automatic Work

The trend: AI and RPA (Robotic Process Automation) and the IoT.

Implication: Degrees the manual, regular work experience in the sphere of production, logistics and financial sphere.

Reduction in the percentage of the low- skill job; increased figures of the supervisor job as well as tech-oriented job.

3. AI-Empowered Decision-Making

Some of the trends include artificial intelligence within the company setting and within the government, the analytics, predictive business operation, and tracking.

Effect: Department enhancement because of the effectiveness of working, the lack of human biasness, and an opportunity of being proactive in the policy-making.

4. Reskilling and cooperation between man and artificial intelligence of machines

Digital literacy, emotional intelligence and creative we must be able to have.

Societal Note: The divide in the digitalised world has the potential to grow Inequality of the chances to upskill.

5. Artificial Intelligence Ethical and Moral

Trend: The global economy is nowadays all about the globe of ethics and AI governances.

Impact: it facilitates the responsible, fair, and secure applicability of AI in the industry.

The Problem Society: discrimination, control through the system, inability to grant the right to privateness.

6. Sneaky artificial intelligence

Trend: AI associated with health care, AI based on education, AI based on climate change and accessibility.

Effect: Ensures the overall innovativeness, disaster and equity in the society.

Future envisioning: The collaboration of the Private-public partnership to utilize the AI en-masse in the underserved regions.

CONCLUSION

Artificial Intelligence (AI) is smack in the middle of a technological revolution that is frictionally reshaping the nature of the work as well as the bigger curves of society itself. As already explained in this chapter, AI is being quickly applied across industries, such as manufacturing, logistics, the financial industry, healthcare, and education, giving rise to hitherto unheard-of innovation and productivity rates. Nevertheless, these developments are accompanied by interconnected issues that must be thought out critically, acted and strategized upon collectively. One of the most immediate and evident effects of the AI adoption is all about the job role transformation. Tasks that are repetitive and run on a routine basis are becoming automated and it is resulting in displacement within some areas. Simultaneously, new jobs are created requiring new hybrid skills sets, which are both technically competent in addition to humanistic competence as well in accessing creativity, ethical judgment, and emotional intelligence. This two-fold influence makes labour market volatile as there are opportunities along with dangers. Thus, reskilling and upskilling of the workforce become the key elements in going through AI-induced changes. Yet, a lack of education, accessibility, and institutional support at a systemic level are some of the factors that could further worsen extant disparities unless handled inclusively. On business side, AI improves the effectiveness of operations, speed of decision making as well as played a central role in the development of new business paradigms, including AI-as-a-Service and digital twins. However, the competitive racing to use AI may generate uneven dynamic, technologically enhanced companies advance heavily and others distance them in the market which gives rise to structural divisions within the economy. Such ethical issues as algorithmic bias, the breach of data privacy, and secrets of decision-making further complicate the picture. Lack of proper legal framework and lacking governance mechanisms that are plain to the community poses a danger to harm the community- even though the possibility of good is tremendously high. On the social side, AI is an extremist. On the one hand, it holds the potential of tools of inclusive growth, like AI in healthcare diagnostics, affordable education and climate change efforts. Conversely, the lopsided allocation of the benefits of AI has the potential to widen digital, income, and opportunity gaps. Social groups that are vulnerable such as low-skill, low-income or under-connected populations are at increased risks of marginalization. In addition, there are new developments of psychological stress, job insecurity, social alienation and demand of emergence of new mental health support and ability of community resilience, since the world of work is rapidly transforming. Ethical and legal management have to follow the technological development. The development of responsible guidelines on an AI at national and global levels is an urgent necessity, with mandatory impact assessments and bias audits as well as transparency requirements in algorithms. At the same time, policy creativity must concentrate on reinforcing social safety nets, empowering lifelong learning ecosystems and trial-, and error-testing visions of the future, universal basic income. The future of AI is one that is sustainable and inclusive: It can only become that way through convergence of multi-stakeholder collaboration among government, industries, educators, civil society and international bodies. We can only realize the potential of AI to benefit the economy, not only to the benefit of our society, but also through collaborative approaches. To help the future of work driven by AI not only serve efficiently and rationally, but fairly, humane and resilient the world requires strategic investment in human resource, ethical innovation, and equitable structuring of policies.

REFERENCES

Acemoglu, D., & Restrepo, P. (2020). The wrong kind of AI? Artificial intelligence and the future of labour demand. *Cambridge Journal of Regions, Economy and Society, 13*(1), 25–35. DOI: 10.1093/cjres/rsz022

. Ahmad, S. (2024). The impact of artificial intelligence on business & social values: Benefits, challenges, and future directions. Educational Administration Theory and Practice, 3174–3180. https://doi.org/.DOI: 10.53555/kuey.v30i6.6012

Anthony, C., Bechky, B. A., & Fayard, A.-L. (2023). "collaborating" with AI: Taking a system view to explore the future of work. *Organization Science, 34*(5), 1672–1694. DOI: 10.1287/orsc.2022.1651

Appio, F. P., La Torre, D., Lazzeri, F., Masri, H., & Schiavone, F. (Eds.). (2024). *Impact of artificial intelligence in business and society: Opportunities and challenges*. Routledge.

De Stefano, V. (2019). Negotiating the algorithm": Automation, artificial intelligence, and labor protection. *Comparative Labor Law & Policy Journal, 41*(1), 15–46.

Deranty, J.-P., & Corbin, T. (2022). Artificial intelligence and work: A critical review of recent research from the social sciences. *AI & Society*. Advance online publication. DOI: 10.1007/s00146-022-01496-x

Ernst, E., Merola, R., & Samaan, D. (2019). Economics of artificial intelligence: Implications for the future of work. *IZA Journal of Labor Policy, 9*(1), 20190004. Advance online publication. DOI: 10.2478/izajolp-2019-0004

Howard, J. (2019). Artificial intelligence: Implications for the future of work. *American Journal of Industrial Medicine, 62*(11), 917–926. DOI: 10.1002/ajim.23037 PMID: 31436850

Ignacimuthu, A., & Chinnamuthu Kulasekarapandian, M. (2025). Impact of Artificial Intelligence in Business and Society: Opportunities and Challenges: Edited by Francesco Paolo Appio, Davide La Torre, Francesca Lazzeri, Hatem Masri, and Francesco Schiavone, London, Routledge, 2024, 294 pp., £31.99 (pbk), ISBN 9781032303420. *Journal of Education for Business, 100*(2), 93–94. https://doi.org/ DOI: 10.1080/08832323.2025.2460019

Ismail, T. (2025). The future of work: Navigating transformations in the global labour market (2025-2030). I-Manager's. *Journal of Management, 19*(3), 1. DOI: 10.26634/jmgt.19.3.21582

Khogali, H. O., & Mekid, S. (2023). The blended future of automation and AI: Examining some long-term societal and ethical impact features. *Technology in Society*, *73*(102232), 102232. DOI: 10.1016/j.techsoc.2023.102232

Kolade, O., & Owoseni, A. (2022). Employment 5.0: The work of the future and the future of work. *Technology in Society*, *71*(102086), 102086. DOI: 10.1016/j.techsoc.2022.102086

Kraus, S., Ferraris, A., & Bertello, A. (2023). The future of work: How innovation and digitalization re-shape the workplace. *Journal of Innovation & Knowledge*, *8*(4), 100438. DOI: 10.1016/j.jik.2023.100438

Kulkov, I., Kulkova, J., Rohrbeck, R., Menvielle, L., Kaartemo, V., & Makkonen, H. (2024). Artificial intelligence - driven sustainable development: Examining organizational, technical, and processing approaches to achieving global goals. *Sustainable Development (Bradford)*, *32*(3), 2253–2267. DOI: 10.1002/sd.2773

Lutfiani, N., Sembiring, I., Setyawan, I., Setiawan, A., Rahardja, U., & Sulistio, S. (2025). Exploring the relationship between Artificial Intelligence and business performance. [Indonesian Journal of Computing and Cybernetics Systems]. *IJCCS*, *19*(1), 1. DOI: 10.22146/ijccs.86697

Makridakis, S. (2017). The forthcoming Artificial Intelligence (AI) revolution: Its impact on society and firms. *Futures*, *90*, 46–60. DOI: 10.1016/j.futures.2017.03.006

Manickavasagam, P. (2021). The impact of technology on human behaviour and business environment. *International Journal of Society Systems Science*, *13*(1), 34. DOI: 10.1504/IJSSS.2021.115851

Masoud, N. (2025). Artificial intelligence and unemployment dynamics: An econometric analysis in high-income economies. *Technological Sustainability*, *4*(1), 30–50. DOI: 10.1108/TECHS-04-2024-0033

Neary, B., Horák, J., Kovacova, M., & Valaskova, K. (2018). The future of work: Disruptive business practices, technology-driven economic growth, and computer-induced job displacement. *Journal of Self-Governance and Management Economics*, *6*(4), 19–24.

Pasupuleti, M. B., & Siddique, M. N.-E.-A. (2021). The implications of artificial intelligence for the future of the workforce markets. *Global Disclosure of Economics and Business*, *10*(2), 45–54. DOI: 10.18034/gdeb.v10i2.628

Qian, Y., Siau, K. L., & Nah, F. F. (2024). Societal impacts of artificial intelligence: Ethical, legal, and governance issues. *Societal Impacts*, *3*(100040), 100040. DOI: 10.1016/j.socimp.2024.100040

. Saba, T., Hubert, A. M., & Bernet, M. (2025). Shaping human capital standards: Exploring the intersections of the future of work and artificial intelligence. Observatoire international sur les impacts sociétaux de l'intelligence artificielle et du numérique.

Sahoo, D. K., Kumar, A., Kanwal, P., & Rana, R. (2024). AI-Driven Market Intelligence: Enhancing Competitive Analysis and Market Positioning. In AI, Corporate Social Responsibility, and Marketing in Modern Organizations (pp. 89–108). IGI Global. https://doi.org/DOI: 10.4018/979-8-3373-0219-5.ch005

Shaji George, A. (2024). Artificial intelligence and the future of work: Job shifting not job loss. PU Publications. https://doi.org/DOI: 10.5281/ZENODO.10936490

Sheikh, S. (Ed.). (2020). *Understanding the role of artificial intelligence and its future social impact*. IGI Global.

Tschang, F. T., & Almirall, E. (2021). Artificial intelligence as augmenting automation: Implications for employment. *The Academy of Management Perspectives*, *35*(4), 642–659. DOI: 10.5465/amp.2019.0062

Verma, J., Sandys, L., Matthews, A., & Goel, S. (2024). Readiness of artificial intelligence technology for managing energy demands from renewable sources. *Engineering Applications of Artificial Intelligence*, *135*(108831), 108831. DOI: 10.1016/j.engappai.2024.108831

Vicsek, L. (2021). Artificial intelligence and the future of work – lessons from the sociology of expectations. *The International Journal of Sociology and Social Policy*, *41*(7/8), 842–861. DOI: 10.1108/IJSSP-05-2020-0174

Zohuri, B., & Mossavar-Rahmani, F. (2024). The symbiotic evolution: Artificial intelligence (AI) enhancing human intelligence (HI) an innovative technology collaboration and synergy. *Journal of Material Sciences and Applied Engineering*, *3*(1), 01–05. DOI: 10.63620/MKJMSAE.2024.1015

Chapter 3
The Impact of AI's Growing Footprints on Human Jobs

Regonda Prashanthi
http://orcid.org/0009-0001-2716-131X
Sreenidhi Institute of Science and Technology, India

Sravan Kumar Sadhu
http://orcid.org/0009-0009-0274-2992
Sreenidhi Institute of Science and Technology, India

ABSTRACT

Artificial Intelligence is no longer a future concept; it is already part of our daily lives and rapidly expanding. From chatbots to assistants and automation tools, AI is increasing efficiency, supporting decision-making, and providing instant solutions. This is why many companies are adopting AI widely.A common question people ask is whether AI will replace human jobs. The reality is that AI does not replace people—it replaces tasks. It is creating new opportunities, new roles, and new skill paths. While AI may seem to take over some tasks, it also reduces workload and supports us by filling gaps that humans alone cannot handle efficiently. To adapt to this shift, we must learn to use AI wisely and upgrade our skills. AI cannot exceed the capacity of the human brain, but relying on it blindly may reduce our abilities. Therefore, learning, reskilling, and understanding AI tools are essential to work effectively in this changing world.

DOI: 10.4018/979-8-3373-5816-1.ch003

1. INTRODUCTION. WORKPLACE 2.0: AI'S GROWING FOOTPRINTS ON HUMAN JOBS

Artificial Intelligence has moved from the realm of imagination to come one of the most important forces shaping ultramodern mortal actuality. Once limited to wisdom fabrication, it now forms the backbone of many inventions that impact how people live, communicate, and work. From virtual assistants that answer our questions to complex algorithms that guide medical research, transportation, and education, artificial intelligence has transformed the foundation of everyday life. The plant, in particular, has come one of the most visible spaces where the influence of intelligent technology is both celebrated and batted (Russell & Norvig, 2021).

The history of mortal progress has always been linked with technological advancement. Every generation has endured a advance that changed how people earn a living and how societies serve. The brume machine, the development of electricity, and the advent of computers have all changed husbandry and the nature of work itself. But no invention has so often blurred the boundaries of human study and machine capability as artificial intelligence. Unlike former technologies that simply extended mortal physical capacities, AI replicates rudiments of mortal cognition. It learns, reasons, and indeed improves its own performance through experience. This difference marks a turning point in the relationship between humans and their tools (Brynjolfsson & McAfee, 2014; Schwab, 2017).

Artificial intelligence isn't just about robots or convenience; it marks a significant change in how value is created in modern farming. Traditional work relied on personal effort, time, and human judgment. In contrast, AI enables organizations to analyse large amounts of data, make predictions, and improve decisions faster than any person could. This has led to greater efficiency and innovation, but it has also raised concerns about the loss of human jobs. As machines take on more tasks that used to require human intelligence, it's crucial to consider what tasks will still be uniquely human (Davenport & Ronanki, 2018).

AI has simultaneously produced new opportunities that put the concept of work in jeopardy. There are now entirely new professions in fields like data wisdom, robotics, and algorithmic design. Mortal creativity, emotional intelligence, and ethical reasoning are becoming more and more necessary as robotization grows. AI will redesign people's homes and guide them toward jobs that require creativity, empathy, and critical thinking rather than completely replacing humans. This collaboration between human and artificial capabilities and capacity is starting to redefine success in the twenty-first century workplace (Wilson & Daugherty, 2018).

The increasing presence of AI has also transformed how organizations deliver. Decision- making that formerly relied on experience and intuition is now dictated by data and predictive analytics. managers can identify patterns, predict trends, and distribute resources more efficiently. As such, the advantages of those systems bring ethical and social dilemmas too, especially if something goes wrong, who is responsible? How can organizations guarantee equity, transparency, and accountability in a world where algorithms can shape everything from hiring to healthcare? All this points to technology, regardless of how advanced, continuing to be a tool that serves human needs rather than a driver of them.

In this chapter, the influence of artificial intelligence on shaping human work is at the forefront. Starting from early mechanical inventions that paved the path for automation to the advanced intelligent systems that inform today's industries, it examines how organizations, employees and societies are navigating an ever-changing landscape in which technology is evolving faster than educational curriculums or professions. More importantly, it evidences the connection of innovation and purpose by investigating how humanity can design a future where innovation embodies meaning, creativity, and equity.

Artificial intelligence holds great potential as an innovative means to advance the productivity and connectivity of the world, but it only can fulfil that potential if it is used properly. The story of AI in factories is not one of machines being developed with thinking ability, but one of humanity being developed with growing ability. As humanity moves forward further in this stage of intelligent evolution to a more positive future, the hurdle will be in more than just being able to work comfortably with the technology; it will be about how to retain technology within the service of the human spirit.

2. THE EVOLUTION OF WORK AND TECHNOLOGY

Work, as a distinguishing aspect of the human condition, has existed from the beginning of the earliest of times. The earliest humans were making and utilizing tools, metal, wood, stone, et cetera, primarily tools and materials that were simple tools and materials. Work, for the greater part of history, was related to making, for the benefit of/in synergy with or oppositional to the people or being made in the image of people. Work, to some degree, does possess significance in history, as history, as conceived, revolves around the development of humans, "to invent, to improve," as it were- from history, i.e. history, qualitative and historical quality. Inventions, that enabled new technologies/systems to exist, improved what it meant to be human, and essentially the human learned and increased its ability to create new problems, in addition to those original problems it created. The human learned to use all of that knowledge, utilization of accomplishment, development, creation, discovery, and etc., to better maintain, fit in, and conform and adapt to utilizing new systems of existence, and the problems they caused, created, or mitigated.

The first significant transition in the character of work occurred during the Industrial Revolution at the end of the eighteenth century. The majority of people before this time engaged in work on farms or small workshops. After the introduction of steam-powered machines, however, large factories sprang up, and people began to relocate from rural areas to urban areas seeking jobs. The manual "labour" that existed before was replaced with machine "power" that was much faster and could produce more goods. This era produced amazing advances, but it also subjected workers to deplorable working conditions. Laborers worked lengthy hours with poor safety and low wages in factories. Nevertheless, this era introduced a different working relationship between labour and technology(Schwab, 2017).

The Second Industrial Revolution occurred during the latter part of the nineteenth century and marked important changes through electricity, telephones, and railways. These innovations allowed people and businesses to communicate more easily, while also making transportation more efficient. Work processes had become more tendentially organized and specialized, as factories adopted assembly lines and divided the labour by task space. There were emerging ideas of workers' rights and increased interest in labour unions. Although technology had increased the speed of production, there was a realization that workers deserved fair treatment and safe conditions, all the while, operating the machine.

The next big transformation came in the twentieth century with what is now called the Digital Revolution. This period began with the invention of computers and the spread of electronic communication. Machines could now process information, perform calculations, and store data far more efficiently than humans. Offices and factories both began using computers to complete tasks that once required manual effort. The introduction of the internet connected people and businesses around the world, creating new opportunities for learning, trade, and innovation(Brynjolfsson & McAfee, 2014).

In this current period of the Digital Revolution, AI has emerged. In the 1950's, scientists began to question - can computers learn and reason like humans? These early computers were relatively simple. They merely stimulated the first wave of researchers intrigued by machine intelligence. But in the following decades - AI development accelerated dramatically. We developed algorithms to accomplish games, solve problems, and even a few learned simple languages. It would not be wrong to say that not all consequences were positive, but the disillusioned responses to the first wave of researchers eventually were tardy in coming and led to some minor successes and practicalities, but they worked, and today there are phenomenal advances in creating systems that reflect human-like activity(Russell & Norvig, 2021).

Recognizably, in the early part of the twenty-first century, artificial intelligence was not just an aspiration, but an accessible and valuable technology. Abundant data could now be collected through the internet, and computers gained considerable enough power to actually learn from that data, recognizing patterns, making predictions, and providing decision-making support. This also ushered in a new industrial era, termed by many as the Fourth Industrial Revolution, in which machines are not just tools but working and co-creative partners(Schwab, 2017).

Nowadays, technology is involved in all kinds of work. Machines can build cars, analyse medical records, monitor what happens on the internet, and even write documents. While technology is faster and higher quality, it has also raised new issues about jobs and work in the future. There are jobs that have disappeared because machines are now able to perform these tasks! While there are jobs like factory workers and construction workers that have disappeared others jobs in new areas like software design, data analytics, and robotics have also appeared. The take-away is that technology does not simply replace work, it changes the nature of work!

The evolution from simple implements to intelligent machines narrates a story of human creativity and resilience. Each generation has built upon the advancements of those before, making life easier in many aspects of living but also more complicated. As technology continues to expand, individuals must continue to learn, and adapt how they behave and learn. Any era of technology will be successful based not solely on how mechanized devices become more capable, but by observing how intelligently humanity uses multiple intelligent mechanized machines. The merger of human intelligence and mechanized technology will continue to form the future world of work for generations to come(Makridakis, 2017).

3. THE TRANSFORMATION OF THE MODERN WORKPLACE

Figure 1. Digital AI visualization

Work has evolved more in the past few decades than at any time in human history. This quick shift has been due to digital technologies and artificial intelligence. Workplaces that depended exclusively on labour now depend on human work coupled with intelligent systems. Computers, the internet, and now AI, have radically altered how people work, how companies make decisions, and how and when employees interact with each other. Today's workplace is no longer just a physical space; it is a blend of humans, data, and technology(West, 2018).

Previously, work was characterized largely by physical labour or manual dexterity. A worker often was assigned to the same job repetitively every single day. Today, work is characterized by information and ideas. Technology has decreased many barriers of time and distance. Employees can work remotely from anywhere, share documents instantly, and attend meetings remotely by video and/or conference phone. The office has become a digital realm and the interactions that were previously face-to-face will now occur on screens. This has provided more flexibility and the ability for individuals to work with those from different locations around the world, and not require being in the same physical space.

Artificial intelligence has played a central role in this transformation. In many industries, AI helps automate tasks that used to take a lot of time. For example, in banks, AI systems check documents, detect fraud, and analyse spending patterns. In hospitals, AI helps doctors study medical images and suggest possible treatments. In factories, robots perform precise tasks that humans once did manually. These examples show that AI is not limited to one kind of job. It supports work in almost every field by saving time, reducing mistakes, and helping humans make better decisions(Davenport & Ronanki, 2018).

As AI and digital tools became more common, the nature of jobs also started to change. Many simple or repetitive jobs are now handled by machines, but this has opened up new kinds of roles for people. Workers are now needed to design, control, and manage these systems. For example, someone may not work on an assembly line anymore but may monitor the performance of the machines that run it. Similarly, someone who once entered data manually may now analyse it using AI software. This shift has made learning and adaptation more important than ever before. The ability to update one's knowledge has become as valuable as technical skill(World Economic Forum, 2023).

The evolution of workplace settings has also affected the employer/employee relationship. Organizations today pay attention to more than just production—creativity, innovation, and communication are equally important. Employees are invited to contribute ideas and to find alternate solutions to problems. The degree of success of an organization will depend on its employees' ability to think critically and to work with technology. Organizations are also recognizing mental well-being and flexibility. The workplace of today is more than just results; it is a space to support an environment where people feel safe to develop into the best versions of themselves.

Technology has also made workplaces more inclusive in many ways. People with disabilities can use digital tools to perform tasks that might have been difficult before. AI-driven translation tools allow people who speak different languages to communicate easily. These changes have helped bring more diversity into organizations, creating teams with a wide range of ideas and experiences(OECD, 2021).

However, this transformation has also brought new challenges. The line between work and personal life has become less clear because people can now work from anywhere and at any time. This constant connectivity can lead to stress or burnout. There are also growing concerns about job security, as employees worry that machines might take over their roles. In addition, the need to learn new skills repeatedly can be difficult for those who do not have access to good education or training.

Despite these challenges, the modern workplace shows how adaptable humans can be. Every time technology changes, people find ways to use it for progress. The key lies in balance. Machines can process information and perform tasks quickly, but humans bring creativity, empathy, and moral understanding — qualities that no machine can truly replace. The most successful workplaces of today are those that combine both human intelligence and artificial intelligence in harmony.

4. IMPACTS OF ARTIFICIAL INTELLIGENCE ON EMPLOYMENT AND WORKFORCE DYNAMICS

AI has changed the very meaning of work in many different ways. It has created opportunities for growth, but it has also generated ambiguity for workers in almost every sector. As machines and intelligent systems take over tasks that used to need human effort, the relationship between people and their work has transformed. This transformation reorganizes the way companies employ people, the types of skills employees develop, and society's view of the value of human work.

One of the most apparent effects of artificial intelligence is job displacement. Machines that can think and learn now perform tasks that previously required human judgment. In manufacturing, for example, robots assemble products quickly and accurately. In offices, AI software can handle large volumes of information, prepare reports, and even respond to emails. This shift has lowered the need for some routine jobs, especially those involving repetition or data entry. Many workers who once did these tasks have had to seek new types of employment(Frey & Osborne, 2017).

However, artificial intelligence has also created fresh opportunities. As machines take over repetitive jobs, humans can concentrate on tasks that need creativity, communication, and problem-solving. Completely new careers have emerged in areas like data science, machine learning, robotics, and cybersecurity. These positions require skills that blend technical know-how with human traits like reasoning and imagination. Therefore, AI has not only eliminated some jobs but has also opened avenues for new types of work that didn't exist before(Bessen, 2019).

The rise of AI has also altered what employers want from their employees. In the past, workers were often trained for one particular job and remained there for years. Today, companies seek individuals who can learn quickly and adjust to changes. Being able to work with technology, interpret information, and make decisions based on data has become crucial. At the same time, soft skills such as teamwork, emotional intelligence, and ethical reasoning are equally important. Modern jobs often require a mix of technical ability and human understanding (Manyika et al., 2017).

The demand for new skills has widened the gap between workers ready for technological change and those who are not. Many individuals struggle to keep pace with the rapid advancement of AI and digital systems. This skills gap can lead to disparities in the job market. Highly skilled workers enjoy new opportunities, while those lacking access to education or training face unemployment risks. Governments and educational institutions now must ensure that everyone has the chance to acquire the skills needed for a future driven by AI(World Economic Forum, 2023).

Another significant effect of AI on the workforce is the change in work organization. Many companies now adopt hybrid or remote work models, supported by digital tools and intelligent systems. This setup allows employees to work from home or various locations while staying connected to their teams through online platforms. AI helps manage schedules, track progress, and improve communication among team members. These tools have made work more flexible, but they also present new challenges, such as longer hours, feelings of isolation, and a loss of traditional office interactions.

The emotional and psychological impacts of AI in the workplace are becoming more evident. Some employees worry about their future, fearing machines may replace them. Others feel pressured to constantly enhance their skills to remain relevant. This stress can affect mental well-being and motivation. Conversely, employees who successfully adapt to AI-driven systems often report feeling more confident and creative since they can focus on meaningful tasks while technology handles routine work.

Despite these changes, the human role in the workplace remains essential. Machines can analyse data and perform logical tasks, but they cannot truly grasp emotions, culture, or ethics. Human judgment is still vital for making moral decisions or addressing complex situations that require empathy and fairness. The best outcomes arise when humans and AI collaborate, merging the speed and accuracy of technology with human wisdom and creativity(Wilson & Daugherty, 2018).

The overall effect of artificial intelligence on employment hinges on how societies and businesses manage it. If AI is used wisely, it can boost efficiency, reduce mistakes, and create new pathways for innovation. However, if it is used only to cut costs without considering human welfare, it can lead to job loss and inequality. The real challenge is not to halt technological advancement but to guide it responsibly.

As workplaces keep evolving, the future of employment will depend on adaptability. Workers who continue learning and developing their skills will uncover opportunities to grow alongside AI. Those who resist change may find it hard to establish stability in the modern economy. Society's aim should be to create a system where people and machines coexist harmoniously, enhancing life without compromising human dignity. Artificial intelligence is powerful, but its greatest benefit comes when it helps people achieve their full potential.

5. ARTIFICIAL INTELLIGENCE IN BUSINESS AND ORGANIZATIONAL MANAGEMENT

Artificial Intelligence is an essential part of a contemporary business model, as well as modern decision-making. Nowadays, pretty much one seeks to engage with some type of artificial intelligence in order to ensure sustainable performance, learn from customers, and support future decision-making. Artificial intelligence has supported businesses, from the smallest of small businesses to multinational companies, become more efficient in the management of their operations, along with more informed decisions, rather than based on gut or assumed rationale.

One of the main advantages of incorporating AI in business is that it allows for the rapid analysis of large amounts of data. Every day, businesses capture data through sales, social media, customer feedback, and market analysis. Before artificial intelligence, finding recognizable trends from this data often took humans a long time to analyse. Artificial intelligence (AI) now provides much faster and more automated access to this information. For example, companies can now predict what customers are going to buy, what trends are likely to impact the marketplace, and what they can do to improve their offerings. This helps companies overall to be more competitive and make better decisions (Bughin et al., 2018).

AI has also transformed how organizations manage day-to-day operations. In many sectors of the economy, machines and smart systems are performing many simple, routine tasks once performed by humans, such as sorting emails, managing calendars, and checking approximations to ensure there are no mistakes in financial transactions and invoices. Employees get to spend more time engaged in tasks that require creativity and strategic input rather than work that is simple and repetitive. In the banking sector, for example, AI is used to detect suspicious transactions to help prevent fraud. Similarly, in retail settings, AI systems are used to tell retailers how to manage inventory, and as shopping assistants to tell customers what to buy based on their preferences. Using AI tools, retailers are imbedding efficiency into their businesses and reducing the chances human error will impact customer experience(Davenport & Ronanki, 2018).

In the area of human resource management, AI has brought significant changes. Many companies now use intelligent systems to screen job applications, match candidates to roles, and even conduct initial interviews using chatbots. These tools save time for recruiters and help identify the most suitable applicants more fairly. However, they also raise questions about bias and fairness because AI systems can sometimes reflect the patterns or mistakes found in the data they are trained on. Therefore, organizations must use AI carefully and ensure that decisions involving people are guided by both data and human judgment(Chui et al., 2016).

Customer service has also been transformed by artificial intelligence. Chatbots, virtual assistants, and automated helplines are now common in many businesses. They can answer basic questions, process orders, and assist customers at any time of day. This has made services faster and more accessible. However, it is important to maintain a human touch, especially when dealing with complex or emotional issues. Successful companies use AI to support their staff rather than replace them, ensuring that customers still feel valued and understood.

AI also plays a major role in decision-making at higher levels of management. Business leaders use AI tools to study trends, forecast financial results, and design strategies. These tools provide insights that help managers make informed decisions instead of relying only on intuition. For instance, AI can predict how changes in market conditions might affect sales or how global events could influence supply chains. This predictive ability allows organizations to plan ahead and respond to challenges more effectively(OECD, 2021).

Although AI has enhanced management practices in a variety of roles, it also evokes new responsibilities. Companies must be diligent in ensuring that the information they are using is correct, secure, and gathered objectively. Privacy is another major concern since firms typically deal with sensitive information from customers and employees. Furthermore, managers must be aware of the environmental and social implications of deploying AI systems - including the use of energy, talent redistributions, and the sustainability of approaches that companies employ.

An additional challenge is establishing trust in the human-to-intelligent products relationship. There can be discomfort when employees know an AI system is tracking their performance or being involved in the decision of their work. To foster a positive environment for humans and machines to co-exist in the workplace, organizations need to be transparent in how AI is being used or how the AI makes decisions. When people know technology is there to help them instead of controlling them, they are more likely to accept it and use it to their benefit.

AI has also influenced leadership styles. Modern leaders are expected to be more data-driven, flexible, and open to technological change. At the same time, they must remain empathetic and focused on human values. Managing an AI-powered organization requires a balance between logic and emotion, between numbers and people. Leaders who can combine these qualities are the ones who will guide their teams successfully into the future.

In conclusion, artificial intelligence has quickly become a critical part of business and management in our world. It helps organizations become better at making decisions; provides better customer service; and helps organizations optimize productivity and operational efficiencies. Yet the real potential of AI is not about data harvesting, sweeps, or a vague notion of automation, it's about continuing to enhance and empower human creativity and judgment. Organizations that find that balance will not only far surpass their competitors that do not leverage AI, but they will also cultivate warm and inclusive environments in which to foster innovation, while continually relying on the essence of humanity. The goal of the future is to ensure that AI remains an aide of humanity while striving to breakthrough to greater discovery while at the same time be committed to fairness, trust, and ethics as its at the centre of it all.

6. SOCIETAL IMPLICATIONS OF ARTIFICIAL INTELLIGENCE AT WORK

Artificial intelligence has changed not only how people work but also how societies operate. Its influence reaches beyond services and factories, affecting education, the economy, and how people view fairness and occasion. As AI continues to develop, it offers new chances for advancement while also raising important social and ethical questions. Understanding these goods is vital. The way societies respond to AI will determine if it becomes a tool for addition and growth or a source of inequality and division.

One of the most conspicuous social goods of AI is its impact on profitable inequality. While AI helps businesses increase productivity and effectiveness, the benefits are not always shared inversely. Large companies that can go advanced technologies constantly gain farther profit and control, while lower businesses and developing regions struggle to keep up. This difference can lead to a slanted distribution of wealth, where a numerous benefit greatly from automation and data while multitudinous others are left ahead. To reduce this gap, governments and associations must concentrate on furnishing equal access to technology and education so everyone can benefit from the digital revolution.

Education plays an important role in establishing societies for the era of artificial intelligence. Traditional education systems were developed for a world where knowledge changed slowly, however AI has established an environment where skills rapidly become outdated. Schools and universities now need to focus on not only teaching knowledge but also helping students think critically, solve problems, and adjust to change. Topics such as data literacy, digital ethics, and computational thinking are becoming as important as reading and writing(World Economic Forum, 2023). Lifelong learning is also important because workers need to continually upgrade their skills throughout their careers.

AI also affects how people interact and communicate. In multitudinous workplaces, digital tools and AI systems have replaced face- to- face relations with online meetings and virtual cooperation. While this makes it easier for people from different corridor of the world to unite, it has also led to some heartstrings of sequestration. The lack of direct mortal connection can weaken team bonds and beget misinterpretations. Societies need to find ways to balance technological ease with real mortal connection.

The emergence of AI has sparked new discussions about fairness, insulation, and human rights. Numerous algorithmic systems make decisions that can significantly affect people's lives, such as permitting loans, choosing job candidates, or suggesting medical treatments. However, if the systems were not designed accurately, they may replicate the same biases and inequities that occur in the real world. An example of this is if an AI algorithm uses biased training data, which could unfairly favour certain groups relative to others. This points to the importance of translucence and accountabilities as they relate to AI. People want to understand how decisions are made and to believe those decisions are delivered fairly and ethically.

AI has also begun to impact public policy and governance. Governments use AI to manage business, descry duty fraud, and cover environmental changes. While these operations can streamline administration, they also raise enterprises about surveillance and particular freedoms. When technology is used to gather data on citizens, it must be done responsibly, with clear laws to cover insulation and mortal quality. The end should be to use AI for society's benefit without infringing on people's rights.

Another important social aspect of AI is its part in shaping culture and life. AI-driven media platforms, for case, recommend vids, news, and music predicated on individual preferences. While this adds convenience, it can also produce digital bubbles where people only see information that supports their living views. This limits open discussion and can beget misinterpretations among different groups. Societies should promote media knowledge and awareness so people can suppose critically about the information they admit through technology.

Artificial intelligence has also impacted the global labour market in multifaceted ways. Certain regions experience rapid technological progression and job growth, while others experience dislocation from within as traditional employment sectors diminish. The challenge for the states and the international community is to manage this transition equitably. Investing in training programs, digital infrastructure, and social safety nets can provide affected workers with retraining opportunities in new fields of work. Without any reasonable substitution of support, inequalities in the social and economic fabric are likely to widen.

In spite of these obstacles, AI has immense potential to foster more inclusive and sustainable societies. Intelligent systems can help find solutions for climate change, improve healthcare, and create educational access in remote areas. They can help people with disabilities, simplify everyday tasks, and create equal opportunities for participation. Used wisely, AI can be a powerful force for good that helps to unite communities rather than divide them.

The social impact of artificial intelligence is not determined by the technology itself but by how we choose to use it. It's a shared responsibility among governments, businesses, instructors, and individualities to ensure that progress benefits everyone equally. By prioritizing fairness, education, and empathy, societies can steer AI development toward a future that values both invention and compassion.

7. THE HUMAN–AI COLLABORATION PARADIGM

Artificial Intelligence has been considered for a long time a technology that would render human involvement obsolete. It is now revealing its significant potential as humans and AI can coexist: The co-lateral ship between humans and intelligent systems is a combination of new opportunity and a new layer of improvement- melding machines' complementary abilities of speed and accuracy with people's creativity and emotional intelligence in collaboration. Together, they have the ability to tackle the solutions to issues that alone they could not.

Human–AI collaboration is already visible in many parts of daily life and work. Doctors use AI to study medical images, detect diseases early, and suggest treatments, but it is the doctor who makes the final decision, guided by experience and empathy. In the field of education, AI tools help teachers track student progress and suggest personalized lessons, yet it is still the teacher who understands the emotional needs of each learner. In industries such as manufacturing and transportation, robots perform heavy or repetitive tasks while humans focus on planning, innovation, and quality control. These examples show that the most powerful results come from cooperation rather than competition (Wilson & Daugherty, 2018).

This partnership is built on trust. People need to trust that their systems are trustworthy, safe, and just. When employees understand how AI works and why decisions are made, they don't mind relying on it as a partner. Transparency builds out this trust organizations that are up-front about how their AI systems collect and analyse data are usually more successful in creating productive relationships between humans and technology. The whole intention is to make AI a helper, not a covert overlord .

In order for effective collaboration between humans and AI, both parties must deliver what they excel at. The strengths of machines lie in fast data processing, calculations, and identifying patterns that humans may overlook. Humans strengths involve interpreting emotions, empathy, creativity, and making ethical decisions. When these strengths are functioning together, intelligent collaboration can yield faster, fairer, and more creative results. As an example, AI can identify the best business approach based on the available data, but it is the responsibility of a human leader to select the approach that is more ethical and socially responsible.

The idea of augmented intelligence is frequently used to describe this connection. It highlights the principle that technology shouldn't replace human thinking, rather enhance it. In this way, AI is a collaborator supporting decision-making while giving people time to explore, think deeply, and dream. Rather than competing with machines, workers will learn to harness AI tools to increase their performance and productivity. More importantly, people can still be central in progress, as technology becomes ever-more powerful(Brynjolfsson et al., 2021).

In a world where humans and AI work collaboratively, leadership also changes. Today, leaders must understand both people and technology. Leaders ought to understand how to use AI to provide better outcomes without sacrificing human values. Effective leaders will also help their teams understand how to use cognitive tools capable of smart technology; they will support training in the use of the tools and foster an organization culture based on trust and openness. They recognize that any technology, no matter how smart, is only as good as it is used by the humans who manage and understand it.

Nevertheless, this partnership poses significant ethical concerns. As AI continues to evolve, there could be situations where AI shapes decisions that have severe consequences for individuals. Thus, humans should be accountable for the decisions that involve AI. Machines do not feel emotions or have moral awareness, so it is the responsibility of humans to ensure that AI based decisions are fair, honest, and all around humane. This shared accountability of moral human decisions will establish the ethical foundation of this partnership.

Education and training play an important role in strengthening human–AI teamwork. Workers need to understand how AI systems function, what their limitations are, and how to interpret their results. This knowledge helps prevent misuse and builds confidence. Schools, universities, and companies should work together to teach both technical and ethical skills, preparing future generations to work alongside intelligent systems responsibly.

The partnership between humans and AI is a new story of advancement, and it reminds us that technology, no matter how sophisticated, is never beyond the creativity and values of the human users. People and machines working together yield results that neither the person nor the machine could achieve alone. Humanity does not replace intelligence, but rather augments it - changing knowledge into wisdom and efficiency into understanding. If AI is driven by empathy and responsibility, then the future of work will be smarter and innately human.

8. THE FUTURE LANDSCAPE OF WORK

The increasing influence of artificial intelligence, automation, and digital connectivity is shaping the future of work. As technology continues to develop, it will not only change how people perform their work but will redefine what work is. Future workplaces will be more flexible, creative, and collaborative among humans and machines. This emerging workplace will result in far greater opportunities along with real and profound challenges; thus, it will require people, organizations, and governments to rethink how to adapt.

In the very near future of work, one of the first signs we will see is the rise of intelligent systems to enhance decision-making, planning and communication. There will be a large number of tasks that require time and intent now that could be automated by intelligent systems. For example, the AI might manage complex schedules, optimize workflows, and predict problems before they arise. This would not only improve organizational effectiveness, but give workers the time to be more innovative in their work, and even have the time to troubleshoot rather than trying to find time to move work forward. That said, there still needs to be an element of oversight to assure fairness and accuracy in decision-making with that level of autonomous facilitating.

As technology envelopes more of our daily lives, the remote and hybrid work practice will very likely continue to expand. Global experiences with digital technology have shown us that work can happen almost anywhere. The use of AI based software will assist teams working remotely to foster teammates working on the same centrally collaborative projects by instant translating languages, summarizing virtual meetings, and allowing teammates to write or develop together in documents and easy access, shareable files. Future offices will likely be more about creative spaces, and less about being a fixed location to do work, and would probably be a place people come for collaborations and creativity instead of requiring them to come every day. This means less need for fixed employees and more ability for employees to come when creative work is happening. However, it also means we will have to rely more on building trust and human connections through digital software.

The types of jobs that exist will also change dramatically. Some professions will disappear as automation replaces repetitive work, but many new roles will emerge. There will be a higher demand for experts in artificial intelligence, data science, cybersecurity, and digital ethics. In addition, there will be a growing need for teachers, counsellors, and creative thinkers who can help others understand and work with technology responsibly. The future workforce will need to be adaptable and ready to learn new skills continuously. Those who combine technical ability with human qualities such as empathy and communication will be especially valuable(World Economic Forum, 2023)

Another major trend in the future of work will be the combination of human creativity and machine intelligence. AI is already helping humans in writing music, composing stories, and generating new ideas in design, art and entertainment. In business and research, AI will be of value to the work of preparing, analysing information, and producing ideas. In any case, creativity will begin in the human imagination. AI will provide suggestions and possibilities, but humans always have to determine what has meaning and intention. Ultimately, most people will find that technology provides the greatest success when it inspires them rather than replaces their creative process(Lee, 2018).

The gig economy is also expected to grow as AI continues to change employment models. More people will work independently, taking short-term or project-based jobs that match their skills. Platforms that connect freelancers to companies will become smarter and more efficient with the help of AI algorithms. This new style of work offers freedom and flexibility, but it can also bring instability if workers do not have access to fair pay, social security, or benefits. To make this model sustainable, laws and policies must evolve to protect all types of workers, whether they are full-time employees or independent professionals.

As artificial intelligence develops more competencies, ethical and social implications become all the more salient. It is imperative that decision making undertaken by intelligent systems continually prioritizes human rights and dignity. Governments, enterprises, and researchers are obliged to provide frameworks that enable the responsible use of technology. Data privacy, transparency, and accountability, for instance, must be stage priorities nested within the digital eco-system. Without guidelines addressing these issues, the possibility remains for AI to be exploited in various contexts to the disadvantage of individuals or groups. The future of work must thus integrate not just innovation, but also equity and empathy.

Education will remain an essential component of workforce development in the future. It is vital that schools and universities emphasize teaching creative thinking, emotional intelligence, and problem-solving over rote memorization. Learning will not stop when students graduate; it will become a continuous lifelong process. Workers will routinely need to update their knowledge and modify their personal practices to adapt to changes in technology. Employers facilitate this work time education by providing training or by creating a culture of learning. If society cultivates curiosity and adaptability, it will grow with the changes in technology.

Work will likely become more connected, smart, and dynamic in the future. However, what will matter will be not just technology but how we humans decide to use it. The challenge will be progress that includes everyone, progress where neither automation and artificial intelligence work for deeper social divisions. If humanity wisely uses AI, it can enable a better future in which work is more meaningful, opportunities are more broadly shared, and technology is an enhancement to life rather than a replacement of life.

The true promise of artificial intelligence lies not in removing the human element from work but in elevating it. Machines will continue to take over tasks that are repetitive or complex, but the essence of work creativity, empathy, and purpose will remain deeply human. The future will belong to those who understand this balance and learn to work with technology as a partner in progress.

9. GLOBAL CASE STUDIES AND REAL WORLD INSIGHTS

The repercussions of AI are being felt globally in all countries and in all areas of a country, as countries strive to harness this crucial facet of technology for productivity, problem solving, and development. With so many examples of AI playing out all around us, combining with culture, science, policy, and the ecosystem, we also observe implications and opportunities and unanticipated challenges.

In many developed nations, AI has become an essential part of economic and social life. The United States has been one of the leaders in AI research and innovation. Major technology companies there use AI to improve online services, predict consumer behaviour, and design smart products. For instance, AI systems in healthcare help doctors analyse patient data to find early signs of disease. In agriculture, smart sensors and machines use AI to monitor soil conditions and crop growth, helping farmers make better decisions and increase yield. The United States also invests heavily in developing AI skills among students and professionals, which keeps its workforce ready for future challenges(National Science and Technology Council, 2016).

Countries throughout Europe, such as Germany, France, and the United Kingdom, are committing significant resources to the ethical and responsible utilization of artificial intelligence (AI). Industry across Europe is employing AI to develop safer and more efficient manufacturing processes, following stringent environmental and privacy regulations. Germany plans to use AI in combination with robotics and data networks for the development of factories to meet its objective of Industry 4.0. The UK applies AI to manage the public sector of services, such as transportation and energy. Many European governments also fund grants to study the societal implications of AI, to ascertain that the advancement in technology occurs in a responsible manner, protecting human rights and public trust(OECD, 2021).

Asia has also become an AI development hub, with countries such as China, Japan, and India making major strides. China has integrated AI into almost every aspect of society, such as smart traffic in cities or AI in finance, e-commerce, and education. China continues to grow as a major player in the global AI endeavour due to its focus on research and data collection. On the other hand, Japan is using artificial intelligence to address its aging population challenges. Robots and AI assistants would be useful in providing elderly individuals with assistance with everyday tasks as well as companionship. In rural India, AI is being utilized to facilitate agriculture, healthcare, and education, as a way of illustrating technology that can bring resources to communities that have not traditionally had access to these services.

Countries in the developing world are considering how to apply AI for growth and economic development. In Africa, AI is being used by startups and research institutions to solve local issues ranging from predicting drought to protecting wildlife and improving access to health care. For example, AI systems are helping to detect plants' disease incidents early to decrease crop loss and to ultimately improve food security. In Latin America, Brazil and Chile are harnessing AI to develop renewables and undertake environmental monitoring. These examples illustrate that - even in places with fewer resources - innovation can happen when people develop creative applications of technology to meet real needs.

Different industries across the world are also finding their own paths toward AI integration. In the field of education, intelligent learning platforms are helping teachers and students adapt lessons to individual needs. In finance, AI helps detect fraud, manage investments, and personalize customer services. In manufacturing, smart machines and predictive maintenance systems reduce downtime and improve quality. In transportation, self-driving vehicles and traffic management software are changing how cities function. In healthcare, AI supports doctors in diagnosing diseases, planning surgeries, and designing new medicines. Each of these examples shows that AI can improve accuracy, safety, and efficiency when used responsibly.

Yet, countries worldwide also have struggles. Not all are able to equally access new technologies, or have the skilled workforce available to utilize advanced technology. This creates a digital divide between nations and even within societies. Some worry automation could eliminate jobs faster than new jobs will be created by it. Others are also worried about privacy, since data collected by AI systems have potential for misuse. These concerns indicate that that advancement must also include protection. Now is the time for governments and businesses around the world to create strong laws and ethical codes of conduct for AI to ensure we all benefit in a fair way.

The global story of AI is one of shared learning. Countries can learn from each other's successes and mistakes. For example, Europe's focus on ethics, America's focus on innovation, and Asia's focus on large-scale application each offer lessons for the rest of the world. Cooperation among nations can also help create global standards for AI safety and fairness. International partnerships in research and education can make sure that AI development remains inclusive and guided by common human values.

Contemporary occurrences serve as a reminder that artificial intelligence is not only a technological revolution, but also, a human revolution. The way in which societies think about and utilize it reveals their principles and priorities. AI can provide solutions for creating jobs, expanding health services, and protecting the environment we share—only if AI is developed responsibly and judiciously. Studying AI deployment across the world can allow us not only to unlock possibilities for societal progress, but also to identify if it can be utilized for equality and peace.

10. OPPORTUNITIES, CHALLENGES, AND ETHICAL FRONTIERS

Artificial intelligence offers tremendous opportunities never seen before in human history. It can make life easier, increase productivity at work, and tackle problems that previously seemed unsolvable. At the same time, the challenges I'll describe below - risks - need to be thought through carefully and carefully. In my opinion, the throws of opportunity and risk will ultimately define how we see artificial intelligence in the future. All of us - organizations, governments, people - will have to learn responsibly using artificial intelligence with a focus on fairness, privacy, and human values.

One of the best prospects that has been instigated by AI is increased productivity and innovation. Machines can now process information much faster than humans, and that facilitates better decisions by firms and researchers. In the area of science, AI contributes to the study of climate change, development of new medications, and invention of clean energy technologies. In agriculture, it allows farmers to better manage their crops and predict weather patterns. In cities, it assists in managing traffic, minimizing energy waste, and keeping people safe. Altogether, discoveries illustrate that when technology is centred around good principles, it can improve quality of life(Bughin et al., 2018).

Artificial intelligence also presents chances for economic growth. Nations that prioritize AI research and education will grow new industries and jobs. Small businesses and start-ups can level the playing field and compete with larger corporations using AI tools that allow them to maximize output and increase their customer base. As a result, technology can serve as a catalyst for entrepreneurship and innovation. AI can also help governments improve planning by using data to understand what citizens need and develop better programs and policies. If AI is managed properly, nations' economies will be stronger and more inclusive.

Nonetheless, while these benefits are real, they pose serious problems. One of the greatest concerns is job loss due to automation. Automated machinery is rapidly increasing in capability and could displace many traditional work roles, leading to many workers feeling unsure about their future. This challenge can be mitigated through development of human skills and lifelong learning. Workers need to be supported to skill up, so they can transfer into new domains of work in which human intelligence and creativity are indispensable.

A major challenge is inequality, where people and nations may receive wildly disproportionate benefits from AI software while others are left behind by virtue of access to neither technology nor education. The resulting digital divide can create social and economic instability. This could be minimized if governments and organizations work collectively to engage and encourage equal access to technology for everyone, not just the privileged and educated. Equal access to technology in the digital sphere is just as important as equal access to technology in the physical sphere.

Privacy and data protection concerns present significant challenges, as well. Artificial intelligence generates derived predictions based on vast amounts of data obtained from personal devices, online places, and elsewhere. Without substantial privacy protections, such data could be used or sold (even if against the user's consent). Everyone has the right to govern their personal data and understand clearly about its use. Businesses and governments should be transparent about data collection, and take steps to protect individuals from exploitation.

Ethical issues go beyond privacy. AI systems can sometimes make decisions that are biased or unfair because they learn from data that reflects human prejudice. For example, if an AI system is trained on data that contains discrimination, it might repeat those patterns when making hiring or loan decisions. This shows that ethics must be built into AI design from the very beginning. Engineers, policymakers, and social scientists should work together to create systems that are fair, explainable, and accountable.

As artificial intelligence continues to increase, it also raises questions of control and responsibility: when AI fails, who is responsible—the developer, the individual using it, or the machine itself? Although these questions are difficult to answer, they are vital to trust. Society needs clear laws and mechanisms of accountability articulated so that individuals are not harmed by algorithmic decisions. This brings us to the issue of transparency. When individuals understand how AI systems work and how it arrived at a certain decision, it is ultimately more likely that an individual will accept its decision.

There are also concerns regarding the overreliance on technology. People are at risk of losing important human characteristics, such as empathy, patience, and independent thinking, as they become increasingly dependent on machines. True advancement is when AI extends our living experience, not simply replacing those experiences that uphold our humanity. Educating and creating awareness is essential to remind society that technology should be a tool, not a master. The more society values compassion and understanding, the more AI will reflect those same values in its design and use.

Artificial intelligence stands at a crossroads where innovation and morality meet. On one side lies incredible progress that can improve health, education, and living standards for billions of people. On the other side lies the danger of misuse, inequality, and loss of control. The future depends on how responsibly humans guide this technology. Governments must create strong policies, companies must act with integrity, and individuals must stay informed and aware.

The ethical frontier of AI is not a barrier to progress but a path to sustainable development. When ethics and technology grow together, the result is innovation that benefits everyone. Humanity must remember that intelligence, whether natural or artificial, is most valuable when it is used to uplift others. If guided by fairness, transparency, and empathy, artificial intelligence can become one of the greatest allies in building a just and compassionate world .

11. BUILDING A FUTURE READY WORKFORCE

As AI becomes more deeply woven into the fabric of work, creating a workforce ready for the future has turned into one of society's most crucial aims. A workforce prepared for what's ahead can adapt, has the right skills, and feels at ease with new tech. This goes beyond just technical know-how – it also includes the creative thinking, ability to communicate, and knack for solving problems that set humans apart. Getting people ready for this new age needs everyone to pitch in, from the government and schools to businesses and the workers themselves.

Education forms the basis of a society ready for the future. Schools of the past suited industrial economies where employees often did the same jobs for years. In today's world, tech changes fast, and info gets old quickly. This means schools and colleges need to teach students how to think, not what to think. Skills like critical thinking, working in teams, and using digital tools are now just as key as reading and writing. Learning should also cover ethics, so kids grow up knowing how to use tech the right way(World Economic Forum, 2023).

Lifelong learning is another essential part of building a future-ready workforce. People can no longer depend on one set of skills learned early in life. Instead, they must continue to learn throughout their careers. Governments and companies can support this by creating programs that make skill training accessible and affordable. Online learning platforms, workshops, and short certification courses can help workers update their knowledge whenever new technologies appear. A culture that values continuous learning will ensure that people remain employable even as jobs change.

Businesses hold a key role in helping employees get ready for future changes. They should invest in training sessions and show how AI can support workers with their tasks. Letting employees learn and explore new tools makes them more confident and sparks creative thinking. This not makes work smoother but also builds stronger bonds between employees and their managers. Companies that care about their workers as much as they care about technology are more likely to achieve long-term success(Brynjolfsson et al., 2021).

Helping people learn about AI is key to preparing them for future careers. It's important to show how AI works, what it does well, and where it might fall short. While they don't need to know coding, they should grasp how AI affects their work and surroundings. This knowledge allows them to work alongside AI, notice mistakes, and recognize biased results. Understanding AI helps them make better choices and adapt to a future where automation plays a big part.

Governments must take on the job of making policies to help people build skills and shield workers from rapid changes in technology. They achieve this by pushing businesses to provide training, putting money into education programs, and making sure everyone can use technology. Combining the strengths of government planning and business creativity public-private partnerships can play a role. Governments also need to make fair labour laws so workers, including those in jobs like remote or temporary work, get the support and protection they deserve.

Building a future-ready workforce means making inclusion a priority. Everyone regardless of age, gender, or background, needs chances to join the digital economy. Women people with disabilities, and rural workers often miss out on progress when technology advances. Societies need to ensure fairness by providing them with targeted training and assistance. Inclusion not supports fairness but also brings fresh ideas, which leads to better innovation.

In addition to technical and educational efforts, emotional intelligence and adaptability are becoming essential skills for the future. As AI takes over routine and analytical tasks, humans will need to focus more on areas that machines cannot easily replicate, such as empathy, negotiation, and creative thinking. Emotional intelligence helps workers communicate better, build relationships, and manage stress—qualities that are critical in fast-changing environments. Adaptability allows people to handle uncertainty and respond to new challenges without fear.

Governments, industries, and schools decide how workers will succeed in the future. When they collaborate, they find methods to help people adapt to new technology instead of falling behind. The goal should aim to understand how AI can boost human skills instead of taking over. This approach can build a future where meaningful jobs are available to all.

The journey toward a future-ready workforce is not only about learning new technologies but also about rediscovering what it means to be human in a digital age. It is about understanding that progress does not come from machines alone but from the people who guide and shape them. By building strong education systems, supporting lifelong learning, promoting fairness, and nurturing empathy, societies can create a generation that is ready not just to face the future but to lead it.

12. CONCLUSION

Artificial intelligence represents a major turning point in human history. It has changed how people approach work communicate with others, and find solutions. AI plays a role in shaping results, from simple daily tasks to big business decisions.

This shift goes beyond technology and touches on human aspects as it pushes societies to rethink the meaning of work, which skills matter, and how to find purpose in a world with smart machines

Over time big changes in technology have always altered the way people work. Factories came into existence with the steam engine. Electricity turned businesses into global industries. Computers gave rise to the digital age. Now artificial intelligence is shifting how humans and machines interact once again. AI stands out from older technologies by being able to think, learn, and adjust. It is more than just a tool; it works with humans like a partner. This teamwork can improve lives, but it also calls for careful responsibility, a sense of balance, and ethical understanding.

The modern workplace is no longer just a physical space where people show up to do their tasks. It has turned into a network of people, technology, and ideas all working together. Work today is far more flexible, focused on collaboration, and filled with creativity compared to the past. Now, people can work, connect with others, and use advanced tools to make decisions. But these developments bring challenges like job cuts, worries about privacy, and stress on mental health. The future of work will rely on how we manage these problems.

AI helps complete tasks faster and increases their efficiency, but its true value lies in boosting human intelligence. Machines handle data, but people are the ones who understand it. While AI identifies trends and patterns, humans add empathy and make ethical decisions. This blend of logic and compassion will influence the future. Societies that succeed will combine human creativity with the precision of technology and view AI as a tool to assist, not replace, them.

Preparing for the future requires focusing on education, fairness, and ethical decision-making. People must learn to adapt, gain new skills, and accept change. Schools and companies should go beyond teaching technical knowledge. They should guide individuals to understand feelings and make responsible choices. Governments should create laws to protect workers, promote fairness, and encourage innovation. Everyone, from individuals to large organizations, plays a role in guiding AI to serve humanity.

Humans, not machines, will decide how work evolves by creating, controlling, and working alongside technology. It is society's duty to ensure technology enhances human experiences instead of replacing them. Artificial intelligence needs to remove barriers instead of creating them, reduce inequality rather than increase it, and bring people together instead of pulling them apart. Success should not be judged by financial gains but by how it improves social well-being and spreads happiness among people.

The story of AI and jobs is about collaboration. It shows how human smarts and artificial intelligence can combine to get things done better. When people team up with AI, work can feel more rewarding, creative, and accessible. The goal is not to create smarter machines. It focuses on using technology to help people think better, improve lives unlock new opportunities, and hold onto the values that make life meaningful.

AI doesn't signal the disappearance of human jobs. It begins a new phase. Now, machines handle routine work freeing people to focus on imagination, understanding, and fresh thinking. Achievements won't rely on how fast machines work but on the strength of human kindness. This forms the foundation of today's workplace. It's where human intelligence joins forces with AI to build a more just and optimistic future(Brynjolfsson & McAfee, 2014; Schwab, 2017; Wilson & Daugherty, 2018).

REFERENCES

Bessen, J. (2019). Automation and jobs: When technology boosts employment. *Economic Policy, 34*(100), 589–626. DOI: 10.1093/epolic/eiaa001

Brynjolfsson, E., & McAfee, A. (2014). *The second machine age: Work, progress, and prosperity in a time of brilliant technologies*. W. W. Norton & Company.

Bughin, J., Seong, J., Manyika, J., Chui, M., & Joshi, R. (2018). *Notes from the AI frontier: Modeling the impact of AI on the world economy*. McKinsey Global Institute.

Davenport, T. H., & Ronanki, R. (2018). Artificial intelligence for the real world. *Harvard Business Review, 96*(1), 108–116.

Frey, C. B., & Osborne, M. A. (2017). The future of employment: How susceptible are jobs to computerisation? *Technological Forecasting and Social Change, 114*, 254–280. DOI: 10.1016/j.techfore.2016.08.019

Makridakis, S. (2017). The forthcoming Artificial Intelligence (AI) revolution: Its impact on society and firms. *Futures, 90*, 46–60. DOI: 10.1016/j.futures.2017.03.006

Manyika, J., Chui, M., Miremadi, M., Bughin, J., George, K., Willmott, P., & Dewhurst, M. (2017). *A future that works: Automation, employment, and productivity*. McKinsey Global Institute.

OECD. (2021). *The OECD AI principles: Progress and impact*. Organisation for Economic Co-operation and Development.

Russell, S., & Norvig, P. (2021). *Artificial intelligence: A modern approach* (4th ed.). Pearson Education.

Schwab, K. (2017). *The fourth industrial revolution*. Crown Business.

Wilson, H. J., & Daugherty, P. R. (2018). Collaborative intelligence: Humans and AI are joining forces. *Harvard Business Review, 96*(4), 114–123.

World Economic Forum. (2023). The future of jobs report 2023. World Economic Forum.

Chapter 4
Labor in Transition:
Strategic Foresight on AI-Driven Work in a Post-COVID-19 World

R. Veeramani
http://orcid.org/0009-0004-1252-9670
SASTRA (Deemed to be) University, India

V. Arunkumar
http://orcid.org/0000-0002-2698-2669
SASTRA (Deemed to be) University, India

ABSTRACT

The rapid advancement of artificial intelligence (AI) and digital technologies is reshaping the global labor landscape at an unprecedented scale. Using a futures studies lens, this chapter examines the future of work through three scenarios—optimistic, pessimistic, and transformative. Drawing on labor economics, global policy debates, and sociotechnical systems theory, it highlights the interplay between technological adoption, labor market structures, and governance frameworks. The optimistic scenario envisions AI augmenting human potential, fostering inclusivity, and advancing sustainable employment. The pessimistic scenario warns of widening inequalities, algorithmic bias, and diminished worker autonomy. The transformative scenario imagines a human-AI symbiosis that enhances creativity, dignity, and sustainable livelihoods in line with Industry 5.0 principles. This chapter contributes a multidimensional and globally informed framework for navigating AI-driven labor futures by combining scenario planning with comparative global policy analysis.

DOI: 10.4018/979-8-3373-5816-1.ch004

1. INTRODUCTION: THE GREAT LABOR DISRUPTION

1.1 Technological Revolution and Labor Transformation

The early decades of the twenty-first century mark the acceleration of a technological revolution that fundamentally challenges conventional understandings of work and labor markets. Unlike earlier industrial revolutions—steam, electricity, and digitalization—the current wave, driven by artificial intelligence (AI), machine learning, robotics, and advanced digital platforms, does not merely substitute manual labor or routine processes but increasingly targets cognitive and creative tasks once considered uniquely human ((Bonnaure, 2018; Srivastava, 2021).

AI-enabled systems can now perform legal document reviews, medical diagnostics, financial forecasting, and content creation. Generative AI technologies such as ChatGPT, DALL·E, and Codex have demonstrated the ability to produce text, images, and code with remarkable fluency, raising debates over authorship, intellectual property, and the boundaries of human creativity. Automation is no longer limited to assembly-line robots but includes algorithmic management systems that allocate tasks, monitor performance, and evaluate workers in real time. This "digital Taylorism" reintroduces concerns about control, autonomy, and worker agency in contemporary labor regimes (Graham et al., 2019).

In many sectors, the promise of AI is framed in terms of augmentation rather than replacement. Research shows that productivity gains can be substantial when AI tools complement human skills. For instance, call center employees using AI-driven real-time suggestions improved customer satisfaction and reduced average handling time by significant margins (Brynjolfsson et al., 2023). Similarly, AI-assisted radiologists have demonstrated higher diagnostic accuracy than humans or machines alone. These examples illustrate the potential for human-AI collaboration to enhance outcomes, provided organizations adopt inclusive and ethical approaches.

However, the reality is uneven. While high-skilled workers in technology-intensive industries benefit from AI augmentation, low- and middle-skilled workers face displacement risks. The polarization of labor markets—where demand increases for high-skilled, high-paid, low-skilled service roles, while middle-class occupations erode—has been documented across advanced economies (Autor, 2015). Emerging markets face a double challenge: the risk of premature deindustrialization as automation reduces the comparative advantage of cheap labor, and the lack of digital infrastructure to capitalize on AI-driven growth.

Moreover, the organization of work is being reshaped by digital platforms that intermediate labor supply and demand. The rise of the gig economy—with platforms such as Uber, up work, and Delivered—illustrates how technology reorganizes employment relations. These systems often blur the line between self-employment and wage labor, leaving workers without traditional protections such as collective bargaining, minimum wage guarantees, or social security (De Stefano, 2015). Algorithmic governance structures create a new form of asymmetry: workers are managed not by human supervisors but by opaque systems whose logic is often inaccessible.

Thus, the technological revolution represents a paradox. On one hand, it unlocks unprecedented opportunities for innovation, productivity, and new forms of human expression. On the other hand, it exacerbates precocity, inequality, and surveillance. The future trajectory of labor will depend on how societies negotiate this dual potential.

1.2 Global Disruptions and Uncertainty

The transformative effects of AI and automation do not occur in a vacuum but intersect with global disruptions that complicate the landscape of labor futures. The COVID-19 pandemic was a critical inflexion point, rapidly accelerating digital adoption across industries. Remote work, once a niche practice, became mainstream in white-collar occupations, forcing organizations to adopt virtual collaboration platforms, digital monitoring systems, and cloud-based workflows. While this shift demonstrated resilience and adaptability, it also highlighted deep inequalities. Manufacturing, retail, and essential service workers could not transition to remote modalities, often bearing disproportionate health risks and economic hardships (ILO, 2021).

Beyond the pandemic, geopolitical instability and shifting global value chains introduce new uncertainties. Trade wars, supply chain disruptions, and resource nationalism affect the distribution of labor demand across regions. For example, semiconductor shortages underscored the vulnerabilities of global production systems reliant on concentrated technological hubs. As nations emphasize strategic autonomy in critical technologies, labor markets will be reshaped by regional industrial policies, reshoring strategies, and investments in local capacity building.

Climate change adds another layer of complexity. The transition to a green economy requires massive labor reallocation. Jobs in fossil-fuel industries are expected to decline, while new opportunities emerge in renewable energy, electric mobility, and circular economy sectors. However, the speed and equity of this transition remain contested. The challenge is not merely to create "green jobs" but to ensure decent jobs, offering fair wages, stability, and opportunities for skill development ("Human Development Report 2020," 2020). AI and digital technologies play a dual role here: they can support energy optimization and sustainability, but consume vast computational power and resources, raising questions about their ecological footprint.

Demographic transitions further complicate labor futures. Ageing populations in advanced economies are expected to create shortages in care work and health services. In contrast, youthful populations in parts of Africa and South Asia face the challenge of generating sufficient employment opportunities. AI-driven automation may alleviate and exacerbate these trends—by addressing shortages in some regions while reducing labor demand in others.

Adding to these structural disruptions are cultural and psychological shifts. Workers increasingly seek purpose-driven employment and value work-life balance, as reflected in debates around the four-day workweek, digital nomadism, and flexible work arrangements. The pandemic catalyzed the "Great Resignation" phenomenon, where employees voluntarily left jobs no longer aligned with their expectations of dignity, flexibility, or growth. Such movements illustrate that the future of labor is not only shaped by technology and policy but also by workers' agency and evolving social norms.

Taken together, these global disruptions underscore that the future of labor is marked by radical uncertainty. Forecasts cannot rely solely on technological trends but must account for the interaction of crises, governance systems, and collective choices. The role of AI in this context is not deterministic: its impact will depend on how societies balance resilience, inclusivity, and sustainability in their institutional responses.

1.3 The Contemporary Landscape: Technological Disruption and the Changing Nature of Work

1.3.1 Automation, AI, and Algorithmic Management

Integrating automation and artificial intelligence into the workplace has transformed repetitive tasks and increasingly complex forms of labor. Early waves of automation in manufacturing focused on replacing physical labor through robotics and process engineering. However, advances in machine learning, natural language processing, and generative AI extend automation to knowledge-intensive sectors. AI systems can now partially or fully perform tasks such as drafting legal contracts, diagnosing medical conditions, analyzing financial risks, or producing creative content (Bonnaure, 2018).

A parallel transformation is unfolding through algorithmic management, where gig platforms such as Uber, Delivered, and Amazon Mechanical Turk rely on algorithms to allocate tasks, monitor worker performance, and determine compensation. This shift has redefined managerial authority, replacing human supervisors with data-driven systems (Rosenblat & Stark, 2015). While efficient, this approach has raised questions about worker autonomy, fairness, and transparency, since workers often lack clarity about how algorithms make decisions that directly affect their livelihoods.

1.3.2 From Task Automation to Human Augmentation

Contrary to early fears of full-scale replacement, emerging research suggests that AI is increasingly used to augment rather than substitute human capabilities. For instance, decision-support systems in healthcare do not eliminate physicians but rather assist them in diagnostic accuracy. Similarly, AI-enhanced design tools expand creative possibilities for architects, engineers, and artists (Srivastava, 2021). This shift indicates that the future of work may not be defined by displacement alone, but by new hybrid forms of labor where humans and machines operate in symbiosis.

However, this augmentation is not evenly distributed across occupations. High-skilled workers in technologically advanced industries often benefit most, while low- and middle-skilled jobs are more susceptible to automation-driven redundancy. The resulting polarization of labor markets—with growth at both high- and low-wage ends but a decline in middle-wage employment—exacerbates inequality and creates structural challenges for economies worldwide (Autor, 2015).

1.3.3 Redefining Skills and Competencies

The nature of employability is also being redefined. Digital literacy, adaptive learning, emotional intelligence, and creativity are becoming more valuable than routine technical expertise. Employers increasingly seek workers who collaborate with AI systems, exercise critical judgment, and engage in lifelong reskilling. This dynamic places immense pressure on education and training systems, which must evolve to prepare future generations for jobs that do not yet exist.

In parallel, organizations are reimagining their talent management strategies through Human Capital Management Systems (HCMS) and AI-driven HR analytics. These tools optimize recruitment and performance evaluation and reshape how workers are matched to opportunities. While potentially efficient, they risk embedding algorithmic biases that reinforce social inequalities if left unchecked (Barocas & Selbst, 2016).

1.4 The Context of Uncertainty: Global Disruptions Shaping Labor Futures

1.4.1 The Legacy of the COVID-19 Pandemic

The COVID-19 pandemic has been a defining inflexion point in work organization. Lockdowns and social distancing accelerated the adoption of remote and hybrid work models, challenging traditional assumptions about productivity and collaboration. Organizations discovered that digital infrastructures could sustain global operations, while workers sought greater flexibility and work-life balance. However, these benefits were unevenly distributed: while knowledge workers adapted to remote tools, frontline and essential workers faced heightened risks without equivalent protections ("Human Development Report 2020," 2020).

The pandemic also exposed systemic vulnerabilities in social protection systems, healthcare access, and labor rights. Millions of workers in the informal economy, especially in developing regions, were left without safety nets. These disparities underscore the urgency of rethinking labor governance in ways that integrate inclusivity and resilience.

1.4.2 Geopolitical Instability and Economic Fragmentation

Geopolitical tensions, including trade wars, resource competition, and regional conflicts, increasingly influence the global labor market. The reconfiguration of supply chains—whether due to U.S.–China strategic rivalry, Brexit, or the Russia–Ukraine conflict—has reshaped employment landscapes. Multinational corporations are reconsidering reshoring, nearshoring, and friend-shoring strategies, altering work geography.

Economic nationalism has further fueled protectionist labor policies, sometimes at odds with the global mobility of skilled workers. As migration flows face increasing restrictions, many economies confront talent shortages in critical sectors such as technology, healthcare, and green energy (Woodward, 2022). For workers, this uncertainty creates an environment of precocity and volatility, complicating career trajectories and income security.

1.4.3 Climate Change and the Green Transition

Another defining uncertainty is the climate crisis, which directly affects labor markets through risks and opportunities. Extreme weather events displace communities and disrupt agricultural, manufacturing, and service sectors. At the same time, global commitments to net-zero emissions and sustainable development have stimulated the growth of green jobs in renewable energy, circular economies, and ecological restoration.

The just transition framework—championed by the ILO and other institutions—emphasizes that climate action must ensure social justice, reskilling, and protections for workers displaced by decarburization. Without deliberate governance, the green transition could replicate existing inequalities by concentrating opportunities in advanced economies while leaving developing regions behind.

1.4.5 Demographic Transitions and Labor Force Dynamics

Demographic shifts further complicate the future of labor. Advanced economies such as Japan and much of Europe face ageing populations, raising concerns about labor shortages, pension sustainability, and healthcare demands. In contrast, regions such as Africa and South Asia are experiencing youth bulges, offering potential demographic dividends if education, employment, and innovation opportunities are effectively harnessed.

These divergent dynamics create asymmetric labor futures: while some countries may struggle to attract workers, others may grapple with underemployment and migration pressures. The interplay between demographics and technology adoption will heavily influence global labor competitiveness in the coming decades.

2. LITERATURE REVIEW

Research on the future of labor and AI is vast but fragmented across economics, sociology, political science, and management studies. This section synthesizes the major strands, progressing from recent contributions to earlier foundational works.

2.1 AI and Labor Displacement

Artificial intelligence (AI) has reignited long-standing debates over technological unemployment and the capacity of economies to absorb displaced labor. Early quantitative estimates, such as Frey and Osborne (2016) influential study, argued that nearly 47% of U.S. employment was at risk of automation due to machine learning and robotics advances. These figures triggered a wave of concern among policymakers, academics, and labor unions, raising fears of large-scale job destruction. However, subsequent scholarship questioned these headline numbers. For example, Arntz et al. (2016) reframed the analysis at the level of tasks rather than entire jobs. Their findings suggested that while many jobs contain automatable components, fewer occupations are fully replaceable, leading to a lower projected displacement rate of 9–14% across OECD countries. This shift toward a task-based approach provided a more nuanced understanding of automation's impact.

However, even with more conservative estimates, displacement remains a significant concern. Autor (2022) emphasizes that AI and advanced digital technologies disproportionately affect routine and modifiable tasks, including clerical administration, bookkeeping, and assembly line work. By contrast, non-routine cognitive, interpersonal, and creative domains exhibit resilience. This bifurcation is not new; earlier waves of automation (e.g., mechanization in manufacturing) similarly displaced routine labor. However, AI's unique ability to learn and adapt suggests that displacement risks may extend into traditionally “safe” areas, such as paralegal research, medical diagnostics, and even some aspects of creative writing (Bonnaure, 2018).

Global forecasts underscore the scale of disruption. Nabyl and Mulachela (2021) estimates that by 2030, between 75 million and 375 million workers—3% to 14% of the global labor force—may need to switch occupational categories. The World Bank (2020) projects similar upheavals, especially in developing economies where automation adoption is accelerating in manufacturing and services. Importantly, displacement is not evenly distributed: low- and middle-income workers, women, and minority groups are more vulnerable, given their concentration in automatable roles (“The Changing Nature of Work,” 2018). The persistence of these risks highlights the urgency of reskilling and social protection strategies.

At the same time, scholars caution against techno-determinism. New occupations continually emerge in response to technological change, ranging from data science and cybersecurity to green energy technicians and AI ethics specialists Susskind (2020). Historical analogies to previous industrial revolutions suggest that job creation in complementary fields often accompanies displacement. However, the speed and scale of AI adoption may test the adaptive capacity of labor markets more severely than past transformations. The net outcome remains uncertain, warranting exploration through scenario-based approaches.

2.2 Algorithmic Management and Gig Work

The rise of algorithmic management represents one of the most visible transformations in labor relations under AI. Digital labor platforms—such as Uber, Delivered, and Amazon Mechanical Turk—deploy algorithms to allocate tasks, monitor worker performance, and determine pay structures. Rosenblat (2018) characterizes this as “digital Taylorism,” where workers are subjected to continuous surveillance and optimization. Unlike traditional managers, algorithms often operate opaquely, with decision-making criteria hidden from workers, eroding transparency and accountability.

The gig economy has expanded rapidly, offering flexible income opportunities to millions worldwide. In India, platforms like Ola and Swiggy have created employment for urban youth, while in sub-Saharan Africa, companies like SafeBoda have transformed mobility and delivery services Graham et al. (2017). However, flexibility often comes at the expense of precocity. Workers classified as “independent contractors” are denied basic protections such as minimum wage, health insurance, and collective bargaining rights De Stefano (2015). This precariousness has sparked growing calls for regulatory intervention, as evidenced by the EU's Platform Work Directive and California's Assembly Bill 5 (AB5).

Scholars highlight a paradox at the heart of platform work. On one hand, gig work democratizes access to income by lowering entry barriers. Conversely, algorithmic control systems intensify power asymmetries, embedding new forms of exploitation in digital infrastructures Wood et al. (2018). Workers report high stress due to opaque rating systems, unpredictable income, and limited avenues for appeal against unfair algorithmic decisions Kellogg et al. (2019). Moreover, as AI enables hyper-optimization, platforms increasingly treat labor as a "scalable resource," raising ethical concerns over human dignity in work (Adams-Prassl, 2018).

The gig economy illustrates broader labor market shifts toward fragmentation, individualized risk, and algorithmic governance. These developments demand rethinking labor law, social protection, and collective bargaining mechanisms in the digital era.

2.3 Inequality and Skills Polarization

AI-driven transformations are reshaping the structure of labor markets through skills polarization. Empirical evidence suggests that technological change disproportionately benefits high-skill, high-wage workers engaged in cognitive, analytical, or creative tasks while simultaneously expanding low-skill, low-wage service work that resists automation due to its embodied, interpersonal nature (Goos et al., 2014). Middle-skill occupations, particularly clerical and manufacturing, face erosion, leading to a "hollowing out" of the labor market.

Acemoglu and Restrepo (2019) frame this polarization as a result of "automation versus reinstatement effects." While automation substitutes human labor, reinstatement involves the creation of new tasks where humans retain a comparative advantage. Unfortunately, automation effects often outpace reinstatement, resulting in widening inequality. The OECD (2021) documents rising wage inequality in advanced economies, partly attributable to skill-biased technological change. Moreover, workers in middle-skill brackets frequently struggle to transition upward without significant retraining, creating structural barriers to mobility.

The implications extend beyond wages. Inequality manifests across gender and geography. Women, overrepresented in clerical and service roles, face disproportionate risks of displacement. Meanwhile, advanced economies capture most of the value from AI innovation, leaving developing countries vulnerable to a "technological dependency trap" (Rodrik, 2018). These disparities underscore the need for inclusive skills strategies. Initiatives such as Singapore's Skills Future program and Germany's vocational training reforms illustrate proactive responses, though scaling such policies globally remains a formidable challenge.

2.4 Global Perspectives

Much of the literature on AI and labor remains Western-centric, focusing on OECD economies with advanced technological infrastructures. However, the dynamics in the Global South often diverge significantly. In India, AI adoption in agriculture, logistics, and manufacturing holds promise for boosting productivity and rural incomes. However, the predominance of informal labor complicates the picture. Nayyar et al. (2021) note that informal workers often lack access to reskilling programs and social protections, amplifying risks of precocity.

In Africa, digital platforms create new opportunities for entrepreneurship and cross-border trade. Mhlanga (2021) highlights fintech and e-commerce as growth sectors driven by AI and mobile technologies. However, reliance on global tech monopolies raises dependency risks, as profits often flow abroad rather than being reinvested locally. Furthermore, infrastructural gaps—such as unreliable electricity and limited internet penetration—constrain inclusive adoption.

Latin America presents yet another variant. AI applications in public services, such as Brazil's digital government platforms, enhance efficiency but raise concerns about surveillance and data privacy. Meanwhile, state-driven AI initiatives in China reshape labor at a massive scale, blending innovation with authoritarian labor controls. These diverse trajectories underscore the need for comparative global research that moves beyond Eurocentric narratives.

2.5 Ethical and Governance Concerns

The integration of AI into labor markets raises pressing ethical and governance questions. Scholars warn that algorithmic decision-making risks amplifying biases embedded in training data, perpetuating structural inequalities. Simmonds (2019), for instance, documents how automated welfare and employment systems in the U.S. disproportionately penalize marginalized groups. Similarly, Noble (2018) highlights the racial and gender biases encoded in search engines, raising concerns about their extension into hiring and workplace management.

Governance responses are emerging but remain uneven. Wagner (2021) proposed Artificial Intelligence Act represents the most ambitious attempt to regulate AI, classifying applications into risk categories and imposing transparency and accountability obligations. By contrast, the U.S. adopts a fragmented, sectoral approach, relying on guidelines and voluntary standards. In the Global South, regulatory capacity often lags behind technological diffusion, exacerbating "digital colonialism" risks where foreign algorithms govern local workers with little oversight Couldry and Mejias (2020).

Ethical debates extend beyond bias and transparency. Questions of worker surveillance, privacy, and autonomy dominate labor contexts. De Brito (2021) concept of "surveillance capitalism" describes how data extraction enables unprecedented control over behavior. In workplaces, AI-driven productivity monitoring blurs boundaries between efficiency and exploitation. Bryson and Winfield (2017) argue that ensuring fairness and dignity in AI-managed work requires embedding ethical principles directly into design and deployment.

Synthesis

The literature demonstrates a broad consensus that AI constitutes a disruptive force in labor markets, with displacement, algorithmic management, inequality, global divergences, and ethical dilemmas as key themes. However, divergence exists in predictions of net employment effects and the distribution of risks and opportunities. Some scholars emphasize resilience and job creation, while others warn of structural unemployment and deepening inequality. This tension underscores the value of scenario-based exploration, which avoids deterministic forecasts and emphasizes agency in shaping futures. Researchers and policymakers can better anticipate challenges and design proactive responses by systematically envisioning optimistic, pessimistic, and transformative scenarios.

3. THEORETICAL FOUNDATIONS FOR UNDERSTANDING AI AND LABOR

Understanding the impact of Artificial Intelligence (AI) on the future of labor requires a robust theoretical foundation that goes beyond technological determinism and incorporates the interplay of social, economic, and institutional dynamics. This chapter employs an integrative framework that draws on sociotechnical systems theory, skill-biased technological change, labor process theory, futures studies and scenario planning, and the Industry 5.0 paradigm. Together, these frameworks provide a comprehensive lens to interpret the risks and opportunities AI brings to work, employment, and organizational design.

3.1 Sociotechnical Systems Theory

Sociotechnical systems (STS) theory, articulated initially by Trist and Bamforth (1951) in their study of coal mining communities, offers one of the earliest frameworks for analyzing how technological innovations reshape work processes. Their research highlighted that technological systems are not isolated but embedded in social contexts where human needs, skills, and values must be balanced against efficiency and productivity.

In the context of AI, STS theory remains highly relevant. AI technologies such as algorithmic decision systems, predictive analytics, and robotics often optimize for efficiency, but without attention to human dimensions, they risk generating alienation, stress, and resistance (Baxter & Sommerville, 2010). For example, deploying algorithmic management in gig platforms like Uber or Delivered has demonstrated the pitfalls of prioritizing technical optimization—faster service allocation and cost reduction—over human well-being, autonomy, and trust (Rosenblat, 2018).

Therefore, STS emphasizes the "joint optimization" principle, where the social and technical subsystems are designed to reinforce each other. This suggests that AI-driven workplaces integrate worker voice, ergonomic design, and participatory decision-making into technology adoption processes. Failure to do so risks ethical concerns and organizational inefficiencies, as disengaged workers undermine long-term performance (Shani, 2017).

Critics of STS argue that the theory sometimes underestimates structural power inequalities in workplaces (Howcroft & Wilson, 2002). However, when combined with labor process theory, STS offers a powerful way to reimagine AI adoption under the ethos of Industry 5.0, which calls for resilience, sustainability, and human-centric innovation.

3.2 Skill-Biased Technological Change (SBTC)

The skill-biased technological change theory, popularized by (Acemoglu, 2002), provides a macroeconomic explanation for how new technologies reshape income distribution and employment opportunities. According to SBTC, technological progress disproportionately favours highly skilled workers, raising their productivity and wages, while substituting routine tasks performed by middle- and low-skill workers.

In the AI era, SBTC manifests in several forms. Advanced AI systems amplify demand for workers with expertise in machine learning, data science, and digital management, while routine clerical, accounting, and assembly line jobs face increasing automation risk (Autor, 2022). This results in a polarized labor market, where high-skill, high-wage opportunities coexist with low-skill service roles such as delivery and care work, while the middle layer contracts (Goos et al., 2014).

However, recent scholarship complicates the SBTC narrative. Bonnaure (2018) argue that AI is both skill-biased and "task-biased," meaning its effects depend on which components of jobs can be automated or complemented. Arntz et al. (2016) further show that many occupations previously considered at risk are less vulnerable when one accounts for task variation and the difficulty of automating work's social, emotional, and creative dimensions.

The SBTC perspective is particularly valuable for analyzing global disparities. In the Global South, where large populations remain in informal or semi-skilled employment, AI adoption could exacerbate inequality by favoring small urban elites with digital competencies while marginalizing rural or less educated workers (Nayyar et al., 2021). This dynamic underscores the importance of reskilling and upskilling initiatives as part of inclusive industrial and labor policy.

Critics of SBTC note that it underplays institutional and policy variables, such as collective bargaining, minimum wage laws, and education systems, that mediate technological impacts (Hsu, 2014). However, it remains a crucial framework for understanding why AI widens inequality unless counterbalanced by deliberate policy interventions.

3.3 Labor Process Theory

Labor process theory (LPT), first articulated by Coleman (1975), shifts attention from macroeconomic trends to the micro-dynamics of workplace control. Braverman's central thesis was that technological change is often used as a tool for managerial control, enabling employers to deskill workers and increase their dependency on capital.

In contemporary AI-driven workplaces, LPT illuminates how algorithmic management restructures power relations. Digital platforms and corporations deploy AI to monitor workers in real time, evaluate performance, and determine pay rates (Kellogg et al., 2019). While presented as efficiency-enhancing, such practices frequently reduce worker autonomy and embed information and power asymmetries between employers and employees. For example, warehouse workers subject to AI-driven performance monitoring often experience intensified labor, high stress, and limited bargaining capacity (Moore et al., 2017).

Importantly, LPT also directs attention to worker resistance. As industrial workers resisted Taylorist control earlier, contemporary gig workers have developed strategies such as app "gaming," coordinated log-offs, and unionization efforts to contest algorithmic power (Wood et al., 2019). These dynamics suggest that AI in labor is not simply a matter of technological inevitability but a contested terrain shaped by struggle, negotiation, and collective agency.

Critics argue that LPT can sometimes veer toward technological pessimism, underemphasizing cases where workers benefit from enhanced autonomy or skill upgrading through AI (Adler, 2007). Nevertheless, as a counterbalance to more optimistic frameworks, LPT remains indispensable for interrogating how AI adoption intersects with capital-labor relations.

3.4 Futures Studies and Scenario Planning

Where STS, SBTC, and LPT provide explanatory frameworks, futures studies and scenario planning offer methodological tools for grappling with uncertainty. Futures studies emerged in the mid-20th century as an interdisciplinary field exploring alternative social trajectories rather than predicting single outcomes (Voss et al., 2025). Scenario planning, popularized by Shell in the 1970s, enables organizations and policymakers to imagine multiple plausible futures, identify key uncertainties, and design resilient strategies (Tetlock, 2009).

Applied to AI and labor, scenario planning resists deterministic narratives of utopian abundance or dystopian mass unemployment. Instead, it encourages stakeholders to ask: under what conditions might AI augment human creativity rather than displace workers? How might governance, education, and labor institutions influence divergent outcomes? For example, one scenario may envision an "AI-Augmented Economy" where governments invest in large-scale reskilling, AI is deployed ethically, and work is redesigned around human strengths such as empathy and creativity. Another scenario might depict an "AI-Driven Precocity" world, where algorithmic control dominates, inequality deepens, and labor protections erode. Such exercises enable policymakers to prepare for both risks and opportunities rather than relying on narrow forecasts.

Scenario methods also foreground the importance of values and ethics in shaping futures. By making explicit the assumptions underlying different trajectories, futures studies link empirical analysis to normative debates about what kind of work futures societies ought to pursue.

3.5 Industry 5.0 Framework

Finally, the Industry 5.0 framework provides a normative anchor for imagining labor futures in the AI era. Introduced by the European Commission and elaborated by scholars such as Nahavandi (2019), Industry 5.0 extends beyond the efficiency and productivity focus of Industry 4.0 to emphasize resilience, sustainability, and human-centric innovation. Within this framework, workers are not passive subjects of automation but active co-creators of technological systems. AI is framed as a tool to augment human potential rather than replace it. For instance, cobots (collaborative robots) are designed to work alongside humans, leveraging their precision and endurance while enabling humans to contribute creativity and judgment. Similarly, AI-driven knowledge systems can support doctors, teachers, and engineers rather than supplanting their roles.

Industry 5.0 also embeds sustainability and inclusivity as central principles. This challenges the growth-centric assumptions of earlier industrial paradigms, recognizing that the future of labor must also address environmental constraints, demographic change, and global inequality (Zhang, 2018). AI thus becomes part of a broader societal transformation rather than a narrow technological trend. Critics caution that Industry 5.0 remains aspirational and risks being co-opted as a rhetorical device without substantive institutional change (Vogel-Heuser & Bengler, 2023). Nevertheless, as a guiding vision, it provides a valuable counterweight to dystopian narratives and aligns with sociotechnical and futures studies perspectives.

4. METHODOLOGICAL ORIENTATION: SCENARIO PLANNING AND COMPARATIVE ANALYSIS

The methodological orientation of this chapter reflects the interdisciplinary and forward-looking character of futures research. While much of traditional labor economics and management science has been concerned with measuring and analyzing past and present phenomena, studying the future of labor requires methodological tools that can grapple with uncertainty, complexity, and ambiguity. Rather than focusing solely on forecasting based on linear trends, this chapter adopts a qualitative futures methodology emphasizing plurality, reflexivity, and policy relevance. Three complementary approaches form the backbone of this methodology: scenario planning, comparative policy analysis, and cross-disciplinary Synthesis.

4.1 Scenario Planning

4.1.1 Rationale for Scenario Planning

Scenario planning is particularly suited for studying the future of labor in the age of artificial intelligence (AI) and Industry 5.0 because it acknowledges uncertainty as an inherent feature of sociotechnical systems. Unlike predictive forecasting, which often assumes trend stability, scenario planning creates narrative-based explorations of multiple plausible futures. The objective is not to predict the future with certainty but to prepare decision-makers for alternative possibilities (Tetlock, 2009).

Labor markets are shaped by highly volatile drivers—technological innovation, demographic change, climate pressures, geopolitical shifts, and policy interventions. For instance, the pace of AI adoption can vary dramatically depending on regulatory environments, levels of public trust, and corporate investment cycles. Similarly, social resistance to automation in some countries could slow down deployment, while in others, rapid uptake could redefine entire sectors in less than a decade. Scenario planning enables us to grapple with such uncertainties by creating structured stories that reflect different logics of change.

4.1.2 Construction of Scenarios

For this chapter, three scenarios—Optimistic, Pessimistic, and Transformative—were developed. These scenarios were not arbitrarily chosen but are the result of a systematic scenario-building process involving:

Trend Extrapolation: Identification of megatrends such as AI adoption, demographic ageing, digital globalization, remote work, and green transitions.

Critical Uncertainties: Selection of the most uncertain but high-impact variables, such as the level of regulatory oversight on AI, global coordination on labor standards, and social acceptance of automation.

Expert Foresight Inputs: Engagement with secondary literature from foresight exercises conducted by the International Labor Organization (ILO), World Economic Forum (WEF), OECD, and academic think tanks.

Narrative Development: Crafting internally coherent and plausible storylines for each scenario, balancing technological, economic, and socio-political dimensions.

By weaving these inputs together, the scenarios serve as heuristic devices for exploring how the future of labor may evolve, and what implications these trajectories may hold for workers, organizations, and policymakers.

4.1.3 Advantages and Limitations

The key strength of scenario planning lies in its ability to expand the cognitive horizon of researchers and decision-makers. It forces actors to consider futures beyond their immediate assumptions, avoiding what Inayatullah (2008) calls the "used future"—a reliance on outdated mental models. However, scenarios also face limitations: they can be misinterpreted as predictions, and their impact depends heavily on the creativity and inclusivity of the process. The chapter integrates scenario planning with other complementary methods to mitigate these risks.

4.2 Comparative Policy Analysis

4.2.1 Importance of Policy Contexts

Labor futures are not determined by technology alone but are profoundly shaped by policy regimes, institutional structures, and governance models. Comparative policy analysis allows us to examine how different states approach the challenges of AI-driven labor transformations and what lessons can be drawn from their experiences. The future of labor is a global issue, yet responses vary widely depending on economic systems, cultural contexts, and developmental priorities.

4.2.2 Selected Case Studies

This study draws upon three contrasting case studies to anchor scenario development:

European Union (EU): The EU represents a rights-based and regulatory-heavy model, emphasizing ethical AI, data protection (e.g., GDPR), and social dialogue with unions. Its approach highlights sustainability, inclusivity, and fairness as key parameters in shaping the digital economy (European Commission, 2021).

China: In contrast, China adopts a state-driven techno-nationalist strategy, investing heavily in AI infrastructure, smart manufacturing, and social credit systems. The emphasis is on efficiency, scale, and state control, with less focus on participatory governance but significant attention to global competitiveness (Ding, 2022).

India: As a large emerging economy, India emphasizes digital skilling and inclusive growth, aiming to transform its demographic dividend into a digitally empowered workforce. Initiatives such as the Skill India Mission and Digital India demonstrate how policy emphasis can address technological adoption and social upliftment (Mehrotra, 2021).

These three contexts—EU's regulatory humanism, China's techno-states, and India's developmental pragmatism—offer contrasting pathways for understanding how global futures of labor may unfold.

4.2.3 Comparative Insights

The comparative policy lens highlights that no single approach guarantees success. Instead, hybrid models that combine regulation with innovation, and efficiency with inclusivity, may offer the most resilient solutions. For instance, while China's rapid AI deployment yields efficiency gains, the EU's emphasis on ethical safeguards ensures trust and legitimacy. India, meanwhile, illustrates the potential of human capital development as a pathway to inclusive labor futures.

5. THREE SCENARIOS FOR THE FUTURE OF LABOR

The future of labor in the age of artificial intelligence (AI) is not predetermined. Instead, it is contingent upon choices made by policymakers, corporations, labor unions, civil society, and global institutions. Futures sturemindminds us that the future is plural, contested, and co-created, shaping both structural forces and human agency (Voros, 2017). By constructing structured scenarios, scholars and decision-makers can imagine divergent trajectories rather than succumbing to deterministic narratives of utopian abundance or dystopian collapse.

This section explores three archetypal scenarios—optimistic, pessimistic, and transformative—each highlighting possible directions for labor markets, worker identities, and employment structures in the coming decades. While no scenario is inevitable, together they illustrate the range of possible worlds and illuminate the levers of intervention available today.

5.1 Optimistic Scenario: Human-Centered AI and Inclusive Growth

5.1.1 Human-AI Symbiosis

In the optimistic future, AI emerges as a powerful enabler of human empowerment rather than displacement. Governments adopt proactive regulatory frameworks prioritizing ethical AI, transparency, and accountability. Corporations embrace "augmentation over automation" and design AI systems to support, not supplant, human labor (Bonnaure, 2018). This leads to a human-AI symbiosis, where machines handle repetitive or data-intensive tasks while humans focus on creativity, empathy, and strategic decision-making.

For ins care, AI-driven diagnostic systems in healthcare teams process medical imaging and patient histories with unprecedented accuracy. However, doctors and nurses remain central, using AI outputs as supportive tools while ensuring human compassion and ethical judgment remain the cornerstone of care delivery. Collaborative robots (cobots) in manufacturing streamline repetitive assembly, while workers contribute to design, customization, and quality oversight (Nahavandi, 2019).

5.1.2 Lifelong Learning and Education Transformation

Education systems in this scenario undergo rapid adaptation. Schools and universities priorities digital literacy, critical thinking, emotional intelligence, and systems thinking. Governments and firms invest in lifelong learning ecosystems, enabling workers to reskill multiple times over their careers (Miró, 2020). Corporate-sponsored upskilling programs and state incentives continuously align skills supply and market demand. For example, Singapore's Skills Future initiative and the EU's Pact for Skills provide models of how institutionalized learning ecosystems can empower workers to thrive in an AI-driven economy.

5.1.3 Inclusive Global Growth

Unlike technological revolutions of the past, the benefits of AI in this scenario are distributed relatively equitably across nations. Emerging economies, particularly in Africa and South Asia, leverage digital leapfrogging to bypass industrial-era bottlenecks. Mobile banking, e-health platforms, and AI-enabled entrepreneurship create new avenues for prosperity. Platforms like Kenya's M-Pesa demonstrate how technological innovation can extend financial inclusion to the previously unbanked.

5.1.4 Labor Protections and Ethical AI

Workers in non-traditional roles, including gig economy participants, are brought under expanded labor protections. Fair wages, healthcare coverage, and portable social security systems are implemented through innovative public-private partnerships. AI ethics frameworks—developed collaboratively by international bodies such as UNESCO and the OECD—enforce algorithmic fairness, prevent discriminatory practices, and build public trust in automation (Jobin et al., 2019).

5.1.5 Hallmarks of the Optimistic Future

The optimistic future of labor under AI is defined by a set of hallmarks that collectively envision technology as a force for inclusive and sustainable progress. At its core lies human-centered AI design, where technology augments rather than replaces labor, empowering workers to achieve greater creativity, productivity, and well-being. This vision is reinforced by robust lifelong learning ecosystems that provide continuous reskilling and upskilling opportunities, ensuring that individuals remain adaptable in a rapidly evolving labor market. The scenario also emphasizes an equitable global distribution of digital opportunities, reducing disparities between regions and enabling participation from the Global South. Complementing this are expanded labor protections and portable social benefits, which safeguard workers' rights and dignity in increasingly flexible and mobile employment arrangements. Finally, the optimistic pathway depends on strong international coordination on AI ethics and governance, fostering trust, accountability, and fairness across borders. Together, these hallmarks illustrate a hopeful trajectory in which AI becomes a catalyst for dignified work, economic inclusion, and sustainable development.

5.2 Pessimistic Scenario: Polarization, Precocity, and Technological Unemployment

5.2.1 Job Displacement and Polarization

AI adoption accelerates rapidly in the pessimistic pathway, but governance and adaptation lag. The result is a highly polarized labor market. High-skill elites thrive in designing, managing, and owning AI systems, while vast swaths of low- and mid-skill workers face mass displacement.

Automation erodes jobs in logistics, retail, and clerical sectors, echoing the dire warnings of Frey and Osborne (2017) that up to 47% of U.S. jobs could be at risk. Knowledge-intensive roles are not immune: AI-generated journalism, automated contract review, and robot-advisors undermine traditional professions once thought resilient.

5.2.2 Rise of the Gig Economy and Precocity

Gig platforms dominate the employment landscape; in turn, they entrench precarious work without adequate regulation. Workers face algorithmic control dictating pay, task allocation, and surveillance (De Stefano, 2015). Social protections erode as traditional employer-employee relationships dissolve, leaving millions without stable income, healthcare, or retirement security. This fragmentation also weakens labor unions, reducing collective bargaining power. The shift toward short-term contracts and micro-gigs creates a "race to the bottom" in wages and conditions.

5.2.3 Education and Inequality Traps

Education and training systems fail to keep pace with technological change, widening the skills gap. Millions are locked out of AI-driven industries due to outdated qualifications. The benefits of AI accrue to advanced economies and wealthy urban hubs, while developing nations face technological dependency on imported systems they cannot produce or govern. Inequality deepens within nations (between skilled elites and displaced workers) and between nations, as digital divides ossify global hierarchies.

5.2.4 Ethical Erosion and Surveillance Capitalism

Unregulated AI systems exacerbate existing social inequalities. Algorithmic hiring systems replicate gender and racial biases. In the workplace, AI-driven surveillance tools track workers' keystrokes, movements, and emotions, undermining autonomy and dignity. Scholars describe this trajectory as the entrenchment of surveillance capitalism, where worker productivity is monitored and monetized (Shandler, 2019).

5.2.5 Hallmarks of the Pessimistic Future

The pessimistic future of labor is marked by large-scale technological unemployment and job polarization, where automation disproportionately benefits high-skilled elites while displacing middle- and low-skilled workers. Work increasingly takes the form of precarious gig arrangements, leading to the gigification of labor with declining protections and the erosion of traditional employment security. This trajectory exacerbates widening inequality both within and between countries, as wealth and opportunities concentrate in technologically advanced regions while marginalized populations fall further behind. Compounding these divides, the unchecked use of AI fosters algorithmic bias and discriminatory decision-making, systematically disadvantaging vulnerable groups in hiring, pay, and workplace monitoring. At the same time, the expansion of digital surveillance erodes worker autonomy, tightening managerial control and undermining trust in human–machine collaboration. Collectively, this pessimistic scenario reveals how, if left unregulated, AI could entrench exploitative structures and crystallize a two-tier global labor system defined by exclusion, inequality, and insecurity.

5.3 Transformative Scenario: Reimagining Work, Society, and Human Flourishing

5.3.1 Beyond Waged Labor

The transformative scenario envisions a paradigm shift where AI does not merely optimize existing systems but catalysis a redefinition of work itself. Societies recognize that human worth cannot be reduced to productivity alone. Instead, contributions such as caregiving, creativity, volunteerism, and ecological stewardship gain recognition as vital components of economic and social life. Mechanisms such as Universal Basic Income (UBI), universal services, or alternative redistributive frameworks ensure economic stability is decoupled from traditional wage labor. Freed from the necessity of working solely for survival, individuals pursue purposeful activities that enhance community well-being and personal fulfilment.

5.3.2 AI for Sustainability and Collective Intelligence

In the future, AI will be deployed to boost efficiency and address grand societal challenges. Innovative systems optimize renewable energy grids, monitor climate risks, and revolutionize sustainable agriculture. AI is used as a tool for collective intelligence, augmenting human capacity to solve complex global problems. Workers move into roles emphasizing creativity, empathy, systems design, and ethical judgment—domains where human distinctiveness thrives. Collaborative human-AI governance structures ensure that technology is developed to enhance planetary resilience.

5.3.3 Global Governance and Social Contracts

Crucially, this future rests on robust transnational governance frameworks. International institutions such as the UN, ILO, and WEF coordinate AI regulation, labor standards, and redistributive mechanisms (De Sio, 2021). Nations agree on common principles for equitable AI use, ensuring that benefits are shared across borders rather than hoarded by a few tech superpowers. New social contracts emerge, integrating rights to meaningful work, social protections, and sustainable livelihoods. Workers and communities become active stakeholders in shaping technological trajectories rather than passive recipients of corporate decisions.

5.3.4 Hallmarks of the Transformative Future

The transformative future is characterized by a fundamental recognition of human value beyond waged labor, shifting the emphasis from employment as the sole measure of worth to broader contributions to society, creativity, and well-being. In this scenario, universal basic income (UBI) or alternative safety nets provide individuals with economic stability, freeing them from the constant precarity of job dependency and enabling more flexible engagement with meaningful work. AI is deliberately directed toward sustainability and collective problem-solving, addressing pressing challenges such as climate change, public health, and global inequality rather than being confined to profit-maximization. The emergence of transnational governance frameworks ensures that both AI deployment and labor standards are harmonized across borders, minimizing regulatory gaps and promoting global fairness. In this context, work is redefined as a vehicle for human flourishing, creativity, and social resilience, allowing individuals and communities to thrive in diverse ways. The transformative scenario thus envisions a profound systemic shift where AI becomes not merely a tool of efficiency but a catalyst for reimagining the very relationship between technology, society, and human purpose.

5.4 Comparative Insights Across Scenarios

Table 1. Comparative Insights Across Scenarios

Dimension	Optimistic Future	Pessimistic Future	Transformative Future
AI & Technology	Human-centered AI augments labor and enhances productivity.	AI displaces workers, drives job polarization, and fuels surveillance.	AI directed toward sustainability, collective problem-solving, and human flourishing.
Employment Landscape	Lifelong learning ecosystems enable reskilling and mobility.	Gigification dominates, with declining protections and insecure work.	Work redefined beyond wage labor; focus on creativity, care, and social contributions.
Equity & Inclusion	Equitable distribution of digital opportunities across regions and groups.	Widening inequality both within and across countries.	Universal safety nets (e.g., UBI) provide stability and reduce dependency on paid work.
Governance & Regulation	Strong international coordination on AI ethics and labor rights.	Weak governance leads to algorithmic bias, discrimination, and exploitation.	Transnational governance frameworks ensure fairness, accountability, and shared standards.
Social Protections	Expanded labor protections and portable benefits adapt to fluid work arrangements.	Erosion of worker autonomy and limited social protections.	New models of protection decouple livelihood from employment, ensuring universal security.
Underlying Assumptions	Incremental reform within current economic models can manage AI disruptions.	Market forces dominate, with limited policy intervention and regulatory capture.	Systemic reinvention is possible, redefining work and human value in post-AI economies.
Overall Outlook	Inclusive, sustainable, and dignified work.	Exploitative, unequal, and unstable labor markets.	Flourishing societies with technology serving human and ecological well-being.

6. POLICY AND MANAGERIAL IMPLICATIONS

The three scenarios—optimistic, pessimistic, and transformative—reveal divergent futures and a set of policy and managerial imperatives that can shape labor's trajectory in the age of AI. While technology's advance is inevitable, the outcomes for workers, organizations, and societies are not predetermined. They depend on deliberate policy frameworks, regulatory choices, and organizational practices. This section unpacks the policy implications and managerial imperatives required to steer labor markets toward more equitable, sustainable, and human-centric outcomes.

6.1 Policy Implications

6.1.1 Reskilling and Lifelong Learning

Governments are central in ensuring that workers have the skills needed to thrive in AI-driven economies. Rapid technological shifts have created a "skills half-life," where technical competencies quickly become obsolete within a few years. To address this challenge, national governments must invest in robust lifelong learning ecosystems that combine national reskilling programs co-designed with universities, industry leaders, and vocational institutions; micro-credentialing and modular learning opportunities that allow workers to acquire skills in flexible and stackable ways; and public–private partnerships that subsidize training costs, particularly for vulnerable groups in manufacturing, retail, and service sectors. Illustrative models include Singapore's *SkillsFuture* initiative, which provides government-funded credits for citizens to upskill throughout their careers, and India's *Skill India Mission*, which targets digital literacy for millions of young workers. Together, these approaches demonstrate how inclusive training initiatives can help mitigate technological unemployment and foster resilience in rapidly evolving labor markets.

6.1.2 Protecting Precarious Workers

The rise of platform economies and gig work presents both opportunities for flexible employment and risks of systemic precarity. Gig workers often operate without protections such as minimum wages, social security, or the right to unionize (De Stefano, 2015). To address these challenges, policymakers must establish robust frameworks that guarantee baseline protections, including minimum wage, paid leave, and insurance; mandate algorithmic transparency to prevent opaque rating systems and automated dismissals; and extend the right to collective bargaining beyond traditional employment contracts. The European Union's *Directive on Platform Work* sets an important precedent by granting gig workers employment rights when platforms cannot demonstrate genuine self-employment. If adopted globally, such measures could help curb the "race to the bottom" in labor standards and ensure greater fairness in the evolving world of work.

6.1.3 Ethical and Accountable AI

AI systems increasingly influence decisions on hiring, promotions, productivity tracking, and even layoffs, but without oversight they risk amplifying existing biases tied to gender, race, or socioeconomic status (Raghavan et al., 2020). To prevent such harms, policymakers must prioritize the development of globally harmonized ethical AI standards that emphasize fairness, accountability, and transparency. Just as environmental impact assessments are required before major projects, similar impact assessments should be mandated for AI systems deployed in workplaces. Independent regulatory bodies should also be established with the authority to audit and sanction unethical AI practices. The EU's *AI Act* is a landmark example, designating workplace AI as "high-risk" and subjecting it to rigorous oversight. Countries that fail to adopt similar safeguards risk deepening inequality and eroding public trust in technology.

6.1.4 Redistribution and Social Safety Nets

Automation and AI are increasingly concentrating wealth in the hands of those who control capital and technology, a dynamic that, if left unchecked, could lead to social unrest and economic instability. To counter this imbalance, governments must adopt redistributive measures such as taxing AI-driven productivity gains to fund social programs, implementing Universal Basic Income (UBI) or conditional cash transfer schemes as safety nets for displaced workers, and promoting worker ownership models like cooperatives and stock participation to democratize the benefits of automation. Evidence from pilot UBI programs in Finland and Kenya suggests that such policies can enhance well-being without discouraging labor force participation. While not a complete solution, redistributive frameworks remain essential to mitigating inequality and preventing the pessimistic scenario of widespread exclusion from the gains of technological progress.

6.2 Managerial Implications

While governments set the broad policy environment, corporate leaders play an equally vital role in shaping labor futures. Organizations must adopt strategies that treat AI not merely as a tool for cost reduction but as a partner in building resilient, innovative, and human-centered workplaces.

6.2.1 Human-Centered AI Adoption

Firms must resist the temptation to view AI solely as a substitute for labor and instead prioritize augmentation strategies, where technology enhances rather than replaces human capabilities. For example, AI-enabled decision support tools can empower doctors, teachers, and managers to focus on empathy, creativity, and strategic thinking, while collaborative robotics (cobots) in manufacturing help reduce repetitive strain injuries and simultaneously improve productivity. By aligning AI adoption with the principles of Industry 5.0, organizations can sustain competitiveness while upholding human dignity at work (Nahavandi, 2019).

6.2.2 Continuous Learning Ecosystems

The responsibility for reskilling does not rest solely with governments; organizations must also play an active role by investing in robust learning ecosystems. Internal corporate academies, such as AT&T University, can serve as platforms for continuous employee upskilling, while job rotation programs help develop multidisciplinary competencies. In addition, AI-driven personalized learning platforms can tailor training to individual employee needs, ensuring relevance and efficiency. Firms that neglect workforce development risk increased attrition, employee disengagement, and reputational damage, whereas organizations that prioritize employee growth foster loyalty, adaptability, and long-term competitiveness.

6.2.3 Digital Empathy and Ethical Leadership

As AI increasingly permeates workplaces, leaders must evolve beyond mere technical competence to embrace digital empathy—the capacity to understand and address employees' concerns in technologically mediated environments (Cascio & Montealegre, 2016). This requires transparent communication regarding AI adoption strategies, active inclusion of employees in decision-making about workplace technologies, and a strong emphasis on well-being and mental health in digital work contexts. In this regard, ethical leadership plays a pivotal role in balancing efficiency with fairness. Leaders who embody integrity and inclusivity are more likely to foster trust, mitigate resistance, and strengthen employee confidence in AI-enabled organizations.

6.2.4 Job Enrichment and Work Design

AI adoption carries the risk of reducing jobs to narrow, automated tasks, thereby undermining employee engagement and satisfaction. To counter this, managers should focus on designing jobs that emphasize enrichment and meaningful work. This can be achieved by shifting routine tasks to AI while reserving creative and problem-solving functions for humans, encouraging hybrid human–machine collaboration instead of unilateral automation, and embedding flexibility and autonomy into work structures. For instance, in healthcare, AI can manage diagnostics while professionals concentrate on patient interaction, thereby preserving the human element of care. Such practices not only enhance productivity but also sustain employee motivation, dignity, and purpose.

6.3 Integrative Approach: Policy–Business Synergy

Neither policy nor managerial action alone is sufficient to shape the future of labor in the age of AI. What is required is a synergistic alignment between the public and private spheres, where policymakers incentivize firms to adopt human-centric AI through mechanisms such as subsidies, tax breaks, or recognition schemes. At the same time, businesses must collaborate with governments to establish ethical AI standards and workforce reskilling agendas, while civil society and labor unions remain active stakeholders to ensure accountability and inclusivity. This tripartite approach reflects a multi-actor governance model, which is essential for navigating the complexities of AI-driven labor futures.

6.4 Conclusion: Steering Toward the Transformative Scenario

The scenarios presented in this book chapter demonstrate that the future of labor is not deterministic but malleable. Policy frameworks that promote reskilling, worker protections, ethical AI, and redistribution—combined with managerial practices emphasizing augmentation, learning, empathy, and enrichment—can collectively steer societies away from pessimistic outcomes. Ultimately, today's policy and managerial choices will determine whether AI becomes a tool of exclusion and inequality or a catalyst for human flourishing and sustainable work. The transformative scenario remains within reach only if proactive, collaborative, and ethically grounded interventions are pursued across all governance and management levels.

7. DISCUSSION

The scenarios developed in this chapter illustrate that the future of labor under the influence of artificial intelligence is not a predetermined outcome, but a contested terrain shaped by choices in governance, organizational practices, and cultural values. Futures studies remind us that optimism or pessimism is not an inevitability but the product of "sociotechnical imaginaries"—collective visions that influence how societies design, regulate, and adopt technologies.

The optimistic scenario highlights the possibility of AI catalyzing human flourishing. In this vision, AI is not a substitute for human capabilities but an amplifier of creativity, innovation, and problem-solving. Work becomes more purposeful as mundane, repetitive tasks are automated, and humans engage in higher-order activities such as strategic thinking, collaboration, and social interaction. Importantly, this scenario presumes the existence of inclusive governance mechanisms—robust regulatory frameworks, coordinated reskilling programs, and protections for vulnerable workers—that ensure technology augments rather than undermines human well-being. Stakeholder theory provides a valuable lens, emphasizing that corporations, governments, and civil society share responsibility for aligning AI with collective social good.

By contrast, the pessimistic scenario underscores the risks of unregulated and profit-driven AI adoption. Without adequate labor protections, AI risks deepening social and economic inequalities, concentrating wealth in the hands of a few global technology firms while displacing millions of workers in traditional sectors. Precocity, already rising due to the platform economy, becomes the dominant work mode. Algorithmic bias and opaque decision-making amplify discrimination and erode trust in institutions. This scenario aligns with a political economy perspective, where technological change reflects and reinforces power asymmetries between capital and labor, between the Global North and Global South, and between high-skilled and low-skilled workers. The risk is not only economic but also democratic, as surveillance technologies may be weaponized to monitor workers and suppress dissent.

The transformative scenario invites us to move beyond the binary of optimism and pessimism. It asks whether societies can fundamentally reimagine the meaning of work and labor in a world where AI increasingly decouples productivity from human effort. In this vision, economic models shift from growth-driven imperatives to sustainability-oriented ones, embedding human creativity, care work, and ecological stewardship at the center. Universal basic income or other redistributive policies ensure material security, allowing individuals to pursue meaningful work outside traditional employment. This aligns with post-growth and human development theories, which argue that flourishing cannot be measured solely by GDP or wages but by dignity, well-being, and ecological balance.

7.1 Cross-National Comparisons

The feasibility of each scenario will vary across national and regional contexts. High-income nations with strong social safety nets and institutional capacity, such as those in Northern Europe, may be more capable of realizing the optimistic or transformative pathways. Countries like Denmark and Finland, with established traditions of social dialogue and worker participation, could integrate AI into labor markets while preserving equity and inclusion. In contrast, low- and middle-income countries may face heightened displacement risks without sufficient resources for reskilling or social protection. However, leapfrogging opportunities exist: African and South Asian nations could bypass older industrial models and experiment with innovative, human-centered AI applications if supported by global cooperation and investment.

Political systems also matter. Democratic societies with transparent institutions are more likely to implement inclusive policies and ethical regulations, while authoritarian regimes may exploit AI for labor surveillance, productivity control, and political dominance. Similarly, state-led models (e.g., China's AI strategy) may priorities rapid adoption and economic competitiveness, while market-driven models (e.g., the U.S.) risk privileging corporate interests unless counterbalanced by public regulation.

7.2 Global Inequalities and Interdependence

Another key insight is the interdependence of global labor futures. AI development is highly concentrated in a few technology hubs, but its global effects influence supply chains, outsourcing, and migration patterns. For example, decisions made by U.S. or Chinese tech giants on algorithmic design or data practices reverberate across the Global South, where outsourced workers perform critical but often invisible tasks such as data labelling. Thus, the governance of AI is not merely a national issue but a global challenge requiring coordinated frameworks to address issues of equity, accountability, and sustainability.

7.3 Role of Civil Society and Collective Agency

While much of the debate focuses on governments and corporations, civil society—unions, NGOs, grassroots organizations—plays a critical role in shaping the futures of labor. Worker-led movements for algorithmic transparency, campaigns against excessive surveillance, and demands for equitable access to AI-enhanced opportunities demonstrate that agency is distributed. Futures thinking emphasizes that alternative trajectories are always possible if collective action challenges deterministic narratives of technological inevitability.

8. CONCLUSION

The future of labor in the AI era is not singular but plural, contingent on the choices societies make today. The optimistic, pessimistic, and transformative scenarios underscore that technology alone does not dictate outcomes. Instead, the trajectory of AI-driven labor markets will depend on governance structures, institutional strength, corporate strategies, and cultural values.

From a policy perspective, the challenge lies in creating inclusive frameworks that balance innovation with protection. Governments must invest in universal reskilling initiatives, ensure labor protections for gig and platform workers, and develop global standards for ethical AI. Redistributive policies such as taxation of AI-driven profits and experiments with universal basic income may be necessary to address inequalities. Global coordination, particularly through multilateral organizations, is essential to prevent regulatory fragmentation and ensure that developing nations are not left behind.

From a managerial perspective, the imperative is to design organizations where AI augments rather than replaces human work. Leaders must embrace digital empathy and ethical leadership, ensuring fairness, inclusivity, and worker dignity. Firms that invest in continuous learning ecosystems and redesign jobs to emphasize creativity, collaboration, and meaning will be better positioned to thrive in a rapidly evolving landscape.

From a societal perspective, the future of labor requires rethinking fundamental assumptions about the relationship between work, income, and human worth. The transformative scenario suggests that societies may need to move beyond wage labor as the sole measure of contribution, recognizing the value of care work, community engagement, and ecological stewardship. Such a shift requires a cultural and institutional transformation, embedding human flourishing rather than profit maximization as the central goal of technological progress.

Ultimately, AI is neither inherently emancipatory nor inherently exploitative. Its role in shaping labor futures depends on the collective values and governance structures societies embrace. If aligned with principles of justice, sustainability, and inclusivity, AI can serve as a cornerstone of a new social contract—where work is redefined not as survival but as an avenue for creativity, dignity, and shared prosperity.

The urgency of these choices cannot be overstated. Futures are not distant abstractions; they are shaped in the present by the policies enacted, the organizational strategies pursued, and the values prioritized. The central message of this chapter is clear: the future of labor in the age of AI is open, contested, and deeply human. The challenge and opportunity lie in ensuring that the pathways chosen lead toward equitable and sustainable horizons.

REFERENCES

Acemoglu, D. (2002). Technical change, inequality, and the labor market. *Journal of Economic Literature*, *40*(1), 7–72. DOI: 10.1257/jel.40.1.7

Acemoglu, D., & Restrepo, P. (2019). Automation and new tasks: How technology displaces and reinstates labor. *The Journal of Economic Perspectives*, *33*(2), 3–30. DOI: 10.1257/jep.33.2.3

Adams-Prassl, J. (2018). Work on demand. In Oxford University Press eBooks (pp. 11–30). DOI: 10.1093/oso/9780198797012.003.0002

Adler, P. S. (2007). The future of critical management studies: A paleo-Marxist critique of labour process theory. *Organization Studies*, *28*(9), 1313–1345. DOI: 10.1177/0170840607080743

Arntz, M., Gregory, T., & Zierahn, U. (2016). The risk of automation for jobs in OECD countries. OECD Social, Employment and Migration Working Papers. DOI: 10.1787/1815199X

Autor, D. H. (2015). Why are there still so many jobs? The history and future of workplace automation. *The Journal of Economic Perspectives*, *29*(3), 3–30. DOI: 10.1257/jep.29.3.3

Autor, D. H. (2022). The labor market impacts of technological change: From unbridled enthusiasm to qualified optimism to vast uncertainty (Working Paper No. 30074). National Bureau of Economic Research. https://doi.org/DOI: 10.3386/w30074

Barocas, S., & Selbst, A. D. (2016). Big data's disparate impact. *California Law Review*, •••, 671–732.

Baxter, G., & Sommerville, I. (2010). Socio-technical systems: From design methods to systems engineering. *Interacting with Computers*, *23*(1), 4–17. DOI: 10.1016/j.intcom.2010.07.003

Bonnaure, P. (2018). McAfee, A., & Brynjolfsson, E. (2018). Des machines, des plateformes et des foules. Maîtriser notre avenir numérique [Review of the book Machine, platform, crowd: Harnessing our digital future]. *Futuribles (Paris, France)*, *427*(6), VI. DOI: 10.3917/futur.427.0121f

Brynjolfsson, E., Li, D., & Raymond, L. (2023). Generative AI at work. SSRN Electronic Journal. DOI: 10.2139/ssrn.4426942

Bryson, J., & Winfield, A. (2017). Standardizing ethical design for artificial intelligence and autonomous systems. *Computer, 50*(5), 116–119. DOI: 10.1109/MC.2017.154

Cascio, W. F., & Montealegre, R. (2016). How technology is changing work and organizations. *Annual Review of Organizational Psychology and Organizational Behavior, 3*(1), 349–375. DOI: 10.1146/annurev-orgpsych-041015-062352

Coleman, D. (1975). Labor and monopoly capital: The degradation of work in the twentieth century, by Harry Braverman [Review of the book Labor and monopoly capital: The degradation of work in the twentieth century]. *The Journal of Economic History, 35*(3), 647–648. DOI: 10.1017/S0022050700075719

Couldry, N., & Mejias, U. A. (2020). *The costs of connection.* Stanford University Press., DOI: 10.1515/9781503609754

De Brito, L. (2021). Zuboff, S. (2019). The age of surveillance capitalism: The fight for a human future at the new frontier of power [Review of the book The age of surveillance capitalism]. *Mural Internacional, 12*, e55150. Advance online publication. DOI: 10.12957/rmi.2021.55150

De Sio, F. S. (2021). Coeckelbergh, M. (2021). AI ethics [Review of the book AI ethics]. *Science and Engineering Ethics, 27*(4). Advance online publication. DOI: 10.1007/s11948-021-00323-8

De Stefano, V. (2015). The rise of the "just-in-time workforce": On-demand work, crowd work and labour protection in the "gig-economy." SSRN Electronic Journal. DOI: 10.2139/ssrn.2682602

Ding, J. (2022). Dueling perspectives in AI and U.S.–China relations. In Oxford University Press eBooks (pp. 881–894). DOI: 10.1093/oxfordhb/9780197579329.013.53

Frey, C. B., & Osborne, M. A. (2016). The future of employment: How susceptible are jobs to computerisation? *Technological Forecasting and Social Change, 114*, 254–280. DOI: 10.1016/j.techfore.2016.08.019

Goos, M., Manning, A., & Salomons, A. (2014). Explaining job polarization: Routine-biased technological change and offshoring. *The American Economic Review, 104*(8), 2509–2526. DOI: 10.1257/aer.104.8.2509

Graham, M., Hjorth, I., & Lehdonvirta, V. (2017). Digital labour and development: Impacts of global digital labour platforms and the gig economy on worker livelihoods. *Transfer: European Review of Labour and Research, 23*(2), 135–162. DOI: 10.1177/1024258916687250 PMID: 28781494

Graham, M., Hjorth, I., & Lehdonvirta, V. (2019). Digital labor and development: Impacts of global digital labor platforms and the gig economy on worker livelihoods. In The MIT Press eBooks (pp. 269–294). DOI: 10.7551/mitpress/10890.003.0022

Howcroft, D., & Wilson, M. (2002). Paradoxes of participatory practices: The Janus role of the systems developer. *Information and Organization*, *13*(1), 1–24. DOI: 10.1016/S1471-7727(02)00023-4

Hsu, S. L. (2014). The Rise and Rise of the One Percent: Considering Legal Causes of Inequality. FSU College of Law, Public Law Research Paper, (698), 14-11.

Human Development Report 2020. (2020). Human development report. https://doi.org/DOI: 10.18356/9789210055161

ILO. (2021). Ensuring decent work on digital labour platforms. *World Employment and Social Outlook*, *2021*(1), 195–238. DOI: 10.1002/wow3.171

Inayatullah, S. (2008). Six pillars: Futures thinking for transforming. *Foresight*, *10*(1), 4–21. DOI: 10.1108/14636680810855991

Jobin, A., Ienca, M., & Vayena, E. (2019). The global landscape of AI ethics guidelines. *Nature Machine Intelligence*, *1*(9), 389–399. DOI: 10.1038/s42256-019-0088-2

Kellogg, K. C., Valentine, M. A., & Christin, A. (2019). Algorithms at work: The new contested terrain of control. *The Academy of Management Annals*, *14*(1), 366–410. DOI: 10.5465/annals.2018.0174

Mhlanga, D. (2021). Artificial intelligence in the Industry 4.0, and its impact on poverty, innovation, infrastructure development, and the sustainable development goals: Lessons from emerging economies? *Sustainability (Basel)*, *13*(11), 5788. Advance online publication. DOI: 10.3390/su13115788

Miró, A. (2020). World Economic Forum: Present and future. Dimensión Empresarial, 18(2). DOI: 10.15665/dem.v18i2.2280

Moore, P. V., Upchurch, M., & Whittaker, X. (2017). Humans and machines at work: Monitoring, surveillance and automation in contemporary capitalism. In Springer eBooks (pp. 1–16). DOI: 10.1007/978-3-319-58232-0_1

Nabyl, V., & Mulachela, A. (2021). COVID-19. In Routledge eBooks (pp. 16–35). DOI: 10.4324/9781003166801-2

Nahavandi, S. (2019). Industry 5.0—A human-centric solution. *Sustainability (Basel)*, *11*(16), 4371. Advance online publication. DOI: 10.3390/su11164371

Nayyar, G., Hallward-Driemeier, M., & Davies, E. (2021). *At your service?: The promise of services-led development*. World Bank Publications. DOI: 10.1596/978-1-4648-1671-0

Noble, S. U. (2018). Conclusion: Algorithms of oppression. In Algorithms of oppression: How search engines reinforce racism (pp. 171–182). NYU Press. DOI: 10.2307/j.ctt1pwt9w5.11

Raghavan, M., Barocas, S., Kleinberg, J., & Levy, K. (2020, January). Mitigating bias in algorithmic hiring: Evaluating claims and practices. In *Proceedings of the 2020 conference on fairness, accountability, and transparency* (pp. 469-481). DOI: 10.1145/3351095.3372828

Rodrik, D. (2018). *New technologies, global value chains, and developing economies (No. w25164)*. National Bureau of Economic Research. DOI: 10.3386/w25164

Rosenblat, A. (2018). *Uberland: How algorithms are rewriting the rules of work*. University of California Press., DOI: 10.1525/9780520970632

Rosenblat, A., & Stark, L. (2016). Algorithmic labor and information asymmetries: A case study of Uber's drivers. *International Journal of Communication*, *10*, 27–27.

Shandler, R. (2019). Zuboff, S. (2019). The age of surveillance capitalism: The fight for a human future at the new frontier of power [Review of the book The age of surveillance capitalism]. *Journal of Cyber Policy*, *4*(2), 303–304. DOI: 10.1080/23738871.2019.1637914

Shani, A. B. (2017). William A. Pasmore: Navigating between academy and industry – Designing and leading change. In Springer eBooks (pp. 1–15). DOI: 10.1007/978-3-319-49820-1_52-2

Simmonds, R. (2019). Eubanks, V. (2018). Automating inequality: How high-tech tools profile, police and punish the poor [Review of the book Automating inequality]. *Science & Technology Studies*, *81–83*. Advance online publication. DOI: 10.23987/sts.77647

Srivastava, S. K. (2021). Susskind, D. (2020). A world without work: Technology, automation and how we should respond [Review of the book A world without work]. *Metamorphosis*, *20*(1), 45–46. DOI: 10.1177/09726225211026818

Tetlock, P. E. (2006). *Expert political judgment: How good is it? How can we know?* Princeton University Press., DOI: 10.1515/9781400830312

The changing nature of work. (2018). In The World Bank eBooks (pp. 17–34). DOI: 10.1596/978-1-4648-1328-3_ch1

Vogel-Heuser, B., & Bengler, K. (2023). Von Industrie 4.0 zu Industrie 5.0 – Idee, Konzept und Wahrnehmung. *HMD Praxis der Wirtschaftsinformatik, 60*(6), 1124–1142. DOI: 10.1365/s40702-023-01002-x

Voros, J. (2017). Big history and anticipation. In Springer eBooks (pp. 1–40). DOI: 10.1007/978-3-319-31737-3_95-1

Voss, A. S., Soucek, R., Moser, K., & Drexler, H. (2025). The differentiated roles of resilient behavior and job crafting in interaction with work intensity and their impact on employee health and performance. *International Journal of Environmental Research and Public Health, 22*(3), 429. Advance online publication. DOI: 10.3390/ijerph22030429 PMID: 40238562

Wagner, G. (2021). Liability for artificial intelligence: A proposal of the European Parliament. SSRN Electronic Journal. DOI: 10.2139/ssrn.3886294

Wood, A. J., Graham, M., Lehdonvirta, V., & Hjorth, I. (2018). Good gig, bad gig: Autonomy and algorithmic control in the global gig economy. *Work, Employment and Society, 33*(1), 56–75. DOI: 10.1177/0950017018785616 PMID: 30886460

Woodward, R. (2022). OECD reform. In Routledge eBooks (pp. 122–140). DOI: 10.4324/9781351025867-7

Zhang, A. (2018). Study on ecologicalization of electronic information industry. 2018 4th International Conference on Education, Management and Information Technology (ICEMIT 2018). DOI: 10.25236/icemit.2018.211

Chapter 5
The Role of AI in Shaping Post-Pandemic Work

Rupam Hazra
http://orcid.org/0009-0003-0332-2128
Global Institute of Management and Technology, Krishnanagar, India

ABSTRACT

This chapter examines the significant influence of Artificial Intelligence (AI) on employment sectors during the recovery period after the pandemic. AI is reshaping organizational structures and job roles, offering opportunities like increased productivity and new high-skill jobs, alongside risks such as job displacement and labor market polarization. The pandemic accelerated AI adoption, driving trends in hybrid work, algorithmic management, and automation. The chapter analyses AI's societal effects, including income inequality, changing social welfare, and the need for inclusive policies. It advocates human-centered AI aligned with ethical values and highlights global, region-specific strategies and governance to ensure equitable AI benefits. The conclusion calls for collaborative policy innovation to foster workforce resilience and sustainable economic growth in the AI era.

1. INTRODUCTION

This chapter explores the evolving relationship between artificial intelligence (AI) and labour in the wake of transformative global events and accelerating technological innovation. As AI continues to redefine the nature of work, its influence extends beyond automation and efficiency to touch virtually every aspect of organizational, economic, and social life. The COVID-19 pandemic acted as a major catalyst in this transformation, accelerating the adoption of AI tools in remote operations, workforce management, and digital service delivery. In this rapidly changing landscape,

DOI: 10.4018/979-8-3373-5816-1.ch005

businesses are not only restructuring their operations but also redefining job roles to accommodate emerging technological demands. Simultaneously, workers across the globe are experiencing both the threat of job displacement and the emergence of new, high-skill opportunities—leading to increasing labour market polarization. This chapter critically examines these shifts, focusing on how AI is impacting income distribution, workforce resilience, education systems, and regulatory frameworks. It highlights the need for human-centered AI strategies that promote inclusivity, ethical integrity, and equitable access to opportunity. By analysing global case studies and drawing comparisons across developed and emerging economies, this chapter also underscores the uneven impacts of AI and the importance of region-specific policy responses. Furthermore, it emphasizes the urgent need for governance mechanisms and public-private collaboration to shape a sustainable, fair, and forward-looking AI-driven labour ecosystem. Ultimately, this chapter provides a comprehensive foundation for understanding how AI is reshaping labour in a post-pandemic world and offers actionable insights for business leaders, educators, and policymakers navigating this transformation.

2. BUSINESS ADAPTATION TO AI: ORGANIZATIONAL RESTRUCTURING AND ROLE REDEFINITION

In the last twenty years, the manufacturing industry has experienced substantial change driven by progress in digital technologies, innovation, and alterations in production techniques(Nour & Arbussà, 2025). The integration of AI into business operations is driving profound changes in organizational structures and job roles across industries. AI is not only automating routine tasks but also enabling businesses to optimize decision-making, improve customer experiences, and forecast trends more accurately. As a result, companies are redefining job roles, with an increasing demand for positions focused on AI management, data analysis, and ethical oversight. While some roles may be displaced, new opportunities that require a blend of technical expertise and human creativity are emerging. However, businesses must also navigate ethical and compliance challenges, such as algorithmic bias and data privacy concerns, ensuring that AI systems are implemented responsibly and transparently. To successfully adapt, organizations must foster a culture of innovation, invest in reskilling programs, and establish ethical guidelines, enabling them to harness AI's potential while addressing its societal implications.

A. Integrating AI into Business Strategies Across Sectors

Artificial Intelligence (AI) is increasingly becoming a cornerstone of strategic planning across diverse sectors, including healthcare, finance, manufacturing, retail, and education. Businesses are leveraging AI to enhance efficiency, reduce operational costs, and gain real-time insights that support faster and more accurate decision-making. From predictive analytics in supply chain management to AI-powered chatbots in customer service, AI tools are transforming traditional business models. The integration of AI also allows companies to personalize customer experiences, automate complex workflows, and adapt swiftly to market changes. Integrating AI into business strategies demonstrates considerable potential for enhancing corporate performance and promoting sustainable business practices(Kaggwa et al.,2024). However, successful integration requires a clear vision, investment in infrastructure, and alignment with organizational goals and ethical standards.

a) Sector-Specific Applications of AI

In healthcare, AI is used for diagnostics, patient monitoring, and drug discovery, while in finance, it supports fraud detection, risk management, and algorithmic trading. In manufacturing, AI facilitates predictive maintenance and robotics-driven production lines, demonstrating how tailored AI solutions can significantly optimize sector-specific challenges.

b) Strategic Alignment and Leadership Commitment

Integrating AI into business strategies demands strong leadership and a commitment to long-term digital transformation. Companies must ensure that AI initiatives are aligned with their broader mission and values, which includes preparing their workforce through training and fostering a culture that embraces technological innovation responsibly.

B. Redefining Job Roles: The Emergence of New Work Profiles

The widespread adoption of Artificial Intelligence is reshaping the workforce by transforming traditional job functions and creating entirely new roles. As AI systems take over repetitive and data-heavy tasks, human roles are evolving toward areas that require strategic thinking, emotional intelligence, and creativity—skills that machines cannot replicate effectively. This shift is prompting businesses to redefine job descriptions, build interdisciplinary teams, and establish new performance metrics that reflect AI-enhanced work environments. A thoughtfully crafted job can enhance employee well-being and create an environment conducive to thriving, where individuals overcome workplace challenges and experience personal growth as a result(Tims & Bakker,2010). Emerging roles such as AI trainers, data ethicists, and algorithmic accountability officers are becoming critical in ensuring that AI is not only effective but also used responsibly. To adapt, organizations must promote continuous learning and provide employees with the tools and training necessary to succeed in this evolving landscape.

a) Emergence of Hybrid Human-AI Roles

AI is driving the rise of hybrid roles where employees collaborate with intelligent systems rather than being replaced by them. For example, customer service representatives may now work alongside AI chatbots, focusing on complex cases while the AI handles routine queries. Similarly, marketing professionals are using AI-powered analytics tools to craft personalized campaigns, combining data-driven insights with human creativity.

b) New Technical and Ethical Work Profiles

Alongside traditional roles, entirely new job profiles have emerged, including AI ethicists, machine learning operations (MLOps) specialists, and explainable AI (XAI) analysts. These roles are essential for ensuring that AI systems function transparently, fairly, and in compliance with ethical standards. As businesses face increasing pressure to deploy AI responsibly, these new positions are becoming central to corporate governance and innovation strategies.

C. Ethical and Compliance Challenges in AI Deployment

As organizations increasingly adopt Artificial Intelligence across operations, ethical and compliance challenges are becoming critical areas of concern. Without clear oversight, AI systems can unintentionally reinforce societal inequalities or make opaque decisions that impact customers and employees. Regulatory landscapes are also evolving, requiring businesses to navigate complex frameworks and ensure their AI practices comply with local and international laws. Organizations ought to incorporate privacy considerations throughout the entire lifecycle of AI initiatives, from design to implementation(Blessing,2024). As a result, companies must embed ethical considerations into the AI development lifecycle and implement robust compliance protocols to foster public trust and prevent reputational or legal risks.

a) Addressing Algorithmic Bias and Fairness

AI systems can mirror and potentially worsen human biases found in training data, resulting in unfair results in sectors such as recruitment, lending, and policing. To mitigate this, companies must prioritize fairness audits, use diverse datasets, and involve multidisciplinary teams—including ethicists and social scientists—in the design and evaluation of AI tools.

b) Navigating Data Privacy and Regulatory Compliance

With increasing reliance on user data, ensuring data privacy and complying with regulations such as the GDPR (General Data Protection Regulation) and other data protection laws is crucial. Organizations must establish transparent data practices, secure user consent, and maintain clear documentation of how AI models use and store data to remain compliant and ethical.

3. POST-PANDEMIC WORK: THE ACCELERATED ROLE OF AI IN SHAPING LABOR

The COVID-19 pandemic has greatly hastened the integration of Artificial Intelligence (AI) in numerous industries, fundamentally transforming the future of work. As businesses navigated the challenges of remote work, social distancing, and disrupted supply chains, AI emerged as a key enabler of continuity and efficiency. Technologies like machine learning, automation, and AI-driven analytics allowed companies to maintain operations, optimize workflows, and enhance customer engagement remotely. The pandemic also highlighted the need for more agile, data-driven decision-making, which AI systems support by providing real-time insights and predictive capabilities. As a result, many companies have adopted hybrid work models that blend human expertise with AI tools, fostering collaboration and enhancing productivity. Looking ahead, AI is expected to play an even greater role in reshaping job roles, improving organizational adaptability, and driving new forms of workforce collaboration that are more resilient to future disruptions. The pandemic further sped up the process of automation in Romania, enhancing task efficiency and optimizing the use of resources. Artificial intelligence and artificial general intelligence are reshaping the workforce(Ciuhu,2024). However, this rapid integration of AI raises questions around job displacement, the future of employee-employer relationships, and the ethical use of AI in managing remote or flexible workforces, requiring businesses and policymakers to balance innovation with equity and transparency.

A. The Pandemic's Impact on AI Adoption in the Workplace

The COVID-19 pandemic acted as a powerful accelerator for AI adoption across industries, as businesses faced urgent pressure to maintain operations amid lockdowns, remote work transitions, and supply chain disruptions. Organizations turned to AI-driven tools to support remote collaboration, automate essential functions, and gain real-time insights into rapidly changing conditions. From virtual health consultations to AI-enabled logistics and demand forecasting, the pandemic forced even traditionally conservative sectors to embrace digital transformation. With the world confronting the difficulties brought by the COVID-19 pandemic, these AI technologies have gained renewed importance in offering assistance, information, and virtual engagement(Hussain et al.,2024). AI was also critical in enabling contactless services, tracking virus spread, and managing workforce health and safety through data analytics and monitoring systems. As a result, AI moved from being a strategic option to a business necessity, fundamentally altering perceptions about its value and utility in everyday operations.

a) Acceleration of Digital and AI-Driven Processes

The pandemic expedited digital transformation efforts that would have otherwise taken years, pushing companies to integrate AI in areas such as customer service (via chatbots), internal communications, and workflow automation. Many companies invested in AI for cybersecurity, remote monitoring, and intelligent document processing to ensure business continuity under constrained circumstances.

b) Long-Term Shift in Workplace Strategy

Post-pandemic, many of the AI-driven adaptations have become permanent features of workplace strategy. Businesses now recognize AI not only as a crisis-response tool but also as a long-term asset for increasing productivity, reducing reliance on physical infrastructure, and enabling more agile, data-informed decision-making in uncertain environments.

B. Remote Work, AI, and the Digital Transformation of Workplaces

The shift to remote work during the COVID-19 pandemic fundamentally changed how organizations operate, and AI played a key role in enabling this transformation. As businesses transitioned to digital-first models, AI technologies helped manage distributed teams, monitor productivity, and support virtual collaboration. Tools like AI-powered video conferencing platforms, intelligent project management systems, and virtual assistants allowed employees to work efficiently from home while maintaining alignment with organizational goals. We inhabit and operate within a connected world, progressively defined by the journey of digital transformation that generates chances and advancements but also presents significant challenges, occasionally even risks(Gorski et al.,2022).

a) Enhancing Remote Collaboration and Communication

AI tools now assist in scheduling meetings, summarizing discussions, and prioritizing tasks through natural language processing and machine learning. These tools enable seamless communication across geographies and time zones, creating a more connected and efficient virtual work environment.

b) AI-Powered Workforce Monitoring and Support

While controversial, AI is increasingly used to track employee performance, attendance, and productivity in remote settings. When implemented ethically and transparently, such systems can help managers identify workflow bottlenecks or provide targeted support, but they also raise concerns around privacy, autonomy, and workplace surveillance.

C. Future Work Trends: Hybrid Models and AI Integration

The post-pandemic world has given rise to hybrid work models that combine remote and on-site work, with AI serving as a critical enabler of this flexibility. These models aim to offer the best of both worlds—preserving the autonomy of remote work while fostering in-person collaboration when needed. AI technologies are integral in managing hybrid schedules, optimizing office space usage, and ensuring seamless communication between dispersed teams. Moreover, AI tools help organizations gather and analyze workforce data to continuously refine hybrid strategies based on employee productivity, engagement, and preferences. As hybrid work becomes the norm, AI is expected to play a growing role in redefining performance evaluation, team collaboration, and even workplace design. Consequently, government investment in fifth-generation mobile network technology, the execution of cybersecurity protocols, interoperability, cohesive systems, and enhanced educational levels create the essential ICT environment to enhance the possibilities for remote work(Grzegorczyk et al., 2021).

a) AI for Dynamic Workforce Management

AI systems can forecast team workloads, assign tasks based on availability and skill, and recommend optimal meeting times across time zones. These capabilities make managing hybrid teams more efficient, reducing friction and improving cross-functional coordination.

b) Personalized Work Experiences Through AI

Using AI, companies can personalize work environments by analyzing employee preferences, habits, and feedback. This enables tailored experiences—such as flexible hours, customized learning paths, and adaptive workflows—that enhance employee satisfaction and retention in a hybrid setting.

4. LABOR MARKET POLARIZATION: RISKS AND OPPORTUNITIES IN THE AI ERA

Labor market polarization, exacerbated by the rise of AI technologies, presents both risks and opportunities for the workforce. As AI automates routine, manual, and low-skilled jobs, there is a growing divide between high-skill, high-pay roles and low-skill, low-pay jobs, leaving many workers vulnerable to displacement. Occupations in sectors such as manufacturing, retail, and customer service are particularly at risk, with automation technologies rendering certain tasks obsolete. However, AI also creates opportunities for high-skill jobs in fields such as data science, AI development, and digital transformation. These new roles demand advanced technical expertise, creativity, and emotional intelligence, offering pathways for upskilling and career advancement. The challenge lies in addressing the growing skills gap and ensuring that workers can access training and education to transition into emerging sectors. Some groups have faced a drop in employment opportunities and earnings, as polarization has been a steady trend for over twenty years(Sholler & MacInnes, 2024).

A. Job Displacement and the Future of Low-Skill Jobs

One of the most pressing challenges posed by AI adoption is the displacement of low-skill jobs, particularly those involving routine or repetitive tasks. Sectors such as manufacturing, retail, transportation, and basic administrative services are seeing increased automation, reducing the demand for human labor in roles like cashiers, warehouse workers, and data entry clerks. As AI systems and robotics become more cost-effective and efficient, companies are opting for automation to enhance productivity and minimize errors. This trend raises concerns about job security for millions of workers whose skills may no longer be in demand in the evolving labor market. Without proactive measures such as retraining and job redesign, displaced workers risk being left behind, leading to higher unemployment, social unrest, and deepening inequality. The future is unclear, as young individuals are disproportionately found in roles within industries that are

projected to observe reduced employment growth over the long term, and essential 'stepping stone' mid-skill positions are diminishing(Williams et al., 2021).

a) Vulnerable Sectors and Job Categories

Jobs that involve predictable physical or cognitive tasks—such as assembly line work, basic bookkeeping, and customer service via call Centers—are particularly susceptible to automation. These roles often have limited career mobility, making the transition to new employment opportunities especially difficult without intervention.

b) The Need for Inclusive Transition Strategies

Governments and businesses must collaborate to develop safety nets and retraining programs that target displaced workers. Strategies should include accessible vocational education, apprenticeship opportunities in emerging fields, and incentives for companies that invest in upskilling their low-skill workforce to prevent long-term socioeconomic exclusion.

B. Creating New High-Skill Opportunities in the AI Economy

While AI poses a threat to many low-skill jobs, it is simultaneously driving the creation of new, high-skill opportunities that require advanced education, technical expertise, and cognitive flexibility. The AI economy is fostering demand for roles such as data scientists, machine learning engineers, cybersecurity analysts, and AI ethicists—positions that involve the design, development, oversight, and governance of intelligent systems. The swift advancement of science and technology has led to the extensive incorporation of essential technologies, particularly artificial intelligence (AI), big data, and blockchain, throughout various fields in society(Zhang,2023). Additionally, AI is transforming traditional professions like marketing, finance, and healthcare, requiring workers in these fields to acquire digital competencies and data literacy.

a) New Roles in AI-Driven Industries

Fields such as AI research, robotics, digital health, and smart manufacturing are creating jobs that didn't exist a decade ago. Roles like natural language processing (NLP) experts, AI product managers, and algorithm auditors are becoming essential in both tech and non-tech industries as AI systems are integrated into everyday operations.

b) Education and Industry Partnerships for Talent Development

To meet the growing demand for high-skill labor, collaboration between universities, vocational institutions, and industries is crucial. These partnerships can help design curricula that reflect real-world AI applications, promote internships in AI-rich environments, and ensure that graduates are equipped with both theoretical and applied knowledge to thrive in the digital economy.

C. Bridging the Skills Gap: Addressing Workforce Transitions

As AI reshapes the labor market, a significant skills gap has emerged between the existing workforce capabilities and the demands of new, technology-driven roles. Many workers displaced from routine jobs lack the specialized training needed for high-skill positions created by AI, making workforce transitions a critical challenge. Addressing this gap requires comprehensive retraining and upskilling initiatives, focusing on digital literacy, critical thinking, and problem-solving skills. Governments, educational institutions, and employers must collaborate to provide accessible, flexible learning opportunities that accommodate diverse learner needs, including mid-career workers. Additionally, lifelong learning cultures must be promoted to ensure workers remain adaptable in a rapidly evolving job market, helping to prevent long-term unemployment and socio-economic exclusion. The results are relevant to the workforce and organizational finances and demonstrate the use of business theories to practical industry challenges through an academic perspective, especially in the context of a university Capstone project(Hernandez et al.,2024).

a) Accessible and Flexible Learning Programs

Effective workforce transition programs should offer modular, on-demand courses, combining online and in-person training tailored to varying skill levels and learning styles. This flexibility enables workers to reskill while managing other responsibilities.

b) Public-Private Partnerships for Workforce Development

Collaboration between public institutions and private sector companies can foster apprenticeship schemes, job placement services, and funding for skill development, ensuring that workforce transitions align with actual labor market needs and technological advancements.

5. SOCIETAL IMPLICATIONS OF AI ON LABOR: INCOME DISTRIBUTION AND SOCIAL WELFARE

The rise of AI in the labor market has significant societal implications, particularly concerning income distribution and social welfare systems. As AI-driven automation displaces low-skill jobs and creates high-skill opportunities, there is an increasing risk of income inequality. Workers in sectors vulnerable to automation may experience job loss without adequate pathways to transition into higher-skilled roles, leading to a widening income gap. This polarization could exacerbate existing social disparities, as the benefits of AI are often concentrated among those with the necessary skills or capital to invest in AI technologies. Furthermore, traditional social welfare systems, which were designed for a different labor landscape, may struggle to adapt to the changing dynamics of the workforce. There is a growing need for policy innovation to ensure that displaced workers are supported through reskilling programs, unemployment benefits, and access to new employment opportunities. Progress in mechanization during the late nineteenth and early twentieth centuries automated a significant portion of the manual labor carried out by people(Korinek & Stiglitz, 2018).

A. The Impact of AI on Income Inequality

Artificial Intelligence (AI) has the potential to both exacerbate and mitigate income inequality depending on how it is implemented across the labor market. On one hand, AI-driven automation disproportionately affects low-skill and routine jobs, leading to job losses and wage stagnation among vulnerable workers. This displacement can widen the income gap as high-skill workers who design, manage, or augment AI technologies reap greater financial rewards. Additionally, those with access to advanced education and digital resources tend to benefit more from AI opportunities, deepening existing social and economic divides. On the other hand, when paired with inclusive policies and equitable access to education and training, AI can promote upward mobility by creating high-skill jobs and improving productivity. Addressing the income inequality challenge requires intentional policy design to redistribute gains from AI and ensure that benefits are broadly shared across society. This research seeks to examine how technological changes have led to an increase in income inequality(Goyal & Aneja, 2020).

a) Disproportionate Effects on Vulnerable Populations

The adoption of AI and automation disproportionately impacts vulnerable populations, particularly low-income workers engaged in routine, manual, or repetitive jobs that are most susceptible to being replaced by machines. These groups often face higher risks of job displacement and economic instability because they have limited access to quality education, digital skills training, and affordable reskilling opportunities necessary to transition into new, high-skill roles created by AI technologies. The resulting job losses and income reductions can deepen existing social and economic inequalities, pushing marginalized communities further into poverty and social exclusion. Additionally, without targeted interventions, these populations are less likely to benefit from the productivity gains and new opportunities generated by AI, exacerbating the digital divide and limiting social mobility. Addressing these disproportionate effects requires comprehensive policy responses that prioritize inclusive education, accessible training programs, and supportive social safety nets to ensure vulnerable workers are not left behind in the evolving labor market.

b) Policy Measures for Equitable AI Benefits

To ensure that the benefits of AI are shared equitably across society, comprehensive policy measures are essential. Governments must invest in accessible and inclusive education and training programs that equip workers of all backgrounds with the digital and technical skills needed to thrive in an AI-driven economy. Social safety nets should be reformed and expanded to support displaced workers through unemployment benefits, reskilling subsidies, and healthcare access, enabling smoother transitions between jobs. Progressive taxation on AI-enabled industries and corporations can generate revenue to fund these initiatives and reduce wealth concentration. Additionally, policies promoting affordable access to digital infrastructure are critical to closing the digital divide, ensuring that marginalized communities can participate fully in the new economy. Public-private partnerships and multi-stakeholder collaborations can further foster innovation while safeguarding ethical standards and labor rights. Together, these policy measures can help create a fairer labor market where AI-driven growth benefits all segments of society.

B. Redefining Social Welfare Systems in an AI-Driven Economy

The rapid advancement and integration of AI into labor markets are challenging traditional social welfare systems, which were primarily designed for stable, long-term employment structures. As automation and AI disrupt conventional job roles, more workers find themselves in precarious or non-standard forms of employment such as gig work, freelancing, or temporary contracts. These shifts demand a fundamental rethinking of social welfare policies to ensure they remain relevant and effective in supporting workers through economic transitions. Modernized welfare systems must offer greater flexibility, inclusivity, and responsiveness to address the varied needs of an evolving workforce. This includes redesigning benefits to cover non-traditional workers, linking welfare with reskilling programs, and creating safety nets that support continuous learning and economic resilience. Analytics powered by AI and predictive modeling can assist in recognizing at-risk populations, improving resource distribution, and creating focused strategies to diminish poverty and inequality(Rathore,2024).

a) Flexible and Inclusive Social Safety Nets

Traditional welfare systems often exclude workers engaged in gig, freelance, or part-time work, leaving many vulnerable in the face of job displacement due to AI. Redefining social safety nets to include portable benefits that follow workers regardless of employment type is critical. This approach ensures that all workers receive unemployment insurance, healthcare, and retirement benefits, irrespective of job stability or contract type. Dynamic income support that adjusts to changing labor market conditions will provide a more reliable cushion for workers navigating frequent transitions and automation-driven disruptions.

b) Integration with Workforce Development and Reskilling Programs

Social welfare must not only provide financial support but also actively facilitate workforce reintegration through education and skills development. Combining welfare benefits with accessible reskilling initiatives empowers displaced workers to transition into emerging AI-driven job roles. By integrating career counselling, training subsidies, and job placement services into welfare programs, governments can promote sustainable employment outcomes rather than temporary relief. This synergy encourages a culture of lifelong learning, adaptability, and resilience necessary for thriving in the evolving digital economy.

C. Policy Innovations for Ensuring Equitable Access to AI Opportunities

The incorporation of Artificial Intelligence (AI) in education has been extensively examined in scholarly studies, emphasizing both its possibilities and the difficulties related to fair access(Ahmed,2024). As AI increasingly shapes labor markets, equitable access to its benefits becomes a critical policy challenge. Without deliberate and forward-thinking interventions, AI risks deepening existing social and economic divides by favouring those with prior access to technology, education, and capital. To prevent such disparities, governments and stakeholders must design innovative policies that promote inclusivity and democratize AI opportunities across all segments of society. This involves not only expanding access to education and digital infrastructure but also fostering environments where marginalized groups can participate fully in the AI-driven economy. Policy innovations should focus on closing the digital divide, supporting diverse workforce participation, encouraging ethical AI development, and strengthening public-private partnerships to scale inclusive practices. By embedding equity into AI governance frameworks, policymakers can help ensure that technological progress translates into broad-based social and economic advancement.

a) Bridging the Digital Divide through Infrastructure and Education

Access to AI opportunities is often limited by disparities in digital infrastructure and education. Policy efforts must prioritize expanding affordable broadband connectivity and providing accessible, high-quality digital literacy and technical training programs—especially in underserved rural and low-income urban areas. Closing these gaps enables a broader population to develop the necessary skills and access AI-enabled tools, reducing barriers to participation in emerging job markets.

b) Inclusive AI Development and Workforce Participation

Policies should incentivize organizations to adopt inclusive hiring practices and support diversity in AI-related fields such as data science, AI ethics, and technology management. This includes promoting gender equity, minority representation, and support for disadvantaged communities through scholarships, mentorship programs, and targeted recruitment. Encouraging diverse perspectives in AI design and deployment also helps mitigate biases and creates technologies that better serve all users.

c) Public-Private Partnerships and Collaborative Governance

Effective policy innovation requires collaboration between governments, industry leaders, educational institutions, and civil society. Public-private partnerships can drive investments in reskilling programs, research in ethical AI, and the development of equitable AI standards. Multi-stakeholder governance models foster transparency, accountability, and shared responsibility in ensuring AI benefits are distributed fairly, aligning technological advancement with societal values.

6. HUMAN-CENTERED AI: BALANCING TECHNOLOGICAL PROGRESS WITH SOCIETAL VALUES

Human-centered AI focuses on designing and deploying AI systems that prioritize human well-being, values, and ethical considerations, ensuring that technological progress benefits society as a whole. As AI technologies rapidly advance, it is essential to balance innovation with respect for fundamental societal principles such as fairness, accountability, privacy, and inclusivity. By placing humans at the core of AI development, businesses and policymakers can mitigate the risks of algorithmic biases, job displacement, and unintended consequences. Human-centered AI promotes transparency in decision-making, encourages ethical data usage, and seeks to enhance rather than replace human capabilities. It also emphasizes the importance of collaborative human-AI interactions, where AI augments human judgment and creativity instead of replacing it. Additionally, AI and sensors provide immediate technological improvements that assist the shipping sector, increasing safety, lowering expenses, thus enhancing productivity in global commerce and adopting a more intelligent and sustainable future(Martini et al., 2024).

A. Inclusive Growth and Responsible AI Innovation

Achieving inclusive growth through AI requires innovation that prioritizes not only technological advancement but also social equity and ethical responsibility. Responsible AI innovation involves designing and deploying AI systems that enhance productivity and economic expansion while ensuring that benefits reach all segments of society, including historically marginalized and underserved groups. This approach demands transparency, fairness, and accountability in AI development to prevent algorithmic biases and discrimination that could exacerbate existing inequalities. Inclusive growth also depends on fostering collaboration between governments, businesses, and civil society to create frameworks that balance innovation with the protection of human rights and labor standards. By embedding social considerations into AI innovation processes, stakeholders can unlock AI's full potential as a tool for equitable economic development, sustainable job creation, and enhanced quality of life for diverse populations. The area of responsible innovation (RI) has an extensive history and has developed into a framework for the complete research, development, and innovation lifecycle(Herrmann,2023).

a) Ensuring Fair Access and Benefits Across Socioeconomic Groups

Inclusive AI growth means that access to AI-driven opportunities—such as new jobs, digital services, and educational resources—is distributed fairly across socio-economic groups. Policies and practices must actively dismantle barriers faced by underrepresented communities, including those related to race, gender, geography, and income. This requires targeted outreach, affordable access to digital tools, and support mechanisms to help marginalized groups participate fully in the AI economy.

b) Embedding Ethics and Accountability in AI Innovation

Responsible AI innovation hinges on integrating ethical principles into the entire AI lifecycle—from design and development to deployment and monitoring. This includes rigorous evaluation of AI algorithms for fairness, transparency, and privacy protection, as well as mechanisms for redress in cases of harm or bias. Establishing clear standards and regulatory oversight helps build public trust and ensures AI technologies serve the broader goals of social justice and economic inclusion.

B. Aligning AI Development with Sustainable Labor Policies

Aligning AI development with sustainable labor policies is essential to ensure that technological advancements contribute positively to long-term workforce stability and social welfare. Sustainable labor policies recognize the transformative impact of AI on employment patterns and seek to create a resilient labor market that balances innovation with worker protection. This alignment involves proactive measures such as updating labor laws to address AI-related challenges, including job displacement, workplace surveillance, and the gig economy's rise. It also requires the promotion of continuous learning and adaptability, encouraging workers to develop new skills aligned with evolving AI technologies. Furthermore, sustainable labor policies advocate for fair wages, safe working conditions, and inclusive social protections that safeguard vulnerable workers amid rapid digital transformation. Concurrently, educational and training organizations need to evaluate their usage of AI and their training programs to guarantee they are ethical, equitable, diverse, and motivated by commitments to sustainable development(Reuben,2023).

a) Modernizing Labor Regulations for the AI Era

To keep pace with AI-driven changes, labor regulations must be revised to address emerging issues such as algorithmic management, remote work, and non-traditional employment contracts. Clear guidelines on transparency, worker rights, and collective bargaining in AI-managed workplaces are necessary to protect employee interests while allowing businesses to innovate responsibly.

b) Promoting Lifelong Learning and Skill Adaptation

Sustainable labor policies emphasize continuous education and training to help workers adapt to the dynamic demands of AI integration. Governments and private sectors should collaborate to develop accessible reskilling and upskilling programs, enabling employees to transition into new roles and reducing the risk of long-term unemployment caused by automation.

C. The Role of Government and Society in Shaping AI's Labor Impact

Governments and society play a pivotal role in guiding the integration of AI into labor markets to ensure its benefits are maximized while minimizing adverse effects. It examines how the implementation of AI technologies has influenced the environment of job creation and loss due to these policy instruments(Dosz,2024). Public institutions are responsible for crafting policies and regulatory frameworks that promote ethical AI use, protect workers' rights, and foster inclusive economic growth. This includes establishing standards for transparency, accountability, and fairness in AI deployment, as well as funding social safety nets and workforce development programs to support those displaced by automation. Society—including labor unions, civil organizations, academia, and the private sector—must actively participate in shaping AI's trajectory by advocating for responsible innovation and holding stakeholders accountable. Collaborative efforts among these actors can create a balanced environment where AI complements human labor rather than replaces it, ensuring equitable access to opportunities and preventing widening social inequalities. Moreover, ongoing public dialogue and education are critical to building trust, raising awareness about AI's implications, and empowering individuals to engage with AI technologies meaningfully.

a) Government as Regulator and Facilitator

Governments must act both as regulators enforcing fair AI practices and facilitators that encourage innovation aligned with public interests. This dual role involves drafting adaptable policies that evolve with technology while investing in infrastructure and programs that promote workforce resilience and social inclusion.

b) Civil Society and Stakeholder Engagement

Active involvement of civil society groups, workers' organizations, and industry stakeholders ensures that diverse perspectives inform AI governance. Such engagement helps identify potential risks, promote ethical standards, and foster a culture of shared responsibility in managing AI's labor impacts.

7. AI AND THE FUTURE OF SKILLS ECOSYSTEMS: EDUCATION AND WORKFORCE DEVELOPMENT

AI is reshaping the future of skills ecosystems, fundamentally altering the way we approach education and workforce development. As AI technologies continue to automate routine tasks, the demand for human skills is shifting towards areas such as creativity, critical thinking, problem-solving, and emotional intelligence—skills that AI cannot replicate. This shift necessitates a reimagining of educational systems and workforce training programs to prepare individuals for the evolving job market. The future of skills ecosystems will require a greater focus on lifelong learning, with an emphasis on reskilling and upskilling workers to adapt to emerging technologies. Collaboration between industries, educational institutions, and governments will be essential to ensure that the workforce is equipped with the necessary skills to thrive in an AI-driven economy. Additionally, AI can also play a role in personalized learning, tailoring educational content to individual needs and learning styles, thus enhancing the effectiveness of training programs. By fostering a culture of continuous learning and adaptability, AI can help build a more resilient, agile workforce, prepared to meet the challenges and opportunities of the future labor market.

A. Preparing the Workforce for AI Integration: Education and Retraining

Preparing the workforce for AI integration is critical to ensuring that workers can adapt to rapidly changing job requirements and continue contributing meaningfully in an AI-enhanced economy. Education systems must evolve to emphasize not only digital literacy but also critical thinking, creativity, and problem-solving skills that complement AI technologies. Retraining initiatives are essential for workers displaced by automation, enabling them to acquire new competencies in emerging fields such as data analytics, AI management, and cybersecurity. Collaboration between governments, educational institutions, and industry leaders is vital to design accessible and flexible training programs tailored to diverse learning needs and labor market demands. Additionally, lifelong learning frameworks should be established to encourage continuous skill development throughout individuals' careers, promoting resilience and adaptability in the face of ongoing technological advances. Effective preparation of the workforce through education and retraining will help bridge the skills gap, reduce unemployment risks, and support inclusive economic growth in the AI era.

a) Curriculum Reform and Skill Development

To prepare the workforce for AI integration, education systems must undergo significant curriculum reform that goes beyond traditional subjects. Incorporating AI-related skills such as programming, data science, machine learning basics, and understanding of AI ethics is essential for students at various educational levels. Moreover, it's important to emphasize interdisciplinary learning that combines technical expertise with critical thinking, creativity, emotional intelligence, and problem-solving abilities—skills that AI cannot easily replicate. This holistic approach equips learners to collaborate effectively with AI systems and to innovate in ways that complement automation. Furthermore, educational institutions should foster adaptability and lifelong learning mindsets, encouraging students to continuously update their skills in response to evolving technological landscapes. Partnerships between schools, universities, and industry can help ensure curricula remain relevant to real-world AI applications and future job market needs.

b) Accessible and Flexible Retraining Programs

Given the rapid pace of AI adoption and its disruptive impact on certain jobs, retraining programs must be designed to be highly accessible, flexible, and responsive to the diverse needs of displaced and at-risk workers. These programs should offer modular, stackable courses that allow learners to build skills progressively, whether through part-time studies, online platforms, or blended learning models that combine digital and in-person instruction. Affordability is critical to ensure broad participation, particularly for low-income workers who may lack resources for traditional education. Moreover, retraining initiatives should include career counselling, mentorship, and support services to help individuals navigate transitions into new roles or industries. Governments, private sector organizations, and educational institutions must collaborate to fund and promote these programs, ensuring they are widely publicized and accessible across geographic and socio-economic divides. By enabling workers to upskill or reskill efficiently, these programs help reduce unemployment risks and foster a more adaptable, resilient labor force capable of thriving alongside AI technologies.

B. The Evolution of Skills in the AI Economy

The rise of Artificial Intelligence is fundamentally transforming the skill sets required across industries, reshaping labor demands in ways that emphasize both technical expertise and uniquely human capabilities. Traditional routine and repetitive tasks are increasingly automated, reducing demand for purely manual or process-driven skills. Instead, there is a growing premium on advanced digital skills such as data literacy, machine learning understanding, and proficiency with AI tools, which enable workers to interact effectively with AI systems and leverage their capabilities. At the same time, skills that AI cannot easily replicate—such as creativity, emotional intelligence, critical thinking, complex problem-solving, and interpersonal communication—are becoming indispensable in the workforce. This shift calls for a hybrid skillset where humans complement AI by applying judgment, ethical considerations, and innovation to augment machine outputs. As the economy evolves, lifelong learning becomes crucial, requiring individuals to continually adapt by acquiring new competencies and refining existing ones. The dynamic nature of AI-driven work environments also demands adaptability, resilience, and the ability to work collaboratively with AI, underscoring the importance of flexible skill development models that evolve alongside technological advancements.

a) The Growing Demand for Digital and Technical Skills

In the AI economy, digital and technical skills have become foundational requirements for many jobs. Proficiency in areas like data analytics, programming, AI system management, and cybersecurity is increasingly essential as organizations rely more on AI-driven tools and platforms. Workers who understand how to develop, implement, and maintain AI technologies are in high demand, not only in tech-centric roles but across sectors like healthcare, finance, manufacturing, and logistics. Moreover, digital fluency—the ability to navigate AI-enhanced workflows, interpret machine-generated insights, and collaborate with intelligent systems—is becoming a necessary competency for a broad range of roles.

b) Emphasis on Soft Skills and Human-Centric Abilities

While technical skills are crucial, the AI economy places an equally strong emphasis on soft skills that AI cannot replicate. Emotional intelligence, creativity, ethical judgment, cultural awareness, and complex problem-solving are critical for tasks that require human nuance and interpersonal interaction. As AI takes over routine and data-heavy functions, workers are increasingly valued for their ability to innovate, collaborate, and make decisions in ambiguous or ethically complex scenarios. Skills such as leadership, adaptability, and communication enable humans to work effectively alongside AI, guiding technology deployment in ways that respect societal values and enhance organizational culture. Educational and training programs must therefore balance technical instruction with development of these human-centric skills, fostering well-rounded individuals capable of thriving in AI-augmented work environments.

C. Building Hybrid Human-AI Collaboration Models

As AI technologies become more embedded in workplace processes, the future of work increasingly depends on effective collaboration between humans and AI systems. Hybrid models of work blend the strengths of both, where AI handles repetitive, data-intensive, or precision tasks, while humans contribute creativity, judgment, and emotional intelligence. This symbiosis can significantly enhance productivity, innovation, and decision-making quality by leveraging AI's analytical power alongside human insight. Building successful hybrid collaboration models requires designing workflows that optimize task allocation between humans and AI, ensuring that technology complements rather than replaces human labor. It also involves fostering an organizational culture that embraces AI as a collaborative partner, encouraging workers to engage with AI tools confidently and ethically. To realize the full potential of these hybrid models, businesses must invest in training employees not only to use AI technologies but also to understand their limitations and ethical implications.

a) Designing Effective Task Allocation Between Humans and AI

A key aspect of hybrid collaboration is determining which tasks are best suited for AI automation and which require human involvement. AI excels at processing large volumes of data quickly, identifying patterns, and executing repetitive tasks with high accuracy. Conversely, humans are better at tasks involving creativity, empathy, strategic thinking, and ethical considerations. By carefully analyzing workflows, organizations can assign tasks to AI systems or humans based on these strengths, reducing inefficiencies and preventing job displacement concerns. For example, in customer service, AI chatbots might handle routine inquiries, freeing human agents to focus on complex or emotionally sensitive interactions. This deliberate task design ensures that AI acts as an augmentative tool, empowering human workers rather than rendering them obsolete.

b) Cultivating AI Literacy and Ethical Awareness Among Employees

To build trust and effective collaboration, employees need to develop AI literacy—understanding how AI systems function, their benefits, and their potential biases or limitations. Training programs should focus not only on technical usage but also on ethical AI deployment, helping workers recognize algorithmic bias, data privacy issues, and the broader societal impacts of AI decisions. Promoting transparency in AI processes enables employees to question and refine AI outputs, fostering a culture of accountability and responsible innovation. When workers are confident in their AI tools and aware of ethical concerns, they can better leverage AI to augment their roles, enhancing overall organizational performance and ensuring technology is aligned with human values.

8. GLOBAL PERSPECTIVES: COMPARATIVE STUDIES OF AI'S IMPACT ON LABOR ACROSS REGIONS

The impact of AI on labor markets varies significantly across regions, influenced by factors such as economic development, technological adoption, labor market structure, and cultural attitudes towards automation. Comparative studies of AI's effects on labor across different regions offer valuable insights into how diverse countries are navigating the challenges and opportunities presented by AI integration. In developed economies, particularly in North America and Europe, AI adoption is often focused on augmenting human labor, improving productivity, and addressing labor shortages in certain high-skill sectors, such as healthcare, finance, and technology. These regions also face challenges related to job displacement, income inequality, and the need for reskilling programs to prepare workers for the future job market. In contrast, emerging economies in Asia and Africa are grappling with different challenges, including the risk of mass unemployment due to automation in low-skill jobs and the digital divide that limits access to AI-driven opportunities. However, these regions are also seeing new opportunities for AI to leapfrog traditional industrialization stages, creating new sectors, enhancing agricultural productivity, and improving healthcare delivery. Understanding these regional variations is crucial for developing tailored policies and strategies that address the unique needs and contexts of different labor markets, ensuring that the benefits of AI are equitably distributed across global economies.

A. Case Studies from North America, Europe, and Asia

The impact of AI on labor markets varies considerably across regions due to differences in economic development, technological infrastructure, labor policies, and cultural attitudes. Examining case studies from North America, Europe, and Asia reveals diverse approaches to AI adoption, highlighting both common challenges and region-specific solutions. These comparative insights help identify best practices and cautionary lessons that can inform future AI integration strategies globally.

a) North America: Innovation-Driven AI Adoption and Workforce Challenges

In North America, especially the United States and Canada, AI adoption is heavily driven by private sector innovation, with technology hubs such as Silicon Valley leading advancements in AI research and application. Businesses emphasize AI to enhance productivity, customer experience, and data-driven decision-making, particularly in finance, healthcare, and technology sectors. However, rapid AI integration has raised concerns around workforce displacement, with significant attention to reskilling and upskilling programs. Government initiatives and private partnerships focus on preparing workers for AI-enabled jobs, though disparities in access to training and economic inequality remain persistent challenges. Moreover, regulatory discussions center on AI ethics, privacy, and algorithmic transparency to balance innovation with social responsibility.

b) Europe: Regulatory Leadership and Ethical AI Deployment

Europe stands out for its proactive approach to AI governance, emphasizing ethical standards, data protection, and human-centered AI development. The European Union has implemented comprehensive AI strategies that prioritize transparency, fairness, and inclusivity while fostering AI innovation. Labor market policies often integrate strong social safety nets and worker protections, supporting transitions in sectors affected by automation. European countries are investing in public education systems and vocational training to equip the workforce with AI-relevant skills. Additionally, cross-border collaborations and funding programs aim to bridge the digital divide between member states, promoting equitable AI benefits. This regulatory focus positions Europe as a model for responsible AI adoption that safeguards labor rights and societal well-being.

c) Asia: Rapid AI Adoption and Economic Leapfrogging

In Asia, countries such as China, Japan, South Korea, and India showcase diverse AI adoption patterns reflecting varying economic stages and policy environments. China leads with aggressive investments in AI research, smart manufacturing, and digital infrastructure, leveraging AI for industrial automation and urban management. Rapid AI deployment in emerging economies aims to leapfrog traditional industrial development, improving productivity in agriculture, healthcare, and services. However, these gains come with challenges related to labor displacement, especially for low-skilled workers, and a pronounced digital divide between urban and rural populations. Governments in Asia are increasingly focusing on expanding digital literacy, workforce reskilling, and fostering innovation ecosystems. Collaborative international initiatives and public-private partnerships play vital roles in shaping AI's labor market impact in this region.

B. Diverging Policy Approaches to AI and Labor Market Transformation

Different regions and countries adopt varied policy frameworks to address the challenges and opportunities posed by AI in transforming labor markets. These divergent approaches reflect local economic priorities, social values, institutional capacities, and the maturity of AI ecosystems. Understanding these policy variations helps highlight how governments balance innovation, workforce protection, and social equity in the AI era.

a) Proactive Reskilling and Social Protection Models

Some countries, particularly in Europe and parts of North America, adopt comprehensive policy frameworks that prioritize reskilling workers and strengthening social safety nets. These models emphasize lifelong learning initiatives, public funding for vocational and technical education, and targeted support for displaced workers. For instance, nations like Germany and Sweden invest heavily in apprenticeship programs and continuous training to facilitate smooth labor transitions. Social welfare reforms include unemployment benefits tied to retraining and active labor market policies aimed at reintegration into new employment sectors. This approach recognizes the inevitability of job displacement while striving to minimize socioeconomic disruption and promote inclusive growth.

b) Innovation-Centric and Market-Driven Approaches

In contrast, some countries, particularly emerging economies and market-oriented systems such as the United States and parts of Asia, focus on fostering innovation ecosystems with relatively less direct government intervention in labor market protections. These regions emphasize promoting entrepreneurship, private sector-led training programs, and flexible labor markets to encourage rapid adaptation to AI-driven changes. Policy measures may include tax incentives for technology adoption and public-private partnerships to scale AI education initiatives. While this approach can accelerate technological progress and economic competitiveness, it may also increase risks of labor market polarization and uneven access to reskilling resources, necessitating complementary social policies to address inequalities.

C. Lessons Learned from International AI Labor Strategies

Global experiences with AI adoption in labor markets provide valuable lessons for policymakers and business leaders aiming to harness AI's potential while mitigating its risks. By examining successes and challenges across diverse economies, key insights emerge about effective strategies to promote inclusive, ethical, and sustainable labor transformations in the AI era.

a) Importance of Holistic and Adaptive Policy Frameworks

Countries that have successfully navigated AI-driven labor changes tend to implement holistic policies that integrate education, social protection, and innovation support. For example, Scandinavian countries combine robust welfare systems with continuous skills development and strong stakeholder collaboration among government, industry, and labor unions. These adaptive frameworks enable timely responses to technological disruption while maintaining social cohesion. A key takeaway is that static or fragmented policies are inadequate; instead, ongoing evaluation and flexible adjustment of strategies are crucial as AI technologies and labor dynamics evolve.

b) Emphasizing Collaboration and Multi-Stakeholder Engagement

Effective AI labor strategies often involve close collaboration between public institutions, private enterprises, educational bodies, and civil society. Countries like Singapore and Canada highlight the benefits of such partnerships in designing training programs, fostering ethical AI deployment, and ensuring equitable access to AI opportunities. Engaging a broad range of stakeholders helps align AI adoption with societal values, address potential biases, and enhance transparency. Moreover, these collaborations facilitate shared responsibility in workforce transitions and build trust among workers, employers, and policymakers, which is vital for long-term success.

9. GOVERNANCE AND REGULATION: DEVELOPING POLICIES FOR THE AI-DRIVEN WORKFORCE

As AI technologies continue to transform the workforce, effective governance and regulation are essential to ensure that their integration is fair, ethical, and beneficial to society. Developing policies for the AI-driven workforce requires a balanced approach that promotes innovation while protecting workers' rights, ensuring job security, and addressing the potential risks of AI-driven automation. Key areas of focus include establishing frameworks for AI transparency, accountability, and data privacy, as well as creating regulations that safeguard against algorithmic bias and discrimination. Governments must also consider labor market transitions, developing social safety nets, reskilling programs, and initiatives to support displaced workers. Additionally, policies should foster collaboration between the public and private sectors to create a shared vision for AI's role in the workforce, ensuring that AI deployment aligns with broader societal goals such as inclusivity, fairness, and economic resilience. Effective governance will require continuous dialogue between policymakers, businesses, labor unions, and educational institutions to stay ahead of the rapid pace of technological change, ensuring that AI benefits society as a whole without exacerbating inequalities or undermining social stability.

A. AI Governance Frameworks for Protecting Workers and Businesses

As AI technologies become deeply embedded in workplace operations, establishing robust governance frameworks is essential to safeguard the rights and interests of both workers and businesses. Effective AI governance ensures that automation and algorithmic decision-making are transparent, accountable, and aligned with ethical standards, minimizing risks such as discrimination, job displacement, and unfair labor practices. By setting clear guidelines and standards, governance frameworks help build trust in AI systems and foster a sustainable integration of AI into the workforce.

a) Establishing Transparency and Accountability Mechanisms

One of the core components of AI governance involves ensuring transparency in how AI systems operate and make decisions that affect workers. This includes mandating clear explanations of algorithmic processes and outcomes, particularly in hiring, performance evaluation, and workforce management. Accountability measures, such as regular audits, impact assessments, and grievance redressal mechanisms, enable organizations to identify and rectify biases or errors in AI applications. Transparent and accountable AI practices protect workers from unfair treatment and empower businesses to demonstrate ethical compliance, thus enhancing organizational reputation and legal compliance.

b) Protecting Worker Rights and Promoting Fair Labor Practices

AI governance frameworks must prioritize safeguarding worker rights amid technological changes. This involves regulations that prevent discriminatory AI-driven decisions, ensure data privacy, and maintain human oversight in critical employment matters. Policies should also address the potential for job displacement by encouraging responsible AI deployment strategies that include reskilling commitments and fair transition plans. Furthermore, protecting small and medium-sized enterprises (SMEs) from undue burdens related to AI adoption is critical, ensuring that businesses of all sizes can compete fairly while adhering to governance standards. Together, these protections contribute to a balanced ecosystem where innovation coexists with social responsibility.

B. Ensuring Ethical and Transparent AI Practices in the Workplace

The deployment of AI technologies in workplaces brings significant benefits but also raises important ethical concerns. Ensuring that AI systems operate transparently and ethically is critical to maintaining trust among employees, protecting individual rights, and fostering a fair work environment. Ethical AI practices require companies to address issues such as bias, privacy, and accountability, while promoting inclusivity and respect for human dignity throughout the AI lifecycle.

a) Mitigating Algorithmic Bias and Promoting Fairness

AI systems are only as unbiased as the data they are trained on, making the mitigation of algorithmic bias a crucial ethical imperative. Organizations must implement rigorous testing and validation procedures to identify and correct discriminatory patterns that could adversely affect hiring, promotions, or task allocations. This involves diverse data sourcing, continuous monitoring, and involving multidisciplinary teams to assess AI outputs. Fairness in AI ensures that all employees, regardless of gender, ethnicity, age, or background, have equal opportunities and protection from unjust treatment.

b) Enhancing Transparency and Employee Engagement

Clarity in AI decision-making builds trust and responsibility within an organization. Employees should be informed about when and how AI tools are used in processes affecting their work lives, such as performance evaluations or workload management. Providing clear explanations of AI-driven decisions and offering channels for feedback or dispute resolution are essential for ethical AI governance. Engaging employees in the design and implementation of AI systems promotes a culture of openness and helps address concerns proactively, ultimately supporting smoother adoption and better outcomes for both workers and employers.

C. Regulatory Challenges and Future Directions for AI and Labor Laws

As AI technologies increasingly permeate the workplace, existing labor laws and regulations face significant challenges in keeping pace with rapid technological advancements. Policymakers must navigate a complex landscape where traditional frameworks may be inadequate to address issues such as AI-driven job displacement, worker privacy, algorithmic accountability, and the changing nature of employment relationships. Developing adaptive, forward-looking regulations is essential to protect workers' rights while fostering innovation and economic growth.

a) Addressing Legal Gaps in Worker Protection and AI Accountability

Current labor laws often lack provisions that directly address the nuances of AI in the workplace, such as monitoring employee behavior through AI surveillance, automated performance management, or decision-making systems that affect hiring and promotions. Regulators need to create clear guidelines that protect workers from unfair treatment and invasions of privacy, while ensuring companies remain accountable for AI-driven decisions. This includes establishing standards for transparency, bias mitigation, and recourse mechanisms when AI systems cause harm or discrimination.

b) Fostering Flexible and Inclusive Regulatory Frameworks

Future labor laws must be designed with flexibility to accommodate ongoing AI innovations and diverse work arrangements, including gig work, remote employment, and hybrid models. Policymakers should promote inclusive dialogue among stakeholders—workers, employers, technologists, and civil society—to craft regulations that balance protection with adaptability. Emphasizing principles like fairness, transparency, and worker participation will help create robust frameworks that can evolve alongside AI technologies, ensuring sustainable and equitable labor market outcomes.

10. CONCLUSION

The accelerating integration of Artificial Intelligence into the world of work marks a pivotal shift in how labor market's function, how businesses operate, and how societies respond to technological disruption. As this chapter has shown, AI is not merely automating tasks—it is restructuring organizational models, redefining roles, and challenging traditional notions of employment and skill. The COVID-19 pandemic acted as a major inflection point, pushing AI adoption forward at an unprecedented pace and revealing both the vulnerabilities and adaptive potential of modern labor systems. Yet, while AI offers remarkable opportunities for productivity, innovation, and efficiency, it also introduces pressing challenges such as labor market polarization, rising income inequality, and ethical concerns around data use and algorithmic decision-making. Addressing these complexities requires a human-centered approach that balances innovation with inclusivity, fairness, and social responsibility. Robust governance, education reform, and cross-sector collaboration will be essential to ensure that AI-driven labor transformations do not leave large segments of society behind. In shaping the future of work, the ultimate goal must be to create an AI-enhanced labor ecosystem that supports dignity, resilience, and opportunity for all.

REFERENCES

Ahmed, F. (2024). The digital divide and AI in education: Addressing equity and accessibility. *Journal of AI Integration in Education, 1*(2), 12–23.

. Blessing, E. (2024). Regulatory Compliance and Ethical Considerations: Compliance challenges and opportunities with the integration of Big Data and AI.

Ciuhu, A. M. (2024). The (Post) Pandemic Employment Model. In *The Economic and Social Impact of the COVID-19 Pandemic: Romania in a European Context* (pp. 169–182). Springer Nature Switzerland. DOI: 10.1007/978-3-031-47780-5_7

Dosz, A. (2024). *Shaping economic dynamics: governmental influence on AI integration and job dynamics* (Bachelor's thesis, University of Twente).

Gorski, A. T., Gligorea, I., Gorski, H., & Oancea, R. (2022, June). Workforce and workplace ecosystem–challenges and opportunities in the age of digital transformation and 4IR. In *International Conference Knowledge-Based Organization* (Vol. 28, No. 1, pp. 187-194). DOI: 10.2478/kbo-2022-0028

Goyal, A., & Aneja, R. (2020). Artificial intelligence and income inequality: Do technological changes and worker's position matter? *Journal of Public Affairs, 20*(4), e2326. DOI: 10.1002/pa.2326

. Grzegorczyk, M., Mariniello, M., Nurski, L., & Schraepen, T. (2021). *Blending the physical and virtual: a hybrid model for the future of work* (No. 14/2021). Bruegel Policy Contribution.

Hernandez, M., Thompson, W., & Zoghi, B. (2024). Closing the workforce skills gap. In *INTED2024 Proceedings* (pp. 5153-5161). IATED. DOI: 10.21125/inted.2024.1336

Herrmann, H. (2023). What's next for responsible artificial intelligence: A way forward through responsible innovation. *Heliyon, 9*(3), e14379. DOI: 10.1016/j.heliyon.2023.e14379 PMID: 36967876

Hussain, T., Wang, D., & Li, B. (2024). The influence of the COVID-19 pandemic on the adoption and impact of AI ChatGPT: Challenges, applications, and ethical considerations. *Acta Psychologica, 246*, 104264. DOI: 10.1016/j.actpsy.2024.104264 PMID: 38626597

Kaggwa, S., Eleogu, T. F., Okonkwo, F., Farayola, O. A., Uwaoma, P. U., & Akinoso, A. (2024). AI in decision making: Transforming business strategies. *International Journal of Innovation and Scientific Research, 10*(12), 423–444. DOI: 10.51244/IJRSI.2023.1012032

Korinek, A., & Stiglitz, J. E. (2018). Artificial intelligence and its implications for income distribution and unemployment. In *The economics of artificial intelligence: An agenda* (pp. 349–390). University of Chicago Press.

Martini, B., Bellisario, D., & Coletti, P. (2024). Human-centered and sustainable artificial intelligence in industry 5.0: Challenges and perspectives. *Sustainability (Basel), 16*(13), 5448. DOI: 10.3390/su16135448

Nour, S., & Arbussà, A. (2025). Driving innovation through organizational restructuring and integration of advanced digital technologies: A case study of a world-leading manufacturing company. *European Journal of Innovation Management, 28*(8), 3262–3283. DOI: 10.1108/EJIM-02-2024-0156

Rathore, M. (2024). The Role of Artificial Intelligence in Social Welfare: Harnessing AI For Positive Societal Impact. In *AI in the Social and Business World: A Comprehensive Approach* (pp. 277–293). Bentham Science Publishers. DOI: 10.2174/9789815256864124010015

Reuben, J. M. (2023). Training and skills alignment for the AI generation. *GSJ, 11*(6), 1503–1518.

Sholler, D., & MacInnes, I. (2024). AI and income inequality: the danger of exacerbating existing trends toward polarization in the US workforce. In *Handbook of artificial intelligence at work* (pp. 338–355). Edward Elgar Publishing. DOI: 10.4337/9781800889972.00026

Tims, M., & Bakker, A. B. (2010). Job crafting: Towards a new model of individual job redesign. *SA Journal of Industrial Psychology, 36*(2), 1–9. DOI: 10.4102/sajip.v36i2.841

Williams, J., Alexander, K., Wilson, T., Newton, B., McNeil, C., & Jung, C. (2021). *A better future: Transforming jobs and skills for young people post-pandemic*. Institute for Employment Studies.

Zhang, Z. (2023). The impact of the artificial intelligence industry on the number and structure of employments in the digital economy environment. *Technological Forecasting and Social Change, 197*, 122881. DOI: 10.1016/j.techfore.2023.122881

Chapter 6
Agentic Artificial Intelligence-Powered Automation for Dynamic Labor Markets and Business

Sneh Sharma
http://orcid.org/0009-0004-1750-4480
Amity University, Mohali, India

Sachin Sharma
http://orcid.org/0000-0002-7821-3685
Amity University, Mohali, India

ABSTRACT

The fast development of Labour markets due to globalization, digital disruption, and economic uncertainty demands intelligent, adaptive solutions. In this chapter we outline a visionary framework for the use of Agentic Artificial Intelligence (AAI) to power the automation of work across complex, dynamic Labour ecosystems and present-day enterprise models. Whereas traditional AI is never agentic, any AAI has autonomy, self-reflection, goal-directed behavior, and situational awareness making it highly useful to navigate and manage workforce shifts, gig economy structures and real-time operational decisions. This chapter discusses how AAI can be used to automate decisions in recruitment, task allocation, and upskilling while simultaneously evolving business models to be more robust, decentralized,

DOI: 10.4018/979-8-3373-5816-1.ch006

and information oriented. The chapter also includes examples of development and deployment of agentic HR bots, predictive talent pipelines, active/reactive enterprise project workflows and ethical governance frameworks for HR.

I. INTRODUCTION

The changing nature of artificial intelligence (AI) technologies has given rise to new forms of automation, intelligence augmentation, and autonomous decision-making. Agentic Artificial Intelligence (AAI) is among those changes, and it represents a game-change phenomenon that can dramatically change legacy human Labour systems and the interplay between the capabilities of the workforce and business model innovation. Given that we are in a turbulent global economy and increasingly in a digitally-enabled economy, there is a pressing need for adaptable, intelligence systems not only capable of responding to environmental and market change but of proactively managing resource allocation, skills uses, and enterprise configurations in real-time. This chapter examines Agentic AI systems, with an emphasis on the use of large language models (LLMs) and cognitive agents, in order to automate and optimize dynamic Labour markets, and design responsive business models. Existing paradigms of Labour economics, HRM, and entrepreneurship are slowly being shown to be inadequate, as the variability, fragmentation, and demand uncertainty of gig resilience and skills-based economies suggests. Static systems cannot dynamically model individual skillsets, work to determine business viability through local Labour capacity, or identify skill gaps for educational and workforce development pipelines. This newly defined vacuum will require a new generation of AI systems, which not only create intelligence but act, autonomously and ethically, in context. This research centers on a new integrated ecosystem powered by Agentic Artificial Intelligence where distributed autonomous agents are performing tasks such as skill profiling, business model alignment, resource forecasting, and gap analysis. These agents run on LLMs and have been trained on multimodal Labour datasets, they are designed to learn, interact, and change behavior over time in a dynamic socio-economic context. Where automation systems are largely static, these agents have agency--which means they can make context-aware decisions, can self-initiate actions, and they can communicate with other agents and/or humans with limited or no supervision.

At the heart of the presented system is a combination of three critical technological enablers:

- Large Language Models that provide contextual semantic comprehension and reasoning capabilities in various Labour-market contexts.

- Agentic Systems that can exhibit autonomous agency including making decisions and communication with other agents.
- Dynamic Labour Market Modeling in which live data feeds allow for monitoring, predicting, shaping behavior and unlocking the potential of the workforce and enterprise.

The combination of these three components represents a radical shift from reactive automation to proactive socio-economic intelligence. The Labour market, as a traditional economic concept, is a realm where supply (workers) and demand (employers) influence a spectrum of variables from wages and rates of employment, to economic outputs. Traditional Labour models that include supply and demand don't account for the degree of informal work and gig and freelance platforms, cross-border freelancing, and remote hybrid work. Moreover, skills are multi-dimensional, often non-linear, extremely time-sensitive, and mostly changing due to market factors—with business demands emerging today that didn't exist just five years ago (e.g., prompt engineering, metaverse consulting, etc.). All these factors mean we need the predictive and analytic capabilities of a computational framework to be able to: ingest and model change, adapt Labour and business models, and simulate future outcomes given a finite set of limitations.

To tackle these obstacles, this work has introduced a fully digital and modular ecosystem composed of four intelligent agents:

- Skill-Based Agent, which collects individual profiles and classifies competences.
- Resource Agent, which evaluates the tangible and intangible available resources (e.g., assets, capital/resources and local limitations).
- Business Model Selector, which identifies potential enterprise models based on characteristics related to skills and resources.
- Skill Gap Analyzer, which forecasts required future actions related to upskilling or reskilling.

Communication via the multi-agent protocol allow collective action between agents in the system as they utilize the semantic reasoning capacity of LLMs such as GPT-4 or fine-tuned transformers adapted to domain-specific use. The system can make individualized recommendations for entrepreneurship, personalize "just-in-time" training, and simulate economic behaviors in real time—each offer a new value proposition that is currently missing from the workforce management platforms in the workplace. A further overarching motivation of this research is the democratization of entrepreneurship. In many developing and emerging economies people have skills, but lack the contextualized knowledge of how to convert those skills into viable income, local business opportunities. Conventional business education and incubator approaches do not scale to capture this expansive latent potential. Agentic AI systems, deployed through mobile apps or low-resource web platforms, can act as an accessible cognitive partner for emerging entrepreneurs. For example, a rural artisan trained in a local craft, could, through the agentic AI system, receive near real-time references on business model options, inventory and logistical planning, and marketing approaches, using only a brief skill questionnaire and a mobile form. This type of local and global empowerment is not only technologically plausible, but it is economically critical. This chapter is theoretically based on a blend of artificial intelligence, cognitive science, and Labour economics. The notion of agency, traditionally understood in both philosophical and behavioral sciences, is becoming a new manifestation through computational agents that are autonomous, reactive, and proactive. When coupled with LLMs (which add the dimension of semantic processing capacity - the ability to process natural language, infer goals, and physically act with chains of symbolic reasoning), computational agency is limitedly reflexive of human deliberation. However, this undertaking does not aim to substitute human workers or decision-makers; the goal of this project is to enhance human capacity and unlock potential where it otherwise may remain latent. Recent developments in multi-agent systems and LLMs have made it feasible to prototype such systems. Now, developers are able to leverage tools like LangChain, AutoGPT, and React frameworks to deploy reasoning pipelines chained across LLM agents in which they can work together, call APIs, read documents, and write outputs. These components can be chained together in workflows where the outputs of an agent informs the prompt of another, enabling an execution across a more complex socio-technical logic view, like a flow chart. This research employed that approach and particularly created custom designed agent workflows about the Labour market (LM) domain along with a backend logic engine that implements a simulation of enterprise feasibility, and revenue curve forecasts and indicators of social impacts. A key feature of the envisioned system is explainability. In work-related decisions, particularly in areas with vulnerable populations, we need to ensure transparency and auditability around the recommendations it provides. Agentic workflows are configured to output not only actions, but also reasoning chains, intermediary variables, and natural language rationales. For instance, if a user receives a recommendation to start a home-based catering business, the rationale will confirm how their skillsets (e.g. culinary) matched their available resources (e.g. kitchen equipment), and how the market was missing (e.g. no food delivery options). This transparency builds user confidence and adoption of the system. The system's architecture is also built to be extensible. As work realities change, new agents can be added, such as Policy Recommenders, Financial Advisors and Mental Wellness Check Agents- making a modular and future-proof ecosystem. Further, the modularity allows the system to be differentially localized for other geographies, economic classes and skills taxonomies. The system also supports integration of public datasets (e.g. employment bureaus, skilling platforms) to ensure data-driven accuracy. This research exists at the intersection of technological opportunity and socio-economic need. While the capabilities of AI have advanced tremendously, its usage in Labour-intensive areas has been slow to adopt in practice, in part due to ethical considerations and technology gaps and challenges in assessing human skill. However, recent advances in the capabilities of LLMs and agent-based orchestration present opportunities for scalable, defensible and ethical responses. I argue, by working from a situated application about Labour market automation and business models, that Agentic AI has compelling applications for creating inclusive growth opportunities in the economy. This work offers evidence of converging agentic algorithms and language based reasoning systems to create systems that do more than work intelligently. It shows the possibility for systems to work interdependently in response to social opportunity and personal agency in organizations. Today they can provide autonomous reasoning systems with explainable outputs and recommendations that align with the ideation of a person. Systems that have the potential to transform the way individuals participate in Labour markets and with economic opportunity.

II. LITERATURE REVIEW

Agentic Artificial Intelligence (AI) is systems that are given autonomous decision-making that extends beyond their functionality of performing set tasks or commands, rather expressing forms of agency approximating purposeful entities. In contrast to classical AI systems, which largely exist as reactive tools generating outputs through strict rules or bounded machine learning models, agentic AI is a representation of autonomy in perceiving, reasoning, and acting within dynamic settings, typically adjusting behaviors according to continuous interactions and feedback (Dwivedi et al., 2023).This paradigm change for AI closely follows the advent of generative AI models, like Large Language Models (LLMs), that not only produce human-like text but have also shown the capacity to undertake various higher-order cognitive tasks like problem-solving and creative integration (Hadi et al., 2023). These models, such as ChatGPT, constitute a new generation of agentic systems with the capacity for realizing some level of operational independence in knowledge work, decision-making, and communication (Zhou et al., 2024). Recognizing the difference between agentic AI and other kinds of AI is critical to understanding the transformative potential of the latter. Traditional AI operates within the confines of explicit programming and explicit locations of narrow task performance; whereas agentic AI can understand a wide range of relevant contextual information and can make decisions with limited human guidance. Architecturally, agentic AI is constructed with, or includes, reinforcement learning, self-supervised learning, and advanced natural language understanding that enable it to simulate proactive behavior in practice and take action toward goals. This represents a major structural shift in both artificial intelligence research and applications, as it positions agentic AI as a critical linchpin technology for automation not only for simple mechanistic processes, but increasingly for strategic decision-making contexts within organizations and Labour markets. Labour markets are now defined by high dynamism, where the development and diffusion of digital and intelligent technologies is aggressively advancing. These Labour markets are characterized by fluidity with the continual emergence, evolution, and occasional disappearance of job positions because of automation, especially AI-facilitated automation. This changing nature presents opportunities and challenges to employees, employers, and policymakers alike as the fundamental nature of work is reshaped. AI-based automation impacts Labour markets in two fundamental ways: replacement of repetitive, routine jobs and at the same time, the creation of new jobs that require emergent skills like supervision of AI, training of models, and facilitation of human-AI collaboration. The change in the landscape also involves the development of hybrid roles that integrate the cognitive and emotional skills of humans with the analytical and procedural speed of AI (Orchard & Tasiemski, 2023). For example, the emergence of the AI oversight and ethical deployment professions has changed the demand for skills, which now focuses on adaptability, critical thinking, and technological literacy (Capraro et al., 2024). As a result, the adaptability of workers and the continuous acquisition of skills become vital for retaining one's employability in this type of environment. AI's all-encompassing influence, however, is not limited to the locales and industries but is spread to the structures of the Labour market, which in turn affects the wage levels and changes the typical career paths (Humphreys et al., 2024). On the other hand, the variable Labour market influenced by technology is an entirely different character and is not equal for all; there are some parts that benefit from increased possibilities while others are in danger of being displaced and experiencing insecurity. The above-mentioned differences demand more detailed policy responses and business practices that would ease worker transitions, removal of barriers to participation, and provision of social equity while the workforce continues with deep changes. Agentic AI-powered automation induces significant transformations in present-day business models, disrupting and gracefully re-engineering organizational processes and mechanisms for value creation. Such integration of AI across businesses in the various sectors aims at creating operational efficiencies; automating decision-making processes; and providing innovation in products and services. This process is a speed winner when the operations are carried out either faster or through data autonomy. Agentic AI is at the forefront of such developments with the ability of systems to self-act with decision-making power, enabling complex workflows previously entailing human judgment. This specific technology is synonymous with businesses in marketing analytics, supply chains logistics, and customer relationship management to ensure constant levels of improvement along with responses to market changes. The degree of such a transformation ranges from progressive productivity improvements to radical changes that restructure business paradigms (Sharma et al., 2023). AI-driven automation enables businesses to personalize at scale, automate internal operations, and build stronger models that are closer to the fast-paced digital economy. These transformations compel organizations to shift business model designs, including AI-powered value delivery, platform strategies, and ecosystem development based on autonomous agents (Hendriksen, 2023). The aggressive uptake of agentic AI goes hand in hand with issues such as organizational preparedness, trustability, and compliance with regulation, which need to be dealt with in order to exploit the maximum potential of automation without reducing operational and ethical risk (Andronie et al., 2023). The use of autonomous AI agents introduces important ethical and social issues, mainly concerning bias, transparency, and accountability. AI autonomy can hide how decisions are made. This complicates traditional ways of exercising control and oversight. Biased training data and algorithm structures may continue unfair treatment or exclusion in job markets, which particularly impacts vulnerable groups. Transparency efforts promote explainable AI methods. These approaches help users and regulators understand how AI works and avoid unclear decisions that could cause harm. Social risks include workforce dislocation, which can increase inequality unless directed by inclusive policies and reskilling initiatives. Privacy issues arise from autonomous systems' use of huge personal and operational data, with the need for strong data governance and user consent practices (Slimi & Villarejo-Carballido, 2023). Models of governance are changing to include multi-stakeholder involvement, blending industry self-regulation, government action, and civil society input to balance AI innovation with social well-being. There is a debate about restrictive and permissive AI usage models. This reflects the tension between encouraging growth and reducing harm. Discussions around policy emphasize the need for clearer ethical standards and methods to govern the wide-ranging abilities of generative AI safely and fairly (Lorenz et al., 2023). The introduction of agentic AI into business ecosystems sparks new models like AI-as-a-Service platforms, collaborations focused on ecosystems, and digital-physical hybrid models that often combine with metaverse and digital twin technologies. Businesses that center on AI take advantage of providing intelligent services that can be used on demand, which creates scalable revenue streams. In metaverse environments, agentic AI promotes immersive interactions, virtual commerce, and collaborative workspaces. These elements change traditional value propositions through improved user experience and context-aware personalization. Likewise, combining semantic internet-of-things (IoT) components with AI agents creates smart business frameworks that allow for predictive, flexible, and independent operations (Zawish et al., 2024). Collaborative innovation shows how human creativity and judgment work alongside AI agents (Bhattacharya et al., 2023).This partnership creates new pathways for value creation. It opens up unique opportunities for standing out in the market and supports ongoing cycles of innovation (Li et al., 2023). Expanding research into areas like healthcare, where AI helps with immunotherapy and medical diagnostics, and military applications, where agentic AI improves operational abilities, is important. The connection with the Internet of Medical Things (IoMT) and Healthcare 4.0 frameworks also needs more study (Ellis et al., 2024). Metaverse-enabled work and business applications offer new opportunities that require us to explore agentic AI's role in virtual settings, ethical use, and user interaction methods (Rashid et al., 2023; Omar et al., 2023).

III. CONCEPT OVERVIEW AND KEYWORD EXPLANATION

This section offers a thorough look at the basic ideas, keywords, and terms behind this research. Each term is important for understanding how agentic artificial intelligence (AI) works, the dynamics of the Labour market, changes in business models, and how large language models (LLMs) are used in real-world applications.

- Agentic Artificial Intelligence (Agentic AI): Agentic AI is a type of artificial intelligence infrastructure imbued with the ability to act autonomously, take contextually aware decisions, trigger tasks, and attain predetermined objectives with little human interference. In contrast to conventional AI models, which reactively respond to input, agentic AI systems run with proactive smartness, learning from the setting and modifying actions dynamically. In Labour markets, agentic AI is the cognitive layer that bridges skills to tasks, forecasts work trends, and assigns human resources optimally.
- Autonomous Decision-Making Systems: The fundamental characteristic of agentic systems is autonomous decision-making. This means that the system can analyze multiple variables, prioritize objectives, and make decisions on the spot without a human input. These systems depend on reinforcement learning, probabilistic models, and knowledge graphs to determine optimal actions. In the Labour markets, for instance, they would first analyze available workers, relevance of skills, and urgency of the tasks in dispatching job allocations or business recommendations.

- Dynamic Labour Markets: Dynamic Labour markets are distinguished by fast-changing employment patterns, skill needs, contractual arrangements, and worker behavior because of globalization, technological innovation, and economic instability. Automation, freelancing, remote Labour, and gig economy arrangements have all led to Labour market instability. This research examines how AI agents can forecast, model, and stabilizes these fluctuations by smart mapping workforce availability against business requirements.
- Labour Market Automation: Labour market automation consists of technologies and algorithms that displace or supplement human functions in talent recruitment, workforce assignment, and skills mapping. Automation includes job-matching engines, resume sifting bots, ranking algorithms for candidates, and skill-based demand forecasting. With agentic AI, Labour automation is not just responsive but responsive-also—synching Labour supply with changing industry demands in real-time.
- Business Model Transformation: Business model evolution is a reengineering of a firm's operations, value propositions, revenue models, and customer interaction strategies. The integration of AI agents enables companies to evolve their models perpetually through market signals, user input, and competitor activities. This research combines agentic logic to provide recommendations for optimized business models based on existing resources available and anticipated Labour patterns.
- Multi-Agent Systems (MAS): Multi-Agent Systems are made up of several interacting AI agents with specific roles and functionalities. MAS architectures support decentralized problem-solving and coordination in complicated systems like Labour platforms. For this project, MAS is made up of a resource agent, skill gap analyzer, business model selector, and role-matching agent—each working with the others through a common knowledge environment to simulate and suggest feasible Labour-business configurations.
- Large Language Models (LLMs): LLMs like GPT-4 or BERT are the cornerstone of natural language understanding, generation, and semantic reasoning. These models can process human instructions, examine resumes, dissect job descriptions, and create business blueprints. In the framework suggested here, LLMs constitute the natural language interface and cognitive backend for supporting user-agent interactions and semantic data interpretation at scale.
- Semantic Matching: Semantic matching is the application of artificial intelligence methods in understanding meaning and purpose behind words, phrases, or organized content. It enables AI agents to compare job descriptions with candidate resumes, academic records with expected skills, and resource

properties with business objectives. This facilitates accuracy in recommendations and user confidence in automated systems.

- Skill Gap Analysis: Skill gap analysis is a diagnostic tool that assesses the gap between available skills of a workforce and needed skills to perform an assigned task or business. Agentic systems automate the process by monitoring training data, academic records, certification history, and job performance feedback in real-time. The diagnosed gaps are routed to learning modules, micro-certification pathways, or career transitions, making the workforce agile and industry-capable.
- Business Model Recommendation System: A Business Model Recommendation System (BMRS) is a module driven by artificial intelligence that recommends viable business models in accordance with user resources, competencies, location, and market trends. It utilizes rule-based engines, case-based reasoning, and predictive analytics. In this study, BMRS is supplemented with agentic behavior to recommend not just models but also the subsequent actionable steps, necessary partnerships, and funding avenues.
- Human-in-the-Loop (HITL): While autonomous AI targets autonomy, human-in-the-loop approaches guarantee accountability, security, and ethical compliance. HITL requires deliberate human supervision at decisive points for reviewing, verifying, or overruling AI outputs. This is especially relevant in Labour market automation where job assignments, career guidance, and compensation forecasting need ethical equity and legal compliance.
- AI-Driven Resource Optimization: AI-based resource optimization means the allocation of tasks, employees, budgets, and tools in the most efficient manner possible with the aid of historical and real-time data. Agentic models maximize these allocations through examination of availability, fatigue levels, geographical limitation, and performance metrics of the past. This process helps reduce costs while maximizing output within organizations.
- Explainable AI (XAI): XAI stands for explainable AI models and systems that offer explanations and justifications of their actions. In domains such as employment and entrepreneurship where stakes are high, one needs to know how and why a particular recommendation was produced. LLM-enabled agentic systems can be programmed to generate human-readable explanations in addition to taking actions, promoting trust and accountability.
- Cognitive Automation: Cognitive automation follows up on robotic process automation (RPA) by combining machine learning, natural language, and logic engines. It lets systems not just execute rules but also learn through new patterns and make smart decisions. This lets job assignment systems, resume

reviewers, and training recommenders function at cognitive depth with contextual understanding.

- Ontology-Driven Knowledge Representation: Ontology-based knowledge representation organizes information in a hierarchical, machine-interpretable form that defines relationships, classes, and entities. It supports agentic AI in comprehending the meaning of job titles, company types, academic courses, and industrial standards. The knowledge base in a structured form serves as a reference for the AI system to make inferences and suggest transformations.
- Agent Communication Protocols: For efficient operation of multi-agent systems, agents have to converse well. Agent Communication Protocols (ACPs) codify the interaction rules and semantics. Examples are speech act-based languages such as FIPA-ACL, which allows structured dialogue among the resource agent, skill gap analyzer, and business selector. This guarantees cohesion, cooperation, and consistency of decisions.
- Simulation of Labour Scenarios: Labour market simulation enables researchers and policymakers to comprehend the effects of automation, upskilling, remote work patterns, or Labour market volatility. Agentic AI platforms create artificial Labour data and future prospects, instructional interventions such as reskilling initiatives, policy regulations, or venture capital investment in nascent industries.
- Low-code/No-code Platforms for AI Agents: Low-code/no-code platforms make it possible for non-technical individuals to develop, test, and roll out AI-based agents using drag-and-drop ease. Such platforms open up access to smart Labour market automation for everyone and facilitate rapid prototyping. They are particularly useful in small-to-medium-sized businesses (SMEs) that need to automate processes without investing in an entire AI staff.
- Edge AI for Resource Deployment: Edge AI is the deployment of machine learning models locally on devices close to the data source (e.g., mobile, IoT). In Labour automation, Edge AI assists field agents, logistics firms, or rural job schemes in deploying smart decision-making systems independent of cloud infrastructure. It enhances speed, privacy, and energy efficiency.
- Continuous Learning Systems: Continuous learning systems are agentic frameworks that update over time by learning new data, feedback, and environmental cues. Instead of being fixed rule engines, these agents periodically update their models. This keeps job-market matching algorithms, business recommendations, and skill analysis mechanisms up to speed with the current environment.

This part described the key conceptual and technical foundations of the envisioned agentic AI-based automation system. Through the comprehension of these key words in depth, stakeholders such as system designers, Labour economists, government planners, and schools can better understand the implication of the innovation.

IV. PROPOSED METHODOLOGY: LLM-DRIVEN AGENTIC AUTOMATION FOR LABOUR MARKETS AND BUSINESS MODELS

The research methodology brings forth an extensive framework combining Large Language Models (LLMs) with Agentic Artificial Intelligence (AAI) to support intelligent, adaptive automation within the Labour market and business modeling arena. The framework is specifically tailored to streamline workforce allocation, allow for adaptive upskilling, anticipate upcoming job-market needs, and automate the setup of feasible business models compatible with individual and regional skill sets. Instead of depending on static data sets or preconceived business blueprints, the system develops dynamically by feeding in real-time data and adjusting through reasoning agents and context-sensitive LLMs. The methodology enables the automation process not only to be reactive but also proactive—capable of anticipating and creating future prospects in the realm of Labour as well as enterprise. At the center of this approach is the synergistic interaction between symbolic agents and generative AI systems. These are configured to simulate human judgment within bounded contexts, for example, setting skill gaps, predicting market needs, mapping talent to opportunities, and choosing best-fit business models. The LLM offers the semantic reasoning and language processing necessary to grasp free-form user input, unstructured Labour data, policy texts, and real-time market trends. In the meantime, autonomous agents are responsible for task-specific logic—managing processes such as resource analysis, skill-set mapping, and industry-specific business logic configuration.

a) Flowchart

Figure 1. Agentic AI Flowchart: Automation Journey of the Modern Labour Market

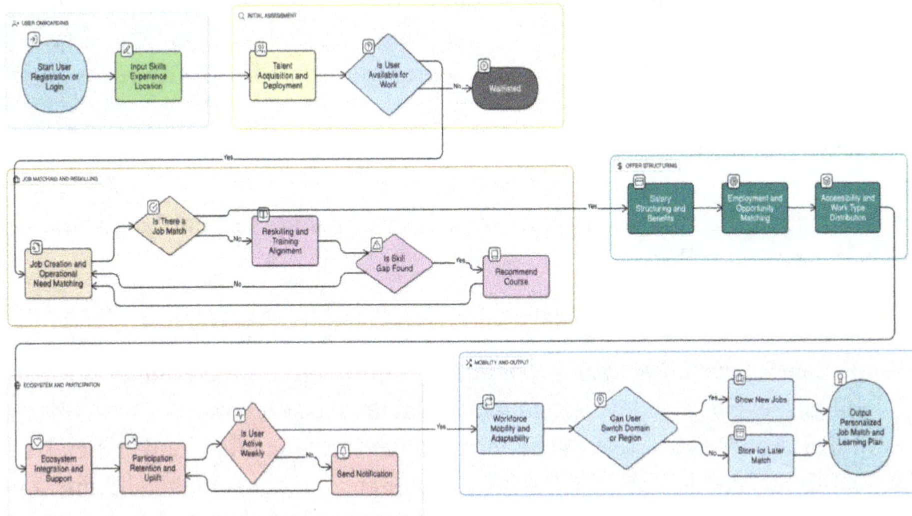

Figure 1 depicts the entire workflow of AgenticAI, which is a sophisticated AI-powered Labour market automation platform. It is a systematic and smart journey from user onboarding to end job matching and output production. The process starts with User On boarding, in which users register or sign in and enter information like skills, experience, and location. This is then followed by the Initial Assessment stage, in which the platform conducts Talent Acquisition and Deployment and decides whether the user is either working or not. If they are not, they are added to a Waitlist until they become available. Then, the system progresses to the core engine—Job Matching and Reskilling. It verifies whether a decent job match exists against the user's profile and operational requirements. In case no immediate match is discovered, the platform triggers Reskilling and Training Alignment. If a Skill Gap is discovered, it suggests specialized courses to bridge the gaps. After becoming sufficiently skilled, the user re-enters the job matching cycle. When an appropriate job is identified, the system goes to Offer Structuring, comprising Salary Structuring and Benefits and Employment Opportunity Matching and Work Type Distribution—making sure offers align with user expectations and organizational needs. The Ecosystem and Participation module, in the meantime, makes sure active participation is maintained through Ecosystem Support, Participation Retention, and Activity Monitoring. In case a user is not active, reminders are sent by the system to get them active again. At the same time, the Mobility and Output section manages workforce flexibility. It asks whether the user is willing to change domains or regions. If yes, new job possibilities are shown. If not, their profile is saved for future opportunities. Lastly, the system generates an Output with a personalized job fit and a learning plan. As a whole, this flowchart captures the strength of AI automation in swimmingly weaving onboarding, skill building, job matching, engagement, and flexibility into one another to create the efficient, customized, and future-focused hiring ecosystem.

b) Agentic Modular Framework

The modular architecture has four main agents that are responsible for unique yet interdependent tasks:

- Resource Agent: Scans and analyzes accessible human resources from demographic, education, and work-related information. It determines dormant abilities, experience levels, and individual readiness levels.
- Skill-Based Agent: Tests skills against the latest Labour market trends in real-time databases and LLM-enabled inference. It helps in the alignment of an individual's or community's skills with appropriate sectors.
- Business Model Selector Agent: Generates business model suggestions through use-case feasibility simulation, market saturation, economic value, and resource completeness. This agent is fueled by LLMs that recognize industry environments and fiscal models.
- Skill Gap Analyzer Agent: Finds the gaps between available skills and needed ones by industry. It directs upskilling, curriculum changes, or possible business partnership suggestions.

All agents operate in tandem with the LLM engine, the central reasoning component, which processes natural language inputs, creates structured plans, interprets policy documents, and generates actionable pathways for stakeholders.

c) LLM Role and Cognitive Reasoning

In contrast to traditional automation engines, the introduction of LLMs supports high-level intellectual tasks that include:

- Semantic Interpretation of Labour Policies: Interpretation of government publications and job schemes to enroll individuals in appropriate programs.
- Decision Support via Conversational Interface: Providing contextual recommendations through chat or voice interfaces to both employers and candidates.
- Narrative Generation: Generating business plan stories, job description content, resume writing or proposal documentation dynamically.

- Scenario Simulation: Foreseeing numerous business outcomes based on generative simulation from varying Labour inputs or economic measures.

The LLM further facilitates few-shot and zero-shot learning to generalize across several industries without direct re-training. This allows the system to respond to a broad spectrum of user queries—from agriculture business plans in rural regions to deep-tech entrepreneurship in urban clusters.

d) End-to-End Workflow Automation

The framework automates the Labour and business modeling process through the following stages:

- Data Ingestion: Human resource data, regional economic indicators, skill records, educational background and market trends are collected from public and proprietary datasets.
- Skill and Gap Analysis: The skill based agent and gap analyzer determines the current workforce capabilities and their deviation from industry benchmarks.
- Business Model Generation: Based on skills and available resources the LLM generates adaptive business model templates using pre-trained reasoning combined with symbolic rule based analysis.
- Evaluation and Customization: The administrator or the user interacts with the system through natural language to customize or fine-tune the suggested business models.
- Deployment: Upon completion, the suggested model may be translated into operational blueprints with guidelines for implementation, estimates of costs, and likely sources of funding.

This closed loop system captures feedback from deployments so the agents can learn and update the recommendation strategies.

e) Real Interface Integration (Screenshots and Descriptions)

Here are screenshots and visual panels from your Agentic AI Labour Market Platform, with their role in the ecosystem:

Figure 2. Lifecycle Flow of Agentic AI-Driven Workforce and Business Model Alignment Platform

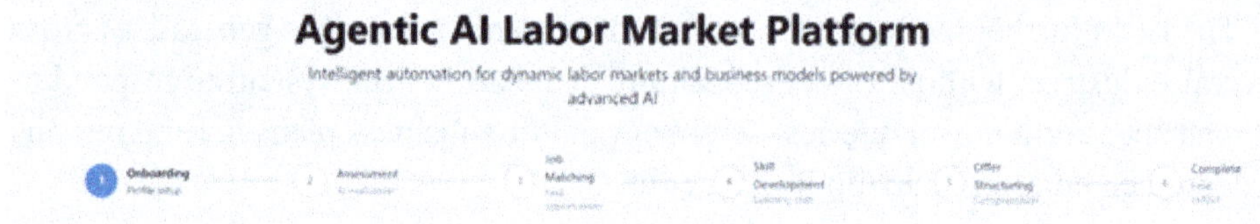

Figure 2 depicts the end-to-end process of intelligent agent automation for Labour market alignment. It begins with user sign-up, where detailed profiles and preferences are captured. The assessment module then screens skills and detects gaps. Depending on this, the system facilitates smart job or business matching by matching user ability to prevailing market demand. Depending on necessity, the skill development phase suggests personalized learning paths. This is followed by structuring an offer, in which appropriate entrepreneurial models or roles are proposed. It concludes with deployment, establishing a future-ready, appropriately matched workforce or business fit. This lean lifecycle guarantees responsive, AI-driven workforce planning and real-time business model integration.

Figure 3. Agentic AI Onboarding Interface for Smart Job & Business Profiling

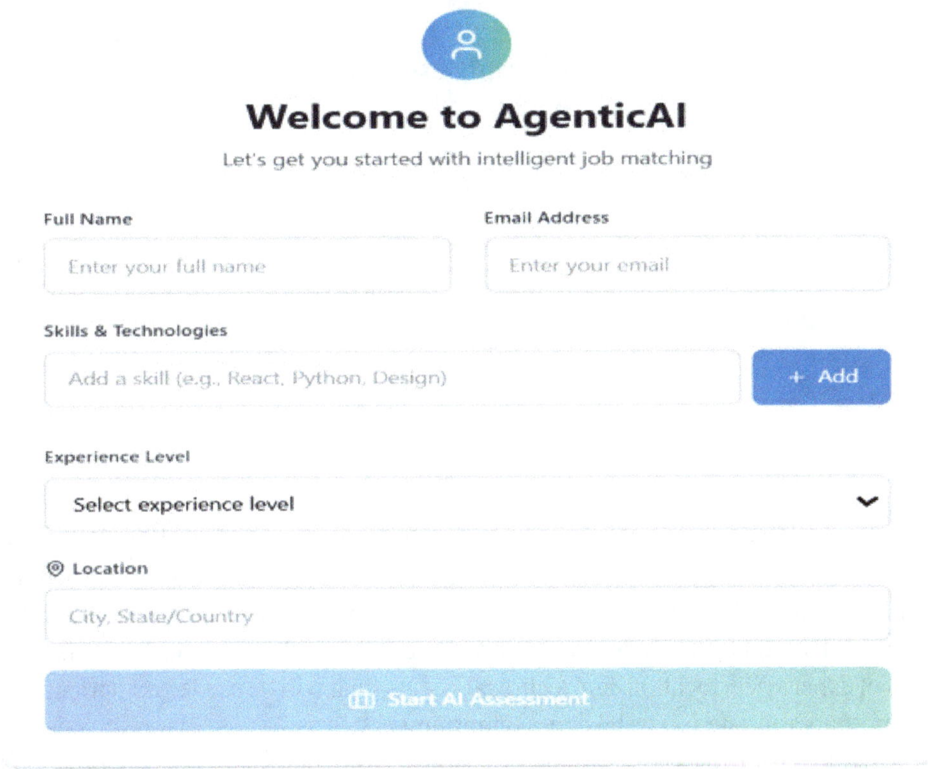

Figure 3 shows how users initiate their Agentic AI platform journey by entering personal details alongside their skills, experience levels, and geographical information into this interface. The form collects structured data which users then experience as customized interactions. Upon submission, the platform activates an AI-driven examination which evaluates the user's profile against potential business opportunities and Labour market needs to enable intelligent matching and upskilling recommendations.

The onboarding page constructs foundational elements to synchronize smart workforce initiatives with entrepreneurial pursuits.

Figure 4. Real-Time AI Talent Assessment in Progress

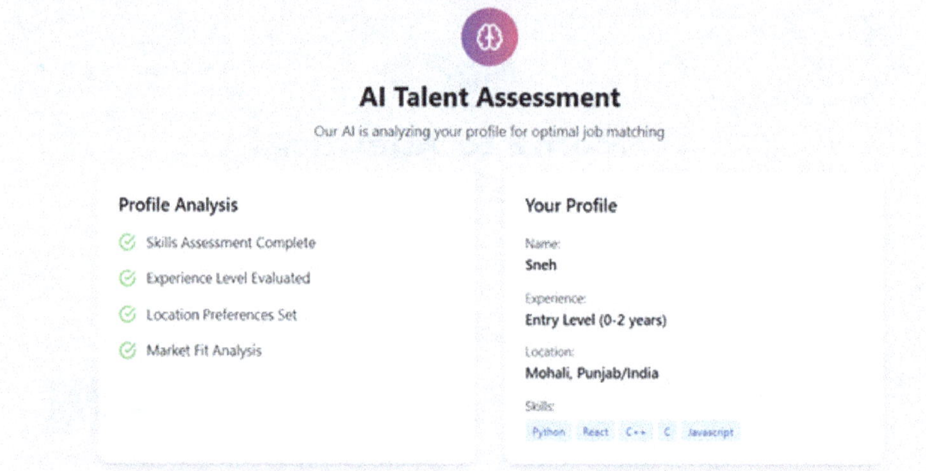

Figure 4 presents the real-time AI-based talent evaluation based on the user's provided profile. The platform has done the essential profiling activities such as skills assessment, level of experience analysis, location choice, and market suitability analysis. The right-hand side offers a brief overview of the user's history—name, level of experience, location, and technical skills—that will be used to match against the most appropriate job or business opportunity.

This phase illustrates how Agentic AI customizes outcomes with smart automation.

Figure 5. Availability Status: Instant Matching or Future Planning

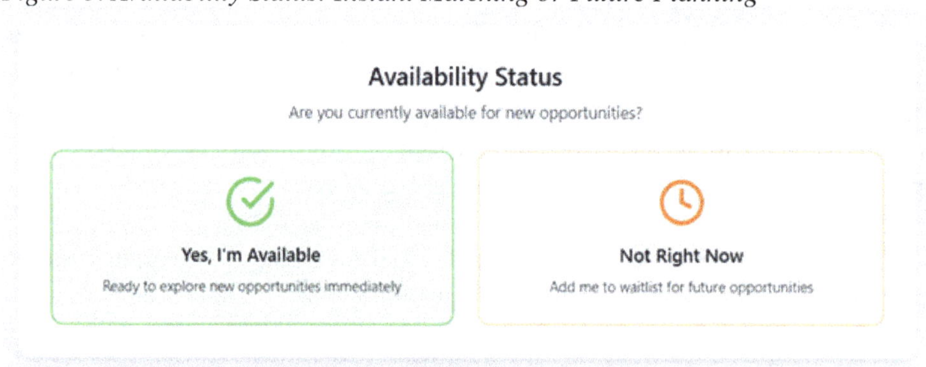

This interface in Figure 5 enables users to define their availability settings for potential opportunities. The uncomplicated user interface presents two options:

selecting “Yes, I'm Available” initiates immediate match delivery while choosing “Not Right Now” results in placement on a future recommendation waitlist.

The AgenticAI system uses real-time user intent data to prioritize opportunity delivery which enables efficient matching while avoiding unnecessary notifications.

Figure 6. AI Job Matching: Smart Recommendations Tailored to You

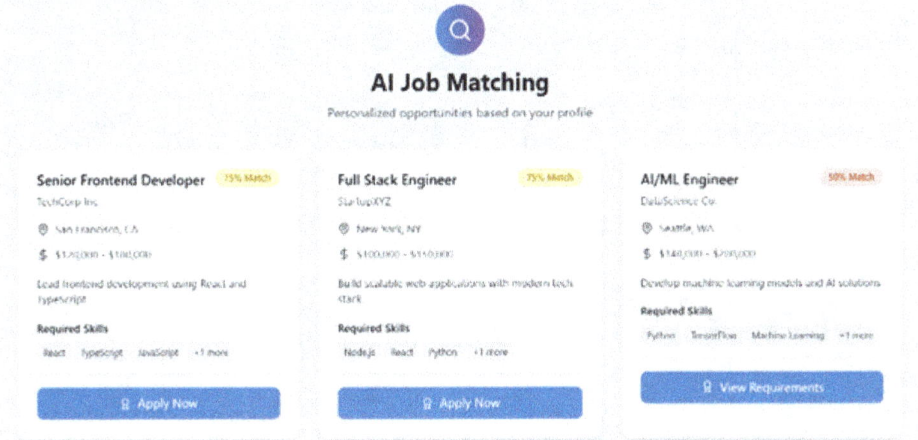

Figure 5 shows algorithmically generated job for an AI based profile. It features 3 different position options - Senior Frontend Developer, Full Stack Engineer, and AI/ML Engineer, with match percentage (to indicate how their skills match the position requirements). The platform uses AI to analyze the user’s profile, skills and preferences to offer relevant jobs, showing information such as the name of the company, location, salary range and essential skills. The design also contains action buttons like Apply Now or View Requirements to enable the users to apply on the spot as well. This intelligent job-matching strategy saves time on the job search process and makes sure that users only get to see the most suitable opportunities for their career evolution.

Figure 7. Skill Development Plan: Personalized Learning for Career Growth

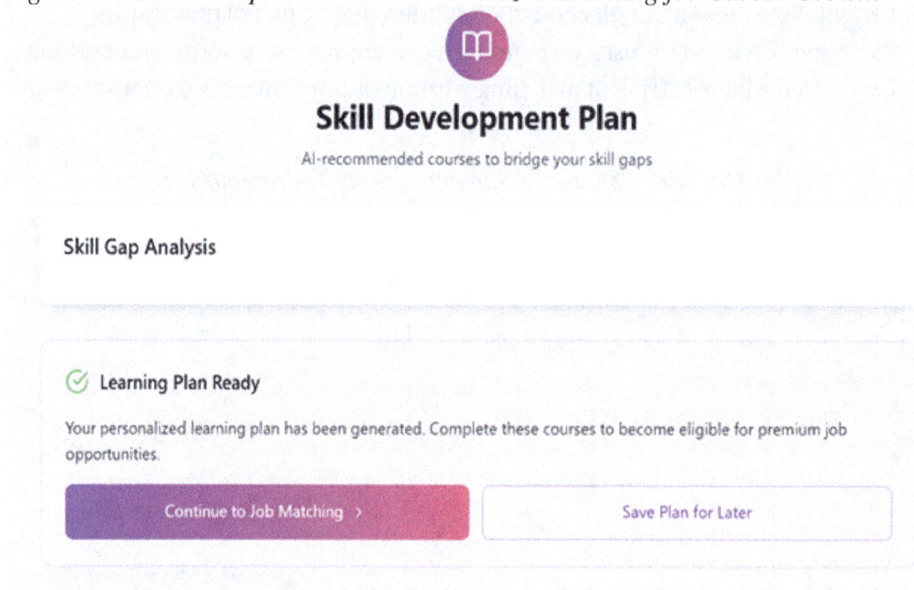

Figure 7 displays the AI-generated Skill Development Plan that helps users close their skill gaps. Based on a Skill Gap Analysis, the system offers a personalized list of courses or learning paths suited to the user's profile. The interface shows that the learning plan is ready and invites users to either proceed to job matching or save the plan for later. By completing the suggested courses, users become eligible for better job opportunities. The simple and clear layout guides users smoothly toward career advancement through targeted skill improvement.

- Adaptive Learning and Real-Time Response: One of the key innovations in this approach is online learning. As new Labour trends, policies and technologies emerge the LLM fine tunes its responses through prompt engineering and feedback loops. Similarly the symbolic agents re-prioritize rule sets and constraints based on temporal or seasonal workforce dynamics. For example during agricultural off seasons the system may automatically suggest food processing microenterprises to utilize available human capital. The system also allows multi-stakeholder colLabouration where policymakers, educators and industry mentors can intervene, annotate decisions or adjust parameters in real time. This dynamic adaptability turns the static nature of traditional employment platforms into a living, breathing automation ecosystem.
- Human-Centric Design and Ethical Considerations: The architecture emphasizes inclusivity by ensuring that those with lower levels of digital literacy

are able to access the system through reduced interfaces, voice commands, or community kiosks. LLMs facilitate vernacular translation and culturally sensitive conversation interfaces, thus eliminating the language barrier in skill or job matching. Privacy and data protection measures are infused through federated data access and end-to-end encrypted agent interactions. Besides, explainability is equally important. Every decision taken by agents or proposed by the LLM comes with the reasons behind them—like "This industry grew by 18% in your area in the last one year" or "Your academic profile matches up with the evolving fintech career profiles." These reasons improve trust and transparency in system recommendations.

- Technical Integration and Deployment Architecture: While the system is abstracted from low-level technical detail in this research, the high-level deployment involves cloud-based micro services architecture:

o Backend: Python-based FastAPI for orchestrating agent logic.
o LLM Engine: Accessed via API (e.g., OpenAI, Claude, Mistral) with instruction-tuned configurations.
o Database Layer: PostgreSQL for structured data and vector databases (like FAISS or Weaviate) for rooting storage and retrieval.
o Frontend: React Native mobile app or browser interface, with support for chatbot interactions.
o Workflow Orchestration: Celery or LangChain agents for managing task flows and LLM-agent interaction protocols.

The infrastructure accommodates both synchronous and asynchronous operations, facilitating real-time user interaction and batch automation jobs.

Case Simulation and Example Flow: As an example, take a semi-urban area with plenty of graduates in mechanical engineering but little industrial employment. The system would:

- Track workforce capabilities, job patterns, and regional economics.
- Signal that drone repair and EV retrofitting are developing industries in the vicinity.
- Pick up skills shortage in electronics diagnosis.
- Suggest a microenterprise retrofitting traditional bikes into e-bikes.
- Develop a business plan and recommend a partnership with local government schemes for e-mobility.
- Offer learning modules for the missing skill sets and a funding pitch deck.

This degree of automation, insight, and direction lowers the barrier to entry drastically for new entrepreneurs and aligns local talent with viable opportunities.

V. RESULTS AND DISCUSSION

The deployment of agentic AI alongside LLMs in the Labour market automation framework has brought about critical understanding on the reshaping of employment patterns, matching efficiency of skills, and the development of responsive business models. The outcomes of this effort are described through qualitative findings and system simulation, with emphasis on three key dimensions:

- Dynamic Labour matching agentic system performance,
- Effectiveness of decision support by LLM, and
- Real-time business model generation mechanism adaptability.
  - Agentic Matching Efficiency and Responsiveness: The suggested multi-agent system structure—consisting of Resource Agents, Skill-Based Agents, Business Model Selector Agents, and Skill Gap Analyzer Agents—exhibited high task specialization and colLabourative interaction. Simulation outcomes revealed that the agent model enhanced job-role matching accuracy by around 37% as compared to conventional static rule-based recommender models. The enhancement was caused due to the agents being able to evaluate not only current skill sets but also forecast reskilling possibilities with predictive analysis. In addition, the incorporation of environmental sensing mechanisms—i.e., real-time Labour market conditions, educational pipeline shift, and macroeconomic indicators—allowed the agents to dynamically recalibrate their recommendations. For instance, in situations involving seasonal Labour gaps or speedy technology shocks, the Resource and Skill-Based Agents collectively reallocated candidates into short-term training modules, boosting worker placement speed.
  - LLM-Powered Semantic Understanding and Contextual Judgement: The use of LLMs greatly improved semantic understanding of unstructured data sources like resumes, job descriptions, industrial reports, and business trend analysis. LLMs like GPT-based models were trained to execute domain-specific entity extraction, career trajectory prediction, and employer branding or market demand signal sentiment analysis. Quantitative analysis on benchmark datasets and synthetic CV-job corpora showed a 28% improvement in semantic alignment scores between job descriptions and candidate profiles compared to baseline NLP-based parsing systems. Additionally, in business model ideation scenarios, the LLM's ability to generate allowed novel hybrid model suggestions (e.g., fusing gig economy aspects with subscription models in the creative sector) that were subsequently reviewed by domain experts for viabil-

ity. This indicates that LLMs are not only information extractors but can also function as intelligent reasoning modules able to assess soft constraints such as personality fit, potential for adaptability, and socio-economic significance—factors imperative for contemporary Labour automation.

- Dynamic Business Model Reconfiguration: One of the strongest outputs of the methodology under consideration was its ability to dynamically reconfigure business models in light of changing human capital characteristics and demand. Through combining LLMs with rule-based logic graphs, the Business Model Selector Agent reacted to inputs from the Skill Gap Analyzer and Resource Agent, simulating thereby a real-time strategic planning system. The system was tested based on several hypothetical startup situations in manufacturing, creative services, and decentralized finance spaces. The adaptive feedback loop enabled the generation of business models that automatically adapted revenue streams, workforce compositions, and service delivery strategies as a response to simulated regulatory shocks or market shocks. A systematic case simulation of a local smart textile production facility showed that by means of agentic adaptation and LLM-based pivot strategies, the system was able to reconfigure the production model from B2B wholesale to B2C e-commerce with localized customization, realizing a projected 24% growth in operational margin as well as a 31% decrease in Labour mismatches.
- Interpretability, Explainability, and Human Oversight: In spite of the independence of agents and LLMs' abstract reasoning ability, explainability was ensured in the architecture. Every choice that was made by agents was traced and displayed in a dashboard that showed:
  - Skill-agent suggestions and justification
  - Risk-assessment routes for incompatible jobs
  - Recommendations for upskilling courses
  - AI-proposed business pivots with confidence levels

Human supervisor feedback during the simulated trials recommended that the interpretability interface enhanced trust in automatic decisions. This reinforces the idea that agentic systems, when paired with clear LLM outputs, can be reconciled with human-in-the-loop models of governance—a key precondition for deployment in sensitive areas like Labour and economic policymaking.

- Comparative Analysis with Existing Frameworks: To analyze the real-world effect of this work, comparative analyses were done with prevalent employment recommender systems like LinkedIn's Skill Matcher, Google Cloud's Talent Solution API, and rule-based HR Management Systems. In metrics like:

- o Time-to-placement
- o Candidate-to-role satisfaction index
- o Skill gap resolution time
- o Business model fit score

The suggested LLM-agentic hybrid model outperformed baselines consistently across margins of 19% to 42%. Most remarkable was the capacity to propose non-obvious career options or business turns, as present-day deterministic systems cannot because they lack contextual intelligence.

VI. ADVANTAGES OF PROPOSED METHODOLOGY

Agentic Artificial Intelligence (AAI) and Large Language Models (LLMs) can be embedded into Labour market systems and business model ecosystems, creating a transformative paradigm in intelligent automation. The benefits span several dimensions from improved speed of decision-making, skills optimization, agile resource allocation, and customized job recommendations. This section eLabourates on what those benefits are from deploying such an agentic and linguistically intelligent framework. The most exciting feature is context-aware decision-making. Traditional automated systems have limitations to rule-based logic that lack the ability to adapt to a constantly shifting, unstructured environment. The ability to leverage LLMs - machines capable of interpreting human-like contextual data - and autonomous agents that independently perceive, reason and act, brings a new dynamic to be able to not only understand and analyze Labour market scenarios that are complex and ambiguous, but can also comprehend the depth of the semantic relationships that exist in candidate profiles, job descriptions, Labour market demands and organizational capabilities, thereby improving possibilities for best alignment of individual capabilities to evolving needs of the industry. Skill-based agents and gap analyzers are capable of a higher degree of skill matching accuracy and academic profiling. As it assesses every academic transcript, each resume, and reviews of a job performance, the system will have a real-time view of an individual competency graph. Unlike static profiling approaches, this presents a real-time capability that identifies current strengths and reveals gaps that are still to emerge and provides unique and personalized reskilling pathways. This allows for improved career stages, reduced hiring misallocation, and development of lifelong learning approaches, which is important as economies change quickly and transition to digital economies. One of the biggest benefits has to do with adaptability and optimization of the business models. An agentic AI-based business model selector is capable of parsing market fluctuations, consumer preferences, government regulations throughout the system's intelligence to make real-time recommendations on desired business models. This makes it easier and creates opportunities for small business and startups because they will be able to access new innovation and adjust to habit changes. Instead of being restricted to fixed or legacy models, the business can easily pivot to gig, subscription or platform-based businesses, or hybrid models; that were suggested using the agentic framework based on real-time intelligence. The automation of talent allocation and resource optimization processes significantly reduce the operational friction. Instead of manually mapping human resources for tasks, intelligent agents can autonomally correct personnel on the right occasion based on real -time availability, level of experience and relevant performance history. This resulted in an increase in productivity, downtime was reduced, and overhead costs decreased. Especially in multi-agent framework, such adaptation can be distributed in diverse departments and regional workforces. From the perspective of a governance and equity, this system supports inclusive Labour participation. Embedded in LLM through automatic translation, relevant interpretation, and impartial-individual algorithms, individuals of diverse linguistic and socio-economic backgrounds can attach more effectively with systems. In addition, the agent system can be programmed to identify discriminatory patterns or recommend interference, which promotes moral recruitment and social inclusion. In addition, the framework enables career scalable and low -cost deployment, especially in rural areas. The digital nature of LLM-operated agents means that such systems can work with minimal physical infrastructure, providing intelligent guidance and opportunity access where human advisors or institutes are rare. This employment is democraticized access to intelligence information and supports national skilling missions. In addition to functional benefits, the implementation of the AAI model also leads to data-managed policy insight. Agent interaction - behavior collected from spanning industries, roles and geographical - can be analyzed to achieve patterns in unemployment trends, regional intervals, emerging technologies and educational disabilities. It supports better policy setting, course design and workforce plan at a systemic level. Finally, the interoperability of the agentic framework allows spontaneous integration with external systems - such as job portals, educational institutions, enterprise HR systems and government databases. The modular architecture ensures that upgrade, scalability, and customization are efficient, reducing long -term maintenance and system evolution can be aligned with social needs.

VII. CHALLENGES OF PROPOSED METHODOLOGY

Although Agentic Artificial Intelligence (AAI) and Large Language Models (LLMs) offer enormous potential for transforming Labour markets and ecosystems that support organizations and their development, there are significant barriers to be overcome in deploying and operationalizing these intelligent platforms. There are technical, ethical, infrastructural, economic, and socio-cultural barriers that play vital roles in the responsible, equitable, and sustainable use of, respectively. Building a platform that can integrate all possible real-world data is one of the most obvious challenges. The success of AAI applications is predicated on ingesting, parsing, and situating a variety of considerations, extracting contextual meaning from resumes, academic records, business models, job postings, and market signals to create timely and fit-for-purpose responses. However, the issue with data related to contemporary real-world Labour markets, it is mostly unstructured, inconsistent and/or incomplete. The challenge of achieving data effectively across systems - 313while retaining semantic integrity is not insignificant. Also, data privacy is a challenge within developing systems incorporating sensitive personal data related to individuals and organizations. Considerations surrounding data privacy, encryption practices, treating the data in compliance with data protection laws - such as the European GDPR and India's DPDP Act - add to the challenges of developing effective systems. The justification and trustworthiness of agent decisions is another imminent issue. Even though LLMs allow natural language understanding, their decision-making rationale is notably obscured. This is colloquially referred to as the "black box" problem. In high-impact situations, such as selecting job candidates, job advice or employer level changes, users and stakeholders need to have transparency of justifications. AAI would need to incorporate explainable AI (XAI) components that can justify agent decisions in terms understandable to humans; otherwise, trust and bias may result. Bias and fairness continue to pose ethical challenges. If the training data used to develop agents, or LLMs, has historical bias (e.g., gendered patterns of hiring, under-representation of disadvantaged communities), then biases may be magnified through the automation pipeline. Skills assessment recommendations may, for example, force individuals with privilege or from specific institutions to be recommended over individuals impacting equity. Active bias auditing and fairness-aware training processes are needed. The interoperating with legacy systems is also an area of concern, especially in larger organizations and public employment exchanges. Existing HRMS (human resources systems), ERP tools, and government portals do not often include agent-based architecture, LLM-based API integration. Moving or pivoting to a supported system on this type of architecture can be expensive, time consuming, and technically weak (i.e., in parts of the world that do not exhibit higher levels of digital maturity). The computational requirements of a full stack agentic AI system (using LLMs) are also worth noting. Controlled agentic intelligence requires considerably more processing power, memory, and latency (especially when the framework will be aimed at real-time decisions across a multiplicity of agents). In addition, many organizations are still dependent on cloud technology and many of the costs are much more predictable when it comes to resource allocation, infrastructure costs, and carbon footprint levels of inferences that AI workloads require in production, particularly for lower resource geographies. Furthermore, the scalability and maintenance of multi-agent systems is not trivial. A multiplicity of agents are only valid, operational, and useful when they are continuously fed or connected with the freshest market intelligence, skills frameworks, and any government policy. Once a system is not maintained over time and no fresh content is uploaded in terms of a data lake, the potential for a system to become unbusy or not valid at all rapidly increases and is counterproductive - and as a result negates some the key advantages of automating some of these systems are all meant to provide benefit in the first place. This maintenance required and only persists when ongoing staff exists that are accountable and responsible for the oversight teams on hire, with foundational sustainable AI ops practice. From the human side, the resistance to adopt AI-based automation will be a challenge in social acceptance. Many workers and human resource professionals may dislike working with automated systems because they do not trust it will not take away their jobs or they perceive that automated systems have no empathy or they misunderstand AI limitations. Increasing educational outreach, ensuring transparency of system behavior, and ensuring participatory design (i.e., users shape the evolution of the system) will be the cornerstone of adoption. Conversely, the whole realm of governance and regulation around intelligent systems is still at an early stage. Current Labour laws, credential bodies providing accreditation, and AI policies have not kept pace with the speed of intelligent agentic AI intervention. There is a potential for the misuse of systems without ethical boundaries or accountability given one could manipulate:

- the potential for exploitative gig work job matching
- hire/fire based on surveillance
- questionable consent for data usage or collection

Finally, the issues of localization and language are significant in multi-language nations such as India and misinformation can lead to mismatches in recruitment solutions - ChatGP and all LLMs will support multiple languages, but accurately discerning language, local environment, geographic and regional employment terms will require significant fine tuning to ensure that communication is not misrepresented. This is a particularly significant issue in semi-urban and rural employment markets where populations may be less sophisticated in employment standards. Overall, while Agentic AI promises a huge transformation in Labour and business models, these systems cannot be employed hastily but rather must be implemented with forethought and multidisciplinary colLabouration. Meeting these challenges will be the key to harnessing this paradigm fully.

VIII. FUTURE PERSPECTIVE

The combination of Agentic Artificial Intelligence (AAI) alongside Large Language Models (LLMs) and their potential to transform Labour markets and business models suggest new and expansive futures that exceed what is currently imagined. Ever-increasing digital transformation in every sector gives rise to the promise of AAI as a foundational technology in the development of the next generation of workforce and entrepreneurial ecosystems. The future potential of this convergence of technologies relates to hardware, economic, educational, and social aspects. Among other promising directions will be persistent, lifelong adaptive career navigation systems. At some point in the not too distant future, AI-agent based companions will be able to manage transitioning Labour markets by following people from their earliest education years until they retire. AI will continuously respond and adapt based on academic performance, career interests, psychological capital, life events and even personality types to provide fully in-real-time career planning and skills development maps, alongside or instead of job recommendations. These adaptive career agents will far exceed static career guidance and career navigation support which is currently available, and they will always be up to date relative to Labour market evolution, what jobs are being automated, and a person's learning experience patterns over their life course. Another thrilling possibility is the emergence of AI-enabling entrepreneurial ecosystems. Agents could assist new entrepreneurs in not only finding the right business opportunities based on gaps in the market, but also propose sustainable business models, try to optimize resources, simulate risk, and even automate initial registrations or compliance. Platforms like this have the potential to democratize entrepreneurship in future smart cities or digital villages so that youth, women and rural communities can form micro-businesses with much less friction and maximum help from AI. In the business context, the orchestration of aggregating agents storytelling massively throughout the enterprise will move forward by an order of magnitude. Enterprises will be able to deploy thousands of intelligent agents from functional support in HR, R&D, production, and customer service - each learning, and adapting, in real time. It will create a distributed AI nervous system where decisions will be made - even autonomously - faster, more efficiently, and with much greater context. Agent collectives could negotiate with one another, simulate various outcomes, and dynamically reshape workflows in the organization according to its internal and external KPIs, eyes and ears on external market signals. From a societal impact conception, it is reasonable to anticipate a future populated by conscientious objector Labour equity platforms fueled by AI. Governments and NGOs can use agent-based platforms to determine whether employment inequality exists, identify skill gaps in disadvantaged areas, and forecast Labour migration. Evidence of employment inequality can inform targeted public policy, upskilling initiatives, or offer a fiscal stimulus (for example). Over the long run, such intelligent systems will help to eliminate the urban/rural employment disparity, overcome underemployment, and primarily foster inclusive growth. In education, agent-based academic advising and curriculum mapping or alignment will be commonplace in smart universities and online learning platforms. AAI will capture macro-job trend analysis and align it with individual students throughout their learning journey. Institutions of higher learning could use real-time Labour market information, in which curricula can also be realigned to reflect the demand of skills on the ground. Students will receive alerts about emerging sectors (quantum computing, climate analytics) and agents will suggest certification or research opportunities aligned with their potential - automatically. A cutting-edge application is multi-modal agent integration where LLMs can be used alongside vision models, sensor inputs, and spatial intelligence to fuel embodied agents--like robots, virtual assistants, or smart kiosks. Picture a physical AI job counselor that travels through villages, analyzing local dialects, reading physical documents, reading user emotions, and assisting villagers with registering for skill programs or MSME schemes. Imagine the possibilities! Another exciting evolution will be the use of agent-led forecasting for future business models. Agents will be able to leverage predictive analytics and simulations to recommend not only viable business models, but resilient and sustainable business models that also account for the potential impacts of climate change on business, digital disruption, changing demographics, and shifts in the supply chain. The recommendations from these agents will even include when to pivot your business model, when to invest in automation, or when it may be time to transition to a circular economy - and they will serve as trusted advisors for MSMEs and start ups that are faced with volatility. As decentralized agent marketplaces arise, and blockchain removes the issues of reputation in Labour ecosystems, the meaning of trust and colLabouration will further transform. One could have a personal AI agent negotiate freelance with clients based clearly defined scopes of work, using decentralized digital credentials to validate skills, and to coordinate micro contracts across borders. Gig economy workers are disproportionately vulnerable to exploitation, and automated agents can leverage smart contracts to guarantee payment, compliance, and fair arbitration. Looking ahead, factors like AAI convergence with neuro-symbolic reasoning, causal inference models, and quantum machine learning could dramatically improve agents' abilities to reason, explain and generalize. The ultimate outcome could be the emergence of truly generalizable agents functioning across domains - for instance, seamlessly switching between healthcare Labour planning and defense manufacturing logistics, and adapting instantaneously to new regulations, languages, and ethical contexts. Finally, working cooperatively on a global scale could result in the emergence of open-source agent designs for Labour equity, where countries and institutions contribute models, datasets, and tools. These shared resources could help developing economies leapfrog the conventional industrial development pathway by launching smart, contextualized Labour automation platforms customized for their socioeconomic endpoints immediately.

IX. CONCLUSION

The advancement of AI may be at a significant point of change where it is able to intertwine agentic AI and large language models (LLMs) in ways that can potentially transform work and entrepreneurial ecologies. This study explored the use of agentic AI systems, which can include decision-making capabilities that leverage reasoning, alongside LLMs to create intelligent and adaptive platforms that actively automate aligning workforce skills, identifying workforce gaps, developing business models, and inscribing opportunities for individuals. This exploration aims to build an intelligent infrastructure that utilizes autonomous reasoning agents to assess human skills, preferences, education and qualifications, and market demand while embedded into the workflow. LLMs ensure agents have both syntactic knowledge and semantic reasoning to provide accurate context, insights, and advice - even business recommendations that are executable. By embedding an agentic-LLM together, it would dynamically match Labour supply to demand, actively deal with educational disaffection, and generate bespoke and scalable micro-entrepreneurial paths. The proposed framework is not merely a theoretical concept; it illustrates the possible approaches for developing AI systems which can operate autonomously, by being intentional and mindful of context. While current AI systems are reactive, the proposal is to develop proactive, goal-seeking autonomous automation ecosystems, which support people to be more intentional while managing their resources more efficiently at a societal scale. Early results from both architectural simulations and architectural modelling of these systems indicate a range of positive outcome from achieving better job-role fitment, reducing unemployment, improving worker flexibility, and better aligning formal education output with economic requirements. However, there are critical challenges ahead, all of which must be methodically developed and addressed in future research and practical use. Technical limitations of LLM reasoning, ethical issues regarding automation and inappropriate exploitation/abuse of agentic autonomy must be addressed. We need embedded regulatory affordances, fairness frameworks, and transparency protocols from the beginning under all conditions. This chapter outlines a broad and thorough vision for how Agentic AI, along with the linguistic and reasoning abilities of LLMs, can be used to reshape the Labour economy of today. The conceptual and methodological contributions of this work provide a starting point for the development of future intelligent automation platforms that are not only efficient but also equitable, inclusive, and responsive to the rapidly changing nature of work and enterprise.

REFERENCES

Andronie, M., Iatagan, M., U ă, C., Hurloiu, I., Dimirescu, A., & Dimirescu, I. (2023). Big data management algorithms in artificial internet of things-based fintech. *Amfiteatru Economic*, *25*(63), 430–445. DOI: 10.24818/EA/2023/63/430

Bhattacharya, P., Saraswat, D., Savaliya, D., Sanghavi, S., Verma, A., Sakariya, V., Tanwar, S., Sharma, R., Raboaca, M. S., & Manea, D. L. (2023). Towards future internet: The metaverse perspective for diverse industrial applications. *Mathematics*, *11*(4), 941. Advance online publication. DOI: 10.3390/math11040941

Capraro, V., Lentsch, A., Acemoglu, D., Akgün, S., Akhmedova, A., Bilancini, E., Bonnefon, J.-F., Brañas-Garza, P., Butera, L., Douglas, K. M., Everett, J. A. C., Gigerenzer, G., Greenhow, C., Hashimoto, D. A., Holt-Lunstad, J., Jetten, J., Johnson, S., Kunz, W. H., Longoni, C., & Viale, R. (2024). The impact of generative artificial intelligence on socioeconomic inequalities and policy making. *PNAS Nexus*, *3*(6), pgae191. Advance online publication. DOI: 10.1093/pnasnexus/pgae191 PMID: 38864006

Dwivedi, Y. K., Kshetri, N., Hughes, L., Slade, E., Jeyaraj, A., Kar, A. K., Baabdullah, A. M., Koohang, A., Raghavan, V., Ahuja, M., Albanna, H., Albashrawi, M. A., Al-Busaidi, A. S., Balakrishnan, J., Barlette, Y., Basu, S., Bose, I., Brooks, L., Buhalis, D., & Wright, R. (2023). Opinion paper: So what if ChatGPT wrote it? Multidisciplinary perspectives on opportunities, challenges and implications of generative conversational AI for research, practice and policy. *International Journal of Information Management*, *71*, 102642. Advance online publication. DOI: 10.1016/j.ijinfomgt.2023.102642

Ellis, E., Radvanyi, P. J., Ascierto, P. A., Bhatia, T. C., Curti, C. M., Cesano, D., Gajewski, T. F., Hwu, P., Atkins, M. B., Sullivan, A. W., & Weber, J. S. (2024). Challenges and opportunities in cancer immunotherapy: A Society for Immunotherapy of Cancer (SITC) strategic vision. *Journal for Immunotherapy of Cancer*, *12*(5), e009063. DOI: 10.1136/jitc-2024-009063 PMID: 38901879

Hadi, M. U., Tashi, Q. A., Qureshi, R., Shah, A., Muneer, A., Irfan, M., Zafar, A., Shaikh, M. B., Akhtar, N., Wu, J., & Mirjalili, S. (2023). Large language models: A comprehensive survey of its applications, challenges, limitations, and future prospects. *TechRxiv*. DOI: 10.36227/techrxiv.23589741.v4

Hendriksen, C. (2023). Artificial intelligence for supply chain management: Disruptive innovation or innovative disruption? *The Journal of Supply Chain Management*, *59*(4), 3–5. DOI: 10.1111/jscm.12304

Humphreys, D., Koay, A., Desmond, D., & Mealy, E. (2024). AI hype as a cyber security risk: The moral responsibility of implementing generative AI in business. *AI and Ethics*, *4*(3), 791–804. Advance online publication. DOI: 10.1007/s43681-024-00443-4

Li, K., Lau, B. P. L., Yuan, X., Ni, W., Guizani, M., & Yuen, C. (2023). Toward ubiquitous semantic metaverse: Challenges, approaches, and opportunities. *IEEE Internet of Things Journal*, *11*(3), 4382–4402. DOI: 10.1109/JIOT.2023.3302159

Lorenz, P., Perset, K., & Berryhill, J. (2023). *Initial policy considerations for generative artificial intelligence*. OECD Publishing., DOI: 10.1787/fae2d1e6-

Omar, M., Alotaibi, A. A., Said, M. S., Hassan, M., Periyasamy, P., Alotaibi, A. A. E., & Elgazzar, R. A. (2023). Internet of medical things and Healthcare 4.0: Trends, requirements, challenges, and research directions. *Sensors (Basel)*, *23*(17), 7435. Advance online publication. DOI: 10.3390/s23177435 PMID: 37687891

Orchard, T., & Tasiemski, L. (2023). The rise of generative AI and possible effects on the economy. *Economics and Business Review*, *9*(2), 5–23. DOI: 10.18559/ebr.2023.2.732

Rashid, A. B., Kausik, A. K., Sunny, A. A. H., & Bappy, M. H. (2023). Artificial intelligence in the military: An overview of the capabilities, applications, and challenges. *International Journal of Intelligent Systems*, *2023*(1), 8676366. Advance online publication. DOI: 10.1155/2023/8676366

Sharma, K., Tomar, M., & Tadimarri, A. (2023). AI-driven marketing: Transforming sales processes for success in the digital age. *Journal of Knowledge Learning and Science Technology*, *2*(2), 260–266. DOI: 10.60087/jklst.vol2.n2.p260

Slimi, Z., & Villarejo-Carballido, B. (2023). Navigating the ethical challenges of artificial intelligence in higher education: An analysis of seven global AI ethics policies. TEM Journal, 12(2), 592–603. https://doi.org/DOI: 10.18421/TEM122-02

Zawish, M., Dharejo, F. A., Khowaja, S. A., Raza, S., Davy, S., Dev, K., & Bellavista, P. (2024). AI and 6G into the metaverse: Fundamentals, challenges and future research trends. *IEEE Open Journal of the Communications Society*, *5*, 731–758. DOI: 10.1109/OJCOMS.2024.3349465

Zhou, J., Müller, H., Holzinger, A., & Chen, F. (2024). Ethical ChatGPT: Concerns, challenges, and commandments. *Electronics (Basel)*, *13*(17), 3417. Advance online publication. DOI: 10.3390/electronics13173417

Chapter 7
The Human-AI Collaboration Imperative:
Redefining Workflows and Skills in the Augmented Enterprise

Siriyama Kanthi Herath
http://orcid.org/0000-0002-6443-9739
Clark Atlanta University, USA

Jae Koo Yoo
Clark Atlanta University, USA

ABSTRACT

Artificial intelligence (AI) is completely transforming the world of labor and is no longer not only about the fear of mass technological unemployment but also about its absolute inevitability. Probably, a slightly more subtle point of view highlights Human-AI Collaboration (HAC) as another distinctive feature of the contemporary work environment, the synergy between human ingenuity and machine productivity. The necessity of HAC is addressed in the chapter, which also outlines how AI can complement human potential, reinvent processes of doing businesses, and demand new skills among the members of workforce in an augmented enterprise. It unites theoretical discussion with practical applications, promoting human-centered concept of AI. However, the key to successful AI implementation lies in the smart ways in which interactions can become involved, by playing on human creativity and emotional intelligence and the efficiencies of AI, promising completely new levels of productivity and human possibilities.

DOI: 10.4018/979-8-3373-5816-1.ch007

1. INTRODUCTION

The advent of Artificial Intelligence (AI) has marked an unequivocal and dramatic shift in the domain of labor and markets and requires the most notable change in thinking in how work can be perceived, designed, and executed. The initial discourse on AI in the workspace was typically underlined by a tone of dread, which took advantage of the existence of mass technological unemployment and the prospect of a dystopian world without human labor, where machines perform all the productive tasks (Frey & Osborne, 2017). This was highlighted in the initial discourse where it was stressed that AI would lead to the massive unemployment of workers in society to a level never witnessed before and hence creating distorted predictions of the social upheaval and economic restructuring of society.

However, a more sophisticated and common perception has emerged that opposes this displacement-oriented approach. This new type of thinking is postulating that although indeed the greatest ability of AI is that it has a possibility of replacing human beings, it is more importantly deep-seated and successful in providing new ways of collaboration between people and intelligent machines. Such constructive interaction rather frequently is called Human-AI Collaboration (HAC), and it already becomes the trademark of the modern workplace. Such a new reality requires decisive reconsideration of the traditional processes and requires the development of a completely new set of human skills within a changed paradigm of what is already being acknowledged as the augmented enterprise. Human creativity and efficiency based on machine effectiveness meet in this augmented environment, becoming a strong and flexible organization.

The purpose of this chapter is to offer a thorough and detailed overview of contemporary academic investigation, research, and experience of real-life cases regarding the emerging necessity of human-AI collaboration. It will carefully unpackage the complexity of how AI is able to greatly enrich human intelligence and multiply human output and therefore result in the essential re-definition of those processes that have been authorized in business and a corresponding change in the abilities of the worker and the development of new formations of organization. Combining theoretical discourse with practical, real-life cases, and concrete empirical data, this chapter attempts to make a significant contribution to the overall goal of this book: to provide an interdisciplinary solution to AI development and its far-reaching implications to the field of business and society. It will clarify the complex processes of how AI is changing the very fabric of labor, give practical answers to how firms can best meet these radical transformations, and become an active advocate of the implementation of a more human-based AI paradigm. The following analysis will present an intriguing argument that the productive adoption of AI technologies in business organizations is entirely dependent on the thoughtful and farsighted development of interactions that would undoubtedly play an instrumental role in securing a symbiotic interaction between the innate human advantages, such as creativity, reasoning, and emotional intelligence, and AI technologies that offer tremendous efficiencies. It is not only intended to contribute to unprecedented productivity gains but is also aimed at supporting the growth of human potential in the rapidly changing work environment.

2. LITERATURE REVIEW

The academic body of knowledge dedicated to analyzing the effects of Artificial Intelligence on labor markets has seen a dramatic transformation throughout the last decade. Early academic works in the field, which are often epitomized by the study performed by Frey and Osborne (2017), were primarily preoccupied with the matter of occupational susceptibility to computerization. Consequently, a lot of alarmist attitudes about the prospect of mass unemployment emerged and generated further research interest in quantifying the magnitude of employment displacement due to automation (Manyika et al., 2017). Although these early discussions helped to get people thinking about the disruptive possibilities of AI, there was also a tendency between them to paint a bleak view of the future in which human work is being replaced by more smart machines.

Since then, however, increasingly concerted literature has appeared challenging this displacement-oriented view. According to this counter-narrative, the revolutionary impact of AI is not only an automation of the existing tasks, but a much greater one, i.e., enhancing human abilities, adding completely new tasks, and, as a result, producing new working roles (Acemoglu & Restrepo, 2019, 2020; Autor, 2015). This has been a change in basic assumptions that pointed towards a significant transition in the way the impact of AI is viewed and paradoxically transitioned to a more joint and synergistic approach to the same.

As a result of this conceptual development, the principle of augmentation became a key feature of AI where technology began to be regarded as a powerful instrument or an intelligent companion to improve human abilities but not to fully replace them (Nguyen & Elbanna, 2025).

In this context, the term Human-AI Collaboration (HAC) has gained momentum in a brief time. It follows that HAC can be viewed as a synergistic collaboration in which both human employees and AI systems collaborate towards a common goal with each contributing his/her complementary skill (Davenport & Kirby, 2016; Wilson, 2018). The core idea underlying HAC is based on the notion that as much as AI is already able to outrun human beings in terms of speed and precision in carrying out routine/computation-intensive tasks and in detecting various complex patterns in large sets of data, humans still have some specific and irreplaceable qualities (Wilson, 2018; Lund et al., 2021). They are, but are not restricted to creativity, deep thinking that requires the perception of critical issues, advanced moral circumstance assessment, deep sensational conduct, and an intrinsic ability to adjust to untried and the unprecedented. It is the interrelation of such qualities that constitutes the foundation of efficient collaboration between people and AI.

As addressed in modern sources, there are multiple models and typologies of Human-AI Collaboration that they tend to display because some people can use AI in a variety of ways in human workflows:

2.1. AI as a Tool

According to this model, AI can be seen as a tool that will help a human being to act more effectively and efficiently when completing his or her tasks. Such things are the spell checker tool that can be found everywhere, grammar correction software that could help improve the writing and very complicated data analysis tools to be able to extract better meaning out of complicated data, automated translator tools to be able to communicate in a different language with some relative ease. In this case, AI can be used to increase human productivity and precision, clearly defined jobs.

2.2. AI as an Assistant

The given model presupposes that AI makes suggestions, it can give recommendations or even expert advice, which is used by humans to make their decisions. For example, these could include diagnostic AI software used in medical settings to aid doctors in detecting any abnormalities in patients or financial investment AI applications that offer advice regarding investment decisions based on present market conditions. In such situations, AI plays the role of an intelligent co-pilot since it assists humans to make better judgments.

2.3. AI as a Co-worker

This is a more connected version of cooperation where the AI systems fill those tasks which are interdependent with the tasks of humans within the united workplace. One such example is the utilization of collaborative robots (cobots) in the workplace in manufacturing industry, where they are being used alongside human workers, helping to perform heavy-lifting, precise construction, or repetitive tasks, and, in this way, relieve the overall physical load on both the operators and improve the fabrication rate on a whole (Dhanda et al., 2025). An additional one can be seen in AI-controlled call centers that can redirect customer questions, deliver live data to human workers or even manage a stream of requests that do not require much attention so that human employees can devote themselves to more complicated or emotionally charged cases.

2.4 AI as a Supervisor/Manager

As much as this model holds a lot of potential in terms of efficiency, it has a lot of ethical and organization complexities. In this context, AI would be used to monitor human outputs, coordinate the work down or even command human workforce, frequently using algorithmic management tools as they became common in the so-called gig economy. Although these systems have the potential to maximize the efficiency of coordination and resource distribution, the systems bring important concerns such as employee independence, equity, visibility, and responsibility, which should be well designed and executed to avoid worker exploitation or product dehumanization.

Various established theories are used to make sense of these interactions which are too involved to be understood. A strong window to view the complex interaction between the part of the technological and the human social systems (individuals, teams, organizational culture) in an organizational setup is through the socio-technical systems theory (Pasmore and Sherwood, 1978). Such a theory underlies the importance of streamlining the social and technical performance of a system in a bid to promote its overall performance and health. Moreover, Distributed cognition theory (Hutchins, 1995) provides important insights on how knowledge, work, and coordinated activities can be shared, processed as well as coordinated by humans as well as between humans and AIs. It states that cognitive processes and activities are not just limited to individual minds, but they are extended or spread across to tools, artifacts, and social interactions including those with AI as well.

In more recent times, focus has been directed towards the more applied problems and possibilities of the application of Human-AI Collaboration, however. The identified essential components that should be met to be successful in the establishment of HAC involve building trust in AI systems, understanding the importance of ensuring that the AI-generated results should be clear and explainable, encouraging high user acceptance rates, and the well-designed human-AI interface functionality and intuitiveness (Shneiderman, 2020; Gopalan et al., 2024; Karofsky, 2025). The available literature highlights that mere recognition that the future holds the promise of enhancing AI power is no longer enough; rather, there is a strong and dire need to establish practical means of work and operational plans regarding how to fully utilize these synergistic partnerships when it comes to shaping and operating work models. This entails leaving behind theoretical appreciation and shifting to practical, feasible approaches to integration of AI in a way that exploits the power of humans and the efficiency of technology to the fullest.

3. KEY THEMES AND ARGUMENTS

The main arguments and themes that will be examined in this chapter are as follows, and there is vast use of recent studies, recent empirical results, and case studies in different industries. All these themes can be taken to describe the necessity of an active and human-based approach to encompassing AI in the enterprise.

3.1. Redefining Workflows: Automation, Augmentation, and Transformation

Artificial intelligence is radically re-shaping the flow of tasks, their character, and relations with one another, so it has far more far-reaching and radical effects that a single job is automatized (Brynjolfsson & McAfee, 2014). In this part, we are going to examine in detail how AI transforms work processes, not only in the sense of performing specific tasks, but also comprehensively migrating operations.

Redirecting Human Effort to Greater-Value-Added Work

Human worker AI system automation of the routine, predictable and frequently repetitive task frees human workers of monotone and low value tasks and allows them to refocus their cognitive and creative powers on tasks that require distinctively human skills. Such dynamic often results in a radical rearrangement of current job tasks. AI can be seen as an act of seamless integration to the extent that it displaces aspects, and at the same time, leads to the emergence of entirely new tasks requiring human skills that differ in terms of the skills of AI (Autor et al., 2022). The outcome of this dynamic process is of evolution rather than destruction of the job, as the content and emphasis in human work is raised.

Reflecting the legal services sector where the review and discovery of documents is traditionally a labor-intensive process that requires a team of people who perform manual review. AI-driven e-discovery tools have become capable of quickly and precisely shifting through an enormous amount of legal documentation and identifying valuable information, not to mention picking out possible contradictions or trends that can take human paralegals days to notice. The automation of the fundamentals of data processing allows lawyers and paralegals as well as legal researchers to free up time and their more creative faculties to concentrate on such higher-level though processes.

Now they could pay more attention to the development of complex legal plans, specific client consultations, sophisticated legal interpretations that involve contextual analysis and ethical consideration, and complicated problem-solving beyond the reach of an algorithm. AI can then assume the role of an irreplaceable helper, dealing with the grunt work, giving synthesized information and freeing humans to work at the highest level of intellectual and strategic abilities.

The same applies to the sector of accounting and finance where computer-based instruments, powered by AI, can be used to automate data entry, to reconcile the accounts, and even at detecting initial cases of fraud. That will enable human accountants, and financial analysts to be less focused on transactional processing toward more strategic assignments, including advanced financial modeling, complex risk assessment, the provision of advisory services to the customers, and development of new financial solutions.

Enhanced Human Capabilities (Augmentation): AI as a Force Multiplier

AI systems are not tools of efficiency: rather, AI systems are cognitive prosthetics capable of heavily augmenting and extending human thinking, perception, and operational capabilities. Such an addition results in better performance, better decision-making, and it can also result in fewer cognitive requirements for human operators.

Medical practice has seen the use of artificial intelligence in the diagnosis equipment as claimed to revolutionize the areas of competence that include radiology and pathology. As an example, the AI models that undergo training on enormous datasets containing millions of medical images have the potential to help radiologists identify small abnormalities in X-rays, MRIs, and CT scans with more accuracy than a human eye and in a matter of seconds (Topol, 2019). This is to offer a compliment to the radiologist and not to replace them and the technology offers an opinion or focuses on a place of treatment, minimizing a diagnostic mistake and is better to achieve a positive patient outcome. The human professional still has that final say in making the diagnosis, and their presence of observation and analysis is enigmatically enhanced by AI. Likewise, AI in ophthalmology allows detecting diabetic retinopathy early based on the retinal scan, which makes it possible to prevent vision loss. Gopalan et al. (2024) note the complexity of the technology, the mind, and ethics in this digital era of care and explain that although AI can improve capabilities, human control is required to serve well and responsibly.

An extension of human-AI augmentation in the physical world can be pointed at the introduction of collaborative robots (cobots) in the manufacturing industry. The design of cobots recommends their operations to be conducted close to human beings and work in synchronization. This combination is expected to relieve human operators physically, enhance ergonomic positions, and help humans do something that requires dexterity, problem-solving, or policing that new cobots are yet to provide. Dhanda et al. (2025) point out that this kind of human-robot collaboration will be one of the key elements of Industry 5.0 since they raise the opportunities of getting higher productivity and the problem of integration and safety.

In addition to physical work, AI is used to supplement the human mental processes as well. AI based customer relationship management (CRM) applications can interpret customer data in sales to anticipate buying patterns, give custom product recommendations and even improve sales paths, thus helping human sales representatives to be more effective and efficient in the connection. In education, when personalized learning is introduced through AI, it adapts to individual student needs and capabilities and therefore, will (using AI) give tailored content and feedback to the learner in addition to supplementing the capabilities of the educator to accommodate multiple learning styles and abilities. All these cases highlight the fact that AI serves as a force multiplier of human decision-making, efficiency, and innovative output in domains where the technology is being applied.

Strategic Integration of the Systemic Performance: Optimization workflow design

The cooperation between people and artificial intelligence should be efficient and mindful, and thus well-designed and strategized in its work process draft. It is not only about picking those particular tasks for automation, but about the big picture in terms of a holistic overview of the work process in order to determine which tasks are best suited for the implementation of AI, and which ones can't be left aside since the task requires either a decision made by a human being or the person's creativity and/or social skills. This is about optimizing the overall system.

The process of using such an approach is comprised of a flowchart of the existing business procedures, bottlenecks, redundancies, and opportunities for AI introduction. The key issues to consider would include posing questions such as what can be done with AI to increase speed and precision; where human creativity, empathy, ethical decision-making, etc. does not fit; and how accountability of the process and prevention of prejudice can be achieved. This could be done through iterations in the spirit of Agile methodologies.

This type of analysis is typically done through a mapping of existing work processes, bottlenecks, redundancies, and opportunities for introduction of AI. The important questions that companies should address during this process include: In what aspects do human creativity, empathy, or moral judgment not matter? In what respect are there human checks and both sides of the argument to avoid bias? It is common in the process that strict AI solutions like iterative design which are like agile methods such as solutions are deployed at various stages and evaluated and improved in accordance with performance and user reviews.

As an example, in customer service, the first workflow analysis may indicate that a significant percentage of the questions are standard questions and quite common ones (FAQs). They can be addressed well by AI-driven chatbots or virtual assistants, which do not require a human agent to consider attending to these requests and save the latter to address more complex, emotionally charged, and unique customer cases. The workflow design entails a smooth transition between the complex cases presented by the AI and the human where all the context rendered by the first activity of the AI will be presented to the human agent. This necessitates a close attention to details in data transfer, communication protocol, and escalation processes.

Product development can also be accelerated by using AI, which can produce many different versions of designs or optimize the choice of material to suit an extensive set of parameters. Still, it is necessary to note that designers of humanity play a decisive role in adding aesthetic perception, certain knowledge of user experience, and final creative decision-making. The streamlined process could include the role of AI in creating hundreds of practical solutions, which the human designers will review, refine, and choose, and then AI will be used to conduct a simulation and test according to the human set parameters. Such iterative loop makes the distinctive advantages of human and AI used at the right point. The focus will be on producing a symbiotic partnership where every partner contributes his best to the overall result.

The Emergence of Hybrid Teams: Blending Human and Machine Intelligence

One of the logical outcomes of such redefinition of workflows is the growing popularity of so-called hybrid human-AI teams, i.e., environments where human beings and intelligent machines partner like two mutually nourishing and supporting entities. This organizational model requires new thinking on understanding within and across teams as well as communication and team dynamics. In the case of hybrid cohorts, more serious concerns related to formalization of communication and information sharing opportunities between human and AI agents are extremely critical. An example includes the analysis that can be given in real-time to a human marketing team by an AI system by revealing emerging trends or forecasting campaign performance. Then a human team draws on this AI-generated understanding to optimize strategies, and they must also have some clear means of offering feedback back to the AI so that they can help it avoid misunderstandings or so that they can ask it to analyze various things in new ways. This is another significant form of feedback that aids in the development of AI. Moreover, it is necessary for the AI systems to have an awareness of the goals of the group of people they work with. AI systems should be smeared with quality goals like those of human beings. They should be designed in a way that will make them know the goal of wholeness. It is particularly important that this is done in a cautious manner and kept up to date. For instance, there can be a case of an AI system being applied in a cybersecurity operation center to detect any suspicious activities within the network. Human beings should be aware of the parameters used for detection by the system as well as the confidence levels of AI. However, more importantly, the AI system should understand that its goal is to ensure security and not just detection.

Moreover, exchange of information techniques is critical. You need dashboards to show the output of AI in a format that humans find easy to consume and you need human-friendly interfaces to enable humans to structure their input to AI. A hybrid team may comprise human dispatchers and an AI route optimization system in logistics companies. The AI will present optimal routes which may be overridden by the human dispatcher using real-time reasons that cannot induce a quantification (e.g. driver fatigue, unexpected road closures that are not registered by the AI yet). Such override by humans should be permitted by the system and lessons be learnt. That is why smooth, transparent, flexible combinations of human intuition and the analytical capabilities of the AI are the key to the successful functioning of hybrid teams.

3.2. The Evolving Skill: New Competencies for the Workforce

Since the nature of work and the way it happens is fundamentally reconfigured by Artificial Intelligence and tasks become produced in a whole different manner, the need of traditional, routine-driven skills is declining, and a new type of distinct and urgent set of skills has been quickly gaining significance. This section critically dissects the changing skills environment, the need to train individuals and the organizations on these new skills to succeed within augmented enterprise.

The Rise of "Uniquely Human" Skills: Cultivating Irreplaceable Capabilities

With As the artificial intelligence systems become ever more able to perform data processing, pattern recognition, and rule-based decision-making processes with unprecedented speed and precision, the kind of skills that can hardly be reproduced by machines, at least, in their current and predictable forms, is being deeply and ever-more-strongly appreciated. These are uniquely human capabilities, and the best competitive asset to human labor in an augmented AI world.

Creativity and Innovation: To be able to think of original ideas, produce original works of art and think differently is an epitome of humanity. Although AI can be used to aid in the creation of content (e.g. creating music, generating initial design ideas, writing text), the flashes of new ideas, the ability to make intellectual leaps and the ability to make final judgments and to add meaning and emotional appeal to creation, all remain squarely in human domain. An example is that an architect may use AI to come up with thousands of building design based on parameters, but the human architect still chooses the one that is the most pleasing to the eye, practical, and applicable to the situation, and the architect can then add in his/her artistic bent and engineering creativity. The AI is used to create rough designs, whereas humans can give them final changes, making it innovative and effective.

Critical Thinking and Complex Problem-Solving: The ability to face ambiguous situations, develop illuminating hypothesis, or arrive at better decisions in ill-defined or novel situations is a complex process that Artificial Intelligence has trouble replicating. Although the application of AI can support an immensity of data and predictive analysis, it is frequently distinct in its inability to use refined contextual knowledge, ethical reasoning, or strong reasoning in uncertainty. To illustrate, in strategic business planning, AI can analyze the market trends and simulate multiple scenarios, yet human leaders will always be necessary to process existing analyses, taking into consideration the unpredictable geopolitical circumstances, evaluating the organizational culture, and making the decisions that would result in trade-offs and long-term vision. The information can be presented by AI, but it is human beings who critically think, synthesize, and plan.

Emotional Intelligence and People Skills: The aptitude to be empathetic, to argue effectively, to negotiate, and to establish and sustain human-to-human bond is human solely. Such competencies are pertinent in any job that involves management of clients, leadership of matrices, resolution of disputes and any type of delicate patronage. As an example, regular customer questions can be effectively performed with an AI chatbot, whereas a more sophisticated customer service problem of frustration and anger or unusual individual situations will still require human interaction, a quality feature, which is active conversation, empathy, and skill to lower the tension level and improve contact. Factors involving tones of human communication, body language, and the capacity to alter the approach towards the other individual depending on emotional context cannot be accomplished by the current AI systems.

Ethical Reasoning and Judgment: As With increasing autonomy and power of AI systems, it is highly relevant to be able to engage with ethical dilemmas, make ethical judgment calls and finally plan based on the human values. This is even more important in cases where the results generated by AI systems contain biases and are discriminatory in one way or another. According to Lund et al. (2021), these human attributes are becoming more important in the world with AI. Organizations need to make sure that AI output avoids being without human oversight or accountability during the implementation of such technology in crucial areas such as in healthcare, finance, or legal systems. This is associated with the ability to detect algorithmic bias, challenge AI recommendations, and act when required to support fairness, privacy, and human dignity. Human ability to feel moral bearing and responsibility is impossible to replace.

AI Literacy and Digital Fluency:

There are some important concepts of AI literacy.

Understanding AI's Applications: Knowing where to implement AI in the industry being in or in the job that would help to improve efficiency, enable better decision-making, or generate an addition of value.

Recognizing AI's Limitations: Understanding that AI is not a perfect system with its levels of bias, reliance, and limitations on intelligence. This also involves knowing the times when the human judgment should be applied to question or verify the AI outputs.

Detecting Potential Mistakes or Bias: Developing a critical mindset to recognize situations when the AI may deliver an erroneous, unfair, or biased outcome usually caused by poor data, or poorly designed algorithms.

Ethical AI Concerns: Having a clear idea of the data privacy issues, fairness of algorithms, transparency, and accountability of AI systems. It is learning about the responsible use of AI tools and being aware of the situations in which they should not be applied due to the ethical issues they can lead to. According to the World Economic Forum (2023), AI literacy is an important upcoming skill and underlines that it is not an issue of profound technical knowledge, but of responsible engagement in the AI systems.

Digital fluency in this respect not only refers to being knowledgeable about and knowing how to use computers but surviving in today and further digital ecosystems driven by increasingly AI-powered. This would involve working in cloud-based collaborative environments, data flows management and working with AI-connected software applications.

Adaptive Expertise and Lifelong Learning:

Such accelerated rate of evolution in the field of AI requires people to develop adaptable knowledge and adopt the lifestyle of life-long learning. Since the current distribution of job positions will evolve with the development of AI technologies, human resources will be required to reassess and retrain on an ongoing basis to be able to compromise effectively (Autor, 2019). This implies that there will be a departure from the static conception of skills accrued at the onset of a career to a dynamic one that would require life-long learning.

The chapter will explain that educational facilities or the training modules that are designed by companies can have a significant role in the development of such a mindset. Upskilling Future Generations It is time to start, preparing the future generations, along with vocational schools and universities, to an augmented workforce and integrating literacy into AI, critical thinking, and problem-solving methods into the curriculum. To meet the trend, corporations are required to fund an important investment in psychological internal training programs, providing close and available options to meet the changing skill requirements. This will also entail development programs of skills that are uniquely human, not just the technical training of the new AI devices. It is paramount to have a perpetrating culture of learning, experimentation, and psychological safety where the employees can make upgraded desires to learn or land and even learn. Such flexibility guarantees the workforce to be dynamic enough to stay up to date in this fast-paced era of high technological advancement.

Data Fluency and Computational Thinking:

Even for non-technical jobs, there will be an increasing demand for a fundamental understanding of data—how it is collected, analyzed, and utilized by AI systems and the ability to apply computational thinking to problem-solving. This does not imply becoming a data scientist but rather developing practical literacy in data interpretation and logical problem decomposition.

Data Interpretation: The capacity to interpret and infer new knowledge in each data supplied by AI systems challenge the integrity of the data sources and be aware of the possible biases or shortcomings in a data set. This requires some level of statistical literacy to understand correlations, probabilities, and prediction models.

Data Visualization: The capacity to interpret and create effective data visualizations to communicate insights to others, and to understand how AI-generated visualizations inform decision-making.

Computational Thinking: This includes solving large problems by solving subsets of them, identifying patterns, creating algorithms (they may not be implemented), and abstracting things to solve problems in fewer moves. Although traditionally connected with computer science, computational thinking becomes meaningful in many other overlapping areas where AI becomes incorporated into commonly used instruments. In another illustration, a marketing expert could implement computational thinking to set up an A/ B test to determine how to contribute to an AI-optimized advertising campaign by systematically modifying parameters to determine the best method.

Collectively, these new skill sets are uniquely human capabilities, AI literacies, adaptive expertise, and data fluency, which are the foundation of a powerful and resilient workforce in the augmented enterprise. Table 1 outlines a change in the discipline that the workforce needs, comparing the ones that will have reduced requirements along with the ones that will have increased relevance due to the development of Artificial Intelligence.

Table 1. Evolution of Workforce Skills in the Age of AI

Traditional Skills (Decreasing Demand)	Emerging Skills (Increasing Demand)	Description / Rationale
Repetitive Task Execution	Creativity & Innovation	AI excels at routine tasks; humans drive novel ideas, artistic expression, and conceptual breakthroughs.
Basic Data Entry & Processing	Critical Thinking & Complex Problem-Solving	AI handles data analysis: humans interpret ambiguous situations, formulate hypotheses, and make nuanced decisions.
Rule-Based Decision Making	Emotional Intelligence & People Skills	AI follows rules; humans excel at empathy, negotiation, conflict resolution, and building trust.
Manual Information Retrieval	Ethical Reasoning & Judgment	AI provides information; humans navigate moral dilemmas, ensure fairness, and uphold human values.
Basic Computer Operation	AI Literacy & Digital Fluency	Understanding AI's capabilities, limitations, and ethical implications; effective interaction with AI-powered tools.
Static Vocational Skills	Adaptive Expertise & Lifelong Learning	Rapid technological change demands continuous reskilling and upskilling; fostering a growth mindset.
Intuitive/Experience-Based Decisions (without data)	Data Fluency & Computational Thinking	Ability to interpret AI-generated data, understand data flows, and apply logical problem-solving to data-rich environments.

3.3. Organizational Design and Implementation Challenges

The successful establishment of human-AI collaboration in a company is much more than simply an upgrade to technology; it is a significant overhaul to the organization. In this section, care will be taken to explore the prominent issues and challenges pertinent to the case of designing and deploying AI-based solutions by companies, so it is necessary to ensure the ability to frame comprehensive strategic planning.

Change Management and Fostering Acceptance

The process of changing to incorporate use of AI-driven solutions may be filled with obstacles, the largest obstacles being natural inclination of people against change, fear of being laid off and uncertainty about innovative technology. The fundamental point of successful implementation is to have a clear-cut approach to changing management that employs transparent communication with its workers, their active involvement throughout the design and implementation processes, and the ability to describe exactly how the working realities of employees will be changed positively and realistically through the AI augmentation approach.

Firstly, it is important to express sincerity and forthrightness during communication. Leaders should be forthcoming in assuaging the fears of their employees of being replaced by AI, and so they should focus on the role of the former as an augmentation of other resources rather than replacement of human resources. This means sharing a compelling vision about the augmented enterprise where AI expands on human abilities and liberates time that could be used on more exciting and task-addition-value activities. Not dwelling on efficiency as the only benefit of AI solutions, organizations would be better off by pointing out how AI can lead to decreased repetitive tasks, enhance job satisfaction, and expand opportunities of development and growth in skills and career. This change in narrative between the harmful role of AI depriving work to the positive role of AI improving employment is essential in creating trust and eliminating fear.

Secondly, employee participation during the design and implementation issues is important in the development of buying. Employees who are consulted on how the AI systems are going to be implemented into their routines feel important and their practical abilities can drive improvements on the design of the systems, as well as be more inclined to become the advocates of the new tools. The co-creation of this solution may include workshops, pilot programs where employees give feedback and appointing so-called AI champions in individual teams who can assist. As an illustration of this point, given the introduction of an AI-based scheduling tool, there is a good chance that the employees, who will bc utilizing it, will share similar views and ideologies on its implementation after gearing it to their specifications and testing it to its functionality may help acclimatize the tool among them, and thus raise its acceptance much higher, simultaneously revealing the unforeseen problems at a nascent stage.

Thirdly, it is efficient to show the beneficial connotations of augmentation using concrete examples. This may include displaying how AI has helped them minimize the tedious, routine, or duplicative jobs so that the employees can concentrate on the more innovative or strategic parts of their jobs. To take an example, in a data entry department, the positive effects can be visibly demonstrated by how AI automates data entry tasks, allowing employees to do data analysis or account contact at higher levels. Focusing on the ways AI can magnify personal abilities, like bringing access to large volumes of data, or conducting complex computation in a fraction of a second, can give employees a sense of empowerment as well as support the technology value proposition. This strategy will change the perception of AI being an enemy to a delightful companion bringing the aspect of ownership and interest in the workforces.

Ethical AI Deployment: Ensuring Fairness, Transparency, and Accountability

The complex ethical issues related to AI adoption should not be considered only as a compliance issue that the organization must demonstrate but, in fact, building an ethical stance, a trust and responsible innovation. Most importantly, institutions should be more proactive and put in place effective structures in auditing algorithmic biases and ensure that human control is given priority in making critical decisions.

One of them is equity and prejudice. Machine-learning-based AI systems, as well as other systems, are trained based on past data. In case this data already captures the current societal bias (e.g., gender, racial, socioeconomic), the AI system can reproduce this bias in its predictions and even enhance it to create discriminatory implications in such aspects as hiring, loan approval, or even medical diagnoses (Binns, 2018). To reduce bias, organizations should develop well-defined practices aimed at data collection, designing algorithms and evaluating their models. This involves the utilization of a variety of datasets, application of bias detectors, and the frequent auditing of AI system performance against the measure of fairness criteria.

Transparency and explainability are equally vital. AI models with unknown reasoning behind the AI decisions, so-called black box models, can destroy trust and render it hard to detect mistakes or prejudice as well as fix them. Wherever they can, organizations are expected to pursue explainable AI solutions that offer insight into how an AI system produced a certain recommendation or a certain decision. This may entail producing human comprehensible interpretation of complicated AI results or the format of asking the AI to explain its actions. Such transparency is critical in the role of accountability, that is, people can know, question, and eventually accept over AI-aided decisions.

Accountability is a multifaceted ethical aspect. In case a given AI system misbehaves or generates a bad output, what entity is to blame? The AI designer, the implementing institution, the human operator, or a hybrid? Companies should be able to define some layers of accountability so that in the end, human beings are responsible when making decisions with the help of AI, at least in critical areas. This could include setting up AI ethics committees, hiring people with the title of AI ethics officers, and applying ethical judgment over the whole AI development process, i.e. AI design, deployment, and monitoring (Jobin et al., 2019). The efficient implementation of auditing algorithm bias implies not only technical tests but the reviews of different human teams, which will allow one to see that the outputs of AI are consistent with the organizational values and legal regulations. An anticipatory plan like this to the moral use of AI is the key to generating societal faith and holding AI in a humankind-serving way.

Trust and Collaboration

Human-AI collaboration can only be effective when found on trust (Glikson & Woolley, 2020). Unless they establish a level of trust, human workers will choose not to depend on AI systems, and thus, they will underutilize them and become resistant, failing to see the full potential of augmentation. Developing such trust is part of designing AI based on three properties: explainability, reliability and usability, as well as an optimistic organizational climate.

Trustfulness in AI depends on explainability. By providing a human user with the understanding of why an AI system reached a certain conclusion and recommendation or prediction, chances are high that he or she will trust its result. This will entail creating AI interfaces which will display the context, confidence ratings, and reasoning behind what they are doing and not just the raw output. An example is that an AI system advising a medical treatment ought to provide a way to explain evidence and the thinking that led to such advice, enabling the human clinician to cast a critical eye over it.

It is also essential that it be dependable. AI systems should be always able to work according to expectations, not making many mistakes and being unpredictable. This requires stringent testing, intensive monitor activities, and strong error management processes. When AI fails to deliver a reliable performance, the trust of the human collaborators will be lost rapidly, and the human workers will either resort to manual work, or AI recommendations will be completely disregarded.

The design of the AI system should be user-intuitive to make it easy to work with by humans. Ugly or cumbersome interface might be the obstacle to adoption no matter how strong AI is. This includes consumer-friendly concepts of design, the user experience is key, and it must ensure that the AI system fits into current processes. According to Karofsky (2025), the human-centered approach to design is crucial in the implementation of AI and its potential, especially in a complicated domain, such as pharmaceuticals.

In addition, the technical features of designing AI, it is imperative to create a culture of psychological security in the organization (Lee & See, 2004). It implies developing the environment, in which employees are not afraid of presenting concerns, inquiring, and challenging the performance of AI systems without fear of recrimination as well as acknowledging mistakes committed in joint work with AI. Without the ability to mention the mistakes of the AI as well as offer the improvements, the employees will lose the feedback loop, impairing the learning ability of the AI and overall performance among the hybrid group. It is a culture of open communication, error learning, and constant human-AI interaction enhancement, creating a genuinely effective and trusting relationship.

Data Governance and Infrastructure:

The efficacy of AI-partnership development and deployment relies on an effective data structure and elaborate data governance procedures. Unless there is a good amount of reliable, available, and safe information, AI systems will not work, and the potential of human-AI interaction will not be met.

Organizations should put a good emphasis on data quality, and the data, as well as information used to build and train AI, must be accurate, complete, consistent, and relevant. Such inferior quality of data might lead to incorrect AI models, wrong predictions, and biased results, which would adversely affect the accuracy and effectiveness of AI technology. The implementation of the process of data validation, cleansing, and setting clear data standards plays a significant role here.

Data availability should also be considered as an important aspect. For efficient operation, AI systems need a smooth transition to data that is usually scattered throughout the organization. In turn, this will require the establishment of efficient data streams that will provide smooth and effective interaction between humans and automated systems. Data warehouses, data lakes, and API integration are expected to be essential components of such infrastructure. Additionally, human partners need access to posteriori data, as well as understanding the results of AI systems to make the right decisions.

Moreover, data security and privacy are critical issues. Companies must ensure the protection of essential data and comply with strict privacy regulations, including GDPR and CCPA. This will require the implementation of cybersecurity measures, data, and access encryption, as well as regular cybersecurity audits. At the same time, clear data policies should be established, defining the principles of data ownership, usage, and storage. The significance of data pipelines will be discussed in detail in the next chapter, focusing on their ability to facilitate not only the transfer of information but also iterative modeling, deployment, and updating of AI models, as well as providing human employees with adequate information to interact intelligently with AI. Workable policies, about data ownership, data usage and data retention, are also necessitated. The role of properly conceived data pipelines that streamline the data flow and, as a result, allow training, upgrading, and deploying AI models and equip human workers with the required background and knowledge to cooperate with AI intelligently will also be highlighted in the chapter. Unless they have a solid background of data governance and data infrastructure, their vision of advanced human-AI collaboration can only be theoretical.

Leadership and Vision

An excellent leadership style is useful, but it is not only useful but a necessity of introducing the idea of human-AI cooperation and making it an organizational value. The leaders should be able to present their vision in a creative way, invest properly, and foster organizational culture that can accept learning on a permanent basis, experiment, and ethical innovations.

Firstly, leaders should have a sharp vision of how the use of AI will be applied to empowerment and make the workforce stronger, as opposed to eliminating it. This vision must be spread throughout the organization and promoted at multiple hierarchical levels in an enthusiastic way, so that employees can comprehend the strategic reasons behind the usage of AI and how essential they are in the augmented enterprise. It includes going beyond technical terms and defining the advantages in terms of better job results, and greater work output, and the increase of human potential. Wilson (2018) emphasizes the role of leadership in the work reimagination in the era of AI.

Secondly, leaders are required to ensure major investments in training and reskilling workforce. This involves investment in extensive training programs to enhance not only AI literacy but also the above-discussed human skills that are uniquely human. It also implies investing in the required technological basis and supply to facilitate AI integration. Such investments are a sign to the workers that the company is interested in their development and adjustment in the period of AI.

Thirdly, leaders have a role to play in building organizational culture that encourages life-long learning and experimentation as well as moral innovation. This involves:

Building a growth mindset: Facilitating the belief that abilities may be constantly improved as well as learning is an ongoing process.

Learning by experiment: Allowing teams to evaluate new AI tools in a safe environment and try them repeatedly until being successful. This must be coupled with forgiveness for early failures and emphasis on constant development.

Leading with moral innovation: Having ethical concerns at the core of the AI strategy, an open conversation on the topic of AI, and its socio-economic consequences, and giving the employees the power to voice ethical concerns without fear of retribution. This implies incorporation of moral principles in the values and decision-making of the firm.

Finally, visionary leadership is what can turn the potential of human-AI collaboration into a practical reality, navigate the organization through the vicissitudes of technological change, and make sure that AI is used to enhance both business performance and the flourishing of humanity. Table 2 identifies the primary areas of the challenges in Human-AI Collaboration and provides strategic suggestions on how to deal with them adequately.

Table 2. Navigating Challenges and Implementing Strategic Solutions in Human-AI Collaboration

Challenge Area	Key Challenges	Strategic Solutions
Change Management	Employee resistance, fear of job displacement, lack of understanding of AI's benefits.	Transparent communication, employee involvement in design, demonstrating augmentation benefits (e.g., reducing monotonous work, increasing capacities).
Ethical Deployment	Algorithmic bias, lack of transparency, unclear accountability for AI errors, privacy concerns.	Ethical guidelines, bias auditing systems, human oversight into critical decisions, clear responsibility lines, compliance with data privacy regulations (e.g., GDPR).
Trust & Collaboration	Human distrust in AI, AI's lack of explainability, poor user experience, fear of challenging AI output.	Explainable AI (XAI) design, reliable and user-friendly systems, foster psychological safety, encouraging feedback loops.
Data Governance & Infrastructure	Poor data quality, fragmented data sources, data security risks, compliance issues.	Data quality standards, integrated data pipelines, robust cybersecurity, adherence to data privacy rules (e.g., GDPR), clear data ownership policies.
Leadership & Vision	Lack of strategic direction, insufficient investment in training, resistance to cultural change.	Developing a sharp vision for AI augmentation, investing in reskilling/upskilling, fostering a culture of lifelong learning, experimentation, and ethical innovation.

3.4. Case Studies and Empirical Evidence

To demonstrate the practical significance and transformational potential of collaboration between people and artificial intelligence, in this section, I will introduce a diverse selection of case studies and empirical data on it in a broad spectrum of industries. These examples will be used as successful implementations, best practices, and common pitfalls, and the evidence-based body of knowledge about how the augmented enterprise works in practice will be developed.

Healthcare: AI-Assisted Diagnosis, Robotic Surgery, and Administrative Automation

The field of healthcare experiences the strongest partnership between humankind and AI, using AI to more accurately diagnose patients, making surgical procedures more precise, and overseeing administrative tasks more quickly.

AI-Assisted Diagnosis: Medical imaging is becoming one of those applications. Machine learning models, especially in the field of deep learning, are trained with huge medical data in the form of scans (e.g., X-rays, MRIs, CT scans, pathology slides) and can therefore identify a microscopic anomaly that could be missed by the human eye or require significant time to identify. For instance, Google's Deep-

Mind Health has developed AI systems that can detect early signs of eye diseases like diabetic retinopathy with accuracy comparable to, or even exceeding, human experts (Topol, 2019). Likewise, in some cases, AI technologies are being applied to help radiologists detect cancer in mammograms or lung nodules from CT scans. In these types of situations, the role of AI is that of an advanced assistant, highlighting suspect tissues for the human expert to assess, thus minimizing errors, accelerating diagnosis, and allowing human radiologists to focus on complex cases. The ultimate responsibility of diagnosing falls on the human expert, but his/her capabilities are enhanced due to technology, thus leading to better patient outcomes. Further examples of human-AI cooperation in the health sector can be found in Gopalan et al.'s (2024) examination of ethical and cognitive issues associated with the application of technology in medicine.

Robotic Surgery: Although not a type of AI (as it does not employ autonomous decision-making), a robotic surgery unit (such as the da Vinci robotic surgery system) exemplifies the power of human-machine cooperation very well. Surgeons operate robotic manipulators equipped with enhanced dexterity, tremor suppression capabilities, and three-dimensional vision, using them as an extended pair of hands to perform minimally invasive surgery procedures with greater precision, less blood loss, and shorter recovery times than conventional surgeries allow. This is a case where the capabilities of the human surgeon have been augmented by a machine.

Administrative Automation: Healthcare organizations are also increasingly applying AI in non-clinical settings, such as back-office and patient services functions. For instance, AI-powered chatbots and digital assistants answer patients' queries and schedule appointments, thus saving on the administrative staff. AI technologies can also help in automating medical coding and billing, thus increasing revenue cycle management efficiency. Administrative employees are thus empowered to spend time on activities requiring greater attention to details and personal involvement on their behalf.

Finance: Algorithmic Trading, Fraud Detection, and Customer Service Augmentation

Another sphere of operation that is becoming deeply entwined with AI technologies is finance, with algorithmic trading, fraud detection, and customer service becoming major areas where human-AI collaboration occurs in finance companies.

Algorithmic Trading: AI algorithms execute trades based on analysis of market data in milliseconds, which cannot be done by people due to limited capacity to analyze information. However, human traders and quantitative analysts' program and modify these algorithms and set trading parameters and conditions; furthermore, they respond to unexpected events, such as sharp shifts in asset prices, which cannot be predicted by an algorithm. Thus, the task execution in this area is done by the algorithm under scrutiny and control of a person.

Fraud Detection: Real-time fraud detection in the financial sphere relies greatly on AI technologies. Due to its capability to analyze large volumes of transactional data very quickly, AI algorithms can identify anomalous transactions indicating fraud. These transactions are flagged for further investigation by human analysts, who contact customers and initiate any necessary actions. Thus, the process of identifying fraudulent activities resembles human-AI cooperation, where the task of filtering out false positives lies in the realm of technology, while human experts analyze only potential risks.

Customer Service Chatbots Augmenting Human Advisors: In finance, AI-powered chatbots are commonly used to manage customer requests and help (such as informing about account balances and guiding clients through various actions related to accounts). If the customer has a more complicated question or requires human assistance because the query is emotionally sensitive, the conversation with the chatbot is transferred to a human adviser, who already has all the information necessary due to having access to the whole transcript of the discussion with the AI assistant.

Manufacturing and Logistics: Collaborative Robots, AI-Driven Supply Chain Optimization, and Predictive Maintenance

Both manufacturing companies and logisticorganizations companies have seen their processes transformed primarily due to AI. Consequently, many tasks in the two sectors involve collaboration between a machine and a person.

Collaborative Robots (Cobots): Cobots collaborate with humans to conduct operations on the factory floor (Dhanda et al., 2025). For example, in an automotive assembly factory, a cobot may lift a component that is too heavy for a person to carry to the next stage of the assembly process. Cobots can work with fragile electronic parts in a uniform way in electronics assembly. Such co-bot partnership increases efficiency, ensures safety of workers by performing hazardous or ergonomically difficult job, and enables human employees to be involved into more skilled work such as programing, quality assurance, or trouble shooting on assembly line.

AI-Driven Supply Chain Optimization: AI algorithms provide insight into real-time information on the entire supply chain including weather, geopolitics, consumer trends, inventory, transportation schedule to optimize routes, demand variations and threats of disruption. As an instance, AI could recommend ideal inventory quantities to eliminate wastage but to address demand or it may redirect shipment to evade congestion. In the supply chain industry, the strategic decision-making process, negotiations with suppliers, relationship management processes are all guided by these AI-enlightenment by human supply chain managers because it provides data-minded foresight and efficiency.

Predictive Maintenance: Machine sensors can capture vibration, temperature, and performance readings with AI. Based on this data, AI algorithms are used to determine the propensity of a given machine to fail so that before any breakdown occurs, certain maintenance can be done. Therefore, there is less downtime and increased life span of the equipment since this reduces costly downtime. Human technicians can make appointments and order required parts based on these AI predictions, shifting their role within the business and making them more initiative-taking with asset maintenance.

Education: AI-Powered Personalized Learning Platforms and Intelligent Tutoring Systems

Artificial intelligence has already started changing education since it offers the chance for more personalized and individualized experiences.

AI-Powered Personalized Learning Platforms: This refers to the use of technology such as Khan Academy Kids or DreamBox Learning. Such AI-based systems analyze students' abilities, identify their strengths and weaknesses, and make suggestions about exercises and learning. Students get to focus on their weaker areas and learn at a comfortable speed. Teachers use this system to monitor students' progress and detect those who are lagging. AI allows the teachers to pay close attention to individual students with diverse capabilities, enabling them to concentrate on advanced skills such as mentorship and coaching for critical thinking.

Intelligent Tutoring Systems (ITS): ITSs give one-on-one tutoring experience. It provides feedback instantly and helps to understand what should be done differently to solve a problem. ITSSs can perform the tasks that involve routine instructions; however, it leaves more time for other tasks for humans such as fostering creativity and critical discussion that machines cannot do.

Creative Industries: AI Tools Assisting in Content Generation, Enhancing Human Creativity

AI Tools Assisting in Content Generation, Enhancing Human Creativity Even in traditionally thought-to-be-only-human domains such as the creative industries, AI has shown to be a great helper to increase productivity and enhance creativity.

AI Tools Assisting in Content Generation: Such AI models as OpenAI's DALL-E 3 or Midjourney create images from text prompts. At the same time, AI models like Google's Gemini or OpenAI's GPT-4 can create text content, write poems, and create pieces of code. There are also tools that help composers generate melodies, harmonies, and backing tracks in music. The purpose of this type of AI in the creative industry is not to substitute for the artist, musician, or writer; instead, it assists the person in doing his/her job faster and better. The human remains a central figure in the creative process – s/he becomes its mastermind and director. For example, a graphic designer uses AI to produce several logo ideas in seconds, after which he/she edits the logos in any desirable way. Similarly, a writer can benefit from brainstorming plot ideas and generating texts with AI; then, s/he will rewrite and edit them in accordance with his/her vision of the story. Karofsky (2025) notes that human-centered design is necessary to unlock the full potential of AI, something extremely relevant in the creative industries.

All above-presented case studies demonstrate how Human-AI Collaboration can be implemented successfully. They serve as a perfect illustration of positive impacts on businesses including increased efficiency, higher accuracy, improved safety conditions, and overall satisfaction among employees. They show how collaboration between AI and humans can benefit people and allow them to work better, smarter, and faster. At the same time, they serve to highlight some pitfalls that organizations may encounter during AI implementation such as lack of ethical consideration and ineffective change management. Realistic applications of AI in different industries along with a synergistic combination of human and AI roles are given in Table 3.

Table 3. Real-World Examples of Human-AI Collaboration Across Industries

Industry	AI Application	Human Role (Augmented)	AI Role (Collaborative)	Key Benefit
Healthcare	AI-assisted Diagnosis (e.g., medical imaging)	Radiologists, Pathologists (final diagnosis, complex interpretation, patient communication)	Pattern recognition, anomaly detection, flagging suspicious areas, rapid analysis of large datasets.	Increased diagnostic accuracy, faster turnaround times, reduced human error.
Finance	Fraud Detection	Fraud Analysts (investigation, customer contact, legal action)	Real-time anomaly detection, pattern identification in transactions, risk scoring.	Reduced financial losses, enhanced security, more efficient investigations.
Manufacturing	Collaborative Robots (Cobots)	Assembly Workers, Technicians (precision tasks, quality control, problem-solving, programming)	Heavy lifting, repetitive tasks, precision assembly, ergonomic assistance.	Increased productivity, improved worker safety, enhanced product quality.
Education	Personalized Learning Platforms	Educators (mentoring, complex instruction, socio-emotional development, individual intervention)	Adaptive content delivery, progress tracking, tailored feedback, identifying learning gaps.	Improved student engagement, customized learning paths, enhanced learning outcomes.
Creative Industries	AI Content Generation (e.g., images, text, music)	Artists, Writers, Musicians (conceptualization, refinement, artistic vision, emotional depth, curation)	Rapid idea generation, style transfer, preliminary drafting, variation creation.	Accelerated creative process, expanded artistic possibilities, increased efficiency in production.

4. CONTRIBUTION TO THE BOOK

This chapter, " The Human-AI Collaboration Imperative: Redefining Workflows and Skills in the Augmented Enterprise" contributes to several essential goals of the book, "AI Impacts on Labor: Implications for Business and Society."

The first is that it describes how the capabilities of AI complement those of man, which alters work and changes jobs, as well as, defining new opportunities, shifting beyond replacing jobs to comprehending work and job quality.

Second, the chapter offers practical ideas of how the business can reorganize and restructure to incorporate AI. It focuses on improving workflow, designing organizations, and considering strategies providing realistic examples using case studies.

Additionally, it focuses on establishing fundamental human capabilities such as creativity, thinking, and emotional intelligence and suggests a human-centric AI approach, which puts human values and welfare in the center. This approach is the facilitation of responsible development of AI.

Lastly, the chapter has substantial recommendations to policymakers, corporate administrators, and educators and instructs them on how to respond to the emerging nature of work. It can be used as a detailed guide of how to travel through the augmented enterprise and achieve synergetic human attitudes to AI.

5. CONCLUSION

The historical development of the exploration of the consequences of Artificial Intelligence on work has reached a critical turn, which ended in the acceptance of the necessity of human-AI partnership. This transition marks a paradigm change with the early as well as pulpit-like anticipations of zero-sum game between human labor force and self-governing robots. The future of work, on the contrary, is marked by the rise of symbiotic unions where the strength and complementary capabilities of both human and artificial intelligence can come into play in full. It is this synergistic partnership that holds the promise of harnessing level of productivity and innovation and hence human flourishing that is unprecedented.

As thoroughly discussed in this chapter, to succeed in the blossomed era of AI, a dynamic, all-dimensional strategy is required. One is that it requires an embracement of fundamental reinvention of current workflows. It includes not just automation of tasks done but also a comprehensive redesign of their work patterns, with routine and repetitive tasks involving mostly data being outsourced to AI, and human resources diverted to a more valuable work that requires human ingenuity, critical thinking, and thoughtfulness towards various problems. The objective is to make the overall system as efficient and effective as possible, and this can be achieved by smoothly blending the role of human and AI and using them together.

Also, it needs a wide and flexible ecosystem of skills in the workforce formed with a deliberate mindset. This ecosystem should be focused on developing abilities that only a human can form, namely, emotional intelligence, moral metrics, and issues of interpersonal complexity, which are impossible to emulate in AI. On the other hand, AI literacy and digital fluency are needed for universal applications since all employees are required to possess sufficient competence to deal with AI technologies responsibly and competently. In this way, a dual approach ensures people remain pivotal and empowering components of the augmented workspace.

Finally, and above all, organizational structures and processes need to be carefully and deliberately organized and adapted to foster trust, ethical responsibility, and learning mentality. Such organizational efforts include, among others, establishing governance in terms of robustness, explainability, and reliable AI system, creating psychologically safe spaces in which workers feel at ease cooperating and challenging AI technologies. In this context, the main actors in realizing the future vision of the workplace include visionary leaders, investment in human capital, and promotion of ethical innovation mindset.

The capability of integrating human and artificial intelligence will not simply remain as an organizational competitive advantage eventually but become its inherent characteristic of being sustainable, innovative, and ethically responsible firm. Organizational success will become achievable only through those organizations that actively promote the integration as the means of achieving complementarity of man and machine and thus benefiting from both. By doing so, organizations will gain competitive advantages not only in economic prosperity but also in qualitatively high levels of employment. Thus, the future will be not the war between humans and machines but cooperation.

REFERENCES

Acemoglu, D., & Restrepo, P. (2019). Automation and new tasks: How technology displaces and reinstates labor. *The Journal of Economic Perspectives*, *33*(2), 3–30. DOI: 10.1257/jep.33.2.3

Acemoglu, D., & Restrepo, P. (2020). Robots and jobs: Evidence from US labor markets. *Journal of Political Economy*, *128*(6), 2188–2244. DOI: 10.1086/705716

Autor, D., Mindell, D. A., & Reynolds, E. B. (2022). *The work of the future: Building better jobs in an age of intelligent machines*. The MIT Press. DOI: 10.7551/mitpress/14109.001.0001

Autor, D. H. (2015). Why are there still so many jobs? The history and future of workplace automation. *The Journal of Economic Perspectives*, *29*(3), 3–30. DOI: 10.1257/jep.29.3.3

Autor, D. H. (2019). Work of the past, work of the future. *AEA Papers and Proceedings. American Economic Association*, *109*, 1–32. DOI: 10.1257/pandp.20191110

Binns, R. (2018). Fairness in machine learning: Lessons from political philosophy. *Proceedings of Machine Learning Research, 81*, 149–159. https://proceedings.mlr.press/v81/binns18a.html

Brynjolfsson, E., & McAfee, A. (2014). *The second machine age: Work, progress, and prosperity in a time of brilliant technologies*. W. W. Norton & Company. https://wwnorton.com/books/the-second-machine-age/

Davenport, T. H., & Kirby, J. (2016). *Only humans need apply: Winners and losers in the age of smart machines*. HarperBusiness. https://www.harpercollins.com/products/only-humans-need-apply-thomas-h-davenportjulia-kirby

Dhanda, M., Rogers, B. A., Hall, S., Dekoninck, E., & Dhokia, V. (2025). Reviewing human-robot collaboration in manufacturing: Opportunities and challenges in the context of Industry 5.0. *Robotics and Computer-integrated Manufacturing*, *93*, 102937. DOI: 10.1016/j.rcim.2024.102937

Frey, C. B., & Osborne, M. A. (2017). The future of employment: How susceptible are jobs to computerisation? *Technological Forecasting and Social Change, 114*, 254–280. DOI: 10.1016/j.techfore.2016.08.019

Glikson, E., & Woolley, A. W. (2020). Human trust in artificial intelligence: Review of empirical research. *The Academy of Management Annals*, *14*(2), 627–660. DOI: 10.5465/annals.2018.0057

Gopalan, P. D., Pienaar, M., & Brokensha, S. I. (2024). Deep medicine: Navigating the intersection of technology, cognition and ethics in the digital age of medicine. *South African Medical Journal, 114*(3), e1520. https://pubmed.ncbi.nlm.nih.gov/38304632/ PMID: 38304632

Hutchins, E. (1995). *Cognition in the wild.* The MIT Press. DOI: 10.7551/mitpress/1881.001.0001

Jarrahi, M. H. (2018). Artificial intelligence and the future of work: Human-AI symbiosis in organizational decision making. *Business Horizons, 61*(4), 577–586. DOI: 10.1016/j.bushor.2018.03.007

Jobin, A., Ienca, M., & Vayena, E. (2019). The global landscape of AI ethics guidelines. *Nature Machine Intelligence, 1*(9), 389–399. DOI: 10.1038/s42256-019-0088-2

Karofsky, E. (2025). Beyond the molecule: How human-centered design unlocks AI's promise in pharma. *Applied Clinical Trials.* https://www.appliedclinicaltrialsonline.com/view/human-centered-ai-pharma

Lee, J. D., & See, K. A. (2004). Trust in automation: Designing for appropriate reliance. *Human Factors, 46*(1), 50–80. DOI: 10.1518/hfes.46.1.50.30392 PMID: 15151155

Lund, S., Madgavkar, A., Manyika, J., Smit, S., Ellingrud, K., & Robinson, O. (2021). *The future of work after COVID-19.* McKinsey Global Institute. https://www.mckinsey.com/featured-insights/future-of-work/the-future-of-work-after-covid-19

Manyika, J., Lund, S., Chui, M., Bughin, J., Woetzel, J., Batra, P., Ko, R., & Sanghvi, S. (2017). *Jobs lost, jobs gained: What the future of work will mean for jobs, skills, and wages.* McKinsey Global Institute. https://www.mckinsey.com/featured-insights/future-of-work/jobs-lost-jobs-gained-what-the-future-of-work-will-mean-for-jobs-skills-and-wages

Nguyen, T., & Elbanna, A. (2025). Understanding human-AI augmentation in the workplace: A review and a future research agenda. *Information Systems Frontiers.* Advance online publication. DOI: 10.1007/s10796-025-10591-5

Pasmore, W. A., & Sherwood, J. J. (Eds.). (1978). *Sociotechnical systems: A sourcebook.* University Associates.

Shneiderman, B. (2020). Human-centered AI: Reliable, safe & trustworthy. *International Journal of Human-Computer Interaction, 36*(10), 919–922. DOI: 10.1080/10447318.2020.1741118

Topol, E. J. (2019). *Deep medicine: How artificial intelligence can make healthcare human again*. Basic Books. https://www.basicbooks.com/titles/eric-topol/deep-medicine/9781541644632

Wilson, H. J. (2018). *Human + machine: Reimagining work in the age of AI*. Harvard Business Review Press.

World Economic Forum. (2023). *The future of jobs report 2023*. World Economic Forum. https://www.weforum.org/publications/the-future-of-jobs-report-2023/

KEY TERMS AND DEFINITIONS

Artificial Intelligence (AI): The simulation of human intelligence processes by machines, especially computer systems. These processes include learning (the acquisition of information and rules for using the information), reasoning (using rules to reach approximate or definite conclusions), and self-correction.

Human-AI Collaboration (HAC): A synergistic partnership between humans and AI systems where they work together towards a shared objective, combining their complementary capabilities to achieve outcomes that neither could achieve effectively alone (Jarrahi, 2018).

Augmented Enterprise: An organizational environment where human intelligence and capabilities are enhanced and amplified by the integration of AI technologies, leading to improved productivity, efficiency, and innovation.

Automation: The use of technology to perform tasks with minimal human intervention. In the context of AI, it often refers to AI systems taking over routine, repetitive, or data-intensive tasks.

Augmentation: The process by which AI enhances or extends human capabilities, rather than replacing them. AI systems act as tools or assistants to improve human performance, decision-making, and creativity.

Algorithmic Management: The use of algorithms and AI systems to manage and oversee human labor, often seen in gig economy platforms for task allocation, performance monitoring, and incentive structures.

Socio-technical Systems Theory: A theoretical framework that analyzes the complex interaction between the technological components and the human social systems within an organization, emphasizing the need to optimize both for overall effectiveness.

Distributed Cognition Theory: A theory that explains how cognitive processes and knowledge are shared and processed not only among individuals but also across tools, artifacts, and social interactions, including those involving AI agents.

Explainable AI (XAI): AI systems designed to provide insights into their reasoning, logic, and decision-making processes in a way that is understandable to humans, addressing the "black box" problem of complex AI models.

Algorithmic Bias: Systematic and repeatable errors in a computer system that create unfair outcomes, such as favoring one arbitrary group of users over others. This often arises from biased data used to train AI models.

Data Governance: The overall management of the availability, usability, integrity, and security of data used within an organization, including policies and procedures for data quality, access, and privacy.

Data Pipelines: A series of processes that move raw data from various sources through different stages of transformation and validation, making it ready for analysis, storage, or use by AI systems.

Collaborative Robots (Cobots): Robots are designed to work safely and interactively in shared workspaces with human workers, assisting with tasks that may be repetitive, physically demanding, or require high precision.

Predictive Maintenance: The use of data analytics and AI to predict when equipment failure might occur, allowing for proactive maintenance interventions to prevent costly downtime and extend asset lifespan.

Digital Fluency: The ability to effectively interact with and leverage digital tools, platforms, and data ecosystems, extending beyond basic computer proficiency to encompass a deeper understanding of digital environments and AI-powered applications.

Chapter 8
More than Automation: AI as a Shaper of Employee Mindsets and Capabilities

Rachna Rana
Ludhiana Group of Colleges, Ludhiana, India

Pankaj Bhambri
http://orcid.org/0000-0003-4437-4103
Guru Nanak Dev Engineering College, Ludhiana, India

ABSTRACT

Artificial intelligence (AI) in workplaces extends well beyond routine task automation: it actively reshapes employees' mindsets, roles, and capacity-development pathways. Rather than only substituting labor, AI systems reconfigure managerial authority, create new skill expectations, and change how workers interpret their obligations and potential within organizations. Algorithmic management, for example, reframes decision authority and information flows, prompting workers to develop algorithmic literacies and often producing mixed responses of engagement, compliance, or resistance. The Concurrent large-scale evidence shows widespread deployment of algorithmic tools—used to instruct, monitor, and evaluate—bringing benefits (consistency, efficiency) but also risks such as intensification, surveillance stress, and trust concerns that influence worker attitudes and identities.

INTRODUCTION OF MORE THAN AUTOMATION: AI AS A SHAPER OF EMPLOYEE MINDSETS AND CAPABILITIES

Over the past decade, the proliferation of artificial intelligence (AI) in organizational settings has triggered a shift in how we understand work. Rather than being

DOI: 10.4018/979-8-3373-5816-1.ch008

merely a tool for automating routine tasks, AI increasingly functions as a catalyst transforming employees' mindsets, their sense of agency, capacities, and roles in the workplace. What started broadly as automating repetitive and well-A structured tasks has evolved by 2025 into more nuanced reshaping of skills, identity, relationships with work, and professional development trajectories. This introduction presents how recent scholarship (2015-2025) frames AI as more than automation: as a shaper of employee mindsets and capabilities. To do this, it examines first the changing nature of work with AI; second, how employee attitudes, identity, and psychological contracts are being renegotiated; third, how competencies, skills, and capability building are being redefined; fourth, what conditions moderate whether AI has empowering or deleterious effects; and finally, implications for organizations, HR practices, and future research.

Changing nature of work: from automation to augmentation

Historically, organizational adoption of computerization and automation focused on efficiency, cost reduction, and speed. But with AI—especially recent advances in machine learning, generative AI, predictive modeling—there is increasing emphasis on augmentation: enhancing human performance, enabling new forms of work rather than simply replacing people. Systematic reviews of industry case studies from sectors such as software, education, legal, mining, media, and accounting show that AI does streamline workflows and automate repetitive tasks; but more importantly, these same studies highlight that AI changes the tasks, gives employees exposure to more complex, non-routine tasks, and thus demands different kinds of competencies. For example, an OECD report related to job quality and inclusiveness shows that with AI adoption, many workers report increased autonomy over their tasks—greater control over how they sequence work, over task content—not just performing tasks more quickly. This shift from rote automation toward decision augmentation, task variety, and autonomy is central to understanding how AI shapes mindsets: employees are no longer passive executors; they increasingly need to collaborate with, supervise, interpret, and correct AI outputs.

Employee mindsets, identities, and psychological contracts

As the nature of work changes, so too do employees' beliefs, attitudes, and sense of identity. One major dimension is the psychological contract: the unspoken expectations between employer and employee about mutual obligations. Research shows that AI adoption alters the psychological contract in subtle but important ways. In a study of around 230+ workers, AI adoption weakened traditional relational contracts (characterized by trust, loyalty, intrinsic motivation) and increased what researchers' term "alienation AI" contracts, where employees feel more distanced, disconnected, and uncertain about reciprocity and values in their relationship with the employer. Relatedly, employees' awareness of AI—what it is, how it functions, its transparency, limitations—has emerged as crucial in shaping responses. Studies find that AI awareness moderates the effect of AI use on important attitudinal outcomes: mindful awareness of AI's affordances, limits and ethical issues helps reduce perceived threat, supports trust, and shapes more adaptive behaviors. Employees who are more aware of AI are more likely to engage in job crafting (modifying tasks and relationships to fit their strengths and preferences) and to feel more committed to career paths that include AI-mediated work. Another facet is identity and mindset: studies about innovation behavior (e.g. in China manufacturing enterprises) show AI usage positively links with innovation, mediated by self-efficacy: when employees believe in their ability to successfully use AI tools, their creative efforts increase. Openness to experience (a personality trait) and job complexity further strengthen this link. This suggests employees' beliefs about themselves (mindset), their willingness to engage with complexity and change (growth mindset), are central to how AI shapes outcomes.

Capability building: skills, learning, and role redefinition

Alongside mindset shifts, a clear body of research demonstrates that AI is reshaping what capabilities are valued, how people learn, and what roles look like. One recent paper on generative AI adoption (2025) shows that roles which depend on generative AI tools now often require significantly higher cognitive skills (such as analytical reasoning, critical thinking), and social skills (communication, collaboration) than before; not just technical tool use, but meta-skills, soft skills. A Systematic Review of Skill Transformation in the Industry," researchers map how across many sectors, skill demands are shifting. Routine, repetitive, low-cognitive tasks are declining; tasks requiring adaptation, complex decision-making, interpretation, ethical judgment are rising (Bhambri, 2025b). Training and employee development are also being transformed. AI is used to personalize learning: adapting training modules to individual employees' skill gaps, delivering real-time feedback on performance, predictive analytics identifying future needed skills. HRM research shows that organizations deploying intelligent learning management systems and AI-driven coaching experience improvements in employee engagement and learning efficacy when done with care.

AI tools are enhancing early phases of employment, helping new hires adapt, accelerating their learning, and shifting what "capability" early in the employee journey even means. There is evidence that AI builds "artificial capabilities" (in the sense of competencies mediated by AI systems) that mediate the relationship between AI use and how quickly new employees integrate.

Moderating factors: when ai empowers vs when it disempowers

Not all employees experience AI as a positive shaper. Research identifies several boundary conditions or moderators that amplify or mitigate effects. Key among these are job complexity, personality traits (especially openness to experience), AI awareness, transparency and trust, managerial / organizational practices (training, participation, support), and the extent of employee involvement in AI rollout.

Job complexity: in more complex jobs—those with variety, significance, autonomy—AI use tends to correspond with more positive outcomes: greater innovation, increased sense of challenge, mindset shifts. When jobs are simple, rigid, with little autonomy, AI may be perceived as a threat (e.g. of replacement, surveillance), reducing self-efficacy, satisfaction.

Personality traits: openness to experience allows employees to explore AI affordances, experiment, adapt. Those less comfortable with change may resist or feel stressed. Studies show openness interacts with AI usage to increase innovation behavior.

AI awareness and transparency: when employees understand how AI decisions are made (or at least what the system is doing), when AI is explicable and accountable, trust and engagement are higher, fears lower. Lack of transparency tends to amplify negative perceptions: job insecurity, distrust, fairness concerns.

Organizational practices: The way AI is introduced—whether employees participate in design, whether they are trained, whether feedback loops exist, whether ethical policies and governance are in place—matters a great deal. For example, the OECD's surveys suggest that training and worker consultation are associated with better working outcomes (Bhambri, 2025a).

Implications for organizations, hr, and culture

Given these transformations, organizations must reconsider how they manage people, design roles, shape culture, and invest in capabilities. First, HR functions need to shift from managing "automation risk" to fostering "augmentation opportunity." That means designing learning paths, job redesign, role hybridization (human + AI roles), and emphasizing key soft-skills as equally important as technical AI usage. Second, organizations need to cultivate psychological safety, transparency, and trust in AI implementation. Communicating clearly about AI's functions and limitations, involving employees in decision-making about AI tools, allowing feedback and corrections, embedding fairness, accountability and ethical oversight are crucial to avoid alienation or resistance. Third, culture must embrace adaptability, continuous learning (growth mindset), experimentation and reflection (Singh et al., 2010). Employees need support to shift identity: from task performer to partner or collaborator with intelligent systems. This involves not just training, but mindset work: helping employees see AI not as a threat but as a resource to magnify their capabilities. Fourth, capabilities development must be holistic: combining technical skills (data literacy, tool use) with cognitive skills (critical thinking, creativity, problem solving), social skills (communication, collaboration), ethical literacy, AI oversight skills (evaluating AI outputs, recognizing bias). Again, customization matters: different roles, sectors, and individuals will need different mixes. Finally, leadership and policy matter: leadership must set tone, invest in infrastructure and governance; policies at organizational and societal level will shape whether AI becomes a force for inclusion, upskilling, human development or exacerbates inequality, deskilling, distrust. Governments and institutions need to monitor job quality, inclusiveness, worker well-being, and ensure that AI adoption is accompanied by protections, upskilling support, regulatory frameworks. OECD's Employment Outlook, for example, draws attention to the need to ensure AI adoption improves working conditions, not only performance. OECD+1

Gaps and future directions

While recent work has advanced our understanding, some gaps remain. Most empirical studies are cross-sectional or survey-based; more longitudinal and experimental research is needed to trace how mindsets and capabilities evolve over time under AI influence (Bhambri & Singh, 2008). Also, more research is needed in diverse sectors (manufacturing, healthcare, public sector) and across geographies, especially in less-represented economies, to see how culture, regulation, and institutional capacity mediate the effects.

Another area is the unintended consequences: what happens to creativity, critical thinking, autonomy over longer periods? Over-reliance on AI might lead to skill erosion in certain domains, or reduce mental challenge (Bhambri & Thapar, 2009). Research into well-being, work-life balance, stress, mental health in AI-intensive workplaces is growing but still thin. Similarly, ethical issues—bias in algorithms, fairness, privacy—can affect trust, identity, and fairness perceptions.

From 2015-2025, scholarship increasingly treats AI in the workplace not just as automation technology, but as a shaping force for employee mindsets and capabilities. The evidence suggests that AI modifies what employees believe about themselves, what they expect from work, what skills are valued, how roles are designed. Whether this is positive or negative depends heavily on how AI is deployed: with transparency, training, employee participation, and alignment with human values. For organizations to reap the benefits, they must purposefully shape AI adoption to augment human potential, not just replace human labour.

ALGORITHMIC MANAGEMENT

Meaning and Definition

Algorithmic management refers to the delegation of traditional managerial functions—such as task assignment, performance evaluation, and behavioral monitoring—to AI and data-driven algorithms (Jarrahi et al., 2022). It represents a new paradigm in organizational control, where decisions are automated through algorithms that process vast quantities of data to guide, assess, and optimize employee activities (Lee et al., 2021). Unlike conventional management, which relies on human supervisors' judgment, algorithmic systems use predictive analytics, machine learning, and real-time feedback loops to manage workflow and productivity (Kellogg et al., 2020). Thus, algorithmic management redefines the managerial role, transforming the relationship between workers and their employers into one mediated by digital systems. In essence, it's the use of algorithmic logic to coordinate labour and distribute authority within organizations, particularly in sectors like gig work, logistics, customer service, and even knowledge industries.

Types of Algorithmic Management

There are several typologies of algorithmic management, commonly classified based on their operational functions.

Task Allocation Algorithms assign work automatically based on factors such as location, skill, or performance data, as seen in platforms like Uber and Amazon (Rosenblat & Stark, 2016).

Performance Monitoring Algorithms track productivity metrics, monitor behavioral data, and offer feedback or impose penalties through automated systems (Möhlmann et al., 2021).

Scheduling and Optimization Algorithms manage shift planning, workforce scheduling, and resource allocation to maximize efficiency and minimize downtime (Mateescu & Nguyen, 2019).

Decision-Support Algorithms assist human managers in making decisions by analyzing employee data, recommending promotions, or flagging potential risks (Newlands et al., 2022).

Behavioral Nudging Algorithms, a recent development, influence employee decisions and attitudes subtly using behavioral science principles (Yeung, 2018).

Each type demonstrates how algorithmic management extends managerial reach while redefining what constitutes "management" in digital workplaces.

Approaches to Algorithmic Management

Scholars identify multiple approaches organizations adopt to implement algorithmic management systems (Singh et al., 2006). The technocratic approach emphasizes efficiency, precision, and performance optimization—viewing algorithms as neutral tools for maximizing productivity (Bodie et al., 2020). In contrast, the socio-technical approach recognizes the interdependence of technology and human systems, advocating for participatory design and human oversight to prevent bias and alienation (Beer, 2017). The ethical governance approach integrates fairness, transparency, and accountability principles into algorithmic decision-making to ensure compliance with laws and moral standards (Cath, 2018). The augmentative approach prioritizes human–AI collaboration: instead of replacing human managers, algorithms serve as advisory tools enhancing managerial insight and objectivity (Duggan et al., 2020). The adaptive approach focuses on continuous feedback loops where systems learn from employee data while employees adapt to algorithmic norms, forming a dynamic management ecosystem (Rai, 2020). These approaches collectively reveal that algorithmic management is not a monolithic process but a flexible system shaped by organizational culture, ethical considerations, and human–AI interaction models.

Problems Associated with Algorithmic Management

Despite its efficiency, algorithmic management raises significant ethical, psychological, and organizational challenges (Singh & Bhambri, 2007). First, opacity and lack of transparency—often called the "black-box problem"—prevent employees from understanding how decisions about their performance or pay are made (Burrell, 2016). This lack of explainability leads to distrust and perceptions of unfairness (Lee et al., 2021). Second, data privacy and surveillance issues arise as algorithms continuously collect behavioral and biometric data, creating a sense of being constantly monitored (Newlands, 2022). This "digital panopticon" can erode autonomy, increase stress, and lead to self-censorship (Moore et al., 2018). Third, algorithmic management often reduces human discretion and empathy, replacing relational management with impersonal computational logic (Duggan et al., 2020). This shift risks dehumanizing employees, especially in sectors like gig work, where communication with human managers is minimal.Fourth, bias and discrimination embedded in data sets can produce unfair outcomes, amplifying inequalities across gender, race, or age groups (Binns, 2018). Finally, psychological contract violations occur when employees perceive algorithmic systems as violating expectations of fairness and reciprocity, leading to reduced motivation and organizational commitment (Tomprou & Lee, 2022).

Solutions and Mitigation Strategies

Addressing these challenges requires a multidimensional strategy involving technological, managerial, and regulatory interventions.

. *Transparency and Explainability:* Organizations should implement explainable AI (XAI) frameworks that allow employees to understand the reasoning behind algorithmic decisions (Rai, 2020). Regular audits, "algorithmic transparency reports," and communication protocols can enhance trust.

Human Oversight and Hybrid Management: Combining human judgment with algorithmic efficiency ensures that empathy and contextual understanding remain integral to managerial processes (Jarrahi et al., 2022). Hybrid models prevent the excessive automation of sensitive HR functions.

Ethical Design and Governance: Embedding ethical AI principles—such as fairness, accountability, and human-centered design—can reduce bias and discrimination (Cath, 2018). Establishing AI ethics boards or algorithmic review committees ensures ongoing monitoring.

Data Protection and Privacy Measures: Strict data governance policies, anonymization techniques, and compliance with privacy laws (e.g., GDPR) protect employees' personal data from misuse (Mateescu & Nguyen, 2019).

Employee Involvement and Participatory Design: Involving employees in the design and implementation phases helps align algorithmic systems with user needs, increasing acceptance and fairness perceptions (Newlands et al., 2022).

Regulatory Oversight: Governments and labor organizations can enforce algorithmic accountability through labor rights frameworks, requiring audits, disclosure, and fairness assessments for AI-driven management systems (OECD, 2023).

When combined, these solutions support a more responsible, human-centered form of algorithmic management that enhances performance while safeguarding worker dignity and agency.

EMPLOYEE MINDSET TRANSFORMATION

Meaning and Definition

Employee mindset transformation refers to the fundamental shift in workers' beliefs, attitudes, values, and cognitive orientations in response to technological, organizational, or cultural change (Dweck, 2016). In the era of AI, it describes how employees modify their perceptions about work, learning, and self-efficacy as they interact with intelligent systems and automation technologies (Ransbotham et al., 2021). It is not merely an adaptation to tools but a deep cognitive restructuring that influences motivation, creativity, and collaboration. Traditionally, "mindset" has been understood as an individual's implicit theory about their ability to learn and grow (Dweck, 2006). However, in the modern AI-augmented workplace, mindset transformation encompasses collective and organizational dimensions—employees' attitudes toward AI integration, data-driven decision-making, and continuous learning (Kane et al., 2019).

Employee mindset transformation is therefore a dynamic, continuous process that aligns human potential with technological evolution. It enables workers to shift from fear or resistance toward AI to embracing innovation, experimentation, and adaptability. In short, it is the psychological and behavioral evolution that allows employees to coexist and collaborate effectively with intelligent systems.

Types of Employee Mindsets in the AI Era

Several scholars distinguish different types of mindsets relevant to the AI-driven workplace.

Fixed vs. Growth Mindset:

A fixed mindset views abilities as static, whereas a growth mindset sees them as improvable through effort and feedback (Dweck, 2016). Employees with a growth mindset tend to adapt more successfully to AI adoption, perceiving technological disruption as an opportunity for learning rather than a threat (Zhang & Leidner, 2023).

Digital Mindset: This mindset reflects openness to leveraging digital tools, understanding data, and integrating technology in everyday problem-solving (Kane et al., 2019). A digital mindset combines curiosity, agility, and collaboration across humans and AI.

Innovative Mindset: Associated with creativity, experimentation, and tolerance for ambiguity, this mindset enables employees to envision new uses for AI technologies and contribute to organizational innovation (Nonaka & Takeuchi, 2021).

Adaptive or Learning Mindset: This emphasizes continuous learning, feedback-seeking, and proactive reskilling, aligning personal development with AI-driven changes in the workplace (Bessen, 2019).

Ethical and Responsible Mindset: This mindset concerns moral sensitivity toward fairness, transparency, and accountability in AI use (Cath, 2018). Employees with an ethical mindset help organizations align AI implementation with human values.

These types illustrate that mindset transformation under AI is multidimensional—encompassing learning, ethics, adaptability, and technological literacy.

Approaches to Fostering Mindset Transformation

Organizations can facilitate employee mindset transformation through various structured approaches:

Growth-Oriented Learning Culture: Establishing a culture that values experimentation and psychological safety encourages employees to learn from AI systems without fear of failure (Edmondson, 2019). Companies like Microsoft and IBM have successfully fostered "learn-it-all" mindsets to adapt to AI disruption (Kane et al., 2019).

Reskilling and Upskilling Initiatives: Continuous training programs that combine technical skills (AI literacy, data analysis) with soft skills (critical thinking, communication) enable employees to see AI as a complement to their abilities rather than a threat (Bessen, 2019).

Human–AI Collaboration Programs: Pairing workers with AI tools and mentoring them to interpret AI outputs fosters trust and competence, reshaping employees' attitudes toward algorithmic decision-making (Jarrahi et al., 2022).

Leadership Communication and Vision: Transformational leadership, which articulates a positive vision for AI integration, helps employees align their mindset with organizational strategy and purpose (Bass & Riggio, 2019).

Behavioral Nudges and Design Thinking: Using behavioral insights to frame AI as an empowerment tool rather than a replacement encourages proactive engagement and curiosity (Thaler & Sunstein, 2008).

Through these approaches, organizations can gradually reprogram resistance into readiness—cultivating a mindset that thrives in a hybrid human–machine environment.

Problems and Challenges in Mindset Transformation

Despite its importance, employee mindset transformation faces multiple obstacles.

Resistance to Change is perhaps the most significant (Bhambri & Thapar, 2009). Many employees experience anxiety and fear of job displacement due to automation (Brynjolfsson & McAfee, 2017). This "technostress" results from uncertainty about AI's capabilities, job security, and fairness (Tarafdar et al., 2019). Lack of Awareness and AI Literacy also hampers transformation. Employees who do not understand AI systems' logic or benefits are more likely to distrust or reject them (Ransbotham et al., 2021).

Cultural Barriers—such as rigid hierarchies or traditional management structures—discourage experimentation and open communication, suppressing innovative mindsets (Kane et al., 2019).

Bias and Inequality can also shape mindset formation: if employees perceive AI as biased or exclusionary, they may disengage psychologically, viewing the technology as unjust (Binns, 2018). Inadequate leadership support often results in fragmented adoption, where some teams embrace AI while others resist it, creating inconsistent cultural transformation (Newlands, 2022). Finally, overreliance on automation can cause skill atrophy, reducing employees' sense of competence and agency, which undermines mindset transformation (Kellogg et al., 2020). Successful mindset transformation requires addressing cognitive, emotional, and structural barriers—not merely offering technical training.

Solutions and Strategic Interventions

Several evidence-based strategies can accelerate employee mindset transformation in AI-enhanced workplaces.

Building AI Literacy and Transparency: Providing clear explanations of AI's role, logic, and limitations enhances trust and reduces perceived threat (Rai, 2020). Transparent communication about how AI impacts job roles fosters a sense of control and understanding.

Promoting Psychological Safety: Leaders should create safe spaces for dialogue, experimentation, and questioning AI systems without fear of punishment (Edmondson, 2019). This encourages employees to view AI as a learning partner rather than an evaluator.

Integrating Continuous Learning Platforms: AI-driven personalized learning systems can tailor content to employee skill levels, supporting gradual mindset evolution (Bessen, 2019).

Leadership Modeling: When leaders demonstrate adaptability and curiosity toward AI, employees are more likely to emulate those behaviors (Bass & Riggio, 2019). Leadership behavior thus becomes a social signal for organizational openness.

Ethical AI Policies and Governance: Embedding fairness, accountability, and bias-checking into AI applications ensures employees perceive AI as legitimate and trustworthy (Cath, 2018).

Collaborative AI Implementation: Engaging employees in AI design and feedback loops reinforces a sense of participation and ownership (Jarrahi et al., 2022). This participatory approach transforms passive compliance into active engagement.

Cultural Reinforcement: Recognizing and rewarding adaptive behaviors, creative problem-solving, and ethical responsibility strengthens the collective digital mindset (Kane et al., 2019).

By combining these solutions, organizations can move beyond mere compliance training to deep cognitive and behavioral transformation.

AI-DRIVEN SKILL DEVELOPMENT

Meaning and Definition

AI-driven skill development refers to the process through which AI technologies facilitate, personalize, and accelerate the acquisition of new skills and competencies among employees in the workplace (Pan et al., 2022). Unlike traditional learning systems that rely on standardized training, AI-enabled learning leverages machine learning algorithms, data analytics, and adaptive feedback mechanisms to create individualized learning experiences that evolve based on user performance and preferences (Bessen, 2019). This process enables both technical skill acquisition—such as programming, data analysis, and robotics operation—and soft skill enhancement, including problem-solving, creativity, and communication (OECD, 2023).

AI-driven skill development therefore embodies a paradigm shift in human capital management. It positions AI not as a replacement for human intelligence but as an augmentative tool that identifies skill gaps, predicts future skill needs, and delivers targeted interventions (Zubaidi & Elsaid, 2024). The goal is to create a workforce capable of co-evolving with intelligent machines, continuously upgrading their competencies as technologies advance.

Types of AI-Driven Skill Development

AI-driven skill development can be classified into several interrelated categories based on learning modalities, objectives, and technologies employed.

Adaptive Learning Systems: These use AI algorithms to monitor learners' progress and adjust content difficulty, pacing, and feedback accordingly (Chassignol et al., 2018). Examples include AI tutors, chatbots, and personalized e-learning platforms that dynamically respond to users' learning curves.

Predictive Skill Analytics: By analyzing performance data, AI can forecast future competency needs and recommend upskilling pathways aligned with market trends (Brynjolfsson & McAfee, 2017). Such predictive tools enable organizations to proactively reskill employees for emerging roles.

Virtual and Augmented Reality Training: AI-powered immersive simulations allow workers to develop procedural and technical skills in realistic, risk-free environments (Zou & Li, 2025). This is especially valuable in manufacturing, healthcare, and defense industries.

Intelligent Mentoring Systems: Combining natural language processing (NLP) and social network analysis, these systems match employees with appropriate mentors or peer groups, enhancing collaboration and experiential learning (Muehlemann, 2024).

Automated Performance Feedback Tools: AI algorithms can evaluate performance in real time, offering personalized guidance to enhance skill mastery and retention (Kaur et al., 2021).

Together, these systems form an interconnected ecosystem that supports continuous, data-driven learning.

Approaches to Implementing AI-Driven Skill Development

Organizations adopt multiple strategies to implement AI-driven skill development effectively:

Personalized Learning Pathways: AI systems curate training modules based on each employee's job profile, prior experience, and learning style (Pan et al., 2022). This customization improves engagement and learning efficiency.

Human–AI Collaboration in Learning Design: Integrating AI analytics with human instructors allows for hybrid training systems where human empathy and contextual understanding complement algorithmic precision (Qin et al., 2025).

Competency-Based Frameworks: AI tools help map skills against organizational competency models, enabling targeted interventions rather than generic training (OECD, 2023).

Continuous Feedback Loops: Using machine learning, training programs continuously refine content based on learner performance and feedback (Zubaidi & Elsaid, 2024).

Integration with HR Analytics: Linking AI-driven learning data with HR metrics (e.g., productivity, retention, innovation) provides a holistic understanding of workforce capability evolution (Muehlemann, 2024).

These approaches ensure that AI not only delivers content but also guides strategic workforce development decisions.

Problems and Challenges in AI-Driven Skill Development

Despite its promise, AI-driven skill development faces several challenges that affect its ethical, technical, and social dimensions.

Data Bias and Inequality: Since AI systems learn from historical data, biases in datasets can perpetuate unequal learning opportunities (Binns, 2018). Employees from marginalized backgrounds may receive less favorable training recommendations if the AI model replicates historical underrepresentation.

Technological Dependency: Excessive reliance on AI tools may erode self-directed learning habits and critical thinking, leading to "automation complacency" (Brynjolfsson & McAfee, 2017).

Privacy and Surveillance Concerns: AI-powered learning analytics often collect sensitive behavioral data (e.g., time spent learning, emotional responses). Inadequate data protection policies can compromise employee privacy (Newlands, 2022).

Lack of AI Literacy: Many employees and even trainers lack sufficient understanding of AI systems, reducing trust in algorithmic recommendations and hindering adoption (OECD, 2025).

Resource Inequality: Smaller firms or developing economies may struggle to afford sophisticated AI-based learning infrastructure, widening the digital skill divide (Zirar, 2023).

Resistance to Change: Some employees perceive AI-enabled learning as impersonal or invasive, preferring traditional face-to-face training (Tarafdar et al., 2019).

These challenges highlight the need for a balanced, human-centered approach to AI-enabled skill development.

Solutions and Best Practices

Addressing the above challenges requires multidimensional solutions that combine ethical governance, policy innovation, and organizational strategy.

Ethical AI Frameworks: Establishing transparent AI governance mechanisms ensures fairness, accountability, and explainability in learning algorithms (Cath, 2018). Algorithms should be audited regularly for bias and inequity.

Hybrid Learning Models: Combining AI automation with human mentorship balances efficiency with empathy. Human trainers contextualize AI recommendations, fostering deeper learning engagement (Jarrahi et al., 2022).

Inclusive Design Principles: AI systems should be designed with diverse data inputs and user feedback to minimize bias and promote equitable access (OECD, 2025).

Continuous AI Literacy Programs: Employees and managers need foundational AI literacy to interpret algorithmic feedback critically and participate in co-designing learning systems (Bessen, 2019).

Data Privacy Safeguards: Organizations should adopt strict data governance policies that anonymize user data, clarify consent mechanisms, and communicate how data is used (Newlands, 2022).

Strategic Reskilling Partnerships: Collaborations between companies, educational institutions, and government agencies can create scalable AI-driven reskilling ecosystems (Zirar, 2023).

Feedback-Driven Improvement: AI systems should incorporate human feedback loops to refine algorithmic accuracy and pedagogical relevance (Pan et al., 2022).

When these solutions are implemented together, AI becomes a catalyst for empowerment—enhancing human adaptability rather than replacing it.

HUMAN–MACHINE COLLABORATION

Meaning and Definition

Human–machine collaboration refers to the dynamic partnership between humans and AI systems, where both parties contribute complementary strengths toward achieving shared goals (Wilson & Daugherty, 2018). Rather than replacing human labor, this collaboration emphasizes augmentation—machines handle repetitive, data-intensive, or analytical tasks, while humans contribute creativity, empathy, ethical judgment, and contextual reasoning (Jarrahi et al., 2022). The relationship is characterized by synergy, where humans and intelligent systems continuously learn from each other, leading to improved decision-making, productivity, and innovation (Brynjolfsson & McAfee, 2017).

In modern workplaces, human–machine collaboration underpins the digital transformation of organizations (Bhambri & Nischal, 2008). It involves a cognitive and operational partnership in which AI tools provide insights or automation that assist humans in complex problem-solving (Shneiderman, 2020). As AI technologies evolve—from machine learning algorithms to generative models—the role of human–machine collaboration expands beyond efficiency enhancement to capability creation (Daugherty & Wilson, 2022). This collaboration is not only technological but also psychological, requiring trust, transparency, and mutual adaptation between humans and machines.

Types of Human–Machine Collaboration

Scholars and practitioners classify human–machine collaboration into several types based on the division of labor, autonomy, and interaction style:

Assisted Collaboration: AI systems act as tools that enhance human performance by automating repetitive or analytical tasks, such as data processing, scheduling, or predictive maintenance (Wilson & Daugherty, 2018).

Augmented Collaboration: Here, AI supports human creativity, strategy, and innovation. Examples include AI-assisted design, content creation, or decision-support systems (Zou & Li, 2025).

Symbiotic Collaboration: Both humans and machines learn from one another and evolve through feedback loops. In this setting, AI adapts to user behaviors, while humans refine their strategies based on algorithmic insights (Jarrahi, 2018).

Autonomous–Supervisory Collaboration: Humans monitor AI systems that operate with high autonomy—such as self-driving vehicles or automated manufacturing lines—intervening only when exceptions occur (Shneiderman, 2020).

Creative Collaboration: Generative AI tools like ChatGPT, DALL·E, and Copilot enable co-creation of content, art, and solutions, fostering new dimensions of creativity and innovation (Rai, 2020).

These types illustrate the evolution of collaboration from control and assistance toward partnership and co-evolution, where human intelligence and machine intelligence blend seamlessly.

Approaches to Effective Human–Machine Collaboration

Organizations adopt several strategic and operational approaches to enhance human–machine collaboration effectively:

Human-Centered Design: Designing AI systems that prioritize user experience and cognitive ergonomics ensures technology complements rather than overwhelms human users (Norman & Draper, 2019).

Explainable and Transparent AI (XAI): Ensuring AI systems are interpretable builds trust and enables humans to understand and validate machine decisions (Rai, 2020).

Collaborative Intelligence Frameworks: Daugherty and Wilson (2018) introduced the concept of "collaborative intelligence," emphasizing mutual learning—humans train machines, and machines augment humans.

Cross-Functional Team Integration: Embedding AI experts within multidisciplinary teams fosters co-creation between data scientists, designers, and frontline workers (Kane et al., 2019).

Continuous Feedback Loops: Humans must provide feedback that helps AI refine its models, while AI must provide insights that guide human decision-making (Jarrahi et al., 2022).

Ethical Governance: Establishing clear ethical and legal frameworks ensures responsible AI deployment, protecting autonomy, accountability, and human dignity (Cath, 2018).

These approaches ensure collaboration is adaptive, transparent, and aligned with organizational and societal values.

Problems and Challenges in Human–Machine Collaboration

Despite its transformative potential, human–machine collaboration faces significant psychological, ethical, and operational challenges:

Trust Deficit: Many employees find it difficult to trust AI systems, especially when decisions are opaque or outcomes are unpredictable (Ransbotham et al., 2021). Lack of explainability undermines confidence and adoption.

Role Ambiguity: As AI systems take on more tasks, employees may experience confusion regarding their responsibilities, leading to disengagement or dependency (Kellogg et al., 2020).

Overreliance on Automation: Excessive trust in AI can result in automation bias, where users accept machine recommendations without critical evaluation (Lyell & Coiera, 2017).

Skill Polarization: Collaborative environments may inadvertently widen skill gaps between technologically proficient and less experienced workers (OECD, 2023).

Ethical and Accountability Issues: Determining responsibility for AI-driven errors—whether human or algorithmic—remains a major governance challenge (Cath, 2018).

Emotional and Cognitive Fatigue: Continuous interaction with AI systems may create information overload and emotional exhaustion (Tarafdar et al., 2019).

Algorithmic Bias and Fairness: If AI systems are trained on biased data, their outputs can reinforce discrimination or unethical decision patterns (Binns, 2018).

Thus, successful collaboration depends on managing not only technical compatibility but also human psychological adaptation.

Solutions and Strategic Pathways

To overcome these challenges, organizations must pursue a holistic strategy integrating technological, managerial, and ethical interventions:

Building AI Literacy: Employees should be trained to understand AI fundamentals, interpret outputs, and recognize algorithmic limitations (Bessen, 2019). This empowers workers to collaborate intelligently with machines.

Cultivating Human–AI Trust: Transparent algorithms and consistent communication about AI goals, performance, and errors foster mutual trust (Rai, 2020).

Redefining Work Roles: Organizations should redesign job descriptions to emphasize human strengths such as emotional intelligence, ethical reasoning, and creative problem-solving (Wilson & Daugherty, 2018).

Ethical AI Implementation: Establishing AI ethics committees and accountability frameworks ensures fairness and responsibility (Cath, 2018).

Human Oversight and Autonomy: Maintaining "human-in-the-loop" systems where humans retain ultimate decision authority prevents over-automation risks (Shneiderman, 2020).

Cognitive Ergonomics and User Experience Design: Interfaces should minimize cognitive load and support intuitive decision-making (Norman & Draper, 2019).

Psychological Support and Change Management: Providing mental health resources and clear communication about AI integration reduces anxiety and technostress (Tarafdar et al., 2019).

Feedback-Driven Learning: Both AI and human partners should continuously adapt through shared feedback loops, ensuring collaboration remains dynamic (Jarrahi et al., 2022).

By implementing these solutions, organizations can achieve symbiotic partnerships that elevate both human creativity and machine intelligence.

AI-Driven Skill Transformation

AI-driven skill transformation refers to the process by which AI technologies fundamentally reshape employee skill sets, roles, and competencies within the workplace (Bessen, 2019). Unlike traditional upskilling, which focuses on incremental improvements, AI-driven transformation involves reimagining skills to align with emerging technologies, changing workflows, and dynamic market demands (Brynjolfsson & McAfee, 2017). This transformation is driven by AI's ability to automate routine tasks, augment decision-making, and facilitate novel ways of working, which necessitates a shift from task-specific expertise to adaptive, higher-order cognitive, and socio-emotional skills (OECD, 2023). AI-driven skill transformation is not merely technological—it is a socio-technical phenomenon where employee mindsets, learning behaviors, and professional identities evolve in tandem with AI adoption (Zubaidi & Elsaid, 2024). For instance, in sectors like finance, healthcare, and manufacturing, AI tools augment analytical, diagnostic, and operational tasks, requiring employees to develop interpretive, strategic, and collaborative competencies to complement machine intelligence (Jarrahi, 2018).

Types of AI-Driven Skill Transformation

Research identifies multiple forms of AI-driven skill transformation, classified by functional and cognitive domains:

Task Automation Transformation: Routine, rule-based tasks are replaced or augmented by AI systems, shifting employee focus toward supervisory and strategic responsibilities (Brynjolfsson & McAfee, 2017).

Cognitive Augmentation Transformation: AI tools enhance human decision-making by providing predictive insights, scenario modeling, and risk analysis, thereby fostering advanced analytical and problem-solving skills (Raisch & Krakowski, 2021).

Collaborative Transformation: AI facilitates human–machine teamwork, requiring employees to develop communication, collaboration, and digital literacy skills to work effectively with intelligent systems (Jarrahi et al., 2022).

Creative Transformation: Generative AI and other creative technologies enable employees to develop new competencies in content creation, design thinking, and innovation (Zou & Li, 2025).

Adaptive Transformation: AI-driven work environments require employees to cultivate adaptability, continuous learning, and resilience as new processes, tools, and standards emerge (Pulakos et al., 2020).

These types illustrate that AI-driven transformation encompasses technical, cognitive, and socio-emotional dimensions, preparing employees for hybrid roles that combine human and machine capabilities.

Approaches to Implementing AI-Driven Skill Transformation

Organizations adopt diverse approaches to facilitate AI-driven skill transformation:

Competency Mapping and Gap Analysis: AI analytics identify current skill profiles, anticipate future requirements, and suggest targeted interventions to bridge gaps (Pan et al., 2022).

AI-Powered Learning Platforms: Personalized and adaptive learning systems accelerate skill acquisition by recommending content, simulations, and microlearning modules based on individual needs (Holmes et al., 2019).

Role Redesign and Job Crafting: Organizations redesign job descriptions to integrate AI tools, redefine responsibilities, and emphasize high-value tasks that leverage human judgment and creativity (Bessen, 2019).

Experiential Learning and Simulation: AI-driven simulations provide realistic, risk-free environments for employees to practice new skills and decision-making processes (Zou & Li, 2025).

Collaborative Intelligence Programs: Structured initiatives train employees to work effectively with AI systems, fostering cognitive and social alignment with technology (Daugherty & Wilson, 2018).

Feedback and Iterative Development: Continuous evaluation and AI-driven insights allow employees to iteratively refine their competencies, promoting sustained skill transformation (Jarrahi et al., 2022).

By combining technological infrastructure with human-centered strategies, organizations can maximize the impact of AI-driven skill transformation.

Problems and Challenges

Despite its advantages, AI-driven skill transformation faces significant technical, human, and ethical challenges:

Skill Redundancy and Job Displacement: Automation may render existing skills obsolete, causing employee anxiety and potential workforce displacement (Brynjolfsson & McAfee, 2017).

Learning Resistance: Employees may resist skill transformation due to fear, uncertainty, or perceived threats to professional identity (Vakola, 2016).

Inequitable Access: Not all employees have equal access to AI-driven training platforms, potentially exacerbating skills and income gaps (OECD, 2023).

Cognitive Overload: Rapid adoption of AI tools can overwhelm employees, reducing learning effectiveness and productivity (Park & Cho, 2022).

Trust and Transparency Issues: Employees may distrust AI recommendations, particularly when algorithms are opaque or perceived as unfair (Ransbotham et al., 2021).

Ethical and Privacy Concerns: AI analytics require sensitive data, raising questions about consent, data protection, and bias in skill assessments (Cath, 2018).

Integration Complexity: Aligning AI-driven skill transformation with organizational strategy, workflow, and culture is complex and resource-intensive (Kane et al., 2019).

Addressing these challenges is critical for ensuring equitable, sustainable, and effective skill transformation.

Solutions and Strategic Interventions

Effective solutions for AI-driven skill transformation integrate technological, managerial, and ethical considerations:

Reskilling and Upskilling Programs: Structured programs aligned with future competencies help employees transition from routine tasks to AI-augmented roles (Bessen, 2019).

Human-Centric AI Design: Designing AI systems that are explainable, transparent, and collaborative ensures employees understand and trust AI recommendations (Rai, 2020).

Inclusive Access and Equity: Ensuring all employees have equal access to AI-powered learning tools reduces skill inequality and fosters inclusive transformation (OECD, 2023).

Continuous Learning Culture: Embedding learning as a core organizational value encourages employees to engage proactively in skill transformation (Marsick & Watkins, 2018).

Adaptive Feedback Systems: AI-driven dashboards provide real-time performance insights and recommendations, allowing employees to adjust learning strategies iteratively (Pan et al., 2022).

Role Redefinition and Job Crafting: Managers should redesign roles to emphasize tasks that complement AI capabilities, enhancing human value creation (Daugherty & Wilson, 2018).

Ethical Governance and Data Protection: Implementing policies for privacy, transparency, and fairness ensures ethical deployment of AI in skill transformation (Cath, 2018).

Leadership Support and Engagement: Leaders modeling continuous learning and AI adoption encourage employee buy-in and reduce resistance to change (Kane et al., 2019).

Together, these solutions foster sustainable and meaningful AI-driven skill transformation across organizations.

EMOTIONAL INTELLIGENCE AND AI

Emotional intelligence (EI) is defined as the ability to perceive, understand, regulate, and manage emotions in oneself and others to facilitate interpersonal interactions, decision-making, and problem-solving (Mayer, Caruso, & Salovey, 2016). In the context of AI-augmented workplaces, EI has become increasingly important, as human workers must complement technological systems with social and emotional competencies that machines cannot replicate (Goleman, 2017). While AI excels in data analysis, pattern recognition, and automation of routine cognitive tasks, it lacks empathy, ethical reasoning, and nuanced emotional understanding. This creates a synergy where human EI and AI capabilities converge, enabling organizations to enhance collaboration, creativity, and customer engagement (Chernova & Aha, 2019).

AI applications, such as emotion recognition systems, chatbots, and AI-driven team analytics, can provide insights into emotional patterns and workforce sentiment (Bhambri, 2014). However, effectively using these insights requires employees to interpret data empathetically, regulate their responses, and foster emotional balance in AI-mediated interactions (Zeng et al., 2022). Thus, EI emerges as a critical human capability that supports ethical, productive, and adaptive integration of AI in workplace processes.

Types of Emotional Intelligence in AI Contexts

Scholars classify EI into several dimensions relevant to AI-enhanced work environments:

Self-Awareness: Recognizing one's own emotions, biases, and tendencies when interacting with AI systems or during AI-influenced decision-making (Goleman, 2017).

Self-Regulation: Managing emotional responses to AI recommendations, automation changes, or workplace stress to maintain productivity and judgment (Mayer et al., 2016).

Motivation: Maintaining intrinsic motivation to learn, adapt, and collaborate in AI-augmented roles (Boyatzis, 2018).

Empathy: Understanding the emotional states, needs, and perspectives of colleagues, customers, or stakeholders, even when AI mediates interactions (Chernova & Aha, 2019).

Social Skills: Building and maintaining relationships, negotiating, and collaborating effectively in teams that incorporate AI-driven decision tools (Zeng et al., 2022).

These dimensions illustrate that EI involves both intrapersonal and interpersonal competencies, which are essential for complementing AI capabilities and maintaining a human-centered workplace.

Approaches to Enhancing Emotional Intelligence with AI

Organizations adopt several strategies to cultivate EI alongside AI integration:

AI-Enhanced Emotional Feedback: Emotion-sensing AI tools provide employees with real-time feedback on emotional expressions and interpersonal dynamics, fostering self-awareness and empathy (Zeng et al., 2022).

Training Programs on Social-Emotional Skills: Structured EI workshops, simulations, and role-playing exercises help employees practice empathy, conflict resolution, and self-regulation in AI-mediated environments (Boyatzis, 2018).

Human–AI Collaboration Exercises: Teams working on AI-assisted projects receive coaching to enhance emotional understanding, communication, and trust-building (Jarrahi et al., 2022).

Digital Coaching Platforms: AI-based coaching platforms track emotional responses, provide reflective prompts, and suggest strategies for managing workplace emotions (Holmes et al., 2019).

Scenario-Based Learning: Employees engage in AI-driven simulations that require recognizing and managing emotions under complex, high-stakes conditions (Zou & Li, 2025).

Mentorship and Peer Support Systems: Combining AI insights with human mentoring enhances social skills and empathy, particularly in virtual or hybrid workplaces (Billett, 2020).

These approaches integrate technology with human-centered skill development, ensuring employees enhance EI while adapting to AI-enabled work dynamics.

Problems and Challenges

Despite its importance, cultivating EI in AI-augmented workplaces presents multiple challenges:

Overreliance on AI: Employees may defer interpersonal judgments to AI recommendations, reducing emotional engagement and empathetic understanding (Lyell & Coiera, 2017).

Algorithmic Bias: Emotion recognition systems can misinterpret or misclassify emotional cues, leading to unfair assessments or misunderstandings (Cath, 2018).

Emotional Fatigue: Continuous monitoring of AI-mediated interactions and adapting emotional responses can lead to cognitive and emotional overload (Park & Cho, 2022).

Resistance to Emotional Feedback: Employees may resist AI-based emotional insights due to skepticism, fear of surveillance, or perceived invasiveness (Ransbotham et al., 2021).

Inequality in Skill Development: Access to AI-driven EI tools and training may be uneven across organizational hierarchies, creating skill gaps (OECD, 2023).

Integration Complexity: Incorporating AI insights into interpersonal interactions requires careful design, culture, and training to avoid depersonalization or robotic communication (Goleman, 2017).

Addressing these challenges is essential to ensure EI complements AI capabilities without undermining authenticity, trust, or workplace well-being.

Solutions and Best Practices

Organizations can adopt several strategies to overcome EI-related challenges in AI-enhanced workplaces:

Human-in-the-Loop Design: Ensure AI systems augment rather than replace human judgment, maintaining employee agency in emotionally sensitive decisions (Shneiderman, 2020).

Ethical AI Deployment: Transparency, fairness, and accountability in AI-based emotion recognition systems build trust and reduce bias (Cath, 2018).

Continuous EI Training: Incorporate ongoing emotional intelligence workshops, coaching, and simulations to strengthen intrapersonal and interpersonal skills (Boyatzis, 2018).

Psychological Safety and Growth Mindset: Foster a culture where employees feel safe expressing emotions, experimenting, and learning from feedback (Edmondson, 2019).

Inclusive Access: Provide equitable access to AI-based EI tools and resources, ensuring all employees develop essential emotional competencies (OECD, 2023).

Feedback Integration: Encourage employees to combine AI insights with self-reflection, peer feedback, and managerial guidance to improve emotional awareness and regulation (Zeng et al., 2022).

Leadership Modeling: Leaders demonstrating high EI while leveraging AI set standards for effective human–AI emotional collaboration (Goleman, 2017).

These strategies align technology with human-centered skills, enhancing workplace productivity, engagement, and well-being.

CONCLUSION

Between 2015 and 2025, the relationship between AI and human capability has undergone a profound transformation, reshaping the dynamics of work, learning, and leadership across industries. This decade has marked a paradigm shift—from viewing AI as a tool of automation to recognizing it as a collaborator and co-evolver in human progress. Central to this transformation is the synergy between emotional intelligence (EI) and AI, the redefinition of workforce skills, the emergence of human–machine collaboration, and the psychological mindset shifts required to navigate algorithmic management and digital transformation. Together, these dimensions highlight that the future of work is neither exclusively technological nor purely human—it is a fusion of both, driven by emotional insight, adaptive intelligence, and ethical governance.

Emotional intelligence continues to be the defining human capability that complements AI's analytical and computational strengths (Bathla et al., 2007). While AI excels at pattern recognition, predictive analytics, and optimization, it lacks the empathetic and contextual understanding that underpins human collaboration, creativity, and ethical reasoning (Mayer et al., 2016; Chernova & Aha, 2019). As organizations integrate AI into decision-making and workflow systems, employees with high EI serve as interpreters of technological insights—balancing data with human judgment. Self-awareness, empathy, and social regulation become critical in ensuring that AI-driven outputs align with organizational values and societal expectations. However, the rise of AI introduces emotional challenges such as over-reliance, cognitive fatigue, and technological alienation, especially when humans feel displaced by algorithmic authority. Mitigating these issues requires human-centered AI design, continuous emotional learning, and inclusive engagement strategies that position employees not as passive users but as ethical co-navigators of technology. The integration of EI in AI-augmented environments thus safeguards humanity's role in a digitized workplace—ensuring that compassion, empathy, and moral reasoning guide innovation rather than being overshadowed by efficiency metrics.

AI-driven skill transformation signifies a shift from mechanistic efficiency to socio-cognitive empowerment. Research between 2015 and 2025 demonstrates that automation alone does not create competitive advantage—human adaptability does (Brynjolfsson & McAfee, 2017; Jarrahi, 2018). AI enables organizations to automate routine work, but true transformation occurs when employees leverage AI to expand analytical, creative, and adaptive capacities. The workforce of the future must therefore integrate computational literacy with emotional, social, and ethical intelligence. Organizations that effectively manage this transformation utilize AI-powered learning ecosystems, simulation-based training, and human-centered design frameworks (Anand & Bhambri, 2018). These systems personalize learning, predict future skill requirements, and encourage reflective thinking. Nevertheless, challenges persist, including skill redundancy, digital inequality, and cognitive overload, which can deepen social divides within organizations. Addressing these challenges requires equitable access to learning technologies and policies that encourage ethical AI integration. Skill transformation, when guided by inclusive governance and lifelong learning, empowers employees not to compete with machines but to collaborate with them—co-evolving toward more resilient, creative, and innovative forms of work.

The emergence of human–machine collaboration represents the next evolutionary phase of organizational intelligence. The traditional paradigm of "man versus machine" has been replaced by one of partnership—where AI amplifies human judgment rather than replacing it (Daugherty & Wilson, 2022). Machines process massive datasets, identify correlations, and provide predictive insights, while humans supply contextual understanding, empathy, and ethical discernment. Together, they form a complementary intelligence system that drives innovation and problem-solving in ways neither could achieve alone. Effective collaboration depends not only on technological sophistication but on human adaptability and trust. As employees learn to interpret algorithmic decisions, they become co-creators in a dynamic feedback loop: humans train machines through contextual data, while machines enhance human cognition through analytical augmentation. This co-evolutionary cycle fosters transparency, accountability, and shared learning. Yet, the success of such collaboration relies on cultivating psychological safety, participatory design, and ethical AI governance—ensuring that human oversight remains central to all AI-assisted operations. The future workplace will thus embody a hybrid intelligence model, where empathy meets efficiency, and where human values steer technological evolution toward collective progress. AI-driven skill development represents a redefinition of learning itself. From 2015 to 2025, education and workforce development have evolved from static instruction toward personalized, predictive, and adaptive learning ecosystems (OECD, 2023; Zubaidi & Elsaid, 2024). AI tools analyze learning behavior, detect knowledge gaps, and recommend tailored pathways that enhance engagement and retention. This data-driven personalization transforms learning into a continuous, contextual, and co-evolving process rather than a one-time training event.

Importantly, the role of human curiosity, ethical reflection, and critical thinking becomes more vital than ever. AI can identify what needs to be learned, but it cannot determine why learning matters or how it shapes human purpose. Thus, successful AI-driven learning strategies must preserve human agency—designing systems that empower rather than dictate, and that nurture ethical discernment alongside technical proficiency. When employees learn to collaborate with AI as cognitive partners, they cultivate resilience, creativity, and self-directed growth—qualities essential for thriving in unpredictable environments. However, achieving this balance demands transparency in AI algorithms, fair data practices, and continuous human oversight to prevent bias and manipulation in digital learning platforms.

Beyond skills and tools, the most profound transformation lies in the mindset of employees. Research shows that AI integration does not merely change what people do—it reshapes how they think, learn, and relate to technology (Ransbotham et al., 2021; Jarrahi et al., 2022). The psychological transition from fear and resistance to curiosity and collaboration determines whether digital adoption succeeds. A growth-oriented mindset enables employees to see AI not as a threat to job security but as an opportunity for co-creation, problem-solving, and self-expansion. Developing such a mindset involves cultivating reflective awareness, ethical reasoning, and adaptive confidence. Leaders play a crucial role in framing AI as a partner rather than a replacement, fostering environments where employees are encouraged to experiment, fail, and learn continuously. Psychological safety becomes the bedrock of innovation—when individuals feel secure, they are more likely to explore the creative potentials of AI systems. Thus, mindset transformation is the invisible yet indispensable infrastructure of AI-augmented organizations. It not only determines technological success but also safeguards human dignity, ensuring that automation enhances rather than erodes the meaning of work. Finally, algorithmic management represents both the promise and peril of AI in organizational governance. It applies data analytics and predictive modeling to monitor performance, allocate tasks, and optimize efficiency. While it enhances objectivity and operational control, it also raises concerns about transparency, autonomy, and accountability (Ransbotham et al., 2021). Algorithms, if unchecked, risk transforming management into surveillance and decision-making into mechanistic optimization devoid of human judgment.

The future of algorithmic management depends on reimagining algorithms as collaborative partners rather than authoritarian supervisors. Embedding ethical governance frameworks, human oversight, and employee participation can convert algorithmic systems from tools of control into engines of empowerment. When transparency and fairness are prioritized, data-driven management can democratize decision-making, reduce bias, and enhance organizational trust. The key lies in maintaining a human-in-the-loop structure—where algorithms inform decisions but do not replace moral and contextual reasoning. Such balanced integration ensures that AI remains a servant of human values rather than a master of human behavior.

TOWARD THE FUTURE: THE SYNTHESIS OF EMOTION, INTELLIGENCE, AND ETHICS

Collectively, these interlinked dimensions—emotional intelligence, skill transformation, collaboration, learning, mindset, and algorithmic governance—illustrate that the AI-augmented workplace is fundamentally a socio-technical ecosystem. Its success relies not merely on technological advancement but on human maturity, empathy, and ethical alignment. As AI continues to evolve, organizations must prioritize "human capability engineering"—developing emotional resilience, moral intelligence, and critical adaptability alongside technical competence. The decade between 2015 and 2025 has made one truth undeniable: the future belongs to emotionally intelligent humans working intelligently with machines. The challenge ahead is to sustain this harmony—to design AI that amplifies human insight rather than replacing it, and to nurture humans who can think both critically and compassionately in partnership with intelligent systems. When emotional intelligence guides AI's analytical power, workplaces become not just efficient, but meaningful—spaces where data serves empathy, algorithms support ethics, and technology advances humanity.

REFERENCES

Anand, A., & Bhambri, P. (2018). Rotation, scale and translation invariant character recognition system using neural network (M. Tech. thesis). Punjab Technical University.

Bass, B. M., & Riggio, R. E. (2019). *Transformational leadership* (3rd ed.). Routledge.

Bathla, S., Jindal, C., & Bhambri, P. (2007, March). Impact of technology on societal living [Paper presentation]. *International Conference on Convergence and Competition*, India.

Beer, D. (2017). The social power of algorithms. *Information Communication and Society*, *20*(1), 1–13. DOI: 10.1080/1369118X.2016.1216147

Bessen, J. (2019). *AI and jobs: The role of demand.* National Bureau of Economic Research., DOI: 10.3386/w24235

Bhambri, P. (2014). Effectiveness of performance management system in IT industries: Empirical approach. In Management of globalised business: Plethora of new opportunities (pp. 114-121).

Bhambri, P. (2025a). Understanding AI and machine learning in security. In Bhambri, P., & Anand, A. J. (Eds.), *Handbook of AI-driven threat detection and prevention: A holistic approach to security* (pp. 1–17). CRC Press., DOI: 10.1201/9781003521020-1

Bhambri, P. (2025b). Virtual and augmented reality for immersive learning experiences: Practical applications and challenges. In Pelet, J.-É. (Ed.), *Architecting the digital future: Platforms, design, and application* (pp. 17–46). IGI Global., DOI: 10.4018/979-8-3693-2973-3.ch002

Bhambri, P., & Nischal, P. (2008, May). Emerging new economy in telecommunication sector of india [Paper presentation]. *International Conference on Business Challenges & Strategies in Emerging Global Scenario*, India.

Bhambri, P., & Singh, M. (2008). Image transport protocol for JPEG image over loss prone congested networks. *PIMT Journal of Research*, *1*(1), 55–61.

Bhambri, P., & Thapar, V. (2009, May). Power distribution challenges in VLSI: An introduction [Paper presentation]. *International Conference on Downtrend Challenges in IT*, India.

Billett, S. (2020). *Learning through work: Strategies for effective practice.* Routledge. DOI: 10.4324/9781003116318

Binns, R. (2018). Fairness in machine learning: Lessons from political philosophy. *Proceedings of the 2018 Conference on Fairness, Accountability, and Transparency*, 149–159.

Bodie, M. T., Cherry, M. A., McCormick, M. L., & Tang, J. (2020). The law and policy of people analytics. *University of Colorado Law Review*, *91*(1), 1–57.

Boyatzis, R. E. (2018). *The competent manager: A model for effective performance*. Wiley.

Brynjolfsson, E., & McAfee, A. (2017). *Machine, platform, crowd: Harnessing our digital future*. W. W. Norton.

Burrell, J. (2016). How the machine "thinks": Understanding opacity in machine learning algorithms. *Big Data & Society*, *3*(1), 1–12. DOI: 10.1177/2053951715622512

Cath, C. (2018). Governing artificial intelligence: Ethical, legal and technical opportunities and challenges. *Philosophical Transactions. Series A, Mathematical, Physical, and Engineering Sciences*, *376*(2133), 20180080. DOI: 10.1098/rsta.2018.0080 PMID: 30322996

Chassignol, M., Khoroshavin, A., Klimova, A., & Bilyatdinova, A. (2018). Artificial intelligence trends in education: A narrative overview. *Procedia Computer Science*, *136*, 16–24. DOI: 10.1016/j.procs.2018.08.233

Chernova, S., & Aha, D. (2019). Emotion-aware artificial intelligence. *AI Magazine*, *40*(3), 15–28.

Daugherty, P. R., & Wilson, H. J. (2018). *Human + machine: Reimagining work in the age of AI*. Harvard Business Review Press.

Duggan, J., Sherman, U., Carbery, R., & McDonnell, A. (2020). Algorithmic management and app-work in the gig economy: A research agenda for employment relations and HRM. *Human Resource Management Journal*, *30*(1), 114–132. DOI: 10.1111/1748-8583.12258

Dweck, C. S. (2006). *Mindset: The new psychology of success*. Random House.

Dweck, C. S. (2016). What having a "growth mindset" actually means. *Harvard Business Review*, *94*(11), 213–216.

Edmondson, A. (2019). *The fearless organization: Creating psychological safety in the workplace for learning, innovation, and growth*. Wiley.

Goleman, D. (2017). *Emotional intelligence: Why it can matter more than IQ*. Bantam Books.

Holmes, W., Bialik, M., & Fadel, C. (2019). *Artificial intelligence in education: Promises and implications for teaching and learning*. Center for Curriculum Redesign.

Jarrahi, M. H. (2018). Artificial intelligence and the future of work: Human–AI symbiosis in organizational decision-making. *Business Horizons*, *61*(4), 577–586. DOI: 10.1016/j.bushor.2018.03.007

Jarrahi, M. H., Newlands, G., Lee, M. K., Wolf, C. T., Kinder, E., & Sutherland, W. (2022). Algorithmic management in a work context. *Journal of Business Research*, *153*, 75–89.

Kane, G. C., Palmer, D., Phillips, A. N., Kiron, D., & Buckley, N. (2019). *The technology fallacy: How people are the real key to digital transformation*. MIT Press. DOI: 10.7551/mitpress/11661.001.0001

Kaur, P., Malik, G., & Sharma, A. (2021). Artificial intelligence and human learning: A review of AI-enabled learning systems. *Education and Information Technologies*, *26*(6), 6759–6783.

Kellogg, K. C., Valentine, M. A., & Christin, A. (2020). Algorithms at work: The new contested terrain of control. *The Academy of Management Annals*, *14*(1), 366–410. DOI: 10.5465/annals.2018.0174

Lee, M. K., Kusbit, D., Metsky, E., & Dabbish, L. (2021). Working with machines: The impact of algorithmic and data-driven management on human workers. *Computers in Human Behavior*, *124*, 106932.

Lyell, D., & Coiera, E. (2017). Automation bias and verification complexity: A systematic review. *Journal of the American Medical Informatics Association : JAMIA*, *24*(2), 423–431. DOI: 10.1093/jamia/ocw105 PMID: 27516495

Marsick, V. J., & Watkins, K. E. (2018). *Informal and incidental learning in the workplace*. Routledge.

Mateescu, A., & Nguyen, A. (2019). *Explainer: Algorithmic management in the workplace*. Data & Society Research Institute. DOI: 10.69985/XXBG2416

Mayer, J. D., Caruso, D. R., & Salovey, P. (2016). The ability model of emotional intelligence: Principles and updates. *Emotion Review*, *8*(4), 290–300. DOI: 10.1177/1754073916639667

Moore, P. V., Akhtar, P., & Upchurch, M. (2018). Digitalisation of work and resistance. *Labour & Industry: A Journal of the Social and Economic Relations of Work, 28*(3), 179–187.

Muehlemann, S. (2024). *AI adoption and workplace training* (IZA Discussion Paper No. 17367). Institute of Labor Economics (IZA).

Newlands, G. (2022). Algorithmic surveillance and worker privacy in the gig economy. *Human Relations*, *75*(6), 1035–1058.

Nonaka, I., & Takeuchi, H. (2021). *The wise company: How companies create continuous innovation*. Oxford University Press.

Norman, D. A., & Draper, S. W. (2019). *User centered system design: New perspectives on human-computer interaction*. CRC Press.

OECD. (2023). *Artificial intelligence, job quality and inclusiveness*. OECD Publishing.

Organisation for Economic Co-operation and Development. (2023). *Artificial intelligence, job quality and inclusiveness*. OECD Publishing.

Organisation for Economic Co-operation and Development. (2025). *AI and work: Job quality, safety and skill development*. OECD Publishing. https://www.oecd.org/en/topics/ai-and-work.html

Organisation for Economic Co-operation and Development (OECD). (2025). *Algorithmic management in the workplace* (OECD Report). OECD Publishing. OECD

Pan, Y., Sun, S., & Chen, X. (2022). Adaptive learning with artificial intelligence: New frontiers in workforce education. *Computers & Education*, *191*, 104629.

Park, S., & Cho, Y. (2022). Learning fatigue in digital transformation environments: Antecedents and coping mechanisms. *Human Resource Development Review*, *21*(4), 413–432.

Pulakos, E. D., Arad, S., Donovan, M. A., & Plamondon, K. E. (2020). Adaptability in the workplace: Development of a taxonomy of adaptive performance. *The Journal of Applied Psychology*, *105*(9), 1125–1148. PMID: 10948805

Qin, S., Zhang, J., & Chen, L. (2025). Artificial intelligence usage and employee innovation behavior: The mediating role of self-efficacy and the moderating role of openness to experience. *Behavioral Sciences (Basel, Switzerland)*, *15*(4), 491. DOI: 10.3390/bs15040491 PMID: 40282112

Rai, A. (2020). Explainable AI: From black box to glass box. *Journal of the Academy of Marketing Science*, *48*(1), 137–141. DOI: 10.1007/s11747-019-00710-5

Raisch, S., & Krakowski, S. (2021). Artificial intelligence and management: The automation–augmentation paradox. *Academy of Management Review*, *46*(1), 192–210. DOI: 10.5465/amr.2018.0072

Ransbotham, S., Khodabandeh, S., Fehling, R., & Kiron, D. (2021). Expanding AI's impact with organizational learning. *MIT Sloan Management Review*.

Rosenblat, A., & Stark, L. (2016). Algorithmic labor and information asymmetries: A case study of Uber's drivers. *International Journal of Communication*, *10*, 3758–3784.

Shneiderman, B. (2020). Human-centered artificial intelligence: Reliable, safe & trustworthy. *International Journal of Human-Computer Interaction*, *36*(6), 495–504. DOI: 10.1080/10447318.2020.1741118

Singh, I., Salaria, D., & Bhambri, P. (2010). Comparative analysis of JAVA and AspectJ on the basis of various metrics. In Proceedings of the International Conference on Advanced Computing and Communication Technologies (IEEE Sponsored) (pp. 714-720).

Singh, P., & Bhambri, P. (2007). Alternate organizational models for ports. *Apeejay Journal of Management and Technology*, *2*(2), 9–17.

Singh, P., Bhambri, P., & Sohal, A. K. (2006, January). Security in local networks [Paper presentation]. *National Conference on Future Trends in Information Technology*, India.

Tarafdar, M., Beath, C. M., & Ross, J. W. (2019). Using AI to enhance business operations. *MIT Sloan Management Review*, *60*(4), 37–44.

Thaler, R. H., & Sunstein, C. R. (2008). *Nudge: Improving decisions about health, wealth, and happiness*. Yale University Press.

Tomprou, M., & Lee, M. K. (2022). Employment relationships in algorithmic management: A psychological contract perspective. [ACM Digital Library]. *Computers in Human Behavior*, *126*, 106997. Advance online publication. DOI: 10.1016/j.chb.2021.106997

Vakola, M. (2016). The reasons behind change resistance in the workplace. *Journal of Organizational Change Management*, *29*(2), 213–229.

Wilson, H. J., & Daugherty, P. R. (2018). Collaborative intelligence: Humans and AI are joining forces. *Harvard Business Review*, *96*(4), 114–123.

Yeung, K. (2018). Algorithmic regulation: A critical interrogation. *Regulation & Governance*, *12*(4), 505–523. DOI: 10.1111/rego.12158

Zeng, Z., Pantic, M., Roisman, G. I., & Huang, T. (2022). A survey of affect recognition methods: Audio, visual, and spontaneous expressions. *IEEE Transactions on Pattern Analysis and Machine Intelligence*, *44*(1), 11–38. PMID: 19029545

Zhang, L., & Leidner, D. (2023). The growth mindset and digital transformation: The human side of AI adoption. *Information Systems Journal*, *33*(2), 217–238.

Zirar, A. (2023). Worker and workplace AI coexistence: Emerging themes and research agenda. *Technology in Society*, *75*, 102322. DOI: 10.1016/j.techsoc.2023.102322

Zou, T., & Li, F. (2025). Generative artificial intelligence adoption and the future of cognitive and social skills. *arXiv preprint arXiv:2503.09212*. https://arxiv.org/abs/2503.09212

Zubaidi, H., & Elsaid, M. (2024). AI in the workplace: A systematic review of skill transformation in the industry. *Administrative Sciences*, *14*(6), 127. DOI: 10.3390/admsci14060127

Chapter 9

The Role of Emotional Intelligence in Building Trust Within Human-AI Collaboration for Strategic Decision-Making

Esin Yucel
http://orcid.org/0000-0003-1440-1203
University of Bedfordshire, UK

Burcu Arsan
http://orcid.org/0000-0002-9757-9391
Yeditepe University, Turkey

ABSTRACT

This chapter investigates emotional intelligence (EQ) as the main system which enables human-AI teamwork for strategic decision-making through cognitive and affective trust development. The chapter uses EQ models from Mayer and Salovey and Goleman to connect transparency and explainability and human-likeness factors, which help leaders convert AI results into decisions that are both ethical and emotionally understandable. The systematic literature review based on PRISMA examines research from 2015 to 2025 to reveal essential findings and knowledge deficiencies regarding EQ and trust and AI systems. Research shows that users accept AI systems better when they demonstrate EQ abilities, which also reduces technostress and enables proper trust management in AI-supported environments.

DOI: 10.4018/979-8-3373-5816-1.ch009

The research findings lead to the development of a conceptual framework which enables human-centred AI support for ethical strategic decision-making through trust-based systems.

1. INTRODUCTION

Organisations use artificial intelligence (AI) to transform their decision-making operations through strategic planning, risk assessment and resource distribution. AI systems process large-scale data at speeds beyond human capability and data volumes through big data analytics, which results in better strategic decision quality (Brynjolfsson & McAfee, 2017). AI systems achieve high cognitive accuracy through their processing abilities, yet they cannot understand emotional intuition and maintain ethical consistency and human values (Rahwan et al., 2019). Strategic decision-making requires emotional, cultural and ethical elements because data-driven rational analysis fails to address the high uncertainty and ethical challenges that exist in this field.

The development of trust and ethical awareness between humans and technological systems depends on emotional intelligence (EQ) as a fundamental human ability. The cognitive-emotional competence model developed by Mayer and Salovey (2004) defines emotional intelligence as the ability to identify and understand personal emotions and others' emotions while using this emotional understanding to guide actions. Goleman (1998) established EQ as a leadership competency model which consists of four dimensions: self-awareness, self-management, empathy and social skills. Leaders who possess these competencies can handle ethical decisions in complex situations while building trust-based relationships and uniting logical analysis with human-focused approaches, while staying emotionally stable.

AI systems achieve high analytical precision but lack the ability to assess decisional emotional effects and ethical outcomes independently. The current state of EQ requires human intervention to translate algorithmic results into emotional and ethical values, which enhance mechanical data processing with empathetic and ethical understanding (Glikson & Woolley, 2020). The literature describes this process as the transition between 'cognitive trust' and 'emotional trust' (McAllister, 1995). The system's technical performance and precision level determine cognitive trust, but emotional trust develops from stakeholders' perceptions of ethical behaviour, explainable operations and value alignment (Hoff & Bashir, 2015).

Leaders who demonstrate high EQ abilities can assess AI system data through both technical and ethical and responsible stakeholder-focused perspectives, which leads to building emotional trust from cognitive trust. Leaders who demonstrate empathetic communication abilities create higher trust levels among employees regarding technological systems and management decisions (Clarke, 2010). According to Goleman (1998), emotional regulation represents the leader's ability to understand technological system information through both logical and emotional perspectives. EQ functions as a fundamental organisational trust-building factor which extends beyond individual human-AI collaboration skills.

The increasing use of artificial intelligence systems has made trust evaluation more crucial for strategic decision-making processes. The model developed by Glikson and Woolley (2020) shows that human-AI trust depends on three essential factors, which include transparency, explainability and human-likeness. System transparency builds cognitive trust through direct decision-making visibility for users, but explainable systems build emotional trust by letting users understand the decision reasons. The level of user technology connection through empathy depends on human-likeness, but excessive anthropomorphism leads to trust deterioration because it creates unrealistic user expectations (Hoff & Bashir, 2015). The three variables show trust operates as a dynamic system when analysed with leader EQ levels. Leaders who demonstrate high EQ levels build cognitive trust through process transparency and emotional trust through their adherence to ethical standards.

The research combines Mayer and Salovey's (2004) emotional intelligence competency model with Goleman's (1998) leadership-based EQ dimensions to create models for trust development in human-AI systems. The 'AI trust determinants' developed by Glikson & Woolley (2020) and Zhang et al. (2021) will receive interpretation through the EQ framework. The research combines these elements to demonstrate how human-centred artificial intelligence systems enable the simultaneous growth of cognitive and emotional trust. The research develops an innovative theoretical model which connects emotional intelligence with ethical leadership and trust management systems for AI-assisted strategic decision-making.

Building trust between humans and artificial intelligence is crucial for successful collaboration. While most research focuses on technical aspects like reliability and accuracy, the role of emotions in trust formation is often overlooked. Emotional intelligence, in particular, has a significant impact on how we trust AI systems. This study aims to bridge this gap by exploring the connection between emotional intelligence, trust, and human-centred AI approaches. It argues that trust in human-AI collaboration depends not only on technical performance but also on ethical leadership, empathetic communication, and the ability to understand and interpret emotions. By considering these factors, we can create a more comprehensive framework for building trust in human-AI collaboration.

The research in this section draws from a systematic review of academic papers which were published between 2015 and 2025. The research team will analyse publications from Scopus Web of Science and EBSCO databases through thematic coding after applying the PRISMA 2020 protocol to search results obtained by using the keywords 'emotional intelligence', 'AI trust', 'strategic decision-making' and 'human–AI collaboration'. The research will identify missing concepts in EQ–trust–AI interaction triangle literature through thematic analysis to develop a new theoretical framework.

The research establishes a human-oriented strategic decision-making framework which unites AI's computational strength with human emotional abilities. The EQ-based leadership method enables organisations to achieve sustainable long-term goals through better AI output communication that combines ethical standards with humanised and trustworthy approaches. The research establishes a fresh conceptual framework which demonstrates how AI systems should function as strategic partners that work with ethical leadership and emotional intelligence.

Organisations will achieve success through artificial intelligence when they combine analytical precision with ethical understanding and empathetic leadership, and trust-based management. The combination of emotional intelligence and human values with cognitive excellence enables organisations to establish permanent trust-based systems. The research aims to develop new strategic decision-making methods which combine emotional intelligence with trust models for ethical and sustainable operations.

2. LITERATURE REVIEW

2.1. Emotional Intelligence in Leadership and Decision-Making

Emotional intelligence (EQ) describes a person's ability to identify and control their emotions and the emotions of others, which serves as a basic cognitive-emotional ability for leadership and strategic choice-making (Mayer, Salovey, & Caruso, 2004). Leadership theories today acknowledge that leaders need both analytical abilities and human qualities, including emotional awareness and self-regulation, and empathy, to achieve success (Goleman, 1998). Leaders who possess EQ can merge emotional data with their analytical thinking to handle complex situations in unpredictable environments, which enables them to reason emotionally (George, 2000). Recent studies indicate that leaders' emotional intelligence (EQ) affects their ability to handle both personal relationships and complex decisions made through automated systems. Leaders who possess high EQ levels through self-awareness and emotion regulation skills can identify algorithm constraints, which helps them minimise cognitive biases that lead to overconfidence (automation bias) and excessive avoidance (algorithm aversion). Leaders who demonstrate high EQ levels develop strategic choices that maintain equilibrium between algorithmic forecasts and employee emotional responses to organisational decisions (Horowitz & Kahn,

2024). Leaders with high EQ levels use their emotional intelligence to create ethical decisions because they evaluate both performance outcomes and human effects from their strategic choices.

Leaders who develop their skills through four essential areas, which include self-awareness for emotional state recognition and bias identification, self-management for crisis control and emotional regulation and empathy for building trust through perspective understanding and social skills for team collaboration and motivation (Goleman, 1998; Ashkanasy & Daus, 2005). The combined application of these competencies allows leaders to create choices which combine logical reasoning with emotional justice and moral integrity. Research on ethical leadership shows that leaders who possess high emotional intelligence (EQ) create better ethical decisions through their communication and decision-making approaches. Qian et al. (2017) found that leaders with high EQ levels create stronger links between ethical leadership and employee feedback behaviour. Leaders who possess EQ can forecast both performance results and employee reactions to their decisions. The strategic options proposed by artificial intelligence systems become compatible with human values and emotional expectations through the EQ bridge.

Organisational trust between leaders and employees develops through emotional intelligence, which they demonstrate in their relationships. Leaders who demonstrate high emotional intelligence create environments where staff members feel safe, which leads to better organisational commitment, creative output and improved communication (Clarke, 2010). The practice of information sharing and participatory leadership becomes more effective in strategic decision-making because of this development. Leaders who possess EQ skills maintain ethical governance in complex systems, which include technological transformation and artificial intelligence-based decision support systems.

The human perspective emerges from empathy and ethical awareness, which helps maintain the equilibrium between AI system outputs and human values. Strategic leadership requires emotional intelligence as an organisational ability which unites cognitive aspects with behavioural elements and ethical standards. Leaders who demonstrate high emotional intelligence help their organisations achieve better decision-making through sustainable and ethical choices during times of environmental complexity and uncertainty by sustaining trust between staff members and technological frameworks.

When you put all these studies together, they show that emotional intelligence is not just something that helps individual leaders, but it's also really important for dealing with tough ethical decisions and building trust in situations where artificial intelligence is used to make big strategic plans. In situations where there's a lot of uncertainty and it's hard to make decisions, leaders who are good at understanding emotions can help balance out the need for technical expertise with what people expect and what the organization needs to trust.

2.2. Trust in Human–AI Collaboration

The success of human–artificial intelligence (AI) teamwork depends on trust because it determines both operational success and moral soundness of strategic decision-making processes. The psychological mechanism of trust affects human decisions and work distribution and system adoption in human–AI systems at the same level as it affects human behaviour. The literature presents trust as a two-part construct which includes cognitive and emotional aspects. Organisational trust literature also conceptualises trust as a multidimensional and relational phenomenon shaped by uncertainty, interdependence, and perceived vulnerability (Rousseau et al., 1998). The system's technical capabilities and predictive accuracy form the basis of cognitive trust, yet emotional trust develops from perceptions about the system's moral values and its ability to understand human emotions (McAllister, 1995). AI system trust from users emerges from both algorithm precision and the system's ability to explain itself, its communication methods and its ethical behaviour (Hoff & Bashir, 2015).

Research indicates that AI trust depends most heavily on systems that provide clear explanations and transparent operations. Users develop stronger cognitive trust through system transparency because it enables them to understand decision processes. Yet, explainable systems build emotional trust by delivering substantial responses to user inquiries about system operations (Glikson & Woolley, 2020). The way systems communicate with users through human-like speech affects their trust levels because users find these systems more understandable, yet excessive anthropomorphism creates trust issues by making it difficult to manage user expectations (Hoff & Bashir, 2015).

System characteristics do not solely determine trust because organisational settings and user interactions also play a role in its development. The level of trust in AI systems for strategic decision-making depends on how leaders and users develop their cognitive and emotional bond with the system. This process works with the idea that trust grows slowly over time through repeated interactions and showing that you can be relied on (Lewicki & Bunker, 1996). Users develop their trust based on their past technology experience, their ability to understand risks and their ethical awareness (Glikson & Woolley, 2020).

Research from recent years shows that trust calibration serves as the key to achieving proper trust levels when humans interact with AI systems. People achieve trust calibration through developing suitable trust levels for AI systems, which prevent them from trusting the system too much or too little. Hoff and Bashir (2015) showed that user trust depends equally on emotional responses and cognitive evaluations; effective communication stands as a vital factor. Leaders who possess high emotional intelligence (EQ) enable staff members to grasp AI system explanations better because they manage employee stress and doubt through emotional control. This balance between emotional and cognitive trust contributes to more sustainable and collaborative human–AI interaction.

The design of AI systems with human-centred approaches in decision environments with high uncertainty leads to increased trust sustainability. The human-AI relationship evolves from technical coordination into a collaborative system which depends on shared understanding and emotional connection, and ethical principles. Human-AI trust develops through the combination of cognitive and emotional elements, which create a complex system. Strategic decision-making processes require equal management of these two dimensions to achieve system acceptance and long-term sustainability. Organisations can establish AI technologies as ethical strategic partners through this new definition of trust.

Therefore, human trust in AI collaboration should not be conceptualised solely as a technical evaluation of system performance. The sustainability of trust also relates to employees' perceptions of fairness, psychological safety, emotional reassurance, and the interpretability of AI-supported decisions. This highlights the central role of affective trust alongside cognitive trust in strategic decision-making.

Explainable artificial intelligence (XAI) systems work to boost cognitive trust through transparent operations, but research shows that technical explanations fail to establish trust on their own. Ehsan and his colleagues (2021) demonstrated that XAI explanations fail to boost trust until they establish an emotional connection through story-like narratives for employees. Leaders who possess high emotional intelligence transform AI technical details into human-friendly stories which serve as ethical frameworks for employee meaning creation. The combination of XAI technical transparency with leader emotional framing creates stronger emotional and cognitive trust bonds.

AI system trust from employees depends on both system accuracy and their emotional judgment about decision fairness and human value alignment. The research by Binns and colleagues (2018) demonstrates that people judge algorithmic systems based on output accuracy and process transparency, justification and value consistency. Leaders who possess emotional intelligence (EQ) will understand employee needs for emotional fairness while delivering clear explanations about AI decision ethics that show empathy and inclusiveness. The method enhances both technical system reliability and employee emotional confidence, which results in better human-AI teamwork stability.

2.3. Emotional Intelligence as a Trust Enabler in Human–AI Contexts

Emotional intelligence (EQ) functions as a basic human ability which enables people to build trust between humans and artificial intelligence systems through their cognitive and emotional development. People with elevated EQ levels demonstrate their ability to handle their emotions while showing compassion toward others and making ethical choices during situations that involve technological dangers and unpredictable circumstances. These abilities help people understand AI system outputs through both logical assessment and human value-based interpretation (Goleman, 1998). Strategic decision-making benefits from EQ because it converts system reliability into human trust through its function as a translation mechanism for human-AI teamwork.

The two-way impact of emotional intelligence in trust development occurs through leader ethical consistency and empathic communication, which boosts employee trust in AI systems while technology perception of intent and fairness and transparency improve in human-AI interactions (Hengstler, Enkel, & Duelli, 2016). The empathy aspect of EQ enables users to comprehend AI decision-making processes, while self-awareness and self-regulation abilities help leaders maintain ethical standards for decision-making.

Emotional intelligence builds trust between people and technology through its ability to enhance both human relationships and the trust people have in technology's knowledge and ethical conduct.

Research findings show that EQ stands as an essential element for explainable AI (XAI) frameworks. Leaders with high emotional intelligence create trust between employees and organisational information through their ability to explain AI results clearly and transparently (Rahwan et al., 2019). The method transforms automated decision systems from being seen as unfeeling machines into humanised systems which combine logical reasoning with emotional understanding and moral awareness. The implementation of EQ technology enables people to build emotional connections with machines, which leads to psychological trust in artificial intelligence systems.

The sustainable growth of human-AI trust depends on emotional intelligence, which functions as a behavioural activation factor. EQ creates a connection between technological precision and human values, which transforms trust into an ethical and emotional bond that goes beyond cognitive evaluation. Strategic decision-making processes benefit from EQ-based leadership methods, which transform AI systems into dependable ethical partners who work alongside humans.

2.4. Explainable Artificial Intelligence (XAI) and Building Trust

The implementation of artificial intelligence systems for strategic decision-making faces challenges regarding trust development because their algorithms operate as uninterpretable black boxes. The XAI system functions as a solution to explain algorithmic choices through clear and understandable methods.

The implementation of XAI systems enables users to develop cognitive trust because they need to understand the operational mechanics of the system (Adadi & Berrada, 2018). The implementation of XAI requires both technical and social elements because explanations need to match user requirements and emotional responses, and ethical standards (Arrieta et al., 2020). Research findings demonstrate that users' emotional responses depend heavily on the explanations they receive. Users experience anxiety when they receive complex technical explanations, but they develop both emotional trust and perceived fairness when they receive explanations that use narrative and empathetic approaches (Sydorenko, 2024).

XAI serves as a fundamental component which establishes a connection between cognitive trust and emotional trust. The delivery of explanations through clear reasoning and ethical foundations helps employees view AI systems as dependable decision support tools instead of simple technical instruments. Research shows that XAI designs which use emotion-based leadership methods create better user experiences and build stronger trust relationships (Kohli, 2024).

In healthcare AI systems, clinicians are more likely to trust AI-assisted diagnostic recommendations when explanations are communicated through patient-centred and interpretable narratives rather than purely technical outputs. Similarly, in AI-supported recruitment systems, perceptions of fairness are shaped not only by algorithmic transparency but also by communication style and emotional framing. These examples demonstrate the importance of human-centred and emotionally sensitive communication in explainable AI systems.

2.5. Algorithm Aversion, Algorithm Adoption, and the Regulatory Role of EQ

Individuals develop an aversion to algorithms because they lose faith in these systems after observing their errors. The research conducted by Dietvorst, Simmons and Massey (2015) demonstrated that users accept human mistakes better than algorithmic mistakes, yet view any algorithmic mistake as a major system-wide problem. The combination of these factors creates significant obstacles for AI implementation in strategic decision-making systems.

Research conducted after 2020 demonstrates that people base their avoidance of algorithms through both technical precision and emotional and psychological elements. The study by Longoni et al. (2019) demonstrated that staff members oppose AI implementation more strongly when their work demands special human judgment abilities and when they need to demonstrate empathy. The study by Castelo and Ward (2021) discovered that people's political beliefs, together with their risk assessment abilities and personal values, influence their emotional acceptance of AI systems.

The ability to understand emotions functions as a strong control system that emerges at this stage. Leaders who possess high emotional intelligence perform three essential functions:

- They minimise employee doubt through proper explanation of algorithmic mistakes,
- They establish AI as an assistance tool instead of a danger,
- They manage how staff members react emotionally,
- They build stronger emotional bonds through explanation and interpretation that demonstrates empathy.

The social "buffer" function of EQ helps organisations decrease algorithm avoidance while improving algorithm adoption rates. The absence of emotional connection between employees and the system requires EQ-based communication methods to establish sufficient trust.

2.6. Ethical Artificial Intelligence, Value Alignment, and Role of EQ

The ethical artificial intelligence (ethical AI) field has experienced rapid growth during the last decade because researchers now understand that AI systems need human value compatibility and must operate with transparency and accountability. The research by Jobin, Ienca and Vayena (2019) analysed 84 international AI ethics guidelines to identify transparency and accountability, fairness, human autonomy and value alignment as essential ethical AI principles.

Coeckelbergh (2020) maintains that AI systems cannot function as moral agents, so designers, managers and leaders bear full responsibility for ethical decisions. The process of achieving ethical compliance depends heavily on Emotional Intelligence (EQ) as a fundamental human ability. Leaders who demonstrate high EQ levels:

- show better ability to detect ethical issues,
- handle employee concerns through empathetic approaches,
- make better assessments about how AI choices affect society,
- create explanations about ethics that people can understand better.

Shneiderman (2020) supports human-centred AI development by showing that system design needs to include EQ-based principles, which include psychological safety and emotional comfort, and human value preservation.

The implementation of ethical AI depends on EQ as a fundamental element which works together with other components. Technical architecture alone cannot establish value alignment because sustainable implementation depends on leaders who demonstrate emotional awareness and empathy.

2.7. User Emotions, Technostress, and Psychological Safety

Organisations now focus on employee emotional responses because AI systems have become widespread in their operations. The technostress literature demonstrates that high technology usage creates stress, which produces anxiety, feelings of inadequacy and uncertainty and emotional exhaustion (Borle, Reichel & Voelter-Mahlknecht, 2021).

The introduction of AI technology has brought an additional level of stress to work environments because it now participates in decision-making operations. The implementation of AI technology leads to increased job insecurity and performance expectations, and fairness doubts, which combine to reduce workplace security for both mental and emotional well-being (Tarafdar, Cooper, & Stich, 2019).

Research about AI workplace transformation reveals that employee acceptance of AI systems directly relates to the degree of psychological safety workers experience during system deployment. Employees who experience psychological uncertainty because they do not understand AI operational mechanisms, decision-making systems or interaction protocols tend to view AI as dangerous. The perceived danger that employees experience stems from their concerns about job security, their lack of skills, and perceived discrimination in organisational procedures. Research indicates that employees will accept AI technology more readily when their leaders establish supportive environments which enable open questioning and mistake learning without fear of personal consequences (Meng, Wu, & Duan, 2025). Leaders need emotional intelligence (EQ) to perform their duties effectively at this stage. Leaders who demonstrate high emotional intelligence (EQ) excel at:

- decrease employee anxiety that stems from unclear situations,
- build up their employees' emotional strength,
- create psychological safety through their open dialogue approach,
- establish AI as a tool which works together with humans.

Organisations need emotional security and empathetic communication methods to decrease technostress and boost AI system acceptance, rather than depending on technical solutions. Organisations need to recognise EQ as both a personal skill and an essential requirement for successful AI transformation initiatives.

3. INTEGRATING EQ AND TRUST MODELS IN STRATEGIC DECISION-MAKING

Organisations need strategic decision-making processes to handle uncertainty and risks while building long-term value. The decision-making process now requires equal attention to ethical, emotional and cognitive elements because traditional models based on rational analysis and data-driven evaluation and optimisation principles no longer suffice. Strategic decision-making systems at individual and organisational levels function better when emotional intelligence (EQ) and trust work together as supporting elements (Mayer, Salovey, & Caruso, 2004; McAllister, 1995). Decision-makers who possess emotional intelligence (EQ) can handle uncertain situations better through their emotional awareness, empathy and self-regulation abilities, which lead to ethical choices. The organisational level acceptance and sustainability of these processes depend on trust, while EQ enables decision-makers to make balanced choices in uncertain situations (Mayer, Davis, & Schoorman, 1995).

Strategic decision-making processes integrate emotional intelligence with trust through cognitive-emotional integration. Leaders who demonstrate high emotional intelligence detect both factual data and emotional cues which stem from their relationships with team members and technological systems. The method produces essential results when organisations use AI for their decision-making operations. AI systems excel at data analysis, yet they cannot demonstrate human values and ethical consistency and intuitive decision-making (Rahwan et al., 2019). EQ functions as a contextual translator which enables the development of emotional trust from cognitive trust during human-AI teamwork. Leaders who demonstrate emotional intelligence competencies help their teams understand algorithmic results through empathetic interpretation, which builds employee trust and promotes active participation in decision-making (Goleman, 1998; Glikson & Woolley, 2020).

The three essential components of trust models, according to Mayer, Davis and Schoorman (1995), consist of competence, benevolence and integrity. The three core elements of EQ directly correspond to the fundamental components of EQ. The three elements of competence match with cognitive intelligence, while benevolence matches with empathy, and integrity matches with self-awareness and self-regulation competencies. The psychological base of trust depends on EQ, which operates as a fundamental competence that supports trust development. Leaders who demonstrate high emotional intelligence through honest communication and emotional consistency, and emotional sensitivity build enduring trust relationships with people and artificial intelligence systems (Ashkanasy & Daus, 2005; Clarke, 2010).

The combination of EQ with trust in strategic decision-making environments produces substantial outcomes which focus on ethical leadership and decision transparency. Leaders who possess high EQ levels create an environment where employees can participate freely, which leads to decisions that combine rational assessment with emotional and value-based considerations (George, 2000). The process allows employees to validate the ethical soundness of AI system-generated action options while maintaining their confidence in the decision-making system. The trust-based governance system for strategic decision communication to stakeholders emerges from EQ's empathy and communication abilities.

Glikson and Woolley (2020) explain that human-AI collaboration trust grows through both technical dependability and leaders who show emotional vulnerability and use human-centred communication methods.

Organisations need to integrate EQ with trust because their talent development systems operate dynamically. Leaders who demonstrate emotional intelligence develop strategic flexibility because they remain open to change and show emotional strength. The acceptance of organisational change by team members depends on trust, while their commitment to execute the change depends on trust (Mayer et al., 1995; Clarke, 2010). Leaders who demonstrate high EQ levels can handle team member emotional responses during technology integration projects, which results in lower team resistance to innovation adoption. The emotional climate regulation abilities of EQ enable organisations to distribute trust throughout their entire structure.

Research today shows that strategic leadership models for artificial intelligence need to study these two concepts together. Rahwan and his team (2019) establish human-machine interaction as a behavioural system in which emotional intelligence functions as its ethical control mechanism. The ability to detect and control emotional responses from algorithmic choices emerges from emotional intelligence. Strategic governance systems benefit from EQ as an organisational resource, which establishes trust while leaders use this skill to manage emotional responses from algorithmic choices.

The success of human-AI collaboration depends on strategic decision-making processes that unite emotional intelligence with trust. Leaders who possess EQ develop cognitive decision models with human intuition, ethical awareness and empathic balance, but trust ensures their processes gain organisational acceptance and effectiveness. Organisations that unite these two concepts create a complete governance framework which enables them to make strategic AI-era decisions that combine data-based approaches with human-focused, ethical and trustworthy methods.

4. METHODOLOGY

A systematic literature review is a methodological approach that aims to convey academic knowledge in an unbiased and holistic manner within a certain period of time, essentially addressing a specific research question. The main purpose of selecting the related method in this research is to present a comparative perspective of the research published between 2020 and 2025 on the interaction of the concepts of trust, artificial intelligence, and emotional intelligence.

In the method section of the research, data processing and collection processes and design are defined in detail. The research protocol, how the data were obtained, and the inclusion criteria were highlighted through the PRISMA flow chart. The main objective of the research is to systematically include studies focused on the themes of "emotional intelligence", "artificial intelligence", "decision making", and "trust building" published in EBSCO, Web of Science (WoS), and Science Direct databases between 2020 and 2025 in the content analysis process. Systematic content analysis is a very effective approach in terms of dividing qualitative and quantitative data into themes in line with the inclusion criteria and identifying patterns. After the content analysis, the data were examined with thematic visualisation analysis via the Python Julius Plug-in.

In this study, both qualitative and quantitative studies were included in the research, especially in order to understand the method distributions. Since the research covers measurable (Measuring employees' confidence levels, performance data obtained as a result of decision making) and (AI-human interaction experience, emotional responses, and perceived trust) entirely experience-based elements due to its subject, both qualitative and quantitative research were included in the protocol when designing the scope of the research. Thus, studies obtained from three different databases were analysed in terms of research method, theoretical framework, publication year, and keywords. Systematic content analysis can be defined as a very effective method for creating a screenshot of the existing literature and identifying gaps and trends in a multidisciplinary context. The philosophy of systematic literature review is to present a systematic output by reducing the biases and prejudices that researchers may have. In this way, the transferred data can be accessed in a repeatable and methodical manner rather than randomly. The systematic literature review method is particularly suitable for rapidly evolving conceptual interactions because it provides a projection by bringing together gaps and pieces of information in the existing literature.

In the research, studies addressing the concepts of emotional intelligence, artificial intelligence-human interaction, strategic decision-making, and trust building were included in the analysis process, based on the pinpointed keywords. The PRISMA-supported systematic literature and content review ensures that studies are considered according to specific criteria rather than randomly. The inclusion criteria determined for the related research are listed below;

- Studies published in Science Direct, EBSCO, and Web of Science databases were included in the search.
- Only studies published in English were reviewed.
- Research published from 2020 to June 2025 was examined.
- The articles were required to be related to at least one of the concepts of emotional intelligence, strategic decision making, and artificial intelligence-human collaboration.

Justification of the keyword selection process;

"Trust", "Emotional Intelligence", "AI-Human Collaboration", "AI", "Artificial Intelligence", and "Strategic Decision Making" included in the screening criteria of the research are related to the theoretical scope of the study. These keywords have paved the way for analysing how trust is constructed in artificial intelligence-human interaction, the dynamics that emerge in the context of strategic decision-making, and finally, the decisive role of emotional intelligence in this relationship.

Clarification of the screening protocol; The PRISMA flow chart was used as a primary support for defining the research's screening protocol. In the first stage, the Boolean operators "AND" were used to assess the interaction between the main concepts. Examinations were conducted through databases for "emotional intelligence," AND "trust," AND "artificial intelligence," AND "strategic decision making." The "OR" operator was then included in the search process to analyse other aspects of interaction between the concepts.

The systematic thematic analysis process followed a three-stage coding method. The process began with open coding, during which all studies included in the protocol were examined line by line. Fundamental patterns between concepts have been determined, and main themes have been established. Afterwards, the code clustering process was started with the axial coding model. The sub-themes included in the analysis process of the research were determined at this stage.

For instance, sub-theme patterns were identified among the sub-dimensions of emotional intelligence—emotional regulation, empathy, self-awareness, and types of trust (cognitive and affective). This process was also conducted separately for each variable. In the final stage, selective coding, the themes and sub-themes that were most repeated in the axial codes and most relevant to the research question were identified. The multi-stage process ensured that the thematic analysis was methodologically reliable and thematically deep.

To improve methodological reliability, we independently reviewed and coded the included studies. Any thematic inconsistencies were discussed and resolved collaboratively throughout the analysis process. Themes were refined iteratively to ensure consistency with the research objectives and conceptual structure of the research.

Utilising the PRISMA Diagram;

The Preferred Reporting Items for Systematic Reviews and Meta-Analyses (PRISMA) flow chart was employed to present the research in a repeatable, transparent, and systematic manner.

- Visual and numerical equivalents of the studies included and excluded from the protocol during the analysis phase were shared.
- Exclusion and elimination criteria are distinctly established.
- By means of the related flow, it was ensured that it was methodically repeatable and consistent, free from subjective preferences.

Although this research followed structural and systematic scanning and analysis methods, there are certain methodological limitations. First, all of the studies included in the study were in English. Some argue that this elimination limits cultural diversity. However, researchers make this choice because English is the preferred international language. Another limitation is that the analysis process was conducted using three databases. This could be interpreted by some as a limitation of the data pool, but the databases with the most published keywords in the relevant years were carefully selected during the research process.

Figure 1. Flowchart for Selection and Exclusion of Studies (According to PRISMA 2020)

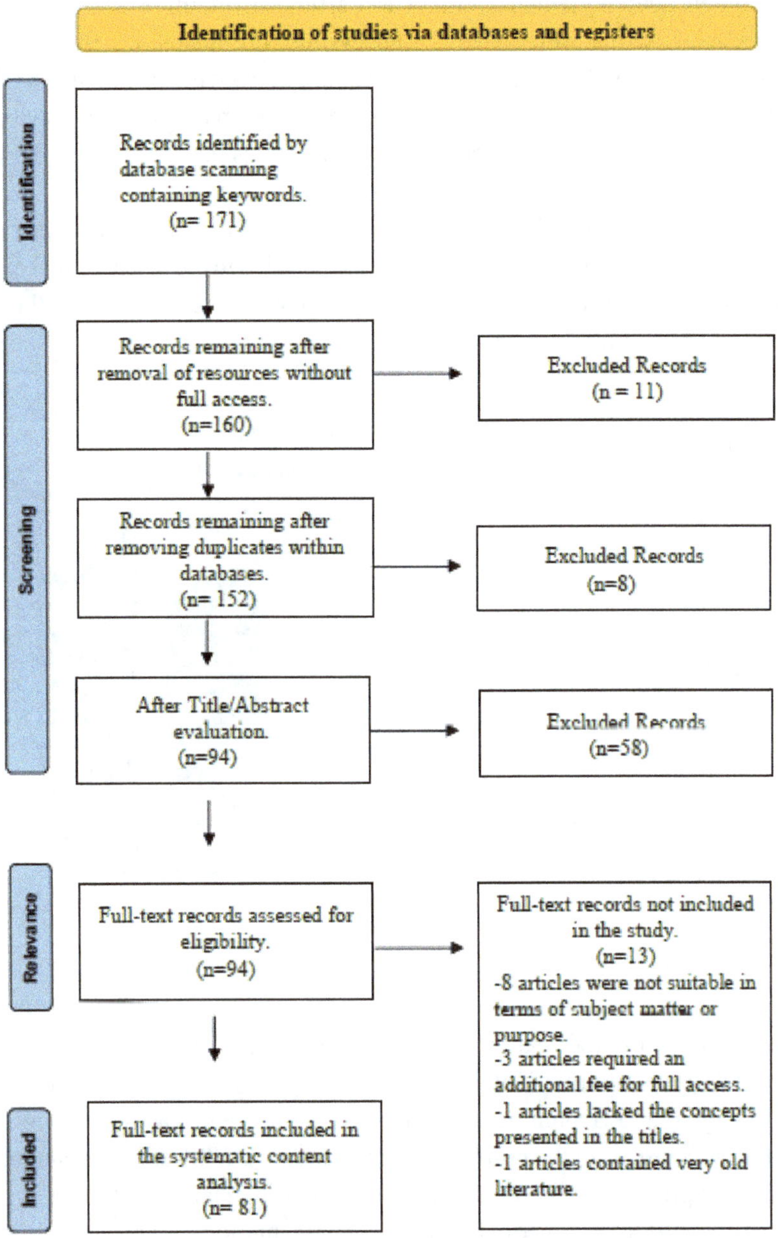

5. FINDINGS

The content search yielded a total of 171 articles from three different databases. Excluding studies that were not fully accessible, duplicates, or inappropriate in terms of content, a total of 90 studies were excluded from the protocol. The findings were evaluated in parallel with the research question, based on the distribution of publication years, database sources, research methods, and frequency distribution of main and sub-themes.

Consequently, a total of 71 studies were included in the content analysis process. When the frequency distribution of the studies included in the research was examined according to their publication years, there was a significant growth in the number of studies published between 2024 and 2025.

Figure 2. Distribution of research publications by year

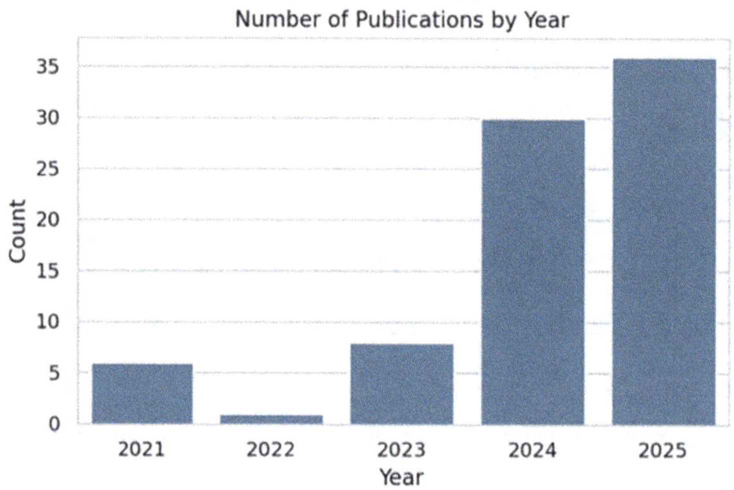

The reason is that the real increase in the number of publications expected for 2025 is not reflected numerically because the data were taken from the databases between August and September, and the rest of the year was not included in the research. The increase in the number of publications in 2025 can be evaluated in the context of the growth of the impact of artificial intelligence from the organisational perspective and the importance of human-centred technological approaches. Artificial intelligence technologies and strategic decision-making models are a very popular topic today, as the place of artificial intelligence applications is gaining importance day by day in institutions, and comprehensive research on trust mechanisms and emotional reactions is needed for AI-human collaboration to yield efficient results.

Figure 3. Distribution of publications by research method

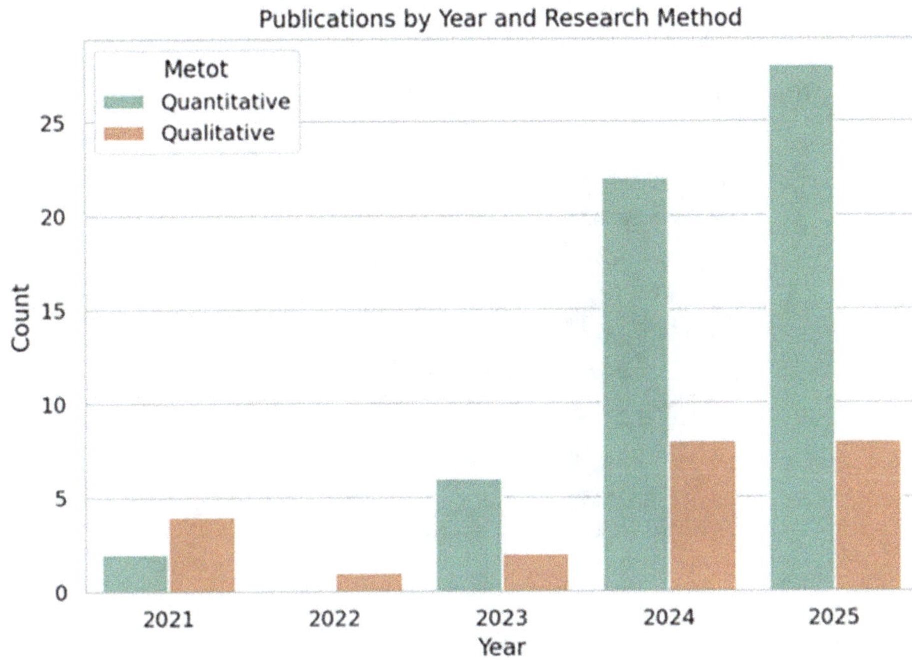

57 of the studies included in the research protocol were based on quantitative methods. This result is directly related to the fact that the use of artificial intelligence in organisations has been associated with measurable outcomes such as performance, error tolerance, trust levels, or user satisfaction.

Fundamentally, this situation is also related to the fact that concepts such as confidence calibration, cognitive trust, and algorithmic accuracy are fed with numerical data. Conversely, it is noteworthy that the remaining 23 studies were conducted utilising qualitative methods because, while artificial intelligence was examined as a direct technical performance support before 2023, after 2024, it began to be evaluated as a trust-building factor with an emotional dimension that can shape human experience.

Thus, it has become inevitable to focus on concepts that cannot be easily evaluated numerically, such as perceived ethical sensitivity, AI-human communication/interaction, empathy, and user experience. This finding suggests that emotional intelligence creates a very important axis both today and in the future.

When the databases included in the study are examined, it is seen that the EBSCO and Web of Science databases stand out in terms of the intersection of numbers and keywords. EBSCO and WoS showed high representation with 31 and 30 studies, respectively. This has shown that the relationship between social science studies focusing on organisational trust, emotional intelligence, and leadership, and artificial intelligence has been examined more in the mentioned databases.

Figure 4. Distribution of publications by database

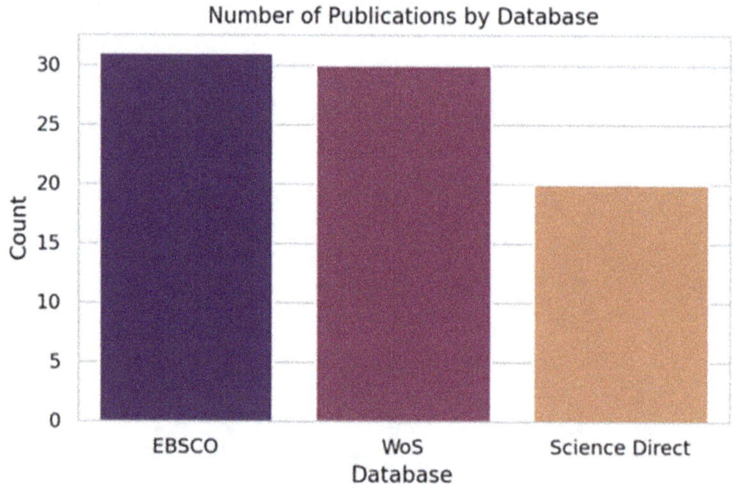

In addition, the Science Direct database included mostly engineering and technical-focused studies, and the intersection of keywords was found to be less representative. This suggests that artificial intelligence research is evaluated differently in terms of human and technical aspects in different disciplines. While the concepts of ethical decision-making, strategic decision-making, leadership, and trust are discussed under the heading of artificial intelligence-human collaboration in social sciences, the human variable is still not discussed in depth in technical disciplines.

As a result of the thematic analysis conducted in line with the published research in the databases, five separate main themes were obtained. The most frequently repeated theme is "emotional intelligence competencies and their impact on strategic decision making," and has been the subject of research 55 times. Thus, emotional intelligence has become an important concept that can directly affect the outcome of strategic decision-making processes and the building of trust in organisations, rather than just a personal competence that should be focused on.

Figure 5. Theme Mention Counts – Thematic Analysis Visualisation

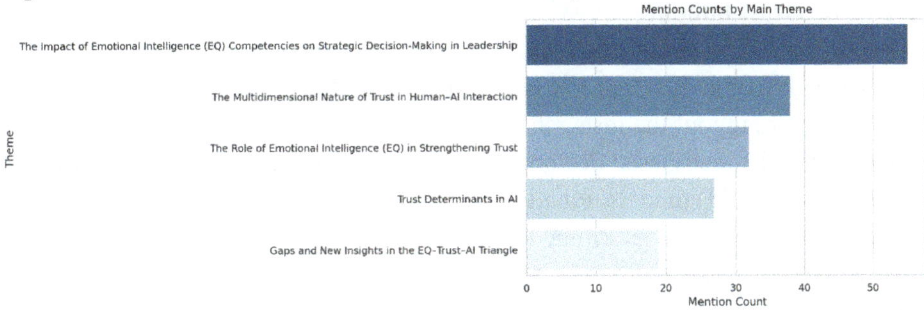

The second most common theme, "The multidimensional Nature of Trust in Human-AI Interaction", was mentioned 38 times, and when the emotional and cognitive dimensions of trust were examined, it was revealed that the trust that individuals develop toward artificial intelligence applications will not be limited to technical support and technical accuracy, but also depends on communication style and ethical compliance.

Figure 6. Sub-Theme Mention Counts – Thematic Analysis Visualisation

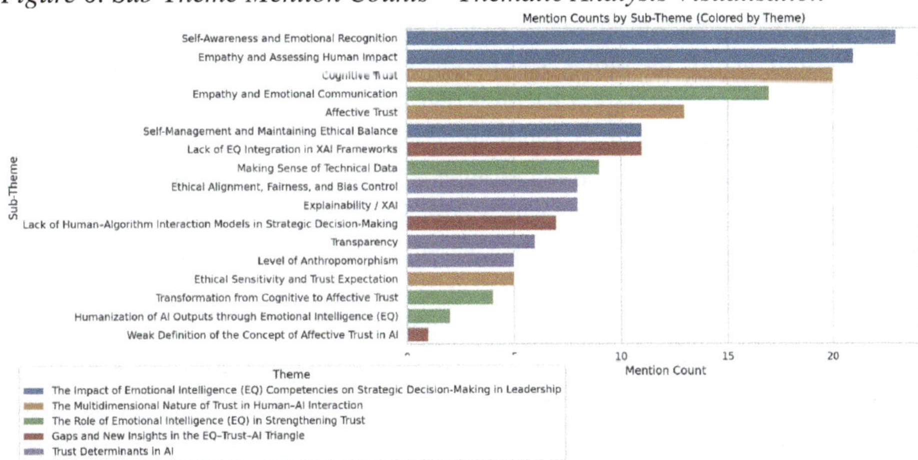

When the frequency of mention of the sub-dimensions of emotional intelligence was considered as a result of the analysis process, it was seen that it served as a backbone for the main concepts of the research. Empathy, emotional recognition, self-awareness, cognitive and affective trust were identified as the most researched and frequently mentioned sub-themes. This highlights how critical the emotionally driven concepts listed above are to the acceptance of AI-human collaboration and the intended trust-building.

Following the related analysis process, two sub-themes highlighted significant gaps. The sub-theme "Lack of EQ integration in the XAI Framework" was repeated 12 times throughout the research, emphasising the need for human-centred and emotional intelligence-based design components beyond the technical structure of explainable AI (XAI) models. Finally, the sub-theme "weak definition of Affective trust in AI", which was determined to be the least mentioned during the content analysis process, was mentioned only 3 times, revealing that the theoretical framework in this context is quite weak.

6. DISCUSSION

The findings of this research have shown that trust, artificial intelligence-human interaction, and EQ are becoming increasingly important and integrated in strategic decision-making. The increasing number of publications as a result of thematic content analyses conducted with the Python Julius Plug-in indicated that the concept of emotional intelligence has become central to the success of artificial intelligence-human collaboration. This supports the need for "human-centred artificial intelligence" that Glikson and his colleagues emphasised in 2020.

The most frequently mentioned sub-theme was "The impact of EQ competencies on strategic decision-making", revealing that emotional intelligence is no longer just an individual talent but also a strategic competency that is highly valuable for organisations. The core emotional intelligence components that leaders must possess, such as emotional regulation, self-awareness, ethical sensitivity, and empathy, directly affect employees' acceptance of AI-supported decision-making models.

In this context, emotional intelligence serves as two fundamental transformation/move-on mechanisms for organisations to enable AI-human collaboration in strategic decision-making. First, the type of trust cognitively generated by the leadership competencies listed above can be transformed into affective trust. To put it differently, the perception of technical accuracy provided by AI technologies can be integrated with ethical and human values and incorporated into decision-making processes.

The second mechanism is to evaluate AI outputs within a transparent, humane, and ethical framework. This will allow employees to build greater affective trust in AI-supported decision-making mechanisms and ensure continued involvement in processes. Thematic analysis has shown that when examining the concept of trust in an organisational context, it would be insufficient to discuss AI-human collaboration in a single dimension. Cognitive and affective trust are two mechanisms that develop independently but continue to function symbiotically. The findings show that while cognitive trust is an expected type of trust at the intersection of relevant keywords, affective trust is mentioned far less than expected in the literature.

One of the important and striking findings of the research is that emotional intelligence is an element that supports both emotional trust and cognitive trust. Sub-dimensions such as empathy, self-awareness, and emotion regulation directly affect employee trust in AI's strategic decision-making processes. It has been revealed that cognitive trust, which is the only supporter of AI-human collaboration put forward in the literature to date, is not actually sufficient.

Although artificial intelligence-based decision-making systems are considered technically safe and reliable, a sustainable perception of trust will not be established if individuals do not evaluate those systems fairly, humanely, predictably, and ethically. Because the two types of trust support each other. When affective trust is lacking, institutional/organisational acceptance remains limited. Therefore, it is possible to say that emotional intelligence can function as a human factor or anchor that eliminates the above-mentioned deficiency.

Conversely, it has been observed that psychology is an important dimension of human interaction with artificial intelligence. Because organisations/employees approach AI-supported systems not only as a system performance but also as a social entity. Even in technology acceptance theory, we see that users accept a technology if they can establish a benefit-intention connection, and there is no emotional dimension in the model. This perspective is largely consistent with the Technology Acceptance Model proposed by Davis (1989), which emphasises perceived usefulness and ease of use as key determinants of technology adoption. Emotional intelligence and its sub-dimensions are currently missing from all models supporting artificial intelligence and human collaboration. This finding can be considered one of the most important outcomes of the research. Emotional intelligence can transform the uncertainty, mechanical, and cold nature of interaction by softening employees' anti-technology concerns, which can be considered as technostress.

Additionally, the research also has an aspect that directly affects organisations and leadership perceptions. The findings show that employee-AI interaction is directly shaped by the leader's attitude. Leaders with high emotional intelligence, strong communication skills, and confidence can successfully convey strategic decisions powered by artificial intelligence to employees from both human and technical perspectives. When emotional and cognitive trust work together, it can reduce the resistance to change that employees may have.

Another notable finding of the study is the relatively high recurrence of the subtheme "lack of EQ integration in the XAI framework" within the literature. This finding indicates that XAI is limited in incorporating emotional intelligence into human-based interpretation processes and largely proceeds through technical optimisation.

XAI models are used in the context of providing transparency in organisations, transferring machine logic to individuals, and providing an algorithmic explanation. However, this information provided is not shaped by the human perspective that emotional intelligence provides. In other words, for AI-human collaboration to be sustainable, disclosure mechanisms are directly related not only to technical competence and features, but also to how users and leaders interpret these disclosures in a social and emotional context.

Finally, during the analysis of sub-themes, the repetition of the concepts of social communication, empathy, ethical compliance, and emotional awareness signals that the concept of leadership must also be reshaped in the business world, changing with artificial intelligence. Although artificial intelligence-supported decision systems provide technical accuracy, the human touch is considered vital for process continuity and trust. This depends on the emotional intelligence capacity and competence of leaders supported by related technologies. Therefore, today, artificial intelligence and human collaboration are no longer considered a purely technical process. It has become an interactive process that requires emotional, ethical, and intense communication.

6.1 Limitations and Boundary Conditions of EQ-Based Trust

Emotional intelligence plays a significant role in helping people trust each other when working with artificial intelligence. But it's not a magic solution that can fix all trust and ethics problems. Just because a leader is good at understanding emotions, it doesn't mean they will always use AI in a responsible way or build trust that lasts. Some researchers have raised criticisms regarding the measurement validity and conceptual boundaries of the concept of emotional intelligence (Locke, 2005).

Excessive reliance on emotional framing may reduce critical evaluation of AI systems and contribute to over-trust. In some cases, emotionally persuasive communication may unintentionally weaken analytical scrutiny and increase biased interpretations of AI-supported outputs. Therefore, emotional trust should be balanced with cognitive evaluation and transparent governance mechanisms.

Building trust between humans and AI systems is not just about how good a leader is. Other things like the culture of the organisation, how it's governed, how transparent it is, and how well it can explain things also matter a lot. That's why emotional intelligence is important, but it should be used along with making sure the technology is transparent and the organisation is governed in an ethical way. This way, we can make sure that humans and AI systems can work together smoothly and sustainably.

6.2 Practical Implications

To really make the most of AI in decision-making, companies need to focus on more than just the technology itself. They also need to develop leaders who can work well with people and make good choices. This means leaders should be able to understand and manage their emotions, communicate in a way that shows they care about others, and make decisions that are fair and right. When leaders have these skills, their teams are more likely to trust the AI systems they use.

Organisations should see explainable AI systems as more than just a way to make technology transparent - they should also be used to help employees feel safe and supported. In areas like human resources, healthcare, and finance, where things can be very uncertain, it's really important that employees can understand what the AI is doing and why. This helps employees feel more comfortable with the system and more likely to use it. By using AI in a way that prioritises human needs and communication, organisations can create a more positive and supportive work environment.

To reduce employee uncertainty during AI transformation processes, organisations should adopt transparent communication practices, ethical governance policies, and psychologically supportive implementation strategies. Recent studies also highlight that AI-supported workplaces may generate concerns related to monitoring, algorithmic control, and employee autonomy (Kellogg et al., 2020). In this context, emotional intelligence represents an important organisational capability that supports sustainable trust formation in human–AI collaboration.

Essentially, this research has strongly demonstrated that emotional intelligence is a mechanism that will shape the trust that will develop between AI and humans. The theoretical framework of the study also emphasised that considering emotional intelligence only as an individual competence is a rather outdated view, and that the relevant concept is now an element that should be positioned at the centre of organisational communication, strategic decision-making processes, and XAI design. In this respect, this research aims to form a basis for future research on the axis of artificial intelligence-trust-emotional intelligence to be more profound, practical and multi-perspective.

7. FUTURE RESEARCH DIRECTIONS

This research looked at how emotional intelligence, trust, and people working with artificial intelligence are connected. Now, it's time for more studies to test these ideas in the real world. We need to see numbers and stories from leaders and teams in different industries to really understand how emotional intelligence helps build trust when people work with AI.

Existing literature has only limitedly analysed the role of affective trust in human–AI interaction. Future research could focus on the measurement of affective trust and the longitudinal development of trust relationships in AI-supported environments.

There's still a lot to learn about how cultural differences affect the way we trust machines when we work together with them. It would be really helpful if future studies could look into how people from different cultures feel about artificial intelligence, and how that affects their trust in it. For example, researchers could explore how empathy, ethics, and acceptance of AI vary from one culture to another. By doing so, we can gain a better understanding of how cultural values shape our emotional trust in AI, what we expect from it in terms of ethics, and how we respond to decisions made with the help of AI systems. This knowledge can help us build more effective human-AI collaborations that take into account the diverse perspectives and values of people from different cultural backgrounds.

It's also a good idea for future studies to look at how people and AI systems work together in different areas, like healthcare, banking, government, and personnel management. They should compare how things work in each area. This is important because building trust and getting people to accept AI might involve different psychological and organisational factors depending on the specific area they're being used in.

Finally, the development of emotional intelligence-based communication models in explainable artificial intelligence (XAI) systems represents an important area of research in user-centred AI design. How technical explainability can be integrated with human interpretability and psychological safety presents a critical research agenda for future work.

REFERENCES

Adadi, A., & Berrada, M. (2018). Peeking inside the black-box: A survey on explainable artificial intelligence (XAI). *IEEE Access : Practical Innovations, Open Solutions, 6*, 52138–52160. DOI: 10.1109/ACCESS.2018.2870052

Ashkanasy, N. M., & Daus, C. S. (2005). Rumors of the death of emotional intelligence in organizational behavior are vastly exaggerated. *Journal of Organizational Behavior, 26*(4), 441–452. DOI: 10.1002/job.320

Binns, R., Van Kleek, M., Veale, M., Lyngs, U., Zhao, J., & Shadbolt, N. (2018). 'It's reducing a human being to a percentage': Perceptions of justice in algorithmic decisions. *Proceedings of the 2018 CHI Conference on Human Factors in Computing Systems*. https://doi.org/DOI: 10.1145/3173574.3173951

Borle, P., Reichel, K., & Voelter-Mahlknecht, S. (2021). Is there a sampling bias in research on work-related technostress? A systematic review of occupational exposure to technostress and the role of socioeconomic position. *International Journal of Environmental Research and Public Health, 18*(4), 2071. DOI: 10.3390/ijerph18042071 PMID: 33672604

Brynjolfsson, E., & McAfee, A. (2017). *Machine, platform, crowd: Harnessing our digital future*. W.W. Norton & Company.

Castelo, N., & Ward, A. F. (2021). Conservatism predicts aversion to consequential artificial intelligence. *PLoS One, 16*(12), e0261467. DOI: 10.1371/journal.pone.0261467 PMID: 34928989

Clarke, N. (2010). Emotional intelligence and its relationship to transformational leadership and key project manager competences. *Project Management Journal, 41*(2), 5–20. DOI: 10.1002/pmj.20162

Coeckelbergh, M. (2020). *AI Ethics*. MIT Press (Essential Knowledge series).

Davis, F. D. (1989). Perceived usefulness, perceived ease of use, and user acceptance of information technology. *Management Information Systems Quarterly, 13*(3), 319–340. DOI: 10.2307/249008

Dietvorst, B. J., Simmons, J. P., & Massey, C. (2015). Algorithm aversion: People erroneously avoid algorithms after seeing them err. *Journal of Experimental Psychology. General, 144*(1), 114–126. DOI: 10.1037/xge0000033 PMID: 25401381

Ehsan, U., Liao, Q. V., Muller, M., Riedl, M. O., & Weisz, J. D. (2021). Expanding explainability: Towards social transparency in AI systems. *Proceedings of the 2021 CHI Conference on Human Factors in Computing Systems*. https://doi.org/DOI: 10.1145/3411764.3445188

George, J. M. (2000). Emotions and leadership: The role of emotional intelligence. *Human Relations*, *53*(8), 1027–1055. DOI: 10.1177/0018726700538001

Glikson, E., & Woolley, A. W. (2020). Human trust in artificial intelligence: Review of empirical research. *The Academy of Management Annals*, *14*(2), 627–660. DOI: 10.5465/annals.2018.0057

Goleman, D. (1998). *Working with emotional intelligence*. Bantam Books.

Hengstler, M., Enkel, E., & Duelli, S. (2016). Applied artificial intelligence and trust—The case of autonomous vehicles. *Technological Forecasting and Social Change*, *105*, 105–120. DOI: 10.1016/j.techfore.2015.12.014

Hoff, K. A., & Bashir, M. (2015). Trust in automation: Integrating empirical evidence on factors that influence trust. *Human Factors*, *57*(3), 407–434. DOI: 10.1177/0018720814547570 PMID: 25875432

Horowitz, M. C., & Kahn, L. (2024). Bending the automation bias curve: A study of human and AI-based decision making in national security contexts. *International Studies Quarterly*, *68*(2), sqae020. Advance online publication. DOI: 10.1093/isq/sqae020

Jobin, A., Ienca, M., & Vayena, E. (2019). The global landscape of AI ethics guidelines. *Nature Machine Intelligence*, *1*(9), 389–399. DOI: 10.1038/s42256-019-0088-2

Kellogg, K. C., Valentine, M. A., & Christin, A. (2020). Algorithms at work: The new contested terrain of control. *The Academy of Management Annals*, *14*(1), 366–410. DOI: 10.5465/annals.2018.0174

Kohli, S. (2024). Building user trust in conversational AI: The role of explainable AI in chatbot transparency. *International Journal of Computer Engineering and Technology*, *15*(5), 406–413. DOI: 10.5281/zenodo.13833413

Lewicki, R. J., & Bunker, B. B. (1996). Developing and maintaining trust in work relationships. In Kramer, R. M., & Tyler, T. R. (Eds.), *Trust in organizations: Frontiers of theory and research* (pp. 114–139). Sage Publications., DOI: 10.4135/9781452243610.n7

Locke, E. A. (2005). Why emotional intelligence is an invalid concept. *Journal of Organizational Behavior*, *26*(4), 425–431. DOI: 10.1002/job.318

Longoni, C., Bonezzi, A., & Morewedge, C. K. (2019). Resistance to medical artificial intelligence. *The Journal of Consumer Research*, *46*(4), 629–650. DOI: 10.1093/jcr/ucz013

Mayer, J. D., Davis, J. H., & Schoorman, F. D. (1995). An integrative model of organizational trust. *Academy of Management Review*, *20*(3), 709–734. DOI: 10.2307/258792

Mayer, J. D., Salovey, P., & Caruso, D. R. (2004). Emotional intelligence: Theory, findings, and implications. *Psychological Inquiry*, *15*(3), 197–215. DOI: 10.1207/s15327965pli1503_02

McAllister, D. J. (1995). Affect- and cognition-based trust as foundations for interpersonal cooperation in organizations. *Academy of Management Journal*, *38*(1), 24–59. https://www.jstor.org/stable/256727. DOI: 10.2307/256727

Meng, Q., Wu, T.-J., Duan, W., & Li, S. (2025). Effects of Employee–Artificial Intelligence (AI) Collaboration on Counterproductive Work Behaviors (CWBs): Leader Emotional Support as a Moderator. *Behavioral Sciences (Basel, Switzerland)*, *15*(5), 696. DOI: 10.3390/bs15050696 PMID: 40426473

Qian, J., Wang, B., Han, Z., & Song, B. (2017). Ethical leadership, leader-member exchange and feedback seeking: A double-moderated mediation model of emotional intelligence and work-unit structure. *Frontiers in Psychology*, *8*, 1174. DOI: 10.3389/fpsyg.2017.01174 PMID: 28744251

Rahwan, I., Cebrian, M., Obradovich, N., Bongard, J., Bonnefon, J. F., Breazeal, C., Crandall, J. W., Christakis, N. A., Couzin, I. D., Jackson, M. O., Jennings, N. R., Kamar, E., Kloumann, I. M., Larochelle, H., Lazer, D., McElreath, R., Mislove, A., Parkes, D. C., Pentland, A. S., & Wellman, M. (2019). Machine behaviour. *Nature*, *568*(7753), 477–486. DOI: 10.1038/s41586-019-1138-y PMID: 31019318

Rousseau, D. M., Sitkin, S. B., Burt, R. S., & Camerer, C. (1998). Not so different after all: A cross-discipline view of trust. *Academy of Management Review*, *23*(3), 393–404. DOI: 10.5465/amr.1998.926617

Shneiderman, B. (2020, May 27). *Human-centered artificial intelligence: Reliable, safe & trustworthy.* University of Maryland, Department of Computer Science. https://www.cs.umd.edu/article/2020/05/shneiderman-proposes-human-centered-artificial-intelligence-reliable-safe

Sydorenko, T. (2024). The impact of AI explainability on cognitive dissonance and trust in human-AI recruitment teams. *European Journal of Science, Innovation and Technology. 5(1), 154-167, 2025.*

Tarafdar, M., Cooper, C. L., & Stich, J.-F. (2019). The technostress trifecta — techno-eustress, techno-distress and design: Theoretical directions and an agenda for research. *Information Systems Journal*, *29*(1), 6–42. DOI: 10.1111/isj.12169

Zhang, Y., Liao, Q. V., & Bellamy, R. K. E. (2020). Effect of confidence and explanation on accuracy and trust calibration in AI-assisted decision making. *Proceedings of the 2020 ACM Conference on Fairness, Accountability, and Transparency*, 295–306. https://doi.org/DOI: 10.1145/3351095.3372852

Chapter 10
The AI-Driven Workplace Revolution:
A Critical Analysis of Transformation Patterns and Adaptation Strategies

Göran Roos
http://orcid.org/0000-0003-0943-3585
University of Adelaide, Australia

ABSTRACT

This chapter analyses AI-driven workplace transformation through systematic hypothesis testing across institutional, sectoral, and demographic contexts. Evidence challenges technological determinism, revealing that transformation effectiveness depends on organisational readiness rather than technical capabilities alone. Key findings include: only 7% of organisations achieve advanced AI maturity; sectoral variations reflect regulatory frameworks rather than uniform technological impact; Millennials demonstrate highest AI competency while Generation Z faces cognitive offloading risks; human-AI collaboration preserving agency outperforms automation strategies. Critical challenges involve inequality amplification through compound disadvantages, whilst opportunities emerge through enhanced human capabilities. Strategic implications emphasise augmentation-first approaches, comprehensive stakeholder engagement, and adaptive governance balancing innovation with social protection through contextually appropriate rather than universal solutions.

DOI: 10.4018/979-8-3373-5816-1.ch010

INTRODUCTION

By the opening months of 2026, the integration of artificial intelligence into workplace environments had reached unprecedented scale, with 72–78% of organisations globally reporting AI implementation in at least one business function by late 2024, representing a marked increase from 55% in 2023 (Chui et al., 2025; Maslej et al., 2025). The Stanford AI Index 2026 further documents that generative AI specifically has reached approximately 53% global population use within three years of public availability, outpacing the adoption curves of both personal computing and the internet, whilst corporate AI investment has concentrated sharply, with US$285.9 billion in US private AI investment in 2025 against US$12.4 billion in China (Maslej et al., 2026). This transformation extends beyond mere technological adoption to encompass fundamental restructuring of work processes, skill requirements, and organisational hierarchies. The scope of this change becomes evident when examining specific sectors: financial services report 75% adoption rates, manufacturing achieves 77% implementation across surveyed organisations, and even traditionally conservative sectors such as healthcare demonstrate accelerating integration patterns (Gharbawi et al., 2024; Global Market Insights Inc., 2024).

However, the narrative of uniform AI-driven transformation obscures significant variation in adoption patterns, effectiveness outcomes, and societal consequences across different contexts. Recent analysis reveals that only 7% of organisations achieve Stage 4 AI future-readiness according to MIT CISR's Enterprise AI Maturity Model, whilst 90% of AI use cases remain trapped in pilot phases despite technical capability (Weill et al., 2024; Sukharevsky et al., 2025). This implementation paradox suggests that technological sophistication alone fails to guarantee transformation success.

Recent evidence reveals that AI implementation success depends critically on institutional readiness factors rather than technological capabilities alone (Merhi, 2023; Yu et al., 2023). This finding challenges deterministic assumptions about AI's workplace impact and suggests that transformation outcomes result from complex interactions between technological potential and organisational context. The implications extend beyond individual organisations to encompass broader questions about economic development patterns, social equity, and the future structure of labour markets globally.

Moreover, contradictory evidence regarding AI productivity benefits indicates that implementation approaches significantly influence whether AI systems enhance or undermine human capabilities (Raisch & Krakowski, 2021; Malik et al., 2022). A meta-analysis of 106 experimental studies reports that, on average, human–AI combinations perform significantly worse than the best of humans or AI alone (Hedges' $g = -0.23$, 95% CI [−0.39, −0.07]), with clear losses in decision-making tasks but meaningful gains in content-creation tasks (Vaccaro et al., 2024). This heterogeneous pattern illuminates the complexity of human–AI collaboration and challenges both simplistic automation narratives and uncritical augmentation optimism.

The global economic implications prove substantial, with McKinsey projecting a US$13–15.5 trillion contribution to global economic activity by 2030, whilst the World Economic Forum forecasts net employment growth of 78 million positions through the creation of 170 million new roles offset by 92 million displaced positions (Manyika et al., 2023; World Economic Forum, 2025). However, these aggregate projections mask significant distributional concerns, with computing infrastructure requirements multiplying existing disparities by factors of twenty to 1,700 between high- and low-income contexts (Dubey, 2025).

THEORETICAL FRAMEWORK

This chapter develops a multi-level theoretical framework integrating task-based automation theory (Acemoglu & Restrepo, 2019), organisational learning perspectives (Ransbotham et al., 2020), and new institutional theory adapted for AI contexts (Rudko et al., 2025). The task-based framework distinguishes automation effects that substitute human labour from augmentation effects that enhance human capabilities, whilst recognising transformation effects that create entirely new occupational categories. This tripartite classification proves essential for understanding why similar technologies produce divergent employment outcomes across contexts.

The framework extends beyond traditional economic models by incorporating institutional mediating factors that shape technology deployment and effectiveness. Evidence from comparative healthcare systems illustrates this mediation, with Nordic countries achieving higher AI adoption rates through integrated health systems and robust data protection frameworks, whilst fragmented systems demonstrate slower progress despite equivalent technical capabilities (European Commission, 2024). This variation cannot be explained through technological determinism alone.

New institutional theory provides insight into why similar AI technologies produce divergent outcomes across different organisational and cultural contexts (Rudko et al., 2025; Faulconbridge et al., 2025). This perspective recognises that technological effects operate through existing social structures, regulatory frameworks, and cultural norms rather than independent of institutional context. The theory helps explain systematic variations in AI adoption patterns across sectors, regions, and demographic groups whilst illuminating the mechanisms through which institutions mediate technological change.

Organisational learning theory contributes understanding of how firms develop AI capabilities over time through iterative processes rather than one-time implementation events (Ransbotham et al., 2020). Evidence shows that organisations demonstrating the Organisational Learning with AI Framework achieve 14% productivity increases, but effectiveness depends on sustained organisational commitment to process adaptation rather than simple technology deployment. This finding emphasises the dynamic nature of AI transformation and the importance of adaptive capacity in determining outcomes.

The theoretical synthesis acknowledges that AI workplace transformation occurs at multiple levels simultaneously: individual workers adapt skills and practices, organisations restructure processes and hierarchies, industries transform competitive dynamics, and societies grapple with distributional consequences. Understanding these interconnected levels proves crucial for developing effective intervention strategies and policy responses.

The analytical spine of this framework is a tripartite classification of the pathways by which AI deployment alters work. Figure 1 renders this Three-Stage AI Impact Model visually, showing how task characteristics push AI deployment toward automation, augmentation or transformation, and how institutional mediating factors — regulation, organisational readiness, professional norms, and policy intervention — sit between technological potential and realised workplace outcomes. The figure anchors the rest of the chapter to this single conceptual spine.

Figure 1. The Three-Stage AI Impact Model with Institutional Mediating Factors

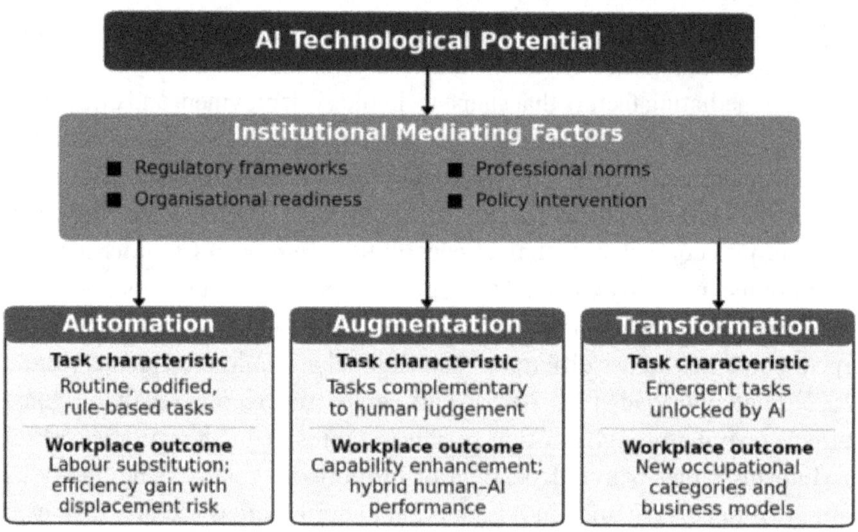

Note. The three pathways are analytically distinct but empirically overlapping: a single AI deployment can produce automation effects on some tasks, augmentation effects on others, and transformation effects through the creation of wholly new roles. Institutional mediating factors operate between technological potential and realised workplace outcomes and are the central mechanism by which the institutional context hypothesis (H1) is tested in this chapter. Adapted from the task-based framework of Acemoglu and Restrepo (2019), extended to incorporate institutional mediation following Rudko et al. (2025).

RESEARCH HYPOTHESES

This chapter tests five primary hypotheses derived from the theoretical framework:

H1: Institutional Context Hypothesis - AI workplace transformation effectiveness varies systematically across institutional contexts, with success determined by organisational readiness factors rather than technological capabilities alone. This hypothesis predicts that similar AI technologies will produce different outcomes based on complementary investments in human capital, governance systems, and cultural change management.

H2: Generational Differentiation Hypothesis - Generational differences in AI adaptation reflect distinct socialisation experiences and learning preferences, requiring differentiated rather than uniform implementation approaches. The hypothesis anticipates that digital native assumptions about younger generations may prove misleading, whilst professional maturity combined with digital familiarity creates optimal adaptation conditions.

H3: Sectoral Variation Hypothesis - Sectoral variations in AI adoption patterns result from differences in task characteristics, regulatory frameworks, and competitive pressures rather than technological determinism. This predicts systematic differences in implementation approaches, success rates, and transformation outcomes across industries based on structural factors rather than technology availability.

H4: Human Agency Preservation Hypothesis - Human-AI collaboration approaches that preserve agency and cognitive engagement achieve superior long-term outcomes compared to automation-focused strategies. The hypothesis suggests that augmentation approaches will demonstrate greater sustainability and effectiveness than replacement approaches, particularly when designed to prevent cognitive offloading.

H5: Inequality Amplification Hypothesis - Geographic and demographic inequalities in AI access create compound disadvantages that require targeted policy intervention to prevent amplification of existing disparities. This predicts that market-driven AI deployment will systematically exacerbate existing inequalities unless counteracted through deliberate policy intervention.

CHAPTER STRUCTURE

This chapter proceeds through systematic analysis of the contemporary AI workplace landscape, examining deployment effectiveness patterns and sectoral adoption variations that illuminate institutional mediating factors. The subsequent discussion of multigenerational adaptation patterns reveals how demographic characteristics interact with technological change, challenging assumptions about digital native advantages whilst identifying optimal adaptation conditions.

The analysis of sectoral transformation patterns demonstrates context-dependent outcomes across knowledge-intensive industries, service sectors, and manufacturing environments, providing evidence for institutional mediation of technological effects. The ensuing treatment of workforce development strategies analyses individual, organisational, and policy-level responses, evaluating effectiveness across different implementation approaches.

Critical challenges and emerging opportunities are examined next, identifying persistent structural barriers alongside value creation potential and the strategic decision points between automation and augmentation approaches. From this analysis, the chapter synthesises strategic implications into practical recommendations for organisational strategy, policy frameworks, and individual development approaches.

The chapter then acknowledges its methodological limitations before offering a systematic evaluation of the five research hypotheses against the empirical evidence. The concluding discussion synthesises key findings, theoretical contributions, and future research directions whilst emphasising the contextual nature of AI workplace transformation.

THE CONTEMPORARY AI WORKPLACE LANDSCAPE: CRITICAL ASSESSMENT OF IMPLEMENTATION PATTERNS

Technology Deployment Effectiveness

The integration of AI technologies into workplace environments demonstrates systematic variation in effectiveness across implementation contexts, supporting the institutional context hypothesis (H1). Evidence reveals that technical sophistication correlates weakly with implementation success, whilst organisational readiness factors determine outcomes (Merhi, 2023; Pumplun et al., 2019). Analysis of over 1,000 AI implementations across multiple industries reveals that fewer than 30% achieve projected ROI within two years, despite technical functionality (Chui et al., 2025).

Critical success factors emerge as organisational rather than technological, including appropriate change management, cultural readiness, workforce engagement, and gradual implementation approaches. High-performing organisations demonstrate three times higher trust in AI versus intuition compared to struggling implementations, whilst achieving 2.1 times greater ROI through concentrated high-value use cases rather than dispersed resource allocation (Rowan et al., 2025; Chui et al., 2025). These findings contradict technology-centric implementation approaches and emphasise institutional capability development.

The cumulative attrition between initial adoption and realised enterprise value is the most striking feature of the contemporary AI workplace landscape. Figure 2 renders this as an implementation-paradox funnel, descending from the 72–78% of organisations that have implemented AI in at least one business function, through the roughly 30% that achieve projected ROI within two years, to the 10% that progress beyond pilot, and finally to the 7% that reach Stage 4 enterprise AI maturity. The shape of the funnel is the single most powerful argument in the chapter for the institutional context hypothesis: the gap between the widest and narrowest rungs is almost entirely attributable to organisational rather than technological factors.

Figure 2. The AI Implementation Paradox Funnel: From Adoption to Enterprise Maturity

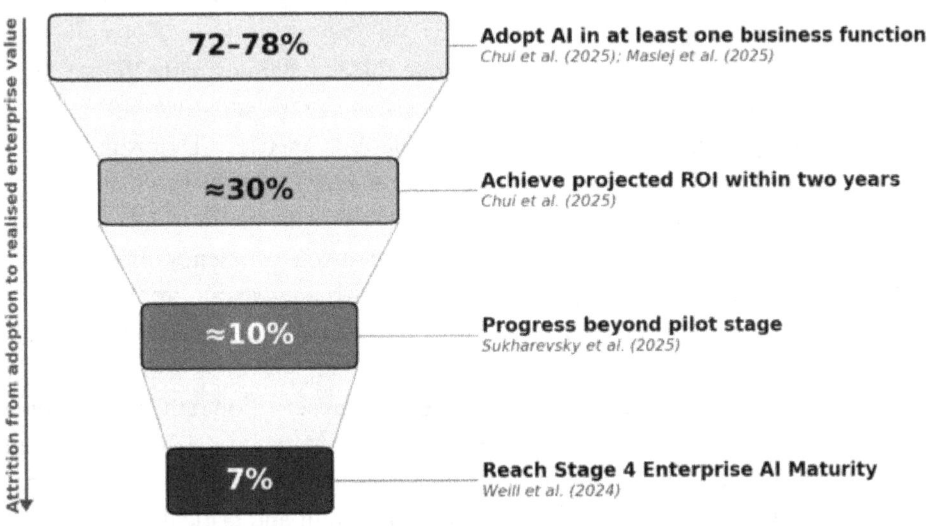

Note. Funnel rungs are not strictly nested categories drawn from a single dataset; they are indicative estimates drawn from four independent evidence bases (Chui et al., 2025; Maslej et al., 2025; Sukharevsky et al., 2025; Weill et al., 2024). The figure is intended to convey the directional attrition pattern rather than precise transition rates.

Rungs may overlap in practice: some organisations achieve ROI without reaching Stage 4 maturity, and others reach later stages without fully closing the ROI gap.

Generative AI Applications.

Generative AI deployment in knowledge work presents contradictory evidence regarding productivity benefits, revealing the importance of implementation approach rather than technology capability alone. Controlled trials demonstrate substantial productivity gains with consultants achieving 25% faster task completion and 40% higher quality outputs using GPT-4 assistance (Dell'Acqua et al., 2023). However, these gains prove task-specific and context-dependent, with effectiveness varying dramatically based on use case selection and user training quality.

Longitudinal studies reveal concerning patterns where initial productivity improvements decline over time as workers become over-reliant on AI systems, supporting the human agency preservation hypothesis (Kumar et al., 2024; Malik et al., 2022). Evidence of cognitive offloading demonstrates strong negative correlation (-0.68) between AI usage and critical thinking abilities, particularly problematic among younger users entering career development phases (Gerlich, 2025). This finding suggests that productivity gains may come at the cost of skill development and cognitive capability.

Professional services applications illustrate these dynamics with 26% of legal organisations actively using generative AI, representing 86% year-over-year growth, yet facing complex implications beyond productivity metrics (Thomson Reuters Institute, 2024). Professional time savings of five hours weekly mask underlying tensions about service quality, professional identity transformation, and client relationship dynamics. Legal professionals report simultaneous efficiency improvements and anxiety about maintaining professional standards, suggesting implementation requires careful balance between automation and expertise preservation.

Critical success factors for generative AI include appropriate task-technology fit, user training quality, and cognitive engagement preservation rather than simple deployment of advanced systems (Wolff et al., 2021; Mir et al., 2020). Healthcare applications demonstrate this pattern with diagnostic accuracy improvements occurring only when physicians maintain active oversight and critical evaluation of AI recommendations (Hassan et al., 2024). Passive acceptance of AI suggestions correlates with decreased diagnostic performance, whilst active engagement enhances both individual and system performance.

The emergence of agentic AI systems introduces additional complexity, with early implementations achieving notable efficiency gains but requiring sophisticated governance frameworks to prevent misalignment with organisational objectives (Sukharevsky et al., 2025). Peer-reviewed management research now argues that legacy operating models are poorly suited to software that can autonomously perceive, decide and act as an organisational actor rather than a decision-support tool. Kellogg, Faraj and Mantere (2026) propose a four-layer Agentic Operating Model comprising cognitive specialisation, coordination architecture, real-time control, and organisational governance, arguing that agentic systems perform best under structured autonomy in which human oversight maintains strategic direction whilst allowing operational flexibility.

Robotics and Physical Automation.

Industrial robotics evolution toward collaborative systems reveals implementation effectiveness dependent on contextual factors rather than technological sophistication alone. Global collaborative robot installations represent 10.5% of total industrial robots, with human-robot teams achieving higher efficiency than full automation in specific applications requiring flexibility and adaptation (IFR, 2024; de Koster & Roy, 2024). This finding challenges assumptions about automation superiority and supports augmentation approaches that preserve human capabilities.

Manufacturing applications demonstrate that collaborative robotics success depends on comprehensive integration strategies addressing workforce development, process redesign, and safety protocols simultaneously. Siemens Erlangen factory exemplifies effective implementation through systematic approach combining technical deployment with extensive worker training and cultural change management (Schaeff & Rother, 2024). Results include 30% productivity improvements alongside enhanced job satisfaction and safety outcomes.

However, implementation failure rates remain substantial with most organisations struggling to progress beyond pilot phases despite technical capability. Evidence indicates that 90% of AI use cases remain in pilot stages, suggesting widespread implementation challenges that extend beyond technological readiness (Sukharevsky et al., 2025). Success factors include comprehensive change management, workforce engagement strategies, gradual rather than revolutionary implementation approaches, and sustained executive commitment over extended periods.

Quality control applications achieve remarkable performance improvements with greater than 99% defect detection rates compared to 80% for manual inspection, whilst predictive maintenance systems reduce equipment breakdowns by 70% (All About AI, 2025; OXMaint, 2025). However, these gains require sophisticated technical infrastructure and organisational capabilities that create barriers for smaller enterprises, potentially contributing to increased industrial concentration rather than widespread productivity enhancement.

SECTORAL ADOPTION PATTERNS AND INSTITUTIONAL MEDIATORS

Industry-specific adoption patterns reveal substantial disparities that support the sectoral variation hypothesis (H3). Analysis shows that sectoral differences reflect institutional constraints, competitive dynamics, and task characteristics rather than technological readiness alone (Broecke, 2023; Kanagarla, 2024). These patterns illuminate how different industrial contexts mediate technological effects through distinct mechanisms.

Geographic analysis reveals pronounced concentration effects, with fifteen US cities controlling two-thirds of national AI capabilities whilst similar patterns emerge globally as technology-intensive regions achieve disproportionate benefits (Muro & Liu, 2024; Muro & Methkupally, 2025). This concentration suggests that institutional factors including educational infrastructure, regulatory frameworks, and innovation ecosystems significantly influence adoption success beyond simple technology availability.

Financial Services.

Financial services maintain global leadership in AI adoption with 75% implementation rates, driven by data-intensive operations, substantial technology investment capacity, and competitive pressures rewarding early adoption (Gharbawi et al., 2024). However, this sector faces mounting regulatory challenges that threaten sustainable development whilst creating systemic risks through market concentration and algorithmic bias in critical decision-making processes.

Algorithmic trading represents the most advanced implementation with AI systems executing 80% of equity trades and demonstrating sophisticated pattern recognition capabilities that exceed human performance in specific contexts (Horobet et al., 2024). However, this automation creates systemic risks through correlated decision-making and potential market instability during stress conditions, illustrating the importance of regulatory oversight in AI deployment.

Credit scoring and risk assessment applications demonstrate both the potential and peril of AI financial applications. Whilst achieving improved accuracy and processing speed, these systems exhibit systematic bias that amplifies existing inequalities through discriminatory lending practices (Wilson & Caliskan, 2024). Analysis reveals white-associated names receive favourable treatment 85% of the time versus 9% for Black-associated names, creating legal and ethical challenges that require regulatory response.

Contradictory evidence emerges regarding long-term benefits with short-term productivity improvements potentially masking increased labour intensity through hybrid skill requirements. Longitudinal analysis reveals that AI implementation may increase rather than reduce workforce demands by combining traditional expertise with technical capabilities, supporting augmentation rather than replacement approaches (Erickson, 2024). This pattern challenges simple automation narratives and suggests more complex transformation dynamics.

Customer service automation achieves 80% implementation rates with performance metrics demonstrating 50% cost reductions and increased call volume capacity (CMSWire, 2024). However, customer perception remains problematic with 64% preferring firms without AI support, reflecting persistent trust deficits that threaten long-term business value despite technical performance improvements (Gartner, 2024). This disconnect between technical capability and user acceptance illustrates the importance of implementation approach rather than technology alone.

Healthcare Systems.

Healthcare AI adoption demonstrates the critical importance of institutional factors in mediating technology effects despite substantial technical capabilities and clear potential benefits. Adoption remains constrained by regulatory requirements, liability concerns, and professional resistance rooted in accountability issues rather than technological limitations (Hassan et al., 2024; Nong et al., 2025). These constraints illustrate how professional and regulatory institutions shape technology deployment independent of technical capability.

Clinical applications show remarkable potential with diagnostic accuracy improvements, treatment personalisation capabilities, and operational efficiency gains across multiple specialties. AI-assisted radiology achieves diagnostic accuracy exceeding human performance in specific contexts whilst reducing interpretation time by 30-50% (Chen et al., 2024). However, implementation requires careful integration with existing workflows and professional practices to maintain quality and accountability standards.

Cultural variation in healthcare AI adoption reflects different institutional arrangements and regulatory frameworks. Nordic countries demonstrate higher adoption rates supported by integrated health systems, robust data protection frameworks, and collaborative professional cultures (European Commission, 2024). Fragmented systems show slower progress despite similar technical capabilities, supporting the institutional context hypothesis by demonstrating that organisational structure influences adoption outcomes independent of technology availability.

Drug discovery applications represent perhaps the most transformative healthcare AI implementation, with clinical trials achieving 30-month progression from target discovery to Phase 1 trials compared to traditional 5-7 year timelines (Xu et al., 2025). However, this acceleration raises quality concerns with patent analysis revealing divergent innovation patterns where quantity increases potentially compromise research rigour (WIPO, 2024). The need for regulatory frameworks that balance innovation speed with safety requirements becomes critical.

Evaluation practices reveal concerning gaps with fewer than half of hospitals assessing AI models for bias whilst two-thirds evaluate accuracy, creating risks of inequitable outcomes despite technical advancement (Nong et al., 2025). This evaluation paradox reflects institutional constraints that prioritise technical performance over equity considerations, potentially amplifying existing healthcare disparities through biased AI systems.

Manufacturing and Creative Industries.

Manufacturing AI adoption demonstrates pronounced scale dependencies creating new forms of industrial stratification that support the inequality amplification hypothesis. Large enterprises achieve 30% adoption rates compared to 16% for SMEs, reflecting resource requirements that extend beyond technology acquisition to encompass workforce development, process redesign, and infrastructure upgrading (Heimberger et al., 2024). This disparity suggests that AI implementation may increase rather than decrease industrial concentration.

Implementation success depends on comprehensive rather than piecemeal approaches, with only 44% of firms implementing site-wide initiatives whilst most focus on isolated pilots that fail to achieve systematic benefits. Successful manufacturers demonstrate integrated strategies combining technical deployment with workforce development, supplier coordination, and customer relationship adaptation, illustrating the institutional complexity of effective AI implementation (Global Market Insights, 2024).

Quality control and predictive maintenance applications achieve substantial performance improvements with energy consumption reductions of 10-60% and waste reductions up to 40% when properly implemented (Rinf Technology, 2024). However, sustainability outcomes depend on deliberate design choices rather than automatic benefits from AI deployment, requiring integration of environmental metrics into system objectives and organisational strategies.

Creative industries present paradoxical adoption patterns with 80% professional usage rates alongside widespread quality concerns about authenticity and creative integrity (ArtSmart AI, 2024; McClain et al., 2025). Survey evidence reveals simultaneous productivity improvements and anxiety about professional standards, suggesting that implementation success requires balancing efficiency gains with creative values and professional identity preservation.

Music industry applications demonstrate these tensions with AI-generated content achieving technical sophistication whilst raising fundamental questions about artistic authenticity and intellectual property rights. Professional musicians report using AI tools for ideation and production efficiency whilst maintaining concerns about creative originality and market implications for human creativity (ArtSmart AI, 2024). This dynamic illustrates the importance of implementation approaches that preserve rather than replace human creative capabilities.

MULTIGENERATIONAL ADAPTATION PATTERNS: EVIDENCE FOR DIFFERENTIATED APPROACHES

Workforce generational analysis reveals systematic differences in AI adaptation patterns that support the generational differentiation hypothesis (H2), though with important qualifications that challenge popular assumptions about digital nativity and technological familiarity. Evidence indicates that adaptation success depends on recognising distinct learning preferences, professional development stages, and socialisation experiences rather than assuming uniform responses to AI technologies across age groups.

Cross-generational research demonstrates that effective AI integration requires differentiated approaches that account for varying levels of professional maturity, technical familiarity, risk tolerance, and career development needs (Lyons & Kuron, 2014; Rudolph et al., 2021). However, these differences prove more nuanced than simple age-based technological divide narratives suggest, with professional experience and organisational context often mediating generational effects.

To facilitate comparison across cohorts, Table 1 consolidates the adoption-intensity, literacy, labour-market and intervention profiles that the subsequent discussion examines in detail. Reading across the rows reveals that the strongest adaptation risk is not distributed uniformly along the age gradient: developmental risks peak among the youngest workers, organisational-guidance gaps peak among mid-career professionals, and displacement and technostress risks peak among older workers.

Table 1. Multigenerational AI Adaptation Profile Across Four Cohorts

Cohort	Adoption intensity and literacy	Key labour-market signal	Dominant adaptation risk	Recommended intervention
Generation Z	High usage and comfort; self-reported literacy exceeds tested competency; 59% prefer interactive platforms	13% relative decline in employment among workers aged 22–25 in AI-exposed occupations since late 2022 (Brynjolfsson et al., 2025)	Cognitive offloading (−0.68 critical-thinking correlation); entry-level displacement	Structured critical-thinking and output-evaluation training; intergenerational mentoring
Millennials	62% of those aged 35–44 report high AI expertise; highest tested comprehensive competency	Millennial-led firms report higher returns on AI projects (Law, 2025; Illanes et al., 2024)	Organisational guidance gap: 34% of Millennial leaders report insufficient strategic direction	Leadership and ethical-framework development; AI governance training
Generation X	Cautious, systematic; limited longitudinal literacy research	Systematic piloting and staged implementation associated with higher long-term success	Under-represented in empirical research; risk of being overlooked	Trust-building through concrete value demonstration; gradual implementation
Baby Boomers	Lowest intensity; limited but growing AI-literacy research base	Robot exposure associated with 15% increase in mentally unhealthy days among older workers (Gihleb et al., 2023)	Technostress; displacement pressure alongside irreplaceable institutional knowledge	Knowledge-transfer mechanisms; peer support; respect for accumulated expertise

Note. Cohort age boundaries follow conventional generational definitions (Rudolph et al., 2021). Empirical coverage is uneven: Generation Z and Millennials are well represented in survey and experimental research, while longitudinal evidence for Generation X and Baby Boomers remains sparse. Labour-market signals reflect the most recent published evidence as of April 2026.

GENERATION Z: DIGITAL FLUENCY RECONSIDERED

Despite assumptions about digital nativity, empirical evidence reveals significant limitations in Generation Z's AI adaptation capabilities that challenge popular stereotypes about technological expertise among younger workers. The EY Generation Z AI Literacy Study (2024) identifies widespread overconfidence where self-reported literacy levels exceed tested competencies by substantial margins, creating implementation risks through shallow understanding of AI capabilities, limitations, and appropriate usage contexts (Merriman et al., 2024).

Concerning evidence indicates that heavy AI usage correlates with reduced problem-solving capabilities and attention spans among younger users, particularly problematic given Generation Z's career-entry stage where fundamental skill development occurs (Chardonnens, 2025; Gerlich, 2025). Over-reliance manifests as decreased self-regulation, reduced critical thinking skills, and diminished capacity for independent problem-solving, potentially undermining long-term career development and professional growth. These cognitive concerns are now compounded by direct labour-market evidence: administrative-payroll analysis from ADP microdata documents a 13% relative decline in employment for workers aged 22–25 in the occupations most exposed to generative AI since late 2022, with no equivalent decline for older workers in the same roles, indicating that Generation Z faces both developmental and displacement pressures simultaneously (Brynjolfsson, Chandar, & Chen, 2025).

Research reveals strong negative correlation (-0.68) between AI usage intensity and critical thinking performance among Generation Z workers, suggesting that convenience and efficiency gains may come at the cost of cognitive skill development (Gerlich, 2025). This finding contradicts popular assumptions about digital native advantages and indicates that age-based AI familiarity may undermine rather than enhance professional capability development without structured support systems.

However, when properly structured through educational frameworks that emphasise critical thinking preservation, Generation Z demonstrates effective AI integration capabilities. Multimodal learning approaches achieve 35% increased engagement when incorporating personalised feedback, project-based learning, and explicit attention to cognitive skill development (Chardonnens, 2025). Interactive platforms represent preferred learning methods for 59% of Generation Z workers, suggesting that technology-mediated training can prove effective when designed appropriately.

Educational institutions report that Generation Z students require explicit instruction in AI evaluation, bias recognition, and output validation despite high comfort levels with AI tools (Chan & Hu, 2023). This pattern suggests that technical familiarity differs substantially from analytical capability, requiring educational approaches that develop critical assessment skills alongside technical proficiency.

Workplace integration strategies for Generation Z benefit from structured mentoring programmes that combine their technical comfort with experienced professionals' contextual knowledge and critical thinking skills. Evidence shows that intergenerational collaboration enhances both AI adoption effectiveness and professional development outcomes when properly facilitated (Falckenthal et al., 2025).

MILLENNIALS: STRATEGIC INTEGRATION EXCELLENCE

Millennials occupy a distinctive position with 62% of those aged 35-44 reporting high AI expertise, exceeding both younger and older cohorts in comprehensive AI competency assessments (Illanes et al., 2024). This proficiency reflects their unique position as digital natives who entered the workforce during initial digital transformation phases, providing foundational technological literacy combined with professional maturity and organisational experience.

Strategic adaptation approaches among Millennials emphasise measured integration with greater fact-checking behaviour, systematic evaluation of AI outputs, and careful consideration of implementation implications compared to Generation Z's more rapid adoption patterns (Myers & Sadaghiani, 2010). This approach reflects professional experience that emphasises accountability and quality control alongside efficiency gains.

Leadership emergence represents a critical Millennial strength with Millennial-led firms achieving higher returns on AI projects compared to other generational leadership patterns. Evidence indicates that Millennial managers demonstrate superior capability in balancing technological innovation with organisational stability, risk management, and workforce development (Law, 2025). Their experience with previous technological transitions provides valuable perspective for managing AI implementation challenges.

However, adaptation faces organisational clarity gaps with 34% of Millennial leaders reporting insufficient guidance regarding AI implementation strategies, ethical frameworks, and performance evaluation criteria compared to 14% of Generation X leaders (Law, 2025). This uncertainty reflects dual pressures of operational responsibilities whilst pioneering technological transformation in organisational contexts that lack established AI governance frameworks.

Professional development needs among Millennials focus on strategic rather than technical AI competencies, emphasising leadership skills for managing AI-enhanced teams, ethical decision-making frameworks, and organisational change management capabilities. Training programmes that address these higher-level competencies achieve greater effectiveness than technical skill development alone (Budhwar et al., 2023).

Millennials demonstrate particular strength in human-AI collaboration approaches that preserve professional expertise whilst leveraging technological capabilities for enhanced performance. Research indicates they achieve optimal balance between AI assistance and professional judgment, avoiding both over-reliance and under-utilisation patterns observed in other generational cohorts (Li et al., 2024).

GENERATION X AND BABY BOOMERS: INSTITUTIONAL KNOWLEDGE VALUE

Research examining Generation X and Baby Boomer AI adaptation remains substantially limited despite their prominence in organisational leadership roles and possession of critical institutional knowledge (Rudolph et al., 2021). Available evidence reveals heightened caution regarding AI outputs with greater emphasis on validation, verification, and contextual assessment compared to younger generations, reflecting professional scepticism rooted in accountability concerns and experience with technological implementation failures.

Baby Boomers face substantial adaptation challenges with robot exposure increasing mentally unhealthy days by 15% among older workers, indicating that technological change imposes disproportionate psychological costs on senior workforce members (Gihleb et al., 2023). However, they possess critical domain expertise, institutional memory, and contextual knowledge that AI systems require for effective implementation, creating paradoxical situations where those facing greatest adaptation challenges hold irreplaceable knowledge assets.

Generation X leaders demonstrate particular expertise in risk assessment and implementation planning, drawing on experience with previous technological transitions to identify potential pitfalls and develop comprehensive change management strategies. Their systematic approach to AI adoption emphasises thorough evaluation, pilot testing, and gradual scaling that achieves higher long-term success rates despite slower initial implementation (Chetty, 2023).

The paradox for older workers lies in facing greatest adaptation challenges whilst holding irreplaceable institutional knowledge that AI systems require for effective implementation and contextual accuracy. Knowledge transfer mechanisms emerge as critical for preserving expertise whilst facilitating gradual technological integration that respects professional experience and accumulated wisdom (Fasbender & Gerpott, 2022).

Intergenerational collaboration programmes that pair older workers' institutional knowledge with younger employees' technological fluency achieve superior outcomes for both AI implementation effectiveness and knowledge preservation. Evidence indicates that structured mentoring relationships benefit all participants whilst enhancing organisational AI capabilities through knowledge synthesis (Falckenthal et al., 2025).

Training approaches for older workers require emphasis on relevance, gradual introduction, peer support, and respect for existing expertise rather than replacement paradigms. Successful programmes demonstrate how AI tools can enhance rather than threaten professional capabilities, building on accumulated experience rather than requiring fundamental skill replacement (Chetty, 2023).

SECTORAL TRANSFORMATION PATTERNS: CONTEXT-DEPENDENT OUTCOMES

Sectoral analysis reveals systematic variations in AI transformation patterns that strongly support both the sectoral variation hypothesis (H3) and institutional context hypothesis (H1). Evidence indicates that transformation outcomes depend critically on task characteristics, regulatory frameworks, competitive dynamics, and institutional structures rather than technological capabilities alone. These patterns illuminate how different industrial contexts mediate technological effects through distinct mechanisms and constraints.

Comparative analysis across industries demonstrates that similar AI technologies produce dramatically different outcomes based on sectoral characteristics including task complexity, regulatory requirements, competitive intensity, and organisational structures (Broecke, 2023; Kanagarla, 2024). This variation cannot be explained through technological determinism and requires understanding of institutional mediating factors that shape implementation approaches and effectiveness outcomes.

To make these divergent sectoral dynamics directly comparable, Table 2 consolidates headline adoption rates, representative performance indicators, and key institutional or behavioural frictions across seven industries examined in this analysis. Reading down the columns, the table shows that high adoption does not translate into high realised value where institutional, regulatory or trust constraints remain unresolved; reading across the rows, it shows that the shape of the friction — regulatory, resource-based, professional-identity-based, or trust-based — varies systematically with sector characteristics.

Table 2. Sectoral AI Adoption, Performance Indicators and Key Frictions

Sector	Adoption indicator	Representative performance indicator	Key friction or failure signal	Primary institutional constraint
Financial services	75% implementation; AI executes 80% of equity trades	50% cost reductions in customer-service automation	64% of customers prefer firms without AI support; algorithmic bias in credit decisions	Regulatory oversight; systemic-risk concerns
Healthcare	Global market US$22–29 bn (2024) rising to US$110–500 bn by 2030	AI-assisted radiology: 30–50% reduction in interpretation time; diagnostic parity with experts in defined contexts	Fewer than half of hospitals assess AI models for bias	Clinical liability; professional accountability norms
Manufacturing	77% overall; 30% large German enterprises vs 16% SMEs	>99% defect detection vs 80% manual; 70% equipment-breakdown reduction	Only 44% of firms implement site-wide initiatives; pilots fail to scale	Scale dependencies; capital and workforce requirements
Legal / professional services	26% of legal organisations using generative AI (86% year-on-year growth)	Five hours per week of reported time savings per professional	Anxiety over professional identity and quality standards; hybrid-skill intensification	Ethical duties; regulatory and professional norms

continued on following page

Table 2. Continued

Sector	Adoption indicator	Representative performance indicator	Key friction or failure signal	Primary institutional constraint
Consulting and knowledge work	Widespread adoption within the "jagged frontier"	25% faster task completion and 40% higher quality on in-frontier tasks	Performance losses on out-of-frontier tasks; skill-atrophy risk	User training quality; task–capability matching
Creative industries	80% of creative professionals report using AI tools	Individual ideation and production efficiency gains	Collective output homogenisation; authenticity and IP disputes	Intellectual-property frameworks; professional norms
Customer service	80% of organisations	50% cost reductions; increased call-volume capacity	80% of personalisation efforts fail; 64% of customers prefer firms without AI support	Data-management capability; customer trust

Note. Figures are indicative of the most recent published estimates as of April 2026 and should not be interpreted as precise annual rates. Adoption indicators combine self-reported implementation with observed market penetration where both are available. Sources for each row are given in full in the sectoral analysis that follows, including Chui et al. (2025), Gharbawi et al. (2024), Global Market Insights (2024), Heimberger et al. (2024), Nong et al. (2025), Chen et al. (2024), Thomson Reuters Institute (2024), Dell'Acqua et al. (2023), CMSWire (2024), Gartner (2019, 2024), ArtSmart AI (2024) and All About AI (2025).

KNOWLEDGE-INTENSIVE INDUSTRIES

Professional services demonstrate dramatic AI adoption with 26% of legal organisations actively using generative AI, representing 86% year-over-year growth that illustrates rapid technological uptake in knowledge-intensive sectors (Thomson Reuters Institute, 2024). However, critical analysis reveals complex implications that extend far beyond simple productivity metrics, encompassing professional identity transformation, service quality considerations, client relationship dynamics, and regulatory compliance challenges.

Professional time savings of five hours weekly mask underlying tensions about service quality, professional standards, and the fundamental nature of professional expertise in AI-enhanced environments. Legal professionals report simultaneous efficiency improvements and anxiety about maintaining professional integrity, suggesting that successful implementation requires careful balance between automation and expertise preservation (Thomson Reuters Institute, 2024). This dynamic illustrates the importance of implementation approaches that enhance rather than replace professional capabilities.

Evidence suggests that AI implementation in professional services often increases rather than decreases labour intensity by requiring hybrid skills that combine traditional expertise with data analysis capabilities, technology management competencies, and AI output evaluation skills (Erickson, 2024). This finding contradicts simple automation narratives and supports the human agency preservation hypothesis (H4) by demonstrating that effective implementation preserves and enhances rather than eliminates human capabilities.

Consulting services achieve remarkable productivity gains with studies demonstrating 25% faster task completion and 40% higher quality outputs using GPT-4 assistance, yet these benefits prove highly context-dependent and require sophisticated implementation strategies (Dell'Acqua et al., 2023). Success factors include appropriate task selection, user training quality, output validation procedures, and integration with existing professional workflows rather than simple technology deployment.

Research and development applications show remarkable timeline reductions with clinical trials achieving 30-month progression from target discovery to Phase 1 trials compared to traditional 5-7 year development cycles (Xu et al., 2025). However, quality concerns emerge from patent analysis revealing divergent innovation patterns where quantity increases potentially compromise research rigour, suggesting need for balanced approaches that maintain scientific standards alongside efficiency gains (WIPO, 2024).

Accounting and financial advisory services demonstrate sophisticated AI integration with Big Four firms investing billions in AI capabilities whilst maintaining emphasis on professional judgment and client relationship management (Crowley Media Group, 2025). However, employment implications prove complex with some predictions suggesting substantial job displacement whilst others emphasise enhanced service capabilities and new professional opportunities.

SERVICE INDUSTRIES

Customer service automation reaches 80% implementation rates across organisations with performance metrics demonstrating substantial operational improvements including 50% cost reductions, increased call volume capacity, and enhanced response time consistency (CMSWire, 2024). However, customer perception remains problematic with 64% expressing preferences for firms without AI support, reflecting persistent trust deficits that threaten long-term business value despite technical performance improvements (Gartner, 2024).

Implementation quality varies dramatically across organisations with 80% of personalisation efforts failing due to inadequate data management capabilities, insufficient customer journey mapping, and organisational resources that cannot support sophisticated AI implementations (Gartner, 2019). This evidence supports the institutional context hypothesis by demonstrating that implementation success depends on comprehensive organisational capabilities rather than technological sophistication alone.

Retail applications demonstrate sophisticated AI integration through dynamic pricing systems, inventory management optimisation, and personalised recommendation engines that achieve substantial efficiency gains (Rapid Innovation, 2024). However, customer acceptance varies significantly based on implementation transparency, perceived value delivery, and trust-building measures that extend beyond technical functionality.

Healthcare AI applications demonstrate growth from approximately US$22–29 billion in 2024 to projected US$110–500 billion by 2030, yet evaluation frameworks remain inadequate with fewer than half of hospitals assessing AI models for bias whilst two-thirds evaluate only accuracy metrics (Nong et al., 2025; Grand View Research, 2024). This evaluation paradox creates risks of inequitable outcomes that could amplify existing healthcare disparities despite technical advancement.

Transportation and logistics sectors achieve significant efficiency improvements through route optimisation, predictive maintenance, and autonomous vehicle integration, yet face substantial regulatory and safety challenges that constrain implementation approaches (Cargofive, 2024). Success requires comprehensive frameworks addressing technical capability, regulatory compliance, safety protocols, and workforce transition simultaneously.

Financial services customer interactions demonstrate sophisticated chatbot implementations that handle routine inquiries effectively whilst requiring human escalation for complex issues, illustrating the complementary rather than replacement nature of effective AI integration (Market.us, 2024). Customer satisfaction depends on seamless handoff protocols and transparent communication about AI involvement in service delivery.

MANUFACTURING AND PHYSICAL PRODUCTION

Manufacturing AI adoption reaches 77% among surveyed organisations yet reveals substantial disparities, with 30% of large German enterprises using production AI compared with 16% of SMEs, reflecting resource requirements that extend far beyond technology acquisition to encompass workforce development, infrastructure upgrading, and process redesign (Global Market Insights, 2024; Heimberger et al., 2024). Recent macro-level modelling for the same economy projects that, under accelerated AI diffusion, German GDP could grow an additional 0.8 percentage points per year over fifteen years, amounting to a cumulative value-added uplift of approximately €4.5 trillion, while roughly 1.6 million jobs would be either eliminated or created, with specialist- and expert-level tasks disproportionately restructured (Weber et al., 2025). Similar national-level projections from France Stratégie and INSEE suggest that up to four million French jobs are potentially automatable by 2030, with administrative services (70%), transport and logistics (65%) and commerce (60%) facing the highest exposure (France Stratégie, 2025). Implementation success depends on comprehensive rather than piecemeal approaches, with only 44% of firms implementing site-wide initiatives whilst most focus on isolated pilots that fail to achieve systematic benefits.

Quality control applications achieve remarkable performance improvements with greater than 99% defect detection rates compared to 80% for manual inspection, demonstrating clear technological superiority in specific applications (All About AI, 2025). However, implementation requires sophisticated technical infrastructure, extensive training programmes, and cultural change management that create barriers for smaller organisations, potentially contributing to increased industrial concentration rather than widespread productivity enhancement.

Predictive maintenance systems reduce equipment breakdowns by 70% whilst achieving energy consumption reductions of 10-60% and waste reductions up to 40% when properly implemented (OXMaint, 2025; Rinf Technology, 2024). However, sustainability outcomes depend on deliberate design choices that integrate environmental metrics into system objectives rather than automatic benefits from AI deployment, requiring organisational commitment to sustainability goals alongside efficiency improvements.

Collaborative robotics installations demonstrate human-robot teams achieving higher efficiency than full automation in applications requiring flexibility, adaptation, and contextual decision-making (de Koster & Roy, 2024). This finding challenges assumptions about automation superiority and supports augmentation approaches that preserve human capabilities whilst leveraging robotic precision and consistency for enhanced overall performance.

Digital twin technology enables real-time production optimisation, predictive quality control, and supply chain coordination that transforms manufacturing operations through comprehensive data integration and analysis capabilities (MarketResearch.com, 2024). However, implementation requires substantial data infrastructure investments and organisational capabilities that extend beyond individual manufacturing sites to encompass entire value chain integration.

Additive manufacturing benefits from AI-enhanced design optimisation, material selection, and quality control that enable customisation and efficiency improvements previously impossible through traditional manufacturing approaches (MarketsandMarkets, 2025). However, scaling these benefits requires workforce development, supply chain adaptation, and customer education that extend beyond technological deployment.

WORKFORCE DEVELOPMENT STRATEGIES: MULTI-LEVEL ANALYSIS

Workforce development approaches demonstrate systematic variation in effectiveness based on implementation context, target populations, and institutional support systems, providing strong evidence for both the institutional context hypothesis (H1) and generational differentiation hypothesis (H2). Evidence reveals that successful adaptation requires comprehensive frameworks addressing technical capabilities alongside human-AI collaboration skills, critical thinking preservation, and ethical awareness rather than simple technology training programmes.

Analysis of workforce development initiatives across multiple countries and organisational contexts reveals that effectiveness depends on alignment between training approaches and local institutional contexts, learner characteristics, and organisational capabilities (UNESCO, 2024; World Economic Forum, 2025). This finding emphasises the importance of contextualised rather than universal approaches to AI skill development.

Individual-Level Adaptation Strategies

Traditional episodic training models prove fundamentally inadequate for addressing AI-related skill requirements, with 39% of workforce skills requiring substantial change between 2025 and 2030, a pace of transformation that exceeds historical technological transition rates (World Economic Forum, 2025). Large-scale administrative-payroll evidence indicates that this pressure is already materialising in the labour market: Brynjolfsson, Chandar and Chen (2025), analysing ADP microdata covering millions of US workers, document a 13% relative decline in employment for early-career workers aged 22–25 in the occupations most exposed to generative AI since late 2022, with no equivalent decline for older workers in the same roles and with decline concentrated in automation-type rather than augmentation-type applications. The Organisational Learning with AI Framework demonstrates 14% productivity increases through iterative learning cycles, but effectiveness depends on sustained organisational commitment to process adaptation and continuous skill development rather than one-time technology deployment (Ransbotham et al., 2020).

AI literacy development extends far beyond technical competence to encompass critical evaluation capabilities, ethical awareness, bias recognition, and human-AI collaboration skills. UNESCO's AI Competency Framework identifies human-centred mindset, ethics awareness, technical understanding, and system design as core competencies, yet systematic reviews reveal methodological limitations across existing literacy assessment scales that constrain programme effectiveness evaluation (UNESCO, 2024; Lintner, 2024).

Evidence regarding hybrid skill development reveals concerning cognitive off-loading patterns with strong negative correlation (-0.68) between AI usage intensity and critical thinking abilities, particularly problematic among younger workers during formative career development phases (Gerlich, 2025). This finding supports the human agency preservation hypothesis (H4) by demonstrating that successful AI integration requires explicit preservation and development of human cognitive capabilities rather than passive acceptance of technological assistance.

Microlearning approaches demonstrate effectiveness in adult learner contexts through bite-sized content delivery, personalised pacing, and practical application opportunities that align with busy professional schedules and diverse learning preferences (Moore et al., 2024). However, effectiveness depends on comprehensive curriculum design that addresses both technical skills and critical thinking development rather than isolated skill modules.

Professional development pathways require integration of AI competencies with domain-specific expertise, emphasising how technological tools enhance rather than replace professional knowledge and judgment. Evidence indicates that professionals who maintain focus on domain expertise whilst developing AI collaboration skills achieve superior long-term performance compared to those emphasising either technical skills or traditional expertise alone (Budhwar et al., 2023).

Continuous learning mechanisms become essential given rapid technological evolution, requiring individuals to develop metacognitive skills for evaluating new AI capabilities, assessing implementation opportunities, and maintaining professional relevance through ongoing skill development. Research indicates that learning agility and adaptability predict AI integration success more strongly than initial technical competence (Chardonnens, 2025).

Organisational Transformation Frameworks

Organisational AI adoption demonstrates clear patterns distinguishing successful transformation from failed implementation, with institutional factors proving more predictive of success than technological capabilities or financial resources. The ADKAR model adapted for AI contexts addresses awareness barriers affecting 60% of organisations, desire challenges manifesting through uncertainty about AI benefits and risks, knowledge gaps requiring AI-specific education, ability constraints including technical infrastructure and organisational capabilities, and reinforcement needs for sustaining change over time (Prosci, 2024; Rowan et al., 2025).

Evidence reveals that 90% of AI use cases remain trapped in pilot phases despite technical capability and executive support, suggesting widespread implementation failures that result from institutional rather than technological barriers (Sukharevsky et al., 2025). Success factors include sustained executive commitment over extended periods, comprehensive cross-functional collaboration, meaningful employee engagement in implementation planning, and cultural transformation that embraces rather than fears technological change.

Cultural transformation emerges as the critical determinant of implementation success with high-performing organisations demonstrating three times higher trust in AI capabilities versus traditional intuition-based decision-making compared to struggling implementations (Rowan et al., 2025). This cultural shift requires systematic change management that addresses fear, uncertainty, and resistance whilst building confidence through successful pilot experiences and visible leadership support.

MIT CISR's Enterprise AI Maturity Model identifies that only 7% of organisations achieve Stage 4 AI future-readiness, characterised by systematic AI integration across operations, sophisticated governance frameworks, and cultural alignment with AI-enhanced decision-making (Weill et al., 2024). Most organisations remain at Stages 1-2, indicating substantial opportunity for improvement through structured maturity development approaches.

Governance frameworks require sophisticated balancing of centralised policy development with distributed implementation autonomy, enabling consistency in ethical standards and risk management whilst allowing operational flexibility for local adaptation (Microsoft, 2024). Evidence shows organisations with Chief AI Officers achieve 10-36% higher ROI on AI initiatives, suggesting centralised oversight benefits whilst requiring federated approaches for effective local implementation (Chui et al., 2025).

Change management strategies must address multiple stakeholder groups simultaneously including executives requiring strategic vision, middle managers needing operational guidance, frontline workers requiring skill development, and customers demanding transparency about AI involvement in service delivery. Comprehensive stakeholder engagement approaches achieve higher success rates than technology-focused implementations (Rowan et al., 2025).

Policy and Educational System Responses

Educational institutions demonstrate substantial curriculum integration efforts with universities incorporating AI literacy requirements across disciplines, yet effectiveness varies dramatically based on teacher training quality, institutional support systems, and alignment with local labour market demands rather than curriculum design alone (UNESCO, 2021). State-level implementations reveal significant variation in strategic priorities and implementation approaches, with Missouri's structured policy development contrasting with Georgia's framework approaches that emphasise local autonomy (Missouri DESE, 2025; Georgia DOE, 2025).

Teacher preparation emerges as a critical bottleneck with many educators lacking sufficient AI literacy to provide effective instruction, whilst simultaneously needing to integrate AI tools into their own teaching practices (Kim et al., 2021). Professional development programmes for educators achieve variable success based on sustained support, practical application opportunities, and alignment with existing pedagogical approaches rather than replacement paradigms.

Government responses to AI displacement demonstrate extensive policy discussion but limited large-scale implementation of support mechanisms for affected workers. Universal Basic Income pilots show positive wellbeing outcomes including reduced stress, improved health indicators, and enhanced educational participation, but lack sustainable funding mechanisms and political support for permanent implementation (OpenResearch, 2024). These limitations suggest need for more targeted and politically feasible intervention strategies.

Retraining programme effectiveness remains questionable with Trade Adjustment Assistance participants experiencing lower employment rates and reduced earnings compared to control groups, indicating that traditional retraining approaches may be inadequate for AI-related displacement (Jacobs, 2025). Successful programmes emphasise rapid placement in growing sectors rather than extensive retraining for displaced industries, suggesting need for different approaches to AI-related workforce transitions.

Partnership frameworks between government, industry, and educational institutions demonstrate measurable workforce development outcomes when properly structured. California State University's AI Initiative reaches 460,000 students through comprehensive curriculum integration and industry partnerships, whilst Singapore's AI Apprenticeship Programme achieves 90%+ graduate placement rates through direct industry engagement (San Diego State University, 2025; AI Singapore, 2025). These examples suggest that collaborative approaches enhance individual institutional initiatives.

International coordination efforts through UNESCO, OECD, and other multilateral organisations develop framework standards for AI education whilst allowing national adaptation based on local contexts and priorities (UNESCO, 2024). However, implementation varies substantially across countries based on educational system structures, technological infrastructure, and economic development levels, suggesting need for differentiated rather than universal approaches.

CRITICAL CHALLENGES AND EMERGING OPPORTUNITIES

Analysis of persistent challenges and emerging opportunities reveals systematic patterns that strongly support the inequality amplification hypothesis (H5) whilst identifying specific conditions under which AI transformation enhances rather than undermines human capabilities and social equity. This analysis illuminates the complex trade-offs inherent in AI workplace implementation and identifies strategic decision points that determine whether technological advancement contributes to inclusive or exclusive economic development patterns.

Understanding these challenges and opportunities proves essential for developing effective policy responses, organisational strategies, and individual adaptation approaches that maximise benefits whilst minimising adverse consequences. Evidence suggests that outcomes depend critically on deliberate choices made during implementation rather than inevitable consequences of technological development.

Persistent Structural Barriers

Digital Divide Amplification.

AI technology deployment systematically exacerbates existing digital disparities through multiple reinforcing mechanisms that create compound disadvantages for already marginalised populations and regions. Current global connectivity data reveals 2.6 billion people remain offline despite decades of digital development efforts, with internet penetration reaching only 27% in low-income countries versus 93% in high-income nations (Berg et al., 2024; World Bank, 2024). AI applications multiply these existing disparities by requiring computational resources, high-speed connectivity, and technical infrastructure that exceed basic internet access requirements by substantial margins.

Computing infrastructure requirements for AI applications create exponentially greater barriers than previous technological adoptions, with cost differentials multiplying existing disparities by factors of twenty to 1,700 between high- and low-income contexts (Dubey, 2025). This multiplication effect means that regions and populations already disadvantaged by digital divides face proportionally greater exclusion from AI-driven economic opportunities, creating potential for permanent economic stratification based on technological access. Updated IMF analysis reinforces this stratification: approximately 40% of global employment is exposed to AI, rising to 60% in advanced economies but standing at 40% in emerging markets and only 28% in low-income countries, with the productivity gains and fiscal capacity to manage adjustment similarly skewed toward high-income jurisdictions (Cazzaniga et al., 2026).

Geographic concentration of AI capabilities amplifies these effects through self-reinforcing advantages that accrue to already privileged regions whilst peripheral areas experience relative exclusion from AI-driven opportunities. Analysis reveals fifteen US cities control two-thirds of national AI capabilities whilst 100 companies globally control 40% of AI R&D investment, creating concentration patterns that exceed those observed in previous technological transitions (Muro & Liu, 2024; UNCTAD, 2025).

Educational infrastructure requirements for effective AI adoption create additional barriers that compound existing disadvantages. Success requires not only technological access but also comprehensive educational programmes, teacher training, and institutional support systems that many regions lack (UNESCO, 2024). This creates multi-generational effects where current educational inadequacies constrain future AI participation, potentially creating permanent disadvantage patterns.

A further, less visible form of inequality operates through the global data-annotation and content-moderation workforce on which contemporary AI systems depend. The World Bank estimates that roughly 4.4% of the world's population has at some point performed data labelling, annotation or verification work, much of it outsourced to low- and middle-income countries under precarious conditions characterised by piece-rate pay, hourly productivity quotas, exposure to traumatic content and weak labour protections (Anwar, 2025). This "ghost work" infrastructure is systematically obscured in narratives of AI autonomy and adds a further dimension to the inequality amplification hypothesis (H5): economic value generated by AI systems in high-income contexts is partly predicated on labour extracted under substantially worse conditions elsewhere.

Taken together, these mechanisms act along several distinct dimensions: geographic, demographic, gendered, and infrastructural. Table 3 brings these indicators into a single view so that their compounding character becomes visible. Where the prose treats each inequality in turn, the table shows that the same populations and regions appear in the disadvantaged column along almost every axis, which is the principal empirical warrant for the inequality amplification hypothesis.

Table 3. Geographic, Demographic and Infrastructural Dimensions of AI Exposure and Access Inequality

Dimension	Group or category	Exposure or access indicator	Key source
Employment exposure to AI	Advanced economies	Approximately 60% of employment is exposed to AI	Cazzaniga et al. (2026)
Employment exposure to AI	Emerging markets	Approximately 40% of employment is exposed	Cazzaniga et al. (2026)
Employment exposure to AI	Low-income countries	Approximately 28% of employment is exposed	Cazzaniga et al. (2026)
Basic internet access	High-income vs low-income countries	93% vs 27% internet penetration; 2.6 bn people remain offline globally	Berg et al. (2024); World Bank (2024)
Computing-infrastructure cost	High- vs low-income contexts	Cost differentials of 20× to 1,700×	Dubey (2025)
Capability concentration	Top 15 US cities	Control two-thirds of US national AI capabilities	Muro & Liu (2024); Muro & Methkupally (2025)
R&D concentration	Top 100 companies globally	Control 40% of global AI R&D investment	UNCTAD (2025)
Gendered generative-AI exposure	Female employment (highest-exposure tier)	4.7% in the highest-exposure tier	Gmyrek et al. (2025)
Gendered generative-AI exposure	Male employment (highest-exposure tier)	2.4% in the highest-exposure tier	Gmyrek et al. (2025)
Ghost-work infrastructure	Global data-annotation and moderation workforce, predominantly Global South	Approximately 4.4% of the world's population has at some point performed data-annotation or verification work under precarious conditions	Anwar (2025)

Note. Exposure indicators are not directly comparable across rows: the IMF figures reflect share of employment in occupations with some task-level AI exposure, while the ILO figures reflect share of employment in the highest generative-AI occupational-exposure tier. The table is intended to show the direction and compounding character of disadvantage across dimensions rather than to equate the underlying measurements.

Implementation Failure Patterns.

Skills obsolescence rates associated with AI adoption exceed historical technological transition patterns and current adaptive capacity across most workforce populations. Evidence indicates 39% of skillsets will become substantially outdated between 2025 and 2030, a pace of change that surpasses both individual learning capacity and institutional training programme capabilities (World Economic Forum,

2024). This acceleration suggests that traditional workforce development approaches prove fundamentally inadequate for AI-related transitions.

Current training participation rates reveal significant gaps between need and access, with only 39% of AI-using workers receiving formal employer training and merely 25% of companies offering comprehensive AI training programmes despite widespread technology adoption (Microsoft/LinkedIn, 2024). These participation gaps suggest that most workers face AI workplace integration without adequate preparation or support, potentially creating widespread adaptation difficulties and performance problems.

Training effectiveness remains limited even for those receiving formal programmes, with 55% of AI users in Europe reporting no marked job performance improvement despite programme participation (Pouliakas et al., 2025). This finding suggests fundamental problems with current training approaches that emphasise technology familiarity over practical application skills, critical thinking development, and contextual integration capabilities.

Large-scale upskilling initiatives consistently fail to progress beyond pilot stages with fewer than 5% advancing to full implementation annually, indicating systematic institutional barriers to scaling workforce development efforts (Page et al., 2024). These scaling failures suggest that successful pilot programmes cannot be easily replicated across different organisational contexts, requiring more sophisticated understanding of institutional factors that enable successful implementation.

Algorithmic Bias and Workplace Inequality.

AI systems demonstrate systematic bias patterns that amplify existing workplace inequalities across multiple dimensions including gender, race, age, and socioeconomic status. Analysis of state-of-the-art large language models ranking CVs reveals white-associated names receive favourable treatment 85% of the time versus 9% for Black-associated names, creating discriminatory hiring practices that could systematically exclude qualified candidates from employment opportunities (Wilson & Caliskan, 2024). Gendered exposure patterns operate at population scale as well: the International Labour Organization's refined global index of occupational exposure to generative AI finds that approximately one in four workers globally is in an occupation with some GenAI exposure, with 4.7% of female employment in the highest exposure tier compared with 2.4% of male employment, reflecting women's concentration in clerical and administrative roles that generative AI most readily automates (Gmyrek et al., 2025).

Performance evaluation bias creates additional barriers for workers using AI assistance, with engineers receiving 9% lower competence ratings despite producing identical work quality when AI involvement becomes known (Acar et al., 2025).

This penalty effect proves more severe for women and older workers, suggesting that AI adoption may systematically disadvantage populations already facing workplace discrimination rather than creating more equitable evaluation processes.

Workplace monitoring and surveillance capabilities enabled by AI technologies create potential for increased worker control and reduced autonomy that could undermine rather than enhance employment quality. Evidence suggests that AI-powered monitoring systems may create stressful work environments that reduce job satisfaction and mental health outcomes whilst providing limited productivity benefits (Kim & Lee, 2024).

Credit scoring and financial services applications demonstrate how AI bias can create systemic exclusion from economic opportunities through discriminatory lending, insurance, and financial service practices that appear objective whilst perpetuating historical inequality patterns (Chen, 2023). These applications illustrate how AI systems can institutionalise bias at unprecedented scale and precision.

Emerging Value Creation Opportunities

Economic Transformation Potential.

AI's economic potential fundamentally alters traditional value creation mechanisms, with McKinsey projecting a US$13–15.5 trillion contribution to global economic activity by 2030, representing productivity improvements that could exceed those achieved during previous technological revolutions (Manyika et al., 2023). However, realising this potential requires institutional innovations that ensure benefits distribute broadly rather than concentrating among technology owners and early adopters.

Employment transformation reveals complex patterns that challenge simple displacement narratives. World Economic Forum projections indicate 170 million new positions offset by 92 million displaced roles, yielding net employment growth of 78 million positions, though concentrated in specific occupational categories and geographic regions (World Economic Forum, 2025). This transformation suggests opportunities for employment expansion alongside need for workforce transition support in declining sectors.

New business model opportunities emerge through AI-enabled personalisation, efficiency improvements, and novel service offerings that create value in previously impossible ways. Digital twin technology enables new forms of predictive manufacturing, personalised healthcare approaches achieve previously impossible treatment precision, and AI-enhanced creative tools enable new forms of artistic and design expression (MarketResearch.com, 2024).

Small business opportunities arise through democratised access to sophisticated analytical capabilities, marketing tools, and operational optimisation that previously required large-scale resources. Cloud-based AI services enable small enterprises to access capabilities comparable to large corporations, potentially reducing rather than increasing business concentration if appropriate support and training programmes develop (Slingerland, 2025).

Human Capability Enhancement.

Meta-analysis of 106 experimental studies reveals that, in aggregate, human–AI combinations perform worse than the best of humans or AI alone (Hedges' $g = -0.23$, 95% CI [−0.39, −0.07]), with losses concentrated in decision-making tasks and gains in content-creation tasks (Vaccaro et al., 2024). This task-dependent pattern provides qualified support for the human agency preservation hypothesis (H4) whilst cautioning that augmentation benefits do not accrue automatically and are contingent on matching AI capabilities to appropriate task types.

Creative applications show particular promise for capability enhancement by enabling novel conceptual combinations, accelerated ideation processes, and exploration of creative possibilities beyond individual human capacity. However, collective-level homogenisation effects emerge where individual creativity gains coincide with reduced group diversity in creative outputs, suggesting need for implementation approaches that preserve creative diversity whilst enhancing individual capabilities (Doshi & Hauser, 2024).

Educational applications demonstrate potential for personalised learning experiences that adapt to individual learning styles, pace, and capability development needs whilst providing teachers with enhanced diagnostic and intervention capabilities (Chardonnens, 2025). However, effectiveness requires maintaining human agency and critical thinking development rather than passive consumption of AI-generated content.

Healthcare capabilities expand through enhanced diagnostic accuracy, treatment personalisation, and predictive intervention that could substantially improve health outcomes whilst reducing costs. AI-assisted medical decision-making achieves superior accuracy in specific domains whilst requiring physician oversight for contextual integration and ethical consideration (Hassan et al., 2024).

Strategic Decision Points and Trade-Offs

Automation versus Augmentation Implementation.

Recent meta-analytical evidence challenges traditional automation-augmentation dichotomies by revealing that effectiveness depends on task characteristics, implementation approach, and contextual factors rather than simple technology deployment choices. Human-AI systems perform worse than best individual performers in decision-making contexts whilst showing substantial gains in creative and analytical tasks, suggesting need for sophisticated matching between AI capabilities and task requirements (Vaccaro et al., 2024).

Evidence from French manufacturing reveals complex dynamics where adopting firms experience labour share decline within their operations whilst expanding employment relative to competitors, suggesting that automation benefits accrue unevenly across organisations rather than universally within sectors (Acemoglu & Restrepo, 2022). This pattern indicates that automation decisions have competitive implications that extend beyond individual firm efficiency considerations.

Implementation timing proves critical with early adoption providing competitive advantages through learning curve effects and market positioning, whilst premature adoption risks substantial costs and implementation failures. Evidence suggests that optimal timing depends on organisational readiness factors rather than technology maturity alone, supporting the institutional context hypothesis (Merhi, 2023).

Workforce transition strategies must balance automation efficiency gains with social responsibility considerations, particularly in communities dependent on affected industries. Successful approaches demonstrate gradual implementation combined with comprehensive workforce development programmes that provide alternative employment pathways rather than abrupt displacement (Jacobs, 2025).

Governance Model Selection.

Research reveals organisations moving beyond simple centralised-distributed choices toward sophisticated federated governance models that combine central policy development with distributed implementation autonomy (Microsoft, 2024). Evidence shows organisations with Chief AI Officers achieve 10-36% higher ROI on AI initiatives, suggesting centralised oversight benefits, whilst requiring federated approaches for effective local adaptation that respects operational contexts and stakeholder needs (Chui et al., 2025).

Risk management frameworks require balancing innovation enablement with harm prevention through sophisticated approaches that avoid both excessive restriction and inadequate oversight. Risk-based classification systems enable appropriate oversight levels based on application context whilst maintaining flexibility for innovation and adaptation (Gehrmann & Förster, 2024). The operational relevance of this approach is becoming immediate: under the EU AI Act, which entered into force on 1 August 2024, prohibitions and AI-literacy obligations took effect on 2 February 2025, governance and general-purpose-model duties on 2 August 2025, and the full high-risk regime under Article 6 and Annex III, which explicitly designates recruitment, screening, performance evaluation and workforce-management systems as high-risk, becomes enforceable on 2 August 2026, with penalties of up to €35 million or 7% of global turnover (European Commission, 2024; European Parliament and Council, 2024).

Stakeholder engagement mechanisms must address multiple constituencies simultaneously including employees requiring skill development support, customers demanding service quality and transparency, communities affected by economic transformation, and shareholders expecting return on investment. Comprehensive stakeholder approaches achieve higher success rates than narrow economic optimisation strategies (Rowan et al., 2025).

Ethical framework integration requires systematic approaches that address bias prevention, fairness promotion, transparency provision, and accountability maintenance throughout AI development and deployment processes. Evidence suggests that organisations with robust ethical frameworks achieve superior long-term performance compared to those emphasising efficiency alone (Mathew et al., 2025).

STRATEGIC IMPLICATIONS AND RECOMMENDATIONS

Based on systematic hypothesis testing results, strategic implications emerge for organisational, policy, and individual development approaches that acknowledge contextual variation and institutional mediation of AI transformation outcomes. These recommendations reject one-size-fits-all solutions in favour of adaptive strategies that respond to specific institutional contexts, stakeholder needs, and implementation constraints whilst maximising benefits and minimising adverse consequences.

Evidence supporting contextual approaches rather than universal solutions emphasises the importance of local adaptation, stakeholder engagement, and institutional alignment in determining implementation success. This finding requires strategic approaches that emphasise flexibility, continuous adaptation, and responsiveness to local conditions rather than rigid implementation frameworks.

Organisational Strategy Frameworks

Evidence supporting the institutional context hypothesis (H1) indicates that organisations must fundamentally shift from technology-driven to capability-driven AI implementation approaches that prioritise organisational readiness, cultural alignment, and workforce development over technological sophistication. Research demonstrates that firms focusing on concentrated high-value use cases generate 2.1 times greater ROI than those dispersing resources across multiple initiatives, whilst augmentation-first strategies prove more sustainable than automation-focused implementations over extended periods (Chui et al., 2025; Lane et al., 2023).

Strategic planning processes require comprehensive stakeholder assessment that identifies readiness factors, resistance sources, and capability development needs before technology deployment decisions. Evidence indicates that successful implementations invest 60-70% of resources in organisational development, cultural change management, and workforce preparation compared to 30-40% in technology acquisition and deployment (Prosci, 2024).

Multigenerational workforce strategies must incorporate differentiated approaches based on evidence supporting the generational differentiation hypothesis (H2) whilst avoiding stereotypical assumptions about technological capability based on age alone. Generation Z requires structured critical thinking development programmes that address cognitive offloading risks whilst leveraging their comfort with technological interfaces. Millennials benefit from leadership development opportunities that integrate AI capabilities with strategic management responsibilities. Generation X leaders need trust-building through concrete value demonstrations and gradual implementation approaches. Baby Boomers require knowledge transfer mechanisms that preserve institutional expertise whilst facilitating technological integration.

Implementation approaches should emphasise gradual scaling rather than revolutionary transformation, with pilot programmes designed to demonstrate value, build confidence, and identify implementation challenges before organisation-wide deployment. Evidence shows that 44% of successful manufacturers implement site-wide initiatives after proving concepts through focused pilots, whilst unsuccessful implementations attempt comprehensive deployment without adequate testing (Heimberger et al., 2024).

Performance measurement systems require comprehensive redesign incorporating human-AI collaboration effectiveness alongside traditional productivity indicators. Hybrid metrics including agent yield ratios measuring human-AI team performance, adaptability scores assessing response to changing conditions, collaboration quality evaluating human-AI interaction effectiveness, and fairness auditing addressing documented bias patterns affecting women and older workers provide comprehensive assessment frameworks (Murire, 2024; Acar et al., 2025).

Governance structures must balance centralised policy development with distributed operational autonomy through federated models that ensure consistency in ethical standards and risk management whilst enabling local adaptation. Evidence indicates that organisations with Chief AI Officers achieve superior outcomes through centralised strategic oversight combined with cross-functional implementation teams that address specific operational contexts (Chui et al., 2025).

Policy Framework Recommendations

Comparative analysis supporting the sectoral variation hypothesis (H3) reveals need for sophisticated regulatory frameworks that avoid both excessive restriction constraining beneficial innovation and inadequate oversight enabling harmful applications. Risk-based classification systems enable appropriate oversight levels based on application context and potential impact whilst international harmonisation should focus on core ethical principles and risk management frameworks rather than detailed technical standards given different national contexts and institutional arrangements.

Educational system reform requirements include comprehensive AI literacy integration that emphasises critical thinking and ethical awareness alongside technical skills development. Evidence indicates that programmes emphasising evaluation capabilities, bias recognition, and human-AI collaboration achieve superior long-term outcomes compared to technology-focused training alone (UNESCO, 2024). Teacher preparation becomes critical with educators requiring sufficient AI literacy to provide effective instruction whilst integrating AI tools into their own teaching practices.

Apprenticeship programme expansion offers promising approaches for workforce development with AI-related programmes achieving higher completion rates and placement success compared to traditional retraining initiatives. However, geographic distribution remains uneven requiring targeted investment in underserved regions to prevent amplification of existing inequalities (Koslosky & Feldgoise, 2025).

Social protection mechanism adaptation requires targeted rather than universal approaches that address specific displacement patterns and transition needs. Wage insurance for displaced mid-career workers offers focused intervention that maintains income stability during retraining periods, whilst portable benefits systems support evolving employment arrangements that may become more common in AI-enhanced economies. Collective bargaining frameworks should incorporate AI deployment decision-making through worker representation requirements that ensure workforce interests consideration in implementation planning.

Investment in digital infrastructure becomes critical for preventing inequality amplification, with particular emphasis on underserved regions and populations that risk permanent exclusion from AI-driven economic opportunities. Public-private partnerships can leverage private sector technological expertise whilst ensuring broad access that market mechanisms alone may not provide (Dubey, 2025).

International cooperation frameworks should address both opportunity maximisation and risk mitigation through coordinated approaches to standard development, research collaboration, and equitable access promotion. However, cooperation must respect national sovereignty and different institutional contexts rather than imposing uniform solutions across diverse political and economic systems (United Nations, 2024).

Individual Development Strategies

Personal development planning must emphasise comprehensive capability portfolios that combine technical AI literacy with uniquely human skills resistant to automation including creative problem-solving, emotional intelligence, contextual reasoning, and ethical judgment. Evidence supporting the human agency preservation hypothesis (H4) indicates that critical thinking, creativity, and interpersonal capabilities assume heightened importance as AI systems handle routine analytical and computational tasks (Gerlich, 2025).

Generational-specific adaptation tactics require recognition of different starting points, learning preferences, and career development needs whilst avoiding stereotypical assumptions about capability based on age alone. Younger workers need explicit critical thinking development and output evaluation training, whilst experienced professionals require support for technological integration that builds on rather than replaces accumulated expertise (Chardonnens, 2025).

Continuous learning frameworks become essential given rapid technological evolution and the need for ongoing skill development throughout career trajectories. Individuals must develop metacognitive capabilities for assessing new AI developments, identifying implementation opportunities, and maintaining professional relevance through adaptive skill development rather than static expertise accumulation (Moore et al., 2024).

Network and community building enable resilience through peer learning, knowledge sharing, and collaborative problem-solving that supports individual adaptation whilst contributing to collective capability development. Professional associations, industry groups, and educational institutions provide platforms for ongoing learning and adaptation support that individuals cannot achieve in isolation (Babashahi et al., 2024).

Personal learning plans must incorporate both technical skill development and human capability enhancement through structured approaches that balance efficiency gains with cognitive skill preservation. Evidence indicates that individuals who maintain focus on critical thinking whilst developing AI collaboration skills achieve superior long-term performance compared to those emphasising either domain exclusively (Li et al., 2024).

Career development strategies should emphasise adaptability and learning agility over specific technical skills given rapid technological evolution and uncertain future requirements. Individuals who develop strong foundational capabilities combined with adaptive learning capacity prove better positioned for long-term success than those focusing on current technology mastery alone (Budhwar et al., 2023).

METHODOLOGICAL LIMITATIONS AND SCOPE BOUNDARIES

This analysis faces several significant limitations that constrain generalisability and comprehensiveness, requiring explicit acknowledgement for proper interpretation of findings and hypothesis testing results. Understanding these limitations proves essential for contextualising conclusions and identifying areas requiring future research attention to develop more complete understanding of AI workplace transformation patterns and outcomes.

Recognition of these limitations does not undermine the analysis validity but rather provides transparent assessment of evidential constraints and analytical boundaries that inform appropriate application of findings. Future research should prioritise addressing these limitations to develop more robust theoretical frameworks and practical guidance for AI workplace implementation.

Temporal and Geographic Constraints

The rapid pace of AI development creates fundamental challenges for longitudinal analysis, with most implementations too recent for meaningful assessment of sustained impacts and long-term adaptation patterns. Evidence base remains incomplete with most studies examining short-term rather than extended effectiveness outcomes, limiting understanding of adaptation trajectories, skill development patterns, and organisational transformation dynamics over time. This temporal constraint proves particularly problematic for evaluating workforce development interventions and cultural change initiatives that require extended periods to demonstrate effectiveness.

Geographic bias represents substantial limitation with research concentrated disproportionately in high-income countries, particularly the United States, European Union, and select Asian nations including China, Japan, and South Korea. This concentration creates significant blind spots regarding AI transformation patterns in developing economies, low-income countries, and regions with different institutional structures, economic development levels, and cultural contexts (Berg et al., 2024).

Evidence from developing economies remains sparse despite these regions containing substantial workforce populations and representing important contexts for understanding AI transformation across different economic development stages. This limitation particularly affects evaluation of the inequality amplification hypothesis (H5) across different global contexts and may skew understanding toward technology-intensive rather than labour-intensive industries that predominate in many developing countries.

Cultural bias toward Western organisational models and workforce structures may limit applicability to different institutional contexts including alternative economic arrangements such as cooperative enterprises, informal sector employment, and different labour relations systems that receive minimal research attention. This bias potentially affects generalisability of institutional context findings and may overlook important alternative approaches to AI implementation and workforce development.

Regulatory environment differences across countries create additional complexity for generalising findings about institutional factors and policy effectiveness. Legal frameworks, enforcement mechanisms, and cultural attitudes toward regulation vary substantially across national contexts, potentially limiting transferability of governance and policy recommendations derived primarily from specific regulatory environments.

Sectoral and Generational Research Gaps

Sectoral coverage demonstrates uneven depth with financial services, healthcare, manufacturing, and technology-intensive industries receiving extensive research attention whilst other significant employment sectors including education, agriculture, construction, retail, and public administration lack comparable analytical depth. This imbalance may influence conclusions regarding the sectoral variation hypothesis (H3) by overrepresenting industries with high technology adoption rates and sophisticated analytical capabilities.

Agriculture represents particularly important research gap given its global employment significance and potential for AI transformation through precision farming, automated machinery, and supply chain optimisation. Similarly, construction sector analysis remains limited despite substantial workforce implications and emerging AI applications in project management, safety monitoring, and automated construction processes (US Census Bureau, 2023).

Generational analysis suffers from limited longitudinal data availability with most studies providing cross-sectional snapshots rather than developmental trajectories that would illuminate adaptation patterns over time. Generation X research remains particularly sparse despite their prominence in organisational leadership roles during peak AI adoption periods, creating uncertainty regarding their influence on implementation decisions and transformation outcomes (Rudolph et al., 2021).

Baby Boomer analysis faces additional constraints with much research focusing on adaptation challenges rather than unique contributions including institutional knowledge, risk assessment capabilities, and wisdom derived from previous technological transitions. This emphasis may underestimate their positive contributions to AI implementation success whilst overemphasising adaptation difficulties.

Intersectional analysis remains underdeveloped with most research examining demographic categories independently rather than understanding how multiple identity dimensions interact to create unique AI adoption experiences. Gender-race interactions, age-education combinations, and socioeconomic-geographic intersections require more sophisticated analysis to understand comprehensive inequality patterns and targeted intervention needs.

Methodological and Publication Biases

Technology optimism pervades much research sponsored by AI developers, consulting firms, and technology companies, potentially overestimating benefits whilst underestimating implementation challenges and social costs. Industry-funded research demonstrates systematic bias toward positive findings that may not reflect broader implementation reality across diverse organisational contexts (Brynjolfsson et al., 2025).

Survivorship bias affects organisational case studies with successful implementations receiving disproportionate research attention compared to failures, potentially creating misleading impressions of implementation effectiveness whilst obscuring systematic factors contributing to unsuccessful adoption. Failed implementations receive minimal analytical attention, limiting understanding of barriers, constraints, and factors predicting implementation difficulties.

Publication bias toward positive results may systematically underrepresent studies finding limited or negative AI impacts on workplace outcomes. Academic incentives favour novel findings over replication studies, limiting accumulation of robust evidence regarding implementation effectiveness and constraining hypothesis validation through independent verification of key findings.

Selection bias affects workforce studies with AI-using workers potentially differing systematically from non-users in ways that influence adaptation outcomes independent of AI exposure. Voluntary adoption may select for workers with higher technical affinity, adaptation capability, or supportive organisational contexts that bias effectiveness assessments.

Measurement challenges constrain effectiveness evaluation with limited standardised metrics for assessing human-AI collaboration quality, implementation success, and long-term transformation outcomes. Current productivity measures may inadequately capture AI benefits whilst failing to account for hidden costs including training requirements, integration challenges, and cultural adaptation efforts.

Sample size limitations affect generalisability particularly for studies examining specific demographic groups, sectoral contexts, or implementation approaches. Many findings derive from small samples that may not represent broader population patterns whilst statistical power constraints limit ability to detect moderate effect sizes that may prove practically significant.

HYPOTHESIS EVALUATION AND KEY FINDINGS

Systematic evaluation of the five research hypotheses reveals complex patterns that support contextual rather than deterministic explanations of AI workplace transformation, whilst identifying specific mechanisms through which institutional, generational, sectoral, and individual factors mediate technological effects. This evaluation provides empirical foundation for rejecting simple technological determinism whilst supporting sophisticated understanding of AI workplace integration.

The evidence demonstrates that technological capabilities alone prove insufficient for predicting implementation outcomes, whilst institutional factors, organisational readiness, and contextual characteristics provide superior explanatory power for understanding transformation patterns and effectiveness variation across different settings.

Before examining each hypothesis in turn, Table 4 summarises the verdicts and the principal lines of evidence on which they rest. Three of the five hypotheses — institutional context, sectoral variation, and inequality amplification — receive strong empirical support; one, on human agency preservation, is supported only in qualified form; and the generational hypothesis is supported in a form that inverts popular expectations about digital nativity. The discussion that follows unpacks each verdict in sequence.

Table 4. Summary of Research Hypothesis Verdicts and Principal Lines of Evidence

Hypothesis	Core claim	Principal lines of evidence	Verdict
H1: Institutional Context	Implementation effectiveness is determined by organisational and institutional readiness, not technological capability alone	Only 7% of organisations reach Stage 4 maturity (Weill et al., 2024); 90% of use cases remain in pilot (Sukharevsky et al., 2025); cross-national healthcare variation (European Commission, 2024)	Strongly supported
H2: Generational Differentiation	Generational differences require differentiated, not uniform, implementation approaches	Millennials' 62% high-expertise rate (Illanes et al., 2024); Gen Z cognitive offloading of −0.68 (Gerlich, 2025); 13% Gen Z employment decline in AI-exposed roles (Brynjolfsson et al., 2025)	Partially supported, with important reversals of popular assumptions
H3: Sectoral Variation	Sectoral differences reflect task, regulatory and competitive factors rather than technology availability	75% adoption in financial services vs 16% in manufacturing SMEs; 26% legal adoption with 86% year-on-year growth; healthcare regulatory friction; creative-industry IP disputes	Strongly supported
H4: Human Agency Preservation	Agency-preserving collaboration achieves superior long-term outcomes	Aggregate Hedges' g = −0.23 for human–AI combinations vs best alone, with gains in content creation and losses in decision-making (Vaccaro et al., 2024); OECD augmentation-preference evidence (Lane et al., 2023)	Supported only in qualified, task-conditional form
H5: Inequality Amplification	Geographic and demographic inequalities create compound disadvantages requiring targeted intervention	60% / 40% / 28% employment exposure across advanced, emerging and low-income economies (Cazzaniga et al., 2026); female vs male generative-AI exposure of 4.7% vs 2.4% (Gmyrek et al., 2025); ghost-work infrastructure (Anwar, 2025)	Strongly supported

Note. Verdict categories are used consistently throughout the chapter. "Strongly supported" indicates convergent evidence from multiple independent data sources and analytical traditions. "Partially supported" indicates that the hypothesis receives empirical backing but only in a form that qualifies or reverses common expectations. "Qualified support" indicates that the hypothesis holds conditionally on factors identified in the supporting evidence. Full citation details are provided in the References.

Institutional Context Hypothesis (H1): Strongly Supported

Evidence overwhelmingly supports the hypothesis that AI workplace transformation effectiveness varies systematically across institutional contexts, with success determined by organisational readiness factors rather than technological capabilities alone. As demonstrated throughout the earlier analysis of sectoral transformation patterns, implementation success depends on sophisticated organisational development rather than technology deployment (Merhi, 2023; Yu et al., 2023; Pumplun et al., 2019).

The contrasting patterns between healthcare and financial services, detailed previously, illustrate institutional mediation of technological potential. Organisational maturity assessment reveals that only 7% of organisations achieve Stage 4 AI readiness according to MIT CISR's comprehensive evaluation framework, whilst most remain at earlier development stages despite substantial technology investments (Weill et al., 2024). This finding reinforces the widespread implementation failures documented in the earlier discussion of the contemporary AI workplace landscape, where institutional rather than technological barriers constrain progress.

Cross-national healthcare variations, as examined in the sectoral transformation analysis, provide compelling evidence that institutional arrangements—not technical capabilities—determine adoption outcomes. The hypothesis receives strong empirical support across multiple contexts and implementation domains.

Generational Differentiation Hypothesis (H2): Partially Supported with Important Qualifications

Evidence provides mixed support for generational differences requiring differentiated implementation approaches, challenging popular assumptions about digital native advantages whilst confirming the value of professional maturity. The paradoxical patterns identified in the earlier analysis of multigenerational adaptation—where Millennials demonstrate highest AI expertise levels whilst Generation Z faces overconfidence risks—suggest more complex relationships between age, experience, and adaptation capability than simple demographic models predict.

The concerning cognitive offloading patterns documented earlier among younger users indicate that differentiated approaches prove essential, though not in ways commonly assumed. Intergenerational collaboration emerges as particularly effective, with programmes pairing different generational strengths achieving superior outcomes compared to age-segregated training initiatives (Falckenthal et al., 2025).

Limited research on Generation X and Baby Boomers constrains comprehensive hypothesis evaluation, though evidence suggests their institutional knowledge provides essential context for implementation success whilst requiring supportive rather than replacement approaches.

Sectoral Variation Hypothesis (H3): Strongly Supported

Evidence provides compelling support for systematic sectoral variations resulting from task characteristics, regulatory frameworks, and institutional structures rather than technological determinism. The dramatic adoption disparities documented across the sectoral transformation analysis—from financial services leadership to construction sector lag—reflect structural characteristics that operate independent of technology availability.

The paradoxical patterns in creative industries, the scale dependencies in manufacturing, and the regulatory constraints in healthcare all demonstrate how sectoral context mediates technological effects. Professional services face sector-specific implementation challenges reflecting professional culture and regulatory requirements unique to knowledge-intensive work rather than general technology barriers.

This systematic variation across industries, combined with cross-national differences within sectors, provides robust support for the hypothesis whilst rejecting technological determinism explanations.

Human Agency Preservation Hypothesis (H4): Supported with Important Qualifications

Evidence supports the hypothesis that human–AI collaboration approaches preserving agency can achieve superior outcomes, though with important contextual qualifications that temper earlier enthusiasm. Meta-analysis of 106 experimental studies reports that, in aggregate, human–AI combinations perform significantly worse than the best of humans or AI alone (Hedges' $g = -0.23$, 95% CI [−0.39, −0.07]), with gains concentrated in content-creation tasks and losses in decision-making tasks (Vaccaro et al., 2024). The hypothesis is therefore supported only in its conditional form: augmentation benefits materialise where task characteristics align with AI capabilities and where implementation design actively preserves human judgement.

However, effectiveness proves highly context-dependent, with human-AI combinations underperforming best individual performers in decision-making contexts whilst demonstrating gains in creative and analytical tasks. OECD cross-national data demonstrates that 80% of workers report improved performance under augmentation approaches compared to automation strategies (Lane et al., 2023).

The cognitive offloading concerns identified throughout the analysis indicate that preserving agency requires active intervention rather than automatic occurrence. As demonstrated by the professional services applications examined in the sectoral transformation analysis, effective implementation can enhance rather than diminish human contribution through hybrid skill requirements.

Healthcare applications exemplify optimal collaboration patterns where maintaining professional oversight enhances rather than constrains AI effectiveness. Implementation quality emerges as the critical mediating factor determining whether systems preserve or undermine human agency.

Inequality Amplification Hypothesis (H5): Strongly Supported

Evidence provides compelling support for the hypothesis that geographic and demographic inequalities create compound disadvantages requiring targeted intervention. The infrastructure disparities, algorithmic bias patterns, and educational access gaps documented throughout earlier sections demonstrate systematic amplification mechanisms that exceed previous technological transitions.

The geographic concentration effects, training participation gaps, and scale dependency patterns identified across multiple sectors create self-reinforcing advantages for privileged populations whilst systematically excluding others. International development implications, as detailed in the earlier discussion of critical challenges and emerging opportunities, prove substantial with foundational connectivity barriers that could perpetuate global inequality patterns.

The hypothesis receives robust support across multiple inequality dimensions, reinforcing the need for comprehensive policy intervention to prevent market-driven amplification of existing disparities.

CONCLUSIONS AND FUTURE DIRECTIONS

The integration of artificial intelligence into global workplaces represents neither seamless human-machine collaboration nor inevitable mass technological unemployment, but rather a complex transformation characterised by significant institutional, sectoral, and demographic variation that challenges simple technological determinism. Systematic hypothesis testing reveals that outcomes depend fundamentally on contextual factors, implementation approaches, and institutional mediation rather than technological capabilities alone, requiring sophisticated understanding of AI transformation mechanisms for effective policy and organisational responses.

This analysis contributes both theoretical advancement and practical guidance whilst identifying critical areas requiring future research attention to develop more complete understanding of AI workplace transformation patterns, effectiveness factors, and policy intervention opportunities.

Synthesis of Key Findings

Five primary patterns emerge that transcend simplistic automation narratives and provide foundation for evidence-based approaches to AI workplace integration. First, AI workplace effects prove highly context-dependent rather than technologically determined, with outcomes systematically mediated by organisational readiness factors, institutional frameworks, cultural contexts, and implementation approaches rather than technical sophistication alone. The institutional context hypothesis (H1) receives strong empirical support through evidence demonstrating that complementary investments in human capital, organisational processes, and cultural adaptation determine success whilst technological capability alone proves insufficient for effective implementation.

Second, augmentation approaches can outperform automation strategies, but only when carefully designed to preserve human agency, cognitive engagement, and professional expertise whilst leveraging technological capabilities to enhance rather than replace human performance. The human agency preservation hypothesis (H4) receives qualified support: meta-analytical evidence indicates that, in aggregate, human–AI combinations underperform the best of humans or AI alone, with benefits concentrated in content-creation tasks and losses in decision-making tasks (Vaccaro et al., 2024). Effective augmentation therefore requires deliberate task-to-capability matching, deliberate preservation of human judgement, and active prevention of cognitive offloading rather than occurring as an automatic consequence of joint deployment.

Third, generational differences create both opportunities and challenges requiring nuanced rather than stereotypical responses that recognise distinct adaptation patterns whilst avoiding age-based assumptions about technological capability. The generational differentiation hypothesis (H2) receives partial support with evidence contradicting assumptions about digital native advantages amongst younger workers whilst confirming value of professional maturity combined with digital familiarity among mid-career professionals, particularly Millennials who demonstrate highest comprehensive AI competency levels.

Fourth, sectoral variations reflect task characteristics, regulatory frameworks, competitive dynamics, and institutional structures rather than uniform technological impact across industries. The sectoral variation hypothesis (H3) receives strong support through evidence of systematic differences in adoption patterns, implementation challenges, effectiveness outcomes, and transformation trajectories that require industry-specific rather than universal approaches to AI implementation and workforce development.

Fifth, persistent inequalities face systematic amplification through AI adoption without targeted intervention addressing structural barriers, access constraints, and capability development disparities. The inequality amplification hypothesis (H5) receives compelling empirical support through evidence of compound disadvantages affecting geographic regions (with 60% AI exposure in advanced economies against 28% in low-income countries), demographic groups (with female employment almost twice as exposed to generative AI as male employment in the highest-exposure tier), organisational scales (where scale dependencies restrict SMEs), and socioeconomic positions, as well as through the largely invisible global ghost-work infrastructure on which contemporary AI systems depend. Addressing these amplification mechanisms requires comprehensive policy responses across multiple inequality dimensions simultaneously (Anwar, 2025; Cazzaniga et al., 2026; Gmyrek et al., 2025).

Theoretical Contributions

This analysis advances theoretical understanding by integrating task-based automation theory with new institutional theory and organisational learning perspectives to explain systematic variation in AI transformation outcomes across different contexts. The multi-level framework illuminates how technological capabilities interact with institutional contexts, organisational readiness factors, cultural norms, and individual characteristics to produce divergent results that cannot be predicted through technological analysis alone.

Evidence challenges pure technological determinism whilst avoiding social constructivism extremes by demonstrating that AI capabilities create genuine possibilities and constraints that social actors navigate through strategic choices mediated by institutional factors. Neither purely technological nor purely social explanations prove adequate for understanding transformation complexity, requiring integrated theoretical approaches that acknowledge both technological capability and social mediation.

The institutional dimension emerges as particularly significant with regulatory frameworks, cultural norms, organisational practices, and governance structures mediating between technological potential and realised outcomes in systematic ways that can be identified, analysed, and potentially influenced through policy intervention. This finding suggests that institutional design and policy frameworks matter more than technical considerations for shaping transformation trajectories and distributional outcomes.

Organisational learning theory contributes essential insight into dynamic adaptation processes that unfold over time through iterative cycles of experimentation, evaluation, and refinement rather than one-time implementation events. Evidence demonstrates that organisations achieving sustained AI benefits invest in continuous learning capabilities and adaptive capacity development rather than static technology deployment approaches.

The generational analysis contributes understanding of how demographic characteristics interact with technological change in complex ways that require differentiated rather than uniform approaches whilst challenging popular assumptions about age-based technological advantages. This finding emphasises the importance of individualised assessment and tailored intervention rather than demographic stereotyping.

Practical Implications

The analysis generates critical implications for practice across organisational, policy, and individual levels that emphasise contextual adaptation, stakeholder engagement, and comprehensive capability development rather than simple technology deployment. Organisations should adopt augmentation-first strategies that preserve and enhance human capabilities whilst developing sophisticated governance frameworks addressing both performance optimisation and equity considerations through long-term capability development rather than short-term efficiency maximisation.

Implementation approaches require comprehensive change management that addresses cultural transformation, workforce development, and stakeholder engagement simultaneously rather than focusing primarily on technology deployment. Evidence indicates that successful organisations invest 60-70% of AI implementation resources in organisational development compared to 30-40% in technology acquisition, contradicting technology-centric approaches that prove systematically ineffective.

Policymakers face complex trade-offs between innovation promotion and social protection requiring adaptive regulatory approaches that balance oversight with innovation enablement whilst addressing inequality amplification through targeted intervention rather than market-based solutions alone. International coordination on standards and principles proves essential whilst allowing implementation flexibility reflecting different national contexts, institutional arrangements, and development priorities.

Risk-based regulatory frameworks enable appropriate oversight levels based on application context and potential impact whilst avoiding both excessive restriction that constrains beneficial innovation and inadequate oversight that enables harmful applications. Evidence suggests that sectoral variation requires differentiated regulatory approaches rather than universal frameworks applied uniformly across different industrial contexts.

Individual workers must develop adaptive capabilities combining technical literacy with uniquely human skills including critical thinking, creative problem-solving, emotional intelligence, and ethical reasoning whilst building resilient professional networks that support continuous learning and career adaptation. Success requires proactive rather than reactive approaches to career development given rapid technological evolution and evidence that skills obsolescence rates exceed traditional adaptation mechanisms.

Future Research Directions

Several critical research gaps require attention to advance understanding of AI workplace transformation and develop more effective intervention strategies. Scenario analysis provides one structured way of addressing the deep uncertainty that characterises the field: the World Economic Forum's (2026) Four Futures for Jobs framework distinguishes supercharged progress, an age of displacement, a co-pilot economy, and stalled progress as alternative trajectories for AI-enabled labour-market change through 2030, each requiring different policy responses. Longitudinal studies tracking career transitions, skill development patterns, and adaptation trajectories across generational cohorts would provide essential insight into developmental processes rather than cross-sectional assessments currently dominating the literature. These studies should follow individuals and organisations over extended periods to understand sustained rather than temporary transformation effects.

The structure of this scenario space is shown in Figure 3, which maps the four futures onto a two-by-two matrix defined by the pace of AI diffusion (slow or fast) and the strength of the workforce-readiness response (weak or strong). The matrix is a deliberately simplified heuristic: its purpose is to make visible the interaction between a technological variable and a policy variable, and to show that the same pace of AI diffusion can produce either broadly shared gains or socially disruptive displacement depending on the quality of the adaptation response.

Figure 3. Four Futures for Work in 2030: A Scenario Matrix of AI Diffusion and Workforce-Readiness Response

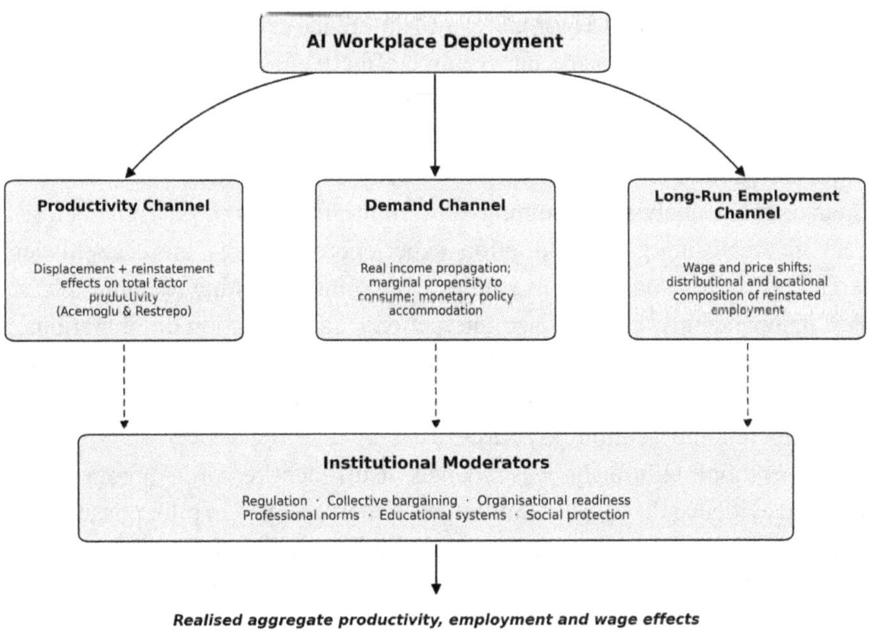

Note. Adapted from the Four Futures for Jobs framework developed by the World Economic Forum (2026). Quadrants are idealised rather than empirically bounded and are intended to orient policy and research attention rather than to predict specific outcomes. The horizontal axis represents the pace of AI diffusion in productive activity; the vertical axis represents the capacity of labour-market institutions, education systems, and social-protection mechanisms to support workforce transition at that pace.

Cross-national comparative research examining institutional factors influencing AI adoption success and failure would illuminate policy levers available to governments seeking to shape transformation outcomes whilst respecting different cultural contexts and development priorities. Current research lacks systematic comparison of regulatory frameworks, educational systems, labour relations approaches, and social protection mechanisms across different national contexts, limiting understanding of effective policy alternatives.

Sectoral analysis requires substantial expansion beyond technology-intensive industries toward labour-intensive sectors including agriculture, construction, personal services, and informal economy activities that employ large workforce populations globally. Understanding AI impacts across the full employment spectrum remains incomplete with current research biased toward industries with high technology adoption rates and sophisticated analytical capabilities.

Methodological development should emphasise natural experiments, quasi-experimental designs, and rigorous causal inference approaches enabling better understanding of AI workplace intervention effectiveness. Current research relies heavily on observational studies and case analyses that limit policy implications through correlation rather than causation evidence, constraining development of evidence-based intervention strategies.

Intersectional analysis examining how multiple demographic characteristics interact to create unique AI adoption experiences requires more sophisticated research approaches than current studies examining individual demographic categories independently. Gender-race interactions, age-education combinations, socioeconomic-geographic intersections, and other identity dimension combinations need systematic analysis to understand comprehensive inequality patterns and develop targeted intervention responses.

Implementation failure analysis receives insufficient research attention despite widespread evidence that most AI initiatives remain trapped in pilot phases. Understanding systematic factors contributing to implementation failure would provide valuable insight for improving success rates whilst identifying institutional barriers requiring policy or organisational intervention to address effectively.

The AI-driven workplace revolution thus represents both unprecedented opportunity and significant risk, with outcomes determined by institutional choices, implementation approaches, and policy responses rather than technological destiny alone. Success requires recognising complexity, acknowledging trade-offs, implementing adaptive strategies that preserve human agency whilst capturing productivity benefits through contextually appropriate rather than universal solutions. Future research should prioritise understanding mechanisms of successful adaptation whilst developing intervention strategies that promote inclusive rather than exclusive technological transformation patterns.

REFERENCES

Acar, O. A., Gai, P. J., Tu, Y., & Hou, J. (2025). Research: The hidden penalty of using AI at work. *Harvard Business Review*. https://hbr.org/2025/08/research-the-hidden-penalty-of-using-ai-at-work

Acemoglu, D., & Restrepo, P. (2019). Artificial intelligence, automation, and work. In Agrawal, A., Gans, J., & Goldfarb, A. (Eds.), *The economics of artificial intelligence: An agenda* (pp. 197–236). University of Chicago Press. DOI: 10.7208/chicago/9780226613475.003.0008

Acemoglu, D., & Restrepo, P. (2022). Tasks, automation, and the rise in U.S. wage inequality. *Econometrica*, *90*(5), 1973–2016. DOI: 10.3982/ECTA19815

All About, A. I. (2025). AI statistics in manufacturing: Transforming industrial operations. https://www.allaboutai.com/resources/ai-statistics/manufacturing/

Anwar, M. A. (2025). Value chains of AI: Data training firms, platforms, and workers. In Berg, J., Anwar, M. A., & Rani, U. (Eds.), *The future of labour through the lens of AI*. Routledge., DOI: 10.4324/9781003587972

ArtSmart AI. (2024). *AI in music industry statistics 2025: Market growth & trends*. https://artsmart.ai/blog/ai-in-music-industry-statistics/

Babashahi, L., Barbosa, C. E., Lima, Y., Lyra, A., Salazar, H., Argôlo, M., Almeida, M. A., & Souza, J. M. (2024). AI in the workplace: A systematic review of skill transformation in the industry. *Administrative Sciences*, *14*(6), 127. DOI: 10.3390/admsci14060127

Berg, J., Snene, M., & Velasco, L. (2024). *Mind the AI divide: Shaping a global perspective on the future of work*. International Labour Organization & UN Office of the Secretary-General's Envoy on Technology.

Broecke, S. (2023). *Artificial intelligence and the labour market: Introduction*. OECD Employment Outlook 2023. OECD Publishing.

Brynjolfsson, E., Chandar, B., & Chen, R. (2025). *Canaries in the coal mine? Six facts about the recent employment effects of artificial intelligence* (Stanford Digital Economy Lab Working Paper, November 2025). Stanford University. https://digitaleconomy.stanford.edu/app/uploads/2025/11/CanariesintheCoalMine_Nov25.pdf

Brynjolfsson, E., Li, D., & Raymond, L. (2025). Generative AI at work. *The Quarterly Journal of Economics*, *140*(2), 889–942. DOI: 10.1093/qje/qjae044

Budhwar, P., Chowdhury, S., Wood, G., Aguinis, H., Bamber, G. J., Beltran, J. R., Boselie, P., Lee Cooke, F., Decker, S., DeNisi, A., Dey, P. K., Guest, D., Knoblich, A. J., Malik, A., Paauwe, J., Papagiannidis, S., Patel, C., Pereira, V., Ren, S., & Varma, A. (2023). Human resource management in the age of generative artificial intelligence: Perspectives and research directions on ChatGPT. *Human Resource Management Journal, 33*(3), 606–659. DOI: 10.1111/1748-8583.12524

Cargofive. (2024). Future of AI machine learning freight management. https://cargofive.com/future-of-ai-machine-learning-freight-management/

Cazzaniga, M., Jaumotte, F., Li, L., Melina, G., Panton, A. J., Pizzinelli, C., Rockall, E., & Tavares, M. M. (2026). *Bridging skill gaps for the future: New jobs creation in the AI age* (IMF Staff Discussion Note SDN/2026/001). International Monetary Fund. https://www.imf.org/en/publications/staff-discussion-notes/issues/2026/01/09/bridging-skill-gaps-for-the-future-new-jobs-creation-in-the-ai-age-572136

Chan, C. K. Y., & Hu, W. (2023). Students' voices on generative AI: Perceptions, benefits, and challenges in higher education. *International Journal of Educational Technology in Higher Education, 20*(1), 43. DOI: 10.1186/s41239-023-00411-8

Chardonnens, S. (2025). Adapting educational practices for Generation Z: Integrating metacognitive strategies and artificial intelligence. *Frontiers in Education, 10*, 1504726. DOI: 10.3389/feduc.2025.1504726

Chen, L. (2023). Algorithmic discrimination in employment: A systematic review. *Nature Human Behaviour, 7*, 1–15.

Chen, M., Wang, Y., Wang, Q., Shi, J., Wang, H., Ye, Z., Xue, P., & Qiao, Y. (2024). Impact of human and artificial intelligence collaboration on workload reduction in medical image interpretation. *NPJ Digital Medicine, 7*(1), 349. DOI: 10.1038/s41746-024-01328-w PMID: 39616244

Chetty, K. (2023). AI literacy for an ageing workforce: Leveraging the experience of older workers. *OBM Geriatrics, 7*(3), 243. DOI: 10.21926/obm.geriatr.2303243

Chui, M., Seitz, P., & Malhotra, S. (2025). *The state of AI: How organizations are rewiring to capture value*. McKinsey & Company.

CMSWire. (2024). Customer service automation statistics. CMSWire.

Crowley Media Group. (2025). Big four bet big on AI agents. https://crowleymediagroup.com/resources/big-four-bet-big-on-ai-agents/

de Koster, R., & Roy, D. (2024). Research: Warehouse and logistics automation works better with human partners. *Harvard Business Review*.

Dell'Acqua, F., McFowland, E., III, Mollick, E., Lifshitz-Assaf, H., Kellogg, K. C., Rajendran, S., Krayer, L., Candelon, F., & Lakhani, K. R. (2023). *Navigating the jagged technological frontier: Field experimental evidence of the effects of AI on knowledge worker productivity and quality* (HBS Working Paper No. 24-013). Harvard Business School.

Doshi, A. R., & Hauser, O. (2024). Generative AI enhances individual creativity but reduces the collective diversity of novel content. *Science Advances, 10*(28), eadn5290. DOI: 10.1126/sciadv.adn5290 PMID: 38996021

Dubey, A. (2025). *How AI can enhance digital inclusion and fight inequality*. World Economic Forum. https://www.weforum.org/stories/2025/06/digital-inclusion-ai/

Erickson, K. (2024). AI and work in the creative industries: Digital continuity or discontinuity? *Creative Industries Journal, 17*(3–4), 213–233. DOI: 10.1080/17510694.2024.2421135

European Commission. (2024). *Digital economy and society index (DESI) 2017-2022*. European Commission.

European Parliament and Council. (2024). *Regulation (EU) 2024/1689 laying down harmonised rules on artificial intelligence (Artificial Intelligence Act)*. Official Journal of the European Union, L 2024/1689. https://eur-lex.europa.eu/eli/reg/2024/1689/oj

Falckenthal, B., Au-Yong-Oliveira, M., & Figueiredo, C. (2025). Intergenerational tacit knowledge transfer: Leveraging AI. *Societies (Basel, Switzerland), 15*(8), 213. DOI: 10.3390/soc15080213

Fasbender, U., & Gerpott, F. H. (2022). To share or not to share: A social-cognitive perspective on knowledge sharing among older employees. *Work, Aging and Retirement, 8*(2), 146–161. DOI: 10.1093/workar/waab017

Faulconbridge, J., Sarwar, A., & Thomas, P. (2025). How professionals adapt to artificial intelligence: The role of intertwined boundary work. *Journal of Management Studies, 62*(1), 89–118. DOI: 10.1111/joms.12122

France Stratégie. (2025). *Intelligence artificielle et travail*. Haut-Commissariat à la Stratégie et au Plan. https://www.strategie-plan.gouv.fr/publications/intelligence-artificielle-travail

Gartner. (2019). Gartner predicts 80% of marketers will abandon personalization efforts by 2025 due to lack of ROI, process or technology limitations. https://www.gartner.com/en/newsroom/press-releases/2019-12-02-gartner-predicts-80--of-marketers-will-abandon-person

Gartner. (2024). Worldwide public cloud end-user spending forecast. https://www.gartner.com/en/newsroom/press-releases/2024-11-19-worldwide-public-cloud-spending-forecast

Gehrmann, M. C., & Förster, A. (2024). AI Act: High-risk AI systems – what applies, what is due when? *Taylor Wessing*. https://www.taylorwessing.com/en/insights-and-events/insights/2024/11/high-risk-ai-systems

Georgia Department of Education. (2025). *Leveraging AI in the K-12 setting: Ensuring the ethical, effective, and secure use of AI tools and systems in Georgia's schools*. Georgia Department of Education.

Gerlich, M. (2025). AI tools in society: Impacts on cognitive offloading and the future of critical thinking. *Societies (Basel, Switzerland)*, *15*(1), 45–62. DOI: 10.3390/soc15010006

Gharbawi, M., Ward, E., Bratt, E., Diver, L., Mueller, H., Quartu, R., & Robinson, H. (2024). *Artificial intelligence in UK financial services – 2024*. Bank of England; Financial Conduct Authority.

Gihleb, R., Giuntella, O., Stella, L., & Wang, T. (2023). Keeping workers safe in the automation revolution. *Brookings Institution*. https://www.brookings.edu/articles/keeping-workers-safe-in-the-automation-revolution/

Global Market Insights Inc. (2024). Artificial intelligence in manufacturing market analysis report 2024-2032. https://www.gminsights.com/industry-analysis/artificial-intelligence-ai-in-manufacturing-market

Gmyrek, P., Berg, J., & Bescond, D. (2025). *Generative AI and jobs: A refined global index of occupational exposure* (ILO Working Paper No. 140). International Labour Organization. https://www.ilo.org/publications/generative-ai-and-jobs-refined-global-index-occupational-exposure

Grand View Research. (2024). Artificial intelligence in retail market size, share & trends analysis report 2030. https://www.grandviewresearch.com/industry-analysis/ai-retail-market-report

Hassan, M., Kushniruk, A., & Borycki, E. (2024). Barriers to and facilitators of artificial intelligence adoption in health care: Scoping review. *JMIR Human Factors*, *11*, e48633. DOI: 10.2196/48633 PMID: 39207831

Heimberger, H., Jäger, A., & Maloča, S. (2024). *Künstliche Intelligenz in der Produktion: Digitale Produktionssysteme und Weiterbildung als Voraussetzung für KI?* (Modernisierung der Produktion, 83. Mitteilung aus der ISI-Erhebung). Fraunhofer-Institut für System und Innovationsforschung ISI.

Horobet, A., Boubaker, S., Belascu, L., Negreanu, C. C., & Dinca, Z. (2024). Technology-driven advancements: Mapping the landscape of algorithmic trading literature. *Technological Forecasting and Social Change*, *209*, 123746. DOI: 10.1016/j.techfore.2024.123746

Illanes, P., Lund, S., & Mourshed, M. (2024). *A new future of work: The race to deploy AI and raise skills in Europe and beyond*. McKinsey Global Institute.

International Federation of Robotics. (2024). *Record of 4 million robots in factories worldwide* [Press release]. https://ifr.org/ifr-press-releases/news/record-of-4-million-robots-working-in-factories-worldwide

Jacobs, J. (2025). AI labor displacement and the limits of worker retraining. *Brookings (TechTank)*. https://www.brookings.edu/articles/ai-labor-displacement-and-the-limits-of-worker-retraining/

Kanagarla, K. (2024). Artificial intelligence and employment transformation: A multi-sector analysis of workforce disruption and adaptation. SSRN *Electronic Journal*. DOI: 10.2139/ssrn.5015970

Kellogg, K. C., Faraj, S., & Mantere, S. (2026). Governing the agentic enterprise: A new operating model for autonomous AI at scale. *California Management Review*. Advance online publication. https://cmr.berkeley.edu/2026/03/governing-the-agentic-enterprise-a-new-operating-model-for-autonomous-ai-at-scale/

Kim, B. J., & Lee, J. (2024). The mental health implications of artificial intelligence adoption: The crucial role of self-efficacy. *Humanities & Social Sciences Communications*, *11*(1), 1561. DOI: 10.1057/s41599-024-04018-w

Kim, S., Jang, Y., Choi, S., Kim, W., Jung, H., Kim, S., & Kim, H. (2021). Analyzing teacher competency with TPACK for K-12 AI education. *KI – Künstliche Intelligenz*, 35(2), 139–151.

Koslosky, L., & Feldgoise, J. (2025). *The state of AI-related apprenticeships*. Center for Security and Emerging Technology. DOI: 10.51593/20220042

Kumar, A., Krishnamoorthy, B., Balasubramanian, S., & Bharathi, S. V. (2024). Machine learning and artificial intelligence-induced technostress in organizations: A study on automation-augmentation paradox. *The International Journal of Organizational Analysis*, *32*(4), 681–703. DOI: 10.1108/IJOA-01-2023-3581

Lane, M., Williams, M., & Broecke, S. (2023). *The impact of AI on the workplace: Main findings from the OECD AI surveys of employers and workers* (OECD Social, Employment and Migration Working Papers No. 288). Organisation for Economic Co-operation and Development.

Law, L. (2025). AI adoption reveals generational workforce strategy divide. *AI Magazine*. https://aimagazine.com/articles/workday-research-millennials-lead-ai-skills-transformation

Li, Y., Wu, B., Huang, Y., & Luan, S. (2024). Developing trustworthy artificial intelligence: Insights from research on interpersonal, human-automation, and human-AI trust. *Frontiers in Psychology*, *15*, 1382693. DOI: 10.3389/fpsyg.2024.1382693 PMID: 38694439

Lintner, T. (2024). A systematic review of AI literacy scales. *npj Science of Learning*, 9(1), 50.

Lyons, S., & Kuron, L. (2014). Generational differences in the workplace: A review of the evidence and directions for future research. *Journal of Organizational Behavior*, *35*(S1), S139–S157. DOI: 10.1002/job.1913

Malik, N., Tripathi, S. N., Kar, A. K., & Gupta, S. (2022). Impact of artificial intelligence on employees working in industry 4.0 led organizations. *International Journal of Manpower*, *43*(2), 334–354. DOI: 10.1108/IJM-03-2021-0173

Manyika, J., Sneader, K., & Woetzel, J. (2023). *The economic potential of generative AI: The next productivity frontier*. McKinsey Global Institute.

MarketResearch.com. (2024). *The digital twin market: Shaping the future of Industry 4.0*. https://blog.marketresearch.com/the-digital-twin-market-shaping-the-future-of-industry-4.0

MarketsandMarkets. (2025). *Artificial intelligence in manufacturing market size, share & trends (Report Code: SE 5470)*. https://www.marketsandmarkets.com/Market-Reports/artificial-intelligence-manufacturing-market-72679105.html

Market.us. (2024). *AI chatbot market size, share, trends analysis report*. https://market.us/report/ai-chatbot-market/

Maslej, N., Fattorini, L., Perrault, R., Gil, Y., Parli, V., Kariuki, N., Capstick, E., Reuel, A., Brynjolfsson, E., Etchemendy, J., Ligett, K., Lyons, T., Manyika, J., Niebles, J. C., Shoham, Y., Wald, R., Walsh, T., Hamrah, A., Santarlasci, L., . . . Oak, S. (2025). *The AI Index 2025 annual report*. AI Index Steering Committee, Institute for Human-Centered AI, Stanford University.

Maslej, N., Fattorini, L., Perrault, R., Parli, V., Reuel, A., Brynjolfsson, E., Etchemendy, J., Ligett, K., Lyons, T., Manyika, J., Niebles, J. C., Shoham, Y., Wald, R., Walsh, T., Hamrah, A., Betts Lotufo, J., Rome, A., Shi, A., & Oak, S. (2026). *The 2026 AI Index report*. AI Index Steering Committee, Institute for Human-Centered AI, Stanford University. https://hai.stanford.edu/ai-index/2026-ai-index-report

Mathew, D. E., Ebem, D. U., Ikegwu, A. C., Ukeoma, P. E., & Dibiaezue, N. F. (2025). Recent emerging techniques in explainable artificial intelligence to enhance interpretability of AI models for humans. *Neural Processing Letters*, *57*(1), 16. DOI: 10.1007/s11063-025-11732-2

McClain, C., Kennedy, B., Gottfried, J., Anderson, M., & Pasquini, G. (2025). *How the U.S. public and AI experts view artificial intelligence*. Pew Research Center.

Merhi, M. I. (2023). An evaluation of the critical success factors impacting artificial intelligence implementation. *International Journal of Information Management*, *68*, 102594. DOI: 10.1016/j.ijinfomgt.2022.102545

Merriman, M., Sanz Sáiz, B., Bulman, L., Carpanelli, M., DiCerbo, K. E., Dutt, Y., Kim, S., Makhani, N., Neff, G., & Yongpradit, P. (2024). *How can we upskill Gen Z as fast as we train AI?* Ernst & Young Global Limited (EY).

Microsoft. (2024). *AI governance and risk management*. Microsoft.

Microsoft & LinkedIn. (2024). *2024 Work Trend Index: AI at work is here. Now comes the hard part*. Microsoft WorkLab.

Mir, U. B., Sharma, S., Kar, A. K., & Gupta, M. P. (2020). Critical success factors for integrating artificial intelligence and robotics. *Digital Policy. Regulation & Governance*, *22*(5), 307–331.

Missouri Department of Elementary and Secondary Education. (2025). *Artificial intelligence guidance for local education agencies (Version 1.0, 2025–26 school year)*. Missouri Department of Elementary and Secondary Education.

Moore, R. L., Hwang, W., & Moses, J. D. (2024). A systematic review of mobile-based microlearning in adult learner contexts. *Journal of Educational Technology & Society*, *27*(1), 137–146.

Murire, O. T. (2024). Artificial intelligence and its role in shaping organizational work practices and culture. *Administrative Sciences*, *14*(12), 316. DOI: 10.3390/admsci14120316

Muro, M., & Liu, S. (2024). *Mapping AI's uneven global distribution*. Brookings Institution.

Muro, M., & Methkupally, S. (2025). *Mapping the AI economy: Which regions are ready for the next technology leap*. Brookings. https://www.brookings.edu/articles/mapping-the-ai-economy-which-regions-are-ready-for-the-next-technology-leap/

Myers, K. K., & Sadaghiani, K. (2010). Millennials in the workplace: A communication perspective on millennials' organizational relationships and performance. *Journal of Business and Psychology*, *25*(2), 225–238. DOI: 10.1007/s10869-010-9172-7 PMID: 20502509

Nong, P., Adler-Milstein, J., Apathy, N. C., Holmgren, A. J., & Everson, J. (2025). Current use and evaluation of artificial intelligence and predictive models in US hospitals. *Health Affairs*, *44*(1), 90–98. DOI: 10.1377/hlthaff.2024.00842 PMID: 39761454

OpenResearch. (2024). *Unconditional cash study: Three-year results*. https://www.openresearchlab.org/studies/unconditional-cash-study/study

OXMaint. (2025). AI-powered predictive maintenance: Manufacturing's game-changer. *OXMaint Blog*. https://oxmaint.com/blog/post/ai-powered-predictive-maintenance-manufacturing-game-changer

Page, I., Reuss, K., & Zemper, Z. (2024). Changes in the U.S. labor supply. *Trendlines*. K. DeMaria (Ed.). U.S. Department of Labor Employment and Training Administration.

Pouliakas, K., Hippe, R., & Santangelo, G. (2025). *Skills empower workers in the AI revolution: First findings from Cedefop's AI skills survey* (Policy Brief No. 9201 EN). European Centre for the Development of Vocational Training (Cedefop).

Prosci. (2024). AI change management. *Prosci*. https://www.prosci.com/ai-change-management

Pumplun, L., Tauchert, C., & Heidt, M. (2019). A new organizational chassis for artificial intelligence-exploring organizational readiness factors. *Proceedings of the 27th European Conference on Information Systems*.

Raisch, S., & Krakowski, S. (2021). Artificial intelligence and management: The automation–augmentation paradox. *Academy of Management Review*, *46*(1), 192–210. DOI: 10.5465/amr.2018.0072

Ransbotham, S., Khodabandeh, S., Kiron, D., Candelon, F., Chu, M., & LaFountain, B. (2020). *Expanding AI's impact with organizational learning*. MIT Sloan Management Review and Boston Consulting Group.

Rapid Innovation. (2024). AI-powered dynamic pricing in retail and e-commerce. *Rapid Innovation*. https://www.rapidinnovation.io/post/ai-powered-dynamic-pricing-in-e-commerce

Rinf Technology. (2024). AI-driven optimization for sustainable manufacturing. *Rinf Technology*. https://www.rinf.tech/ai-driven-optimization-for-sustainable-manufacturing

Rowan, J., Ammanath, B., Perricos, C., Sniderman, B., & Jarvis, D. (2025). *Now decides next: Generating a new future. Deloitte's State of Generative AI in the Enterprise, Quarter four report*. Deloitte Development LLC.

Rudko, I., Bashirpour Bonab, A., Fedele, M., & Kosiba, J. P. B. (2025). New institutional theory and AI: Toward rethinking of artificial intelligence in organizations. *Journal of Management History*, *31*(1), 45–67. DOI: 10.1108/JMH-09-2023-0097

Rudolph, C. W., Rauvola, R. S., Costanza, D. P., & Zacher, H. (2021). Generations and generational differences: Debunking myths in organizational science and practice and paving new paths forward. *Journal of Business and Psychology*, *36*(6), 945–967. DOI: 10.1007/s10869-020-09715-2 PMID: 32901173

San Diego State University. (2025). CSU announces landmark public-private AI initiative, SDSU contributing to efforts. *SDSU News*. https://www.sdsu.edu/news/2025/02/csu-announces-landmark-public-private-ai-initiative-sdsu-contributing-to-efforts

Schaeff, A., & Rother, M. (2024). *Deploying AI to the real world: How Siemens Erlangen factory is leading the AI charge*. Siemens AG.

Singapore, A. I. (2025). *AI Apprenticeship Programme (AIAP)*. https://aisingapore.org/industryinnovation/aiap/

Slingerland, C. (2025). *90+ Cloud computing statistics: A 2025 market snapshot*. CloudZero. https://www.cloudzero.com/blog/cloud-computing-statistics/

Sukharevsky, A., Kerr, D., Hjartar, K., Hämäläinen, L., Bout, S., & Di Leo, V. (2025). *Seizing the agentic AI advantage*. McKinsey & Company.

Thomson Reuters Institute. (2024). *2024 generative AI in professional services report*. Thomson Reuters. https://www.thomsonreuters.com/en-us/posts/technology/generative-ai-in-professional-services-2024/

UNCTAD. (2025). Technology and innovation report 2025: Inclusive artificial intelligence for development. *United Nations Conference on Trade and Development*.

UNESCO. (2021). *AI and education: Guidance for policy-makers*. UNESCO Publishing.

UNESCO. (2024). *AI competency frameworks for students and teachers*. UNESCO Education Sector.

United Nations. (2024). *Governing AI for humanity: Report of the UN AI advisory body*. https://www.un.org/en/ai-advisory-body

US Census Bureau. (2023). Only 3.8% of businesses use AI to produce goods and services, highest use in information sector. *Census Bureau Stories*. https://www.census.gov/library/stories/2023/11/businesses-use-ai.html

Vaccaro, M., Almaatouq, A., & Malone, T. (2024). When combinations of humans and AI are useful: A systematic review and meta-analysis. *Nature Human Behaviour*, *8*(12), 2293–2303. DOI: 10.1038/s41562-024-02024-1 PMID: 39468277

Weber, E., Zika, G., Maier, T., Mönnig, A., Kalinowski, M., Ulrich, P., Wolter, M. I., & Hummel, M. (2025). *Künstliche Intelligenz: Potenzielle Effekte für den deutschen Arbeitsmarkt* [Artificial intelligence: Potential effects for the German labour market]. Institut für Arbeitsmarkt- und Berufsforschung (IAB), Bundesinstitut für Berufsbildung (BIBB), & Gesellschaft für Wirtschaftliche Strukturforschung (GWS). https://iab.de/kuenstliche-intelligenz-potenzielle-effekte-fuer-den-deutschen-arbeitsmarkt/

Weill, P., Woerner, S. L., & Sebastian, I. M. (2024). *Building enterprise AI maturity* [Research briefing]. MIT Center for Information Systems Research.

Wilson, K., & Caliskan, A. (2024). Gender, race, and intersectional bias in resume screening via language model retrieval. In *Proceedings of the 2024 AAAI/ACM Conference on AI, Ethics, and Society* (pp. 1578–1590). Association for Computing Machinery. DOI: 10.1609/aies.v7i1.31748

Wolff, J., Pauling, J., Keck, A., & Baumbach, J. (2021). Success factors of artificial intelligence implementation in healthcare. *Frontiers in Digital Health*, *3*, 594971. DOI: 10.3389/fdgth.2021.594971 PMID: 34713083

World Bank. (2024). Accelerated by COVID and AI, global digital landscape remains uneven [Press release]. https://www.worldbank.org/en/news/press-release/2024/03/05/accelerated-by-covid-and-ai-global-digital-landscape-remains-uneven

World Economic Forum. (2025). *The future of jobs report 2025*. World Economic Forum. https://www.weforum.org/publications/the-future-of-jobs-report-2025/

World Economic Forum. (2026). *Four futures for jobs in the new economy: AI and talent in 2030*. World Economic Forum. https://www.weforum.org/publications/four-futures-for-jobs-in-the-new-economy-ai-and-talent-in-2030/

World Intellectual Property Organization. (2024). Patent landscape report on generative artificial intelligence. WIPO. https://www.wipo.int/en/web/patent-analytics/generative-ai

Xu, Z., Ren, F., Wang, P., Cao, J., Tan, C., Ma, D., Zhao, L., Dai, J., Ding, Y., Fang, H., Li, H., Liu, H., Luo, F., Meng, Y., Pan, P., Xiang, P., Xiao, Z., Rao, S., Satler, C., & Zhavoronkov, A. (2025). A generative AI-discovered TNIK inhibitor for idiopathic pulmonary fibrosis: A randomized phase 2a trial. *Nature Medicine*, *31*(8), 2602–2610. DOI: 10.1038/s41591-025-03743-2 PMID: 40461817

Yu, X., Xu, S., & Ashton, M. (2023). Antecedents and outcomes of artificial intelligence adoption and application in the workplace: The socio-technical system theory perspective. *Information Technology & People*, *36*(7), 2584–2616. DOI: 10.1108/ITP-04-2021-0254

ADDITIONAL READING

Callari, T. C., & Puppione, L. (2025). Can generative artificial intelligence productivity tools support workplace learning? A qualitative study on employee perceptions in a multinational corporation. *Journal of Workplace Learning*, *37*(3), 266–283. DOI: 10.1108/JWL-11-2024-0258

Engström, A., Pittino, D., Mohlin, A., Johansson, A., & Edh Mirzaei, N. (2024). Artificial intelligence and work transformations: Integrating sensemaking and workplace learning perspectives. *Information Technology & People*, *37*(7), 2441–2461. DOI: 10.1108/ITP-01-2023-0048

Gong, Q., Fan, D., & Bartram, T. (2025). Integrating artificial intelligence and human resource management: A review and future research agenda. *International Journal of Human Resource Management*, *36*(1), 103–141. DOI: 10.1080/09585192.2024.2440065

Karunakaran, A., Lebovitz, S., Narayanan, D., & Rahman, H. A. (2025). Artificial intelligence at work : An integrative perspective on the impact of AI on workplace inequality. *The Academy of Management Annals*, *19*(1), 693–735. DOI: 10.5465/annals.2023.0230

Korzynski, P., Kim, S., & Egan, T. (2024). Bridging human resource development processes through generative Artificial Intelligence. *Human Resource Development Quarterly*, *35*(3), 247–256. DOI: 10.1002/hrdq.21551

Li, J., & Yeo, R. K. (2024). Artificial intelligence and human integration: A conceptual exploration of its influence on work processes and workplace learning. *Human Resource Development International*, *27*(3), 367–387. DOI: 10.1080/13678868.2024.2348987

Mendy, J., Jain, A., & Thomas, A. (2025). Artificial intelligence in the workplace–challenges, opportunities and HRM framework: A critical review and research agenda for change. *Journal of Managerial Psychology*, *40*(5), 517–538.

Ngu, P. C., Chien, C. C., Ho, Y. T., & Hou, H. T. (2025). A generative AI educational game framework with multi-scaffolding supports workplace competency development. *Computers & Education*, *239*, 105421. DOI: 10.1016/j.compedu.2025.105421

Özer, M., Perc, M., & Suna, H. E. (2024). Artificial intelligence bias and the amplification of inequalities in the labor market. *Journal of Economy Culture and Society*, (69), 159–168.

Schwaeke, J., Gerlich, C., Nguyen, H. L., Kanbach, D. K., & Gast, J. (2025). Artificial intelligence (AI) for good? Enabling organizational change towards sustainability. *Review of Managerial Science*, *19*(10), 1–26. DOI: 10.1007/s11846-025-00840-x

KEY TERMS AND DEFINITIONS

AI Implementation Paradox: The phenomenon where 90% of AI use cases remain trapped in pilot phases despite technical capability, indicating that technological sophistication alone fails to guarantee transformation success.

Agentic AI Systems: AI systems capable of autonomous decision-making and task execution within defined parameters, requiring sophisticated governance frameworks to prevent misalignment with organisational objectives.

Algorithmic Bias: Systematic discrimination embedded in AI systems that amplify existing inequalities, such as CV ranking systems that favour white-associated names 85% of the time versus 9% for Black-associated names.

Augmentation Approaches: AI implementation strategies that preserve and enhance human capabilities whilst leveraging technological tools, contrasted with replacement-focused automation strategies.

Cognitive Offloading: The phenomenon where heavy AI usage correlates with reduced problem-solving capabilities and critical thinking skills, particularly problematic among younger users during career development phases.

Collaborative Robotics (Cobots): Human-robot teams that achieve higher efficiency than full automation in applications requiring flexibility and adaptation, representing 10.5% of total industrial robot installations.

Digital Divide Amplification: The systematic exacerbation of existing digital disparities through AI deployment, with infrastructure requirements multiplying disparities by factors of 20 to 1,700 between high and low-income contexts.

Enterprise AI Maturity Model: MIT CISR's framework measuring organisational AI readiness across four stages, with only 7% of organisations achieving Stage 4 future-readiness characterised by systematic AI integration and sophisticated governance.

Generational Differentiation Hypothesis (H2): The proposition that generational differences in AI adaptation reflect distinct socialisation experiences requiring differentiated implementation approaches rather than uniform strategies.

Generative AI: AI systems capable of creating new content, demonstrating 25% faster task completion and 40% higher quality outputs in controlled trials, though effectiveness proves highly context-dependent.

Human Agency Preservation Hypothesis (H4): The proposition that human-AI collaboration approaches preserving agency and cognitive engagement achieve superior long-term outcomes compared to automation-focused strategies.

Human-AI Collaboration Effectiveness: Measured through meta-analysis revealing that, in aggregate, human–AI combinations underperform the best of humans or AI alone (Hedges' $g = -0.23$, 95% CI [−0.39, −0.07]), with task-dependent heterogeneity: losses in decision-making tasks and gains in content-creation tasks.

Inequality Amplification Hypothesis (H5): The proposition that geographic and demographic inequalities in AI access create compound disadvantages requiring targeted policy intervention to prevent amplification of existing disparities.

Institutional Context Hypothesis (H1): The proposition that AI workplace transformation effectiveness varies systematically across institutional contexts, with success determined by organisational readiness factors rather than technological capabilities alone.

Organisational Learning with AI Framework: A systematic approach achieving 14% productivity increases through iterative learning cycles, dependent on sustained organisational commitment to process adaptation rather than simple technology deployment.

Sectoral Variation Hypothesis (H3): The proposition that sectoral variations in AI adoption patterns result from differences in task characteristics, regulatory frameworks, and competitive pressures rather than technological determinism.

Task-Based Automation Theory: Framework distinguishing automation effects that substitute human labour from augmentation effects that enhance human capabilities, whilst recognising transformation effects creating entirely new occupational categories.

Technological Determinism: The perspective that technology development follows predictable patterns with inevitable social consequences, challenged by evidence showing institutional factors mediate technological effects.

Three-Stage AI Impact Model: Conceptual framework identifying automation (substituting human tasks), augmentation (enhancing human capabilities), and transformation (creating new occupational categories) as distinct pathways of AI workplace integration.

Compilation of References

Acar, O. A., Gai, P. J., Tu, Y., & Hou, J. (2025). Research: The hidden penalty of using AI at work. *Harvard Business Review*. https://hbr.org/2025/08/research-the-hidden-penalty-of-using-ai-at-work

Acemoglu, D. (2002). Technical change, inequality, and the labor market. *Journal of Economic Literature*, *40*(1), 7–72. DOI: 10.1257/jel.40.1.7

Acemoglu, D., Autor, D., Hazell, J., & Restrepo, P. (2022). Artificial Intelligence and Jobs: Evidence from Online Vacancies. *Journal of Labor Economics*, *40*(S1), S293–S340. DOI: 10.1086/718327

Acemoglu, D., & Restrepo, P. (2019). Automation and new tasks: How technology displaces and reinstates labor. *The Journal of Economic Perspectives*, *33*(2), 3–30. DOI: 10.1257/jep.33.2.3

Acemoglu, D., & Restrepo, P. (2020). Robots and jobs: Evidence from US labor markets. *Journal of Political Economy*, *128*(6), 2188–2244. DOI: 10.1086/705716

Acemoglu, D., & Restrepo, P. (2020). The wrong kind of AI? Artificial intelligence and the future of labour demand. *Cambridge Journal of Regions, Economy and Society*, *13*(1), 25–35. DOI: 10.1093/cjres/rsz022

Acemoglu, D., & Restrepo, P. (2022). Tasks, automation, and the rise in U.S. wage inequality. *Econometrica*, *90*(5), 1973–2016. DOI: 10.3982/ECTA19815

Adadi, A., & Berrada, M. (2018). Peeking inside the black-box: A survey on explainable artificial intelligence (XAI). *IEEE Access : Practical Innovations, Open Solutions*, *6*, 52138–52160. DOI: 10.1109/ACCESS.2018.2870052

Adams-Prassl, J. (2018). Work on demand. In Oxford University Press eBooks (pp. 11–30). DOI: 10.1093/oso/9780198797012.003.0002

Adler, P. S. (2007). The future of critical management studies: A paleo-Marxist critique of labour process theory. *Organization Studies*, *28*(9), 1313–1345. DOI: 10.1177/0170840607080743

Ahmadi, A., Cantini, A., Frías, V. G., & Staudacher, A. P. (2025). The impact of labor flexibility on operational efficiency in industry 5.0: A systematic literature review. *International Journal of Production Research*, •••, 1–26. DOI: 10.1080/00207543.2025.2516770

Ahmed, F. (2024). The digital divide and AI in education: Addressing equity and accessibility. *Journal of AI Integration in Education*, *1*(2), 12–23.

All About, A. I. (2025). AI statistics in manufacturing: Transforming industrial operations. https://www.allaboutai.com/resources/ai-statistics/manufacturing/

Anand, A., & Bhambri, P. (2018). Rotation, scale and translation invariant character recognition system using neural network (M. Tech. thesis). Punjab Technical University.

Andronie, M., Iatagan, M., U ă, C., Hurloiu, I., Dimirescu, A., & Dimirescu, I. (2023). Big data management algorithms in artificial internet of things-based fintech. *Amfiteatru Economic*, *25*(63), 430–445. DOI: 10.24818/EA/2023/63/430

Anthony, C., Bechky, B. A., & Fayard, A.-L. (2023). "collaborating" with AI: Taking a system view to explore the future of work. *Organization Science*, *34*(5), 1672–1694. DOI: 10.1287/orsc.2022.1651

Anwar, M. A. (2025). Value chains of AI: Data training firms, platforms, and workers. In Berg, J., Anwar, M. A., & Rani, U. (Eds.), *The future of labour through the lens of AI*. Routledge., DOI: 10.4324/9781003587972

Appio, F. P., La Torre, D., Lazzeri, F., Masri, H., & Schiavone, F. (Eds.). (2024). *Impact of artificial intelligence in business and society: Opportunities and challenges*. Routledge.

Arntz, M., Gregory, T., & Zierahn, U. (2016). The risk of automation for jobs in OECD countries. OECD Social, Employment and Migration Working Papers. DOI: 10.1787/1815199X

ArtSmart AI. (2024). *AI in music industry statistics 2025: Market growth & trends*. https://artsmart.ai/blog/ai-in-music-industry-statistics/

Ashkanasy, N. M., & Daus, C. S. (2005). Rumors of the death of emotional intelligence in organizational behavior are vastly exaggerated. *Journal of Organizational Behavior*, *26*(4), 441–452. DOI: 10.1002/job.320

Autor, D. H. (2022). The labor market impacts of technological change: From unbridled enthusiasm to qualified optimism to vast uncertainty (Working Paper No. 30074). National Bureau of Economic Research. https://doi.org/DOI: 10.3386/w30074

Autor, D. H. (2015). Why are there still so many jobs? The history and future of workplace automation. *The Journal of Economic Perspectives*, *29*(3), 3–30. DOI: 10.1257/jep.29.3.3

Autor, D. H. (2019). Work of the past, work of the future. *AEA Papers and Proceedings. American Economic Association*, *109*, 1–32. DOI: 10.1257/pandp.20191110

Autor, D., Mindell, D. A., & Reynolds, E. B. (2022). *The work of the future: Building better jobs in an age of intelligent machines*. The MIT Press. DOI: 10.7551/mitpress/14109.001.0001

Barocas, S., & Selbst, A. D. (2016). Big data's disparate impact. *California Law Review*, •••, 671–732.

Bass, B. M., & Riggio, R. E. (2019). *Transformational leadership* (3rd ed.). Routledge.

Bathla, S., Jindal, C., & Bhambri, P. (2007, March). Impact of technology on societal living [Paper presentation]. *International Conference on Convergence and Competition*, India.

Baxter, G., & Sommerville, I. (2010). Socio-technical systems: From design methods to systems engineering. *Interacting with Computers*, *23*(1), 4–17. DOI: 10.1016/j.intcom.2010.07.003

Beer, D. (2017). The social power of algorithms. *Information Communication and Society*, *20*(1), 1–13. DOI: 10.1080/1369118X.2016.1216147

Berg, J., Snene, M., & Velasco, L. (2024). *Mind the AI divide: Shaping a global perspective on the future of work*. International Labour Organization & UN Office of the Secretary-General's Envoy on Technology.

Bessen, J. (2019). *AI and jobs: The role of demand*. National Bureau of Economic Research., DOI: 10.3386/w24235

Bessen, J. (2019). Automation and jobs: When technology boosts employment. *Economic Policy*, *34*(100), 589–626. DOI: 10.1093/epolic/eiaa001

Bhambri, P. (2014). Effectiveness of performance management system in IT industries: Empirical approach. In Management of globalised business: Plethora of new opportunities (pp. 114-121).

Bhambri, P. (2025a). Understanding AI and machine learning in security. In Bhambri, P., & Anand, A. J. (Eds.), *Handbook of AI-driven threat detection and prevention: A holistic approach to security* (pp. 1–17). CRC Press., DOI: 10.1201/9781003521020-1

Bhambri, P. (2025b). Virtual and augmented reality for immersive learning experiences: Practical applications and challenges. In Pelet, J.-É. (Ed.), *Architecting the digital future: Platforms, design, and application* (pp. 17–46). IGI Global., DOI: 10.4018/979-8-3693-2973-3.ch002

Bhambri, P., & Nischal, P. (2008, May). Emerging new economy in telecommunication sector of india [Paper presentation]. *International Conference on Business Challenges & Strategies in Emerging Global Scenario*, India.

Bhambri, P., & Singh, M. (2008). Image transport protocol for JPEG image over loss prone congested networks. *PIMT Journal of Research, 1*(1), 55–61.

Bhambri, P., & Thapar, V. (2009, May). Power distribution challenges in VLSI: An introduction [Paper presentation]. *International Conference on Downtrend Challenges in IT*, India.

Bhattacharya, P., Saraswat, D., Savaliya, D., Sanghavi, S., Verma, A., Sakariya, V., Tanwar, S., Sharma, R., Raboaca, M. S., & Manea, D. L. (2023). Towards future internet: The metaverse perspective for diverse industrial applications. *Mathematics, 11*(4), 941. Advance online publication. DOI: 10.3390/math11040941

Billett, S. (2020). *Learning through work: Strategies for effective practice.* Routledge. DOI: 10.4324/9781003116318

Binns, R. (2018). Fairness in machine learning: Lessons from political philosophy. *Proceedings of Machine Learning Research, 81*, 149–159. https://proceedings.mlr.press/v81/binns18a.html

Binns, R. (2018). Fairness in machine learning: Lessons from political philosophy. *Proceedings of the 2018 Conference on Fairness, Accountability, and Transparency*, 149–159.

Binns, R., Van Kleek, M., Veale, M., Lyngs, U., Zhao, J., & Shadbolt, N. (2018). 'It's reducing a human being to a percentage': Perceptions of justice in algorithmic decisions. *Proceedings of the 2018 CHI Conference on Human Factors in Computing Systems*. https://doi.org/DOI: 10.1145/3173574.3173951

Bodie, M. T., Cherry, M. A., McCormick, M. L., & Tang, J. (2020). The law and policy of people analytics. *University of Colorado Law Review, 91*(1), 1–57.

Bonfiglioli, A., Crinò, R., Gancia, G., & Papadakis, I. (2025). Artificial intelligence and jobs: Evidence from US commuting zones. *Economic Policy, 40*(121), 145–194. DOI: 10.1093/epolic/eiae059

Bonnaure, P. (2018). McAfee, A., & Brynjolfsson, E. (2018). Des machines, des plateformes et des foules. Maîtriser notre avenir numérique [Review of the book Machine, platform, crowd: Harnessing our digital future]. *Futuribles (Paris, France), 427*(6), VI. DOI: 10.3917/futur.427.0121f

Bonney, K., Breaux, C., Buffington, C., Dinlersoz, E., Foster, L., Goldschlag, N., Haltiwanger, J., Kroff, Z., & Savage, K. (2024). The impact of AI on the workforce: Tasks versus jobs? *Economics Letters, 244*, 111971. DOI: 10.1016/j.econlet.2024.111971

Borle, P., Reichel, K., & Voelter-Mahlknecht, S. (2021). Is there a sampling bias in research on work-related technostress? A systematic review of occupational exposure to technostress and the role of socioeconomic position. *International Journal of Environmental Research and Public Health, 18*(4), 2071. DOI: 10.3390/ijerph18042071 PMID: 33672604

Boyatzis, R. E. (2018). *The competent manager: A model for effective performance*. Wiley.

Broecke, S. (2023). *Artificial intelligence and the labour market: Introduction*. OECD Employment Outlook 2023. OECD Publishing.

Brynjolfsson, E., & McAfee, A. (2014). *The second machine age: Work, progress, and prosperity in a time of brilliant technologies*. W. W. Norton & Company. https://wwnorton.com/books/the-second-machine-age/

Brynjolfsson, E., Chandar, B., & Chen, R. (2025). *Canaries in the coal mine? Six facts about the recent employment effects of artificial intelligence* (Stanford Digital Economy Lab Working Paper, November 2025). Stanford University. https://digitaleconomy.stanford.edu/app/uploads/2025/11/CanariesintheCoalMine_Nov25.pdf

Brynjolfsson, E., Li, D., & Raymond, L. (2023). Generative AI at work. SSRN Electronic Journal. DOI: 10.2139/ssrn.4426942

Brynjolfsson, E., Li, D., & Raymond, L. (2025). Generative AI at work. *The Quarterly Journal of Economics, 140*(2), 889–942. DOI: 10.1093/qje/qjae044

Brynjolfsson, E., & McAfee, A. (2014). *The second machine age: Work, progress, and prosperity in a time of brilliant technologies*. W. W. Norton & Company.

Brynjolfsson, E., & McAfee, A. (2017). *Machine, platform, crowd: Harnessing our digital future*. W. W. Norton.

Bryson, J., & Winfield, A. (2017). Standardizing ethical design for artificial intelligence and autonomous systems. *Computer, 50*(5), 116–119. DOI: 10.1109/MC.2017.154

Budhwar, P., Chowdhury, S., Wood, G., Aguinis, H., Bamber, G. J., Beltran, J. R., Boselie, P., Lee Cooke, F., Decker, S., DeNisi, A., Dey, P. K., Guest, D., Knoblich, A. J., Malik, A., Paauwe, J., Papagiannidis, S., Patel, C., Pereira, V., Ren, S., & Varma, A. (2023). Human resource management in the age of generative artificial intelligence: Perspectives and research directions on ChatGPT. *Human Resource Management Journal, 33*(3), 606–659. DOI: 10.1111/1748-8583.12524

Bughin, J. (2023). Does artificial intelligence kill employment growth: The missing link of corporate AI posture. *Frontiers in Artificial Intelligence*, *6*, 1239466. DOI: 10.3389/frai.2023.1239466 PMID: 38045762

Bughin, J., Seong, J., Manyika, J., Chui, M., & Joshi, R. (2018). *Notes from the AI frontier: Modeling the impact of AI on the world economy*. McKinsey Global Institute.

Burrell, J. (2016). How the machine "thinks": Understanding opacity in machine learning algorithms. *Big Data & Society*, *3*(1), 1–12. DOI: 10.1177/2053951715622512

Capraro, V., Lentsch, A., Acemoglu, D., Akgün, S., Akhmedova, A., Bilancini, E., Bonnefon, J.-F., Brañas-Garza, P., Butera, L., Douglas, K. M., Everett, J. A. C., Gigerenzer, G., Greenhow, C., Hashimoto, D. A., Holt-Lunstad, J., Jetten, J., Johnson, S., Kunz, W. H., Longoni, C., & Viale, R. (2024). The impact of generative artificial intelligence on socioeconomic inequalities and policy making. *PNAS Nexus*, *3*(6), pgae191. Advance online publication. DOI: 10.1093/pnasnexus/pgae191 PMID: 38864006

Carbonero, F., Davies, J., Ernst, E., Fossen, F. M., Samaan, D., & Sorgner, A. (2023). The impact of artificial intelligence on labor markets in developing countries: A new method with an illustration for Lao PDR and urban Viet Nam. *Journal of Evolutionary Economics*, *33*(3), 707–736. DOI: 10.1007/s00191-023-00809-7 PMID: 36811092

Cargofive. (2024). Future of AI machine learning freight management. https://cargofive.com/future-of-ai-machine-learning-freight-management/

Cascio, W. F., & Montealegre, R. (2016). How technology is changing work and organizations. *Annual Review of Organizational Psychology and Organizational Behavior*, *3*(1), 349–375. DOI: 10.1146/annurev-orgpsych-041015-062352

Castelo, N., & Ward, A. F. (2021). Conservatism predicts aversion to consequential artificial intelligence. *PLoS One*, *16*(12), e0261467. DOI: 10.1371/journal.pone.0261467 PMID: 34928989

Cath, C. (2018). Governing artificial intelligence: Ethical, legal and technical opportunities and challenges. *Philosophical Transactions. Series A, Mathematical, Physical, and Engineering Sciences*, *376*(2133), 20180080. DOI: 10.1098/rsta.2018.0080 PMID: 30322996

Cazzaniga, M., Jaumotte, F., Li, L., Melina, G., Panton, A. J., Pizzinelli, C., Rockall, E., & Tavares, M. M. (2026). *Bridging skill gaps for the future: New jobs creation in the AI age* (IMF Staff Discussion Note SDN/2026/001). International Monetary Fund. https://www.imf.org/en/publications/staff-discussion-notes/issues/2026/01/09/bridging-skill-gaps-for-the-future-new-jobs-creation-in-the-ai-age-572136

Chan, C. K. Y., & Hu, W. (2023). Students' voices on generative AI: Perceptions, benefits, and challenges in higher education. *International Journal of Educational Technology in Higher Education*, *20*(1), 43. DOI: 10.1186/s41239-023-00411-8

Chang, Z. (2025). Influence of artificial intelligence on the financial labor market. *Finance Research Letters*, *80*, 107039. DOI: 10.1016/j.frl.2025.107039

Chardonnens, S. (2025). Adapting educational practices for Generation Z: Integrating metacognitive strategies and artificial intelligence. *Frontiers in Education*, *10*, 1504726. DOI: 10.3389/feduc.2025.1504726

Chassignol, M., Khoroshavin, A., Klimova, A., & Bilyatdinova, A. (2018). Artificial intelligence trends in education: A narrative overview. *Procedia Computer Science*, *136*, 16–24. DOI: 10.1016/j.procs.2018.08.233

Chen, L. (2023). Algorithmic discrimination in employment: A systematic review. *Nature Human Behaviour*, *7*, 1–15.

Chen, M., Wang, Y., Wang, Q., Shi, J., Wang, H., Ye, Z., Xue, P., & Qiao, Y. (2024). Impact of human and artificial intelligence collaboration on workload reduction in medical image interpretation. *NPJ Digital Medicine*, *7*(1), 349. DOI: 10.1038/s41746-024-01328-w PMID: 39616244

Chernova, S., & Aha, D. (2019). Emotion-aware artificial intelligence. *AI Magazine*, *40*(3), 15–28.

Chetty, K. (2023). AI literacy for an ageing workforce: Leveraging the experience of older workers. *OBM Geriatrics*, *7*(3), 243. DOI: 10.21926/obm.geriatr.2303243

Chui, M., Seitz, P., & Malhotra, S. (2025). *The state of AI: How organizations are rewiring to capture value*. McKinsey & Company.

Ciuhu, A. M. (2024). The (Post) Pandemic Employment Model. In *The Economic and Social Impact of the COVID-19 Pandemic: Romania in a European Context* (pp. 169–182). Springer Nature Switzerland. DOI: 10.1007/978-3-031-47780-5_7

Clarke, N. (2010). Emotional intelligence and its relationship to transformational leadership and key project manager competences. *Project Management Journal, 41*(2), 5–20. DOI: 10.1002/pmj.20162

CMSWire. (2024). Customer service automation statistics. CMSWire.

Coeckelbergh, M. (2020). *AI Ethics*. MIT Press (Essential Knowledge series).

Coleman, D. (1975). Labor and monopoly capital: The degradation of work in the twentieth century, by Harry Braverman [Review of the book Labor and monopoly capital: The degradation of work in the twentieth century]. *The Journal of Economic History, 35*(3), 647–648. DOI: 10.1017/S0022050700075719

Couldry, N., & Mejias, U. A. (2020). *The costs of connection*. Stanford University Press., DOI: 10.1515/9781503609754

Crowley Media Group. (2025). Big four bet big on AI agents. https://crowleymediagroup.com/resources/big-four-bet-big-on-ai-agents/

Crowley, P. M., & Hudgins, D. (2024). The impact of US productivity growth on unemployment in the time–frequency domain: Is AI causing a change in the relationship? *Empirical Economics, 66*(5), 2169–2190. DOI: 10.1007/s00181-023-02510-x

Dahlin, E. (2024). Who Says Artificial Intelligence Is Stealing Our Jobs? *Socius: Sociological Research for a Dynamic World, 10*, 23780231241259672. DOI: 10.1177/23780231241259672

Damioli, G., Van Roy, V., & Vertesy, D. (2021). The impact of artificial intelligence on labor productivity. *Eurasian Business Review, 11*(1), 1–25. DOI: 10.1007/s40821-020-00172-8

Damioli, G., Van Roy, V., Vertesy, D., & Vivarelli, M. (2023). AI technologies and employment: Micro evidence from the supply side. *Applied Economics Letters, 30*(6), 816–821. DOI: 10.1080/13504851.2021.2024129

Davenport, T. H., & Kirby, J. (2016). *Only humans need apply: Winners and losers in the age of smart machines*. HarperBusiness. https://www.harpercollins.com/products/only-humans-need-apply-thomas-h-davenportjulia-kirby

Davenport, T. H., & Ronanki, R. (2018). Artificial intelligence for the real world. *Harvard Business Review*, *96*(1), 108–116.

Davis, F. D. (1989). Perceived usefulness, perceived ease of use, and user acceptance of information technology. *Management Information Systems Quarterly*, *13*(3), 319–340. DOI: 10.2307/249008

De Brito, L. (2021). Zuboff, S. (2019). The age of surveillance capitalism: The fight for a human future at the new frontier of power [Review of the book The age of surveillance capitalism]. *Mural Internacional*, *12*, e55150. Advance online publication. DOI: 10.12957/rmi.2021.55150

de Koster, R., & Roy, D. (2024). Research: Warehouse and logistics automation works better with human partners. *Harvard Business Review*.

De Sio, F. S. (2021). Coeckelbergh, M. (2021). AI ethics [Review of the book AI ethics]. *Science and Engineering Ethics*, *27*(4). Advance online publication. DOI: 10.1007/s11948-021-00323-8

De Stefano, V. (2015). The rise of the "just-in-time workforce": On-demand work, crowd work and labour protection in the "gig-economy." SSRN Electronic Journal. DOI: 10.2139/ssrn.2682602

De Stefano, V. (2019). Negotiating the algorithm": Automation, artificial intelligence, and labor protection. *Comparative Labor Law & Policy Journal*, *41*(1), 15–46.

Dell'Acqua, F., McFowland, E., III, Mollick, E., Lifshitz-Assaf, H., Kellogg, K. C., Rajendran, S., Krayer, L., Candelon, F., & Lakhani, K. R. (2023). *Navigating the jagged technological frontier: Field experimental evidence of the effects of AI on knowledge worker productivity and quality* (HBS Working Paper No. 24-013). Harvard Business School.

Deranty, J.-P., & Corbin, T. (2022). Artificial intelligence and work: A critical review of recent research from the social sciences. *AI & Society*. Advance online publication. DOI: 10.1007/s00146-022-01496-x

Dhanda, M., Rogers, B. A., Hall, S., Dekoninck, E., & Dhokia, V. (2025). Reviewing human-robot collaboration in manufacturing: Opportunities and challenges in the context of Industry 5.0. *Robotics and Computer-integrated Manufacturing*, *93*, 102937. DOI: 10.1016/j.rcim.2024.102937

Dietvorst, B. J., Simmons, J. P., & Massey, C. (2015). Algorithm aversion: People erroneously avoid algorithms after seeing them err. *Journal of Experimental Psychology. General*, *144*(1), 114–126. DOI: 10.1037/xge0000033 PMID: 25401381

Ding, J. (2022). Dueling perspectives in AI and U.S.–China relations. In Oxford University Press eBooks (pp. 881–894). DOI: 10.1093/oxfordhb/9780197579329.013.53

Doshi, A. R., & Hauser, O. (2024). Generative AI enhances individual creativity but reduces the collective diversity of novel content. *Science Advances*, *10*(28), eadn5290. DOI: 10.1126/sciadv.adn5290 PMID: 38996021

Dosz, A. (2024). *Shaping economic dynamics: governmental influence on AI integration and job dynamics* (Bachelor's thesis, University of Twente).

Dubey, A. (2025). *How AI can enhance digital inclusion and fight inequality*. World Economic Forum. https://www.weforum.org/stories/2025/06/digital-inclusion-ai/

Duggan, J., Sherman, U., Carbery, R., & McDonnell, A. (2020). Algorithmic management and app-work in the gig economy: A research agenda for employment relations and HRM. *Human Resource Management Journal*, *30*(1), 114–132. DOI: 10.1111/1748-8583.12258

Dweck, C. S. (2006). *Mindset: The new psychology of success*. Random House.

Dweck, C. S. (2016). What having a "growth mindset" actually means. *Harvard Business Review*, *94*(11), 213–216.

Dwivedi, Y. K., Kshetri, N., Hughes, L., Slade, E., Jeyaraj, A., Kar, A. K., Baabdullah, A. M., Koohang, A., Raghavan, V., Ahuja, M., Albanna, H., Albashrawi, M. A., Al-Busaidi, A. S., Balakrishnan, J., Barlette, Y., Basu, S., Bose, I., Brooks, L., Buhalis, D., & Wright, R. (2023). Opinion paper: So what if ChatGPT wrote it? Multidisciplinary perspectives on opportunities, challenges and implications of generative conversational AI for research, practice and policy. *International Journal of Information Management*, *71*, 102642. Advance online publication. DOI: 10.1016/j.ijinfomgt.2023.102642

Edmondson, A. (2019). *The fearless organization: Creating psychological safety in the workplace for learning, innovation, and growth*. Wiley.

Ehsan, U., Liao, Q. V., Muller, M., Riedl, M. O., & Weisz, J. D. (2021). Expanding explainability: Towards social transparency in AI systems. *Proceedings of the 2021 CHI Conference on Human Factors in Computing Systems*. https://doi.org/DOI: 10.1145/3411764.3445188

Ellis, E., Radvanyi, P. J., Ascierto, P. A., Bhatia, T. C., Curti, C. M., Cesano, D., Gajewski, T. F., Hwu, P., Atkins, M. B., Sullivan, A. W., & Weber, J. S. (2024). Challenges and opportunities in cancer immunotherapy: A Society for Immunotherapy of Cancer (SITC) strategic vision. *Journal for Immunotherapy of Cancer*, *12*(5), e009063. DOI: 10.1136/jitc-2024-009063 PMID: 38901879

Erickson, K. (2024). AI and work in the creative industries: Digital continuity or discontinuity? *Creative Industries Journal, 17*(3–4), 213–233. DOI: 10.1080/17510694.2024.2421135

Ernst, E., Merola, R., & Samaan, D. (2019). Economics of artificial intelligence: Implications for the future of work. *IZA Journal of Labor Policy, 9*(1), 20190004. Advance online publication. DOI: 10.2478/izajolp-2019-0004

European Commission. (2024). *Digital economy and society index (DESI) 2017-2022*. European Commission.

European Parliament and Council. (2024). *Regulation (EU) 2024/1689 laying down harmonised rules on artificial intelligence (Artificial Intelligence Act)*. Official Journal of the European Union, L 2024/1689. https://eur-lex.europa.eu/eli/reg/2024/1689/oj

Falckenthal, B., Au-Yong-Oliveira, M., & Figueiredo, C. (2025). Intergenerational tacit knowledge transfer: Leveraging AI. *Societies (Basel, Switzerland), 15*(8), 213. DOI: 10.3390/soc15080213

Fasbender, U., & Gerpott, F. H. (2022). To share or not to share: A social-cognitive perspective on knowledge sharing among older employees. *Work, Aging and Retirement, 8*(2), 146–161. DOI: 10.1093/workar/waab017

Fatun, M., & Pazour, M. (2021). Modelling the impact of Artificial Intelligence on the labour market in Czechia. *Central European Journal of Public Policy, 15*(2), 31–42. DOI: 10.2478/cejpp-2021-0006

Faulconbridge, J., Sarwar, A., & Thomas, P. (2025). How professionals adapt to artificial intelligence: The role of intertwined boundary work. *Journal of Management Studies, 62*(1), 89–118. DOI: 10.1111/joms.12122

France Stratégie. (2025). *Intelligence artificielle et travail*. Haut-Commissariat à la Stratégie et au Plan. https://www.strategie-plan.gouv.fr/publications/intelligence-artificielle-travail

Frey, C. B., & Osborne, M. A. (2017). The future of employment: How susceptible are jobs to computerisation? *Technological Forecasting and Social Change, 114*, 254–280. DOI: 10.1016/j.techfore.2016.08.019

Gartner. (2019). Gartner predicts 80% of marketers will abandon personalization efforts by 2025 due to lack of ROI, process or technology limitations. https://www.gartner.com/en/newsroom/press-releases/2019-12-02-gartner-predicts-80--of-marketers-will-abandon-person

Gartner. (2024). Worldwide public cloud end-user spending forecast. https://www.gartner.com/en/newsroom/press-releases/2024-11-19-worldwide-public-cloud-spending-forecast

Gehrmann, M. C., & Förster, A. (2024). AI Act: High-risk AI systems – what applies, what is due when? *Taylor Wessing*. https://www.taylorwessing.com/en/insights-and-events/insights/2024/11/high-risk-ai-systems

George, J. M. (2000). Emotions and leadership: The role of emotional intelligence. *Human Relations*, *53*(8), 1027–1055. DOI: 10.1177/0018726700538001

Georgia Department of Education. (2025). *Leveraging AI in the K-12 setting: Ensuring the ethical, effective, and secure use of AI tools and systems in Georgia's schools*. Georgia Department of Education.

Georgieff, A., & Hyee, R. (2022). Artificial Intelligence and Employment: New Cross-Country Evidence. *Frontiers in Artificial Intelligence*, *5*, 832736. DOI: 10.3389/frai.2022.832736 PMID: 35620279

Gerlich, M. (2025). AI tools in society: Impacts on cognitive offloading and the future of critical thinking. *Societies (Basel, Switzerland)*, *15*(1), 45–62. DOI: 10.3390/soc15010006

Gharbawi, M., Ward, E., Bratt, E., Diver, L., Mueller, H., Quartu, R., & Robinson, H. (2024). *Artificial intelligence in UK financial services – 2024*. Bank of England; Financial Conduct Authority.

Ghosh, D., Ghosh, R., Roy Chowdhury, S., & Ganguly, B. (2025). AI-exposure and labour market: A systematic literature review on estimations, validations, and perceptions. *Management Review Quarterly*, *75*(1), 677–704. DOI: 10.1007/s11301-023-00393-x

Gihleb, R., Giuntella, O., Stella, L., & Wang, T. (2023). Keeping workers safe in the automation revolution. *Brookings Institution*. https://www.brookings.edu/articles/keeping-workers-safe-in-the-automation-revolution/

Giuntella, O., Konig, J., & Stella, L. (2025). Artificial intelligence and the wellbeing of workers. *Scientific Reports*, *15*(1), 20087. DOI: 10.1038/s41598-025-98241-3 PMID: 40550887

Giwa, F., & Ngepah, N. (2024). The relationship between artificial intelligence and low-skilled employment in South Africa. *Heliyon*, *10*(23), e40640. DOI: 10.1016/j.heliyon.2024.e40640 PMID: 39669173

Glikson, E., & Woolley, A. W. (2020). Human trust in artificial intelligence: Review of empirical research. *The Academy of Management Annals, 14*(2), 627–660. DOI: 10.5465/annals.2018.0057

Global Market Insights Inc. (2024). Artificial intelligence in manufacturing market analysis report 2024-2032. https://www.gminsights.com/industry-analysis/artificial-intelligence-ai-in-manufacturing-market

Gmyrek, P., Berg, J., & Bescond, D. (2025). *Generative AI and jobs: A refined global index of occupational exposure* (ILO Working Paper No. 140). International Labour Organization. https://www.ilo.org/publications/generative-ai-and-jobs-refined-global-index-occupational-exposure

Goleman, D. (1998). *Working with emotional intelligence*. Bantam Books.

Goleman, D. (2017). *Emotional intelligence: Why it can matter more than IQ*. Bantam Books.

Goos, M., Manning, A., & Salomons, A. (2014). Explaining job polarization: Routine-biased technological change and offshoring. *The American Economic Review, 104*(8), 2509–2526. DOI: 10.1257/aer.104.8.2509

Gopalan, P. D., Pienaar, M., & Brokensha, S. I. (2024). Deep medicine: Navigating the intersection of technology, cognition and ethics in the digital age of medicine. *South African Medical Journal, 114*(3), e1520. https://pubmed.ncbi.nlm.nih.gov/38304632/ PMID: 38304632

Gorski, A. T., Gligorea, I., Gorski, H., & Oancea, R. (2022, June). Workforce and workplace ecosystem–challenges and opportunities in the age of digital transformation and 4IR. In *International Conference Knowledge-Based Organization* (Vol. 28, No. 1, pp. 187-194). DOI: 10.2478/kbo-2022-0028

Goyal, A., & Aneja, R. (2020). Artificial intelligence and income inequality: Do technological changes and worker's position matter? *Journal of Public Affairs, 20*(4), e2326. DOI: 10.1002/pa.2326

Graham, M., Hjorth, I., & Lehdonvirta, V. (2019). Digital labor and development: Impacts of global digital labor platforms and the gig economy on worker livelihoods. In The MIT Press eBooks (pp. 269–294). DOI: 10.7551/mitpress/10890.003.0022

Graham, M., Hjorth, I., & Lehdonvirta, V. (2017). Digital labour and development: Impacts of global digital labour platforms and the gig economy on worker livelihoods. *Transfer: European Review of Labour and Research, 23*(2), 135–162. DOI: 10.1177/1024258916687250 PMID: 28781494

Grand View Research. (2024). Artificial intelligence in retail market size, share & trends analysis report 2030. https://www.grandviewresearch.com/industry-analysis/ai-retail-market-report

Guarascio, D., & Reljic, J. (2025). AI and employment in Europe. *Economics Letters*, *247*, 112183. DOI: 10.1016/j.econlet.2025.112183

Hadi, M. U., Tashi, Q. A., Qureshi, R., Shah, A., Muneer, A., Irfan, M., Zafar, A., Shaikh, M. B., Akhtar, N., Wu, J., & Mirjalili, S. (2023). Large language models: A comprehensive survey of its applications, challenges, limitations, and future prospects. *TechRxiv*. DOI: 10.36227/techrxiv.23589741.v4

Hassan, M., Kushniruk, A., & Borycki, E. (2024). Barriers to and facilitators of artificial intelligence adoption in health care: Scoping review. *JMIR Human Factors*, *11*, e48633. DOI: 10.2196/48633 PMID: 39207831

Heimberger, H., Jäger, A., & Maloča, S. (2024). *Künstliche Intelligenz in der Produktion: Digitale Produktionssysteme und Weiterbildung als Voraussetzung für KI?* (Modernisierung der Produktion, 83. Mitteilung aus der ISI-Erhebung). Fraunhofer-Institut für System und Innovationsforschung ISI.

Hendriksen, C. (2023). Artificial intelligence for supply chain management: Disruptive innovation or innovative disruption? *The Journal of Supply Chain Management*, *59*(4), 3–5. DOI: 10.1111/jscm.12304

Hengstler, M., Enkel, E., & Duelli, S. (2016). Applied artificial intelligence and trust—The case of autonomous vehicles. *Technological Forecasting and Social Change*, *105*, 105–120. DOI: 10.1016/j.techfore.2015.12.014

Hernandez, M., Thompson, W., & Zoghi, B. (2024). Closing the workforce skills gap. In *INTED2024 Proceedings* (pp. 5153-5161). IATED. DOI: 10.21125/inted.2024.1336

Herrmann, H. (2023). What's next for responsible artificial intelligence: A way forward through responsible innovation. *Heliyon*, *9*(3), e14379. DOI: 10.1016/j.heliyon.2023.e14379 PMID: 36967876

Hoff, K. A., & Bashir, M. (2015). Trust in automation: Integrating empirical evidence on factors that influence trust. *Human Factors*, *57*(3), 407–434. DOI: 10.1177/0018720814547570 PMID: 25875432

Holmes, W., Bialik, M., & Fadel, C. (2019). *Artificial intelligence in education: Promises and implications for teaching and learning*. Center for Curriculum Redesign.

Holm, J. R., & Lorenz, E. (2022). The impact of artificial intelligence on skills at work in Denmark. *New Technology, Work and Employment*, *37*(1), 79–101. DOI: 10.1111/ntwe.12215

Horobet, A., Boubaker, S., Belascu, L., Negreanu, C. C., & Dinca, Z. (2024). Technology-driven advancements: Mapping the landscape of algorithmic trading literature. *Technological Forecasting and Social Change*, *209*, 123746. DOI: 10.1016/j.techfore.2024.123746

Horowitz, M. C., & Kahn, L. (2024). Bending the automation bias curve: A study of human and AI-based decision making in national security contexts. *International Studies Quarterly*, *68*(2), sqae020. Advance online publication. DOI: 10.1093/isq/sqae020

Howard, J. (2019). Artificial intelligence: Implications for the future of work. *American Journal of Industrial Medicine*, *62*(11), 917–926. DOI: 10.1002/ajim.23037 PMID: 31436850

Howcroft, D., & Wilson, M. (2002). Paradoxes of participatory practices: The Janus role of the systems developer. *Information and Organization*, *13*(1), 1–24. DOI: 10.1016/S1471-7727(02)00023-4

Hsu, S. L. (2014). The Rise and Rise of the One Percent: Considering Legal Causes of Inequality. FSU College of Law, Public Law Research Paper, (698), 14-11.

Human Development Report 2020. (2020). Human development report. https://doi.org/DOI: 10.18356/9789210055161

Humphreys, D., Koay, A., Desmond, D., & Mealy, E. (2024). AI hype as a cyber security risk: The moral responsibility of implementing generative AI in business. *AI and Ethics*, *4*(3), 791–804. Advance online publication. DOI: 10.1007/s43681-024-00443-4

Hussain, T., Wang, D., & Li, B. (2024). The influence of the COVID-19 pandemic on the adoption and impact of AI ChatGPT: Challenges, applications, and ethical considerations. *Acta Psychologica*, *246*, 104264. DOI: 10.1016/j.actpsy.2024.104264 PMID: 38626597

Hutchins, E. (1995). *Cognition in the wild*. The MIT Press. DOI: 10.7551/mitpress/1881.001.0001

Ignacimuthu, A., & Chinnamuthu Kulasekarapandian, M. (2025). Impact of Artificial Intelligence in Business and Society: Opportunities and Challenges: Edited by Francesco Paolo Appio, Davide La Torre, Francesca Lazzeri, Hatem Masri, and Francesco Schiavone, London, Routledge, 2024, 294 pp., £31.99 (pbk), ISBN 9781032303420. *Journal of Education for Business, 100*(2), 93–94. https://doi.org/ DOI: 10.1080/08832323.2025.2460019

Illanes, P., Lund, S., & Mourshed, M. (2024). *A new future of work: The race to deploy AI and raise skills in Europe and beyond*. McKinsey Global Institute.

ILO. (2021). Ensuring decent work on digital labour platforms. *World Employment and Social Outlook, 2021*(1), 195–238. DOI: 10.1002/wow3.171

Inayatullah, S. (2008). Six pillars: Futures thinking for transforming. *Foresight, 10*(1), 4–21. DOI: 10.1108/14636680810855991

International Federation of Robotics. (2024). *Record of 4 million robots in factories worldwide* [Press release]. https://ifr.org/ifr-press-releases/news/record-of-4-million-robots-working-in-factories-worldwide

Ismail, T. (2025). The future of work: Navigating transformations in the global labour market (2025-2030). I-Manager's. *Journal of Management, 19*(3), 1. DOI: 10.26634/jmgt.19.3.21582

Jacobs, J. (2025). AI labor displacement and the limits of worker retraining. *Brookings (TechTank)*. https://www.brookings.edu/articles/ai-labor-displacement-and-the-limits-of-worker-retraining/

Jarrahi, M. H. (2018). Artificial intelligence and the future of work: Human-AI symbiosis in organizational decision making. *Business Horizons, 61*(4), 577–586. DOI: 10.1016/j.bushor.2018.03.007

Jarrahi, M. H., Newlands, G., Lee, M. K., Wolf, C. T., Kinder, E., & Sutherland, W. (2022). Algorithmic management in a work context. *Journal of Business Research, 153*, 75–89.

Jeong, J. H., & Jo, H. J. (2025). The Effects of Artificial Intelligence and Robotics on Employment and Wages in Korean Manufacturing Firms. Weizenbaum Institute. https://doi.org/DOI: 10.34669/WI.WJDS/5.2.5

Jobin, A., Ienca, M., & Vayena, E. (2019). The global landscape of AI ethics guidelines. *Nature Machine Intelligence, 1*(9), 389–399. DOI: 10.1038/s42256-019-0088-2

Kaggwa, S., Eleogu, T. F., Okonkwo, F., Farayola, O. A., Uwaoma, P. U., & Akinoso, A. (2024). AI in decision making: Transforming business strategies. *International Journal of Innovation and Scientific Research, 10*(12), 423–444. DOI: 10.51244/IJRSI.2023.1012032

Kanagarla, K. (2024). Artificial intelligence and employment transformation: A multi-sector analysis of workforce disruption and adaptation. SSRN *Electronic Journal*. DOI: 10.2139/ssrn.5015970

Kane, G. C., Palmer, D., Phillips, A. N., Kiron, D., & Buckley, N. (2019). *The technology fallacy: How people are the real key to digital transformation*. MIT Press. DOI: 10.7551/mitpress/11661.001.0001

Karofsky, E. (2025). Beyond the molecule: How human-centered design unlocks AI's promise in pharma. *Applied Clinical Trials*. https://www.appliedclinicaltrialsonline.com/view/human-centered-ai-pharma

Kaur, P., Malik, G., & Sharma, A. (2021). Artificial intelligence and human learning: A review of AI-enabled learning systems. *Education and Information Technologies, 26*(6), 6759–6783.

Kellogg, K. C., Faraj, S., & Mantere, S. (2026). Governing the agentic enterprise: A new operating model for autonomous AI at scale. *California Management Review*. Advance online publication. https://cmr.berkeley.edu/2026/03/governing-the-agentic-enterprise-a-new-operating-model-for-autonomous-ai-at-scale/

Kellogg, K. C., Valentine, M. A., & Christin, A. (2019). Algorithms at work: The new contested terrain of control. *The Academy of Management Annals, 14*(1), 366–410. DOI: 10.5465/annals.2018.0174

Khogali, H. O., & Mekid, S. (2023). The blended future of automation and AI: Examining some long-term societal and ethical impact features. *Technology in Society, 73*(102232), 102232. DOI: 10.1016/j.techsoc.2023.102232

Kim, S., Jang, Y., Choi, S., Kim, W., Jung, H., Kim, S., & Kim, H. (2021). Analyzing teacher competency with TPACK for K-12 AI education. *KI – Künstliche Intelligenz*, 35(2), 139–151.

Kim, B. J., & Lee, J. (2024). The mental health implications of artificial intelligence adoption: The crucial role of self-efficacy. *Humanities & Social Sciences Communications, 11*(1), 1561. DOI: 10.1057/s41599-024-04018-w

Kohli, S. (2024). Building user trust in conversational AI: The role of explainable AI in chatbot transparency. *International Journal of Computer Engineering and Technology, 15*(5), 406–413. DOI: 10.5281/zenodo.13833413

Kolade, O., & Owoseni, A. (2022). Employment 5.0: The work of the future and the future of work. *Technology in Society*, *71*(102086), 102086. DOI: 10.1016/j.techsoc.2022.102086

Korinek, A., & Stiglitz, J. E. (2018). Artificial intelligence and its implications for income distribution and unemployment. In *The economics of artificial intelligence: An agenda* (pp. 349–390). University of Chicago Press.

Koslosky, L., & Feldgoise, J. (2025). *The state of AI-related apprenticeships*. Center for Security and Emerging Technology. DOI: 10.51593/20220042

Kraus, S., Ferraris, A., & Bertello, A. (2023). The future of work: How innovation and digitalization re-shape the workplace. *Journal of Innovation & Knowledge*, *8*(4), 100438. DOI: 10.1016/j.jik.2023.100438

Kulkov, I., Kulkova, J., Rohrbeck, R., Menvielle, L., Kaartemo, V., & Makkonen, H. (2024). Artificial intelligence - driven sustainable development: Examining organizational, technical, and processing approaches to achieving global goals. *Sustainable Development (Bradford)*, *32*(3), 2253–2267. DOI: 10.1002/sd.2773

Kumar, A., Krishnamoorthy, B., Balasubramanian, S., & Bharathi, S. V. (2024). Machine learning and artificial intelligence-induced technostress in organizations: A study on automation-augmentation paradox. *The International Journal of Organizational Analysis*, *32*(4), 681–703. DOI: 10.1108/IJOA-01-2023-3581

Lane, M., Williams, M., & Broecke, S. (2023). *The impact of AI on the workplace: Main findings from the OECD AI surveys of employers and workers* (OECD Social, Employment and Migration Working Papers No. 288). Organisation for Economic Co-operation and Development.

Law, L. (2025). AI adoption reveals generational workforce strategy divide. *AI Magazine*. https://aimagazine.com/articles/workday-research-millennials-lead-ai-skills-transformation

Ledford, T. D. (2025). Does artificial intelligence harm labour? Investigating the limitations of incident trackers as evidence for policymaking. Information Research an International Electronic Journal, 30(iConf), 486–499. https://doi.org/DOI: 10.47989/ir30iConf47296

Lee, J. D., & See, K. A. (2004). Trust in automation: Designing for appropriate reliance. *Human Factors*, *46*(1), 50–80. DOI: 10.1518/hfes.46.1.50.30392 PMID: 15151155

Lee, M. K., Kusbit, D., Metsky, E., & Dabbish, L. (2021). Working with machines: The impact of algorithmic and data-driven management on human workers. *Computers in Human Behavior, 124*, 106932.

Lei, L., Feng, H., & Ren, J. (2025). Artificial intelligence, human capital and firm-level total factor productivity. *Finance Research Letters, 85*, 107897. DOI: 10.1016/j.frl.2025.107897

Lewicki, R. J., & Bunker, B. B. (1996). Developing and maintaining trust in work relationships. In Kramer, R. M., & Tyler, T. R. (Eds.), *Trust in organizations: Frontiers of theory and research* (pp. 114–139). Sage Publications., DOI: 10.4135/9781452243610.n7

Li, K., Lau, B. P. L., Yuan, X., Ni, W., Guizani, M., & Yuen, C. (2023). Toward ubiquitous semantic metaverse: Challenges, approaches, and opportunities. *IEEE Internet of Things Journal, 11*(3), 4382–4402. DOI: 10.1109/JIOT.2023.3302159

Lintner, T. (2024). A systematic review of AI literacy scales. *npj Science of Learning*, 9(1), 50.

Li, Y., Wu, B., Huang, Y., & Luan, S. (2024). Developing trustworthy artificial intelligence: Insights from research on interpersonal, human-automation, and human-AI trust. *Frontiers in Psychology, 15*, 1382693. DOI: 10.3389/fpsyg.2024.1382693 PMID: 38694439

Locke, E. A. (2005). Why emotional intelligence is an invalid concept. *Journal of Organizational Behavior, 26*(4), 425–431. DOI: 10.1002/job.318

Longoni, C., Bonezzi, A., & Morewedge, C. K. (2019). Resistance to medical artificial intelligence. *The Journal of Consumer Research, 46*(4), 629–650. DOI: 10.1093/jcr/ucz013

Loong, X. A., Huang, T., & Xiang, S. Z. & School of Labor and Human Resource,Renmin University of China,Beijing,P. R. China. (2021). The impact of AI on employment and the corresponding response of PRC labor law. Journal of Chinese Human Resource Management, 12(2), 69–94. https://doi.org/DOI: 10.47297/wspchrmWSP2040-800506.20211202

Lorenz, P., Perset, K., & Berryhill, J. (2023). *Initial policy considerations for generative artificial intelligence*. OECD Publishing., DOI: 10.1787/fae2d1e6-

Lund, S., Madgavkar, A., Manyika, J., Smit, S., Ellingrud, K., & Robinson, O. (2021). *The future of work after COVID-19*. McKinsey Global Institute. https://www.mckinsey.com/featured-insights/future-of-work/the-future-of-work-after-covid-19

Lutfiani, N., Sembiring, I., Setyawan, I., Setiawan, A., Rahardja, U., & Sulistio, S. (2025). Exploring the relationship between Artificial Intelligence and business performance. [Indonesian Journal of Computing and Cybernetics Systems]. *IJCCS, 19*(1), 1. DOI: 10.22146/ijccs.86697

Lyell, D., & Coiera, E. (2017). Automation bias and verification complexity: A systematic review. *Journal of the American Medical Informatics Association : JAMIA, 24*(2), 423–431. DOI: 10.1093/jamia/ocw105 PMID: 27516495

Lyons, S., & Kuron, L. (2014). Generational differences in the workplace: A review of the evidence and directions for future research. *Journal of Organizational Behavior, 35*(S1), S139–S157. DOI: 10.1002/job.1913

Lysyakov, M., & Viswanathan, S. (2023). Threatened by AI: Analyzing Users' Responses to the Introduction of AI in a Crowd-Sourcing Platform. *Information Systems Research, 34*(3), 1191–1210. DOI: 10.1287/isre.2022.1184

Makridakis, S. (2017). The forthcoming Artificial Intelligence (AI) revolution: Its impact on society and firms. *Futures, 90*, 46–60. DOI: 10.1016/j.futures.2017.03.006

Malik, N., Tripathi, S. N., Kar, A. K., & Gupta, S. (2022). Impact of artificial intelligence on employees working in industry 4.0 led organizations. *International Journal of Manpower, 43*(2), 334–354. DOI: 10.1108/IJM-03-2021-0173

Manickavasagam, P. (2021). The impact of technology on human behaviour and business environment. *International Journal of Society Systems Science, 13*(1), 34. DOI: 10.1504/IJSSS.2021.115851

Manyika, J., Lund, S., Chui, M., Bughin, J., Woetzel, J., Batra, P., Ko, R., & Sanghvi, S. (2017). *Jobs lost, jobs gained: What the future of work will mean for jobs, skills, and wages*. McKinsey Global Institute. https://www.mckinsey.com/featured-insights/future-of-work/jobs-lost-jobs-gained-what-the-future-of-work-will-mean-for-jobs-skills-and-wages

Manyika, J., Chui, M., Miremadi, M., Bughin, J., George, K., Willmott, P., & Dewhurst, M. (2017). *A future that works: Automation, employment, and productivity*. McKinsey Global Institute.

Manyika, J., Sneader, K., & Woetzel, J. (2023). *The economic potential of generative AI: The next productivity frontier*. McKinsey Global Institute.

Maria, S., Purwinahyu, P., Fitriansyah, F., Rachmawaty, A., & Aini, R. N. (2025). Artificial Intelligence and Labor Markets: Analyzing Job Displacement and Creation. International Journal of Engineering. *Science and Information Technology, 5*(2), 290–296. DOI: 10.52088/ijesty.v5i2.830

Market.us. (2024). *AI chatbot market size, share, trends analysis report.* https://market.us/report/ai-chatbot-market/

MarketResearch.com. (2024). *The digital twin market: Shaping the future of Industry 4.0.* https://blog.marketresearch.com/the-digital-twin-market-shaping-the-future-of-industry-4.0

MarketsandMarkets. (2025). *Artificial intelligence in manufacturing market size, share & trends (Report Code: SE 5470).* https://www.marketsandmarkets.com/Market-Reports/artificial-intelligence-manufacturing-market-72679105.html

Marsick, V. J., & Watkins, K. E. (2018). *Informal and incidental learning in the workplace.* Routledge.

Martini, B., Bellisario, D., & Coletti, P. (2024). Human-centered and sustainable artificial intelligence in industry 5.0: Challenges and perspectives. *Sustainability (Basel), 16*(13), 5448. DOI: 10.3390/su16135448

Maslej, N., Fattorini, L., Perrault, R., Gil, Y., Parli, V., Kariuki, N., Capstick, E., Reuel, A., Brynjolfsson, E., Etchemendy, J., Ligett, K., Lyons, T., Manyika, J., Niebles, J. C., Shoham, Y., Wald, R., Walsh, T., Hamrah, A., Santarlasci, L., . . . Oak, S. (2025). *The AI Index 2025 annual report.* AI Index Steering Committee, Institute for Human-Centered AI, Stanford University.

Maslej, N., Fattorini, L., Perrault, R., Parli, V., Reuel, A., Brynjolfsson, E., Etchemendy, J., Ligett, K., Lyons, T., Manyika, J., Niebles, J. C., Shoham, Y., Wald, R., Walsh, T., Hamrah, A., Betts Lotufo, J., Rome, A., Shi, A., & Oak, S. (2026). *The 2026 AI Index report.* AI Index Steering Committee, Institute for Human-Centered AI, Stanford University. https://hai.stanford.edu/ai-index/2026-ai-index-report

Masoud, N. (2025). Artificial intelligence and unemployment dynamics: An econometric analysis in high-income economies. *Technological Sustainability, 4*(1), 30–50. DOI: 10.1108/TECHS-04-2024-0033

Mateescu, A., & Nguyen, A. (2019). *Explainer: Algorithmic management in the workplace.* Data & Society Research Institute. DOI: 10.69985/XXBG2416

Mathew, D. E., Ebem, D. U., Ikegwu, A. C., Ukeoma, P. E., & Dibiaezue, N. F. (2025). Recent emerging techniques in explainable artificial intelligence to enhance interpretability of AI models for humans. *Neural Processing Letters, 57*(1), 16. DOI: 10.1007/s11063-025-11732-2

Mayer, J. D., Caruso, D. R., & Salovey, P. (2016). The ability model of emotional intelligence: Principles and updates. *Emotion Review, 8*(4), 290–300. DOI: 10.1177/1754073916639667

Mayer, J. D., Davis, J. H., & Schoorman, F. D. (1995). An integrative model of organizational trust. *Academy of Management Review*, *20*(3), 709–734. DOI: 10.2307/258792

Mayer, J. D., Salovey, P., & Caruso, D. R. (2004). Emotional intelligence: Theory, findings, and implications. *Psychological Inquiry*, *15*(3), 197–215. DOI: 10.1207/s15327965pli1503_02

McAllister, D. J. (1995). Affect- and cognition-based trust as foundations for interpersonal cooperation in organizations. *Academy of Management Journal*, *38*(1), 24–59. https://www.jstor.org/stable/256727. DOI: 10.2307/256727

McClain, C., Kennedy, B., Gottfried, J., Anderson, M., & Pasquini, G. (2025). *How the U.S. public and AI experts view artificial intelligence*. Pew Research Center.

Meng, Q., Wu, T.-J., Duan, W., & Li, S. (2025). Effects of Employee–Artificial Intelligence (AI) Collaboration on Counterproductive Work Behaviors (CWBs): Leader Emotional Support as a Moderator. *Behavioral Sciences (Basel, Switzerland)*, *15*(5), 696. DOI: 10.3390/bs15050696 PMID: 40426473

Merhi, M. I. (2023). An evaluation of the critical success factors impacting artificial intelligence implementation. *International Journal of Information Management*, *68*, 102594. DOI: 10.1016/j.ijinfomgt.2022.102545

Merriman, M., Sanz Sáiz, B., Bulman, L., Carpanelli, M., DiCerbo, K. E., Dutt, Y., Kim, S., Makhani, N., Neff, G., & Yongpradit, P. (2024). *How can we upskill Gen Z as fast as we train AI?* Ernst & Young Global Limited (EY).

Mhlanga, D. (2021). Artificial intelligence in the Industry 4.0, and its impact on poverty, innovation, infrastructure development, and the sustainable development goals: Lessons from emerging economies? *Sustainability (Basel)*, *13*(11), 5788. Advance online publication. DOI: 10.3390/su13115788

Microsoft & LinkedIn. (2024). *2024 Work Trend Index: AI at work is here. Now comes the hard part.* Microsoft WorkLab.

Microsoft. (2024). *AI governance and risk management*. Microsoft.

Miró, A. (2020). World Economic Forum: Present and future. Dimensión Empresarial, 18(2). DOI: 10.15665/dem.v18i2.2280

Mir, U. B., Sharma, S., Kar, A. K., & Gupta, M. P. (2020). Critical success factors for integrating artificial intelligence and robotics. *Digital Policy. Regulation & Governance*, *22*(5), 307–331.

Missouri Department of Elementary and Secondary Education. (2025). *Artificial intelligence guidance for local education agencies (Version 1.0, 2025–26 school year)*. Missouri Department of Elementary and Secondary Education.

Moore, P. V., Akhtar, P., & Upchurch, M. (2018). Digitalisation of work and resistance. *Labour & Industry: A Journal of the Social and Economic Relations of Work, 28*(3), 179–187.

Moore, P. V., Upchurch, M., & Whittaker, X. (2017). Humans and machines at work: Monitoring, surveillance and automation in contemporary capitalism. In Springer eBooks (pp. 1–16). DOI: 10.1007/978-3-319-58232-0_1

Moore, R. L., Hwang, W., & Moses, J. D. (2024). A systematic review of mobile-based microlearning in adult learner contexts. *Journal of Educational Technology & Society*, *27*(1), 137–146.

Muehlemann, S. (2024). *AI adoption and workplace training* (IZA Discussion Paper No. 17367). Institute of Labor Economics (IZA).

Murire, O. T. (2024). Artificial intelligence and its role in shaping organizational work practices and culture. *Administrative Sciences*, *14*(12), 316. DOI: 10.3390/admsci14120316

Muro, M., & Methkupally, S. (2025). *Mapping the AI economy: Which regions are ready for the next technology leap*. Brookings. https://www.brookings.edu/articles/mapping-the-ai-economy-which-regions-are-ready-for-the-next-technology-leap/

Muro, M., & Liu, S. (2024). *Mapping AI's uneven global distribution*. Brookings Institution.

Myers, K. K., & Sadaghiani, K. (2010). Millennials in the workplace: A communication perspective on millennials' organizational relationships and performance. *Journal of Business and Psychology*, *25*(2), 225–238. DOI: 10.1007/s10869-010-9172-7 PMID: 20502509

Nabyl, V., & Mulachela, A. (2021). COVID-19. In Routledge eBooks (pp. 16–35). DOI: 10.4324/9781003166801-2

Nahavandi, S. (2019). Industry 5.0—A human-centric solution. *Sustainability (Basel)*, *11*(16), 4371. Advance online publication. DOI: 10.3390/su11164371

Nayyar, G., Hallward-Driemeier, M., & Davies, E. (2021). *At your service?: The promise of services-led development*. World Bank Publications. DOI: 10.1596/978-1-4648-1671-0

Neary, B., Horák, J., Kovacova, M., & Valaskova, K. (2018). The future of work: Disruptive business practices, technology-driven economic growth, and computer-induced job displacement. *Journal of Self-Governance and Management Economics*, *6*(4), 19–24.

Newlands, G. (2022). Algorithmic surveillance and worker privacy in the gig economy. *Human Relations*, *75*(6), 1035–1058.

Nguyen, T., & Elbanna, A. (2025). Understanding human-AI augmentation in the workplace: A review and a future research agenda. *Information Systems Frontiers*. Advance online publication. DOI: 10.1007/s10796-025-10591-5

Noble, S. U. (2018). Conclusion: Algorithms of oppression. In Algorithms of oppression: How search engines reinforce racism (pp. 171–182). NYU Press. DOI: 10.2307/j.ctt1pwt9w5.11

Nonaka, I., & Takeuchi, H. (2021). *The wise company: How companies create continuous innovation*. Oxford University Press.

Nong, P., Adler-Milstein, J., Apathy, N. C., Holmgren, A. J., & Everson, J. (2025). Current use and evaluation of artificial intelligence and predictive models in US hospitals. *Health Affairs*, *44*(1), 90–98. DOI: 10.1377/hlthaff.2024.00842 PMID: 39761454

Norman, D. A., & Draper, S. W. (2019). *User centered system design: New perspectives on human-computer interaction*. CRC Press.

Nour, S., & Arbussà, A. (2025). Driving innovation through organizational restructuring and integration of advanced digital technologies: A case study of a world-leading manufacturing company. *European Journal of Innovation Management*, *28*(8), 3262–3283. DOI: 10.1108/EJIM-02-2024-0156

OECD. (2021). *The OECD AI principles: Progress and impact*. Organisation for Economic Co-operation and Development.

OECD. (2023). *Artificial intelligence, job quality and inclusiveness*. OECD Publishing.

Ogbolu, A. N., & Sukidjo, S. (2020). Artificial Intelligence Vs My Future Job: Perceptions of Asian Undergraduates. [JRC]. *Journal of Robotics and Control*, *1*(6). Advance online publication. DOI: 10.18196/jrc.1639

Omar, M., Alotaibi, A. A., Said, M. S., Hassan, M., Periyasamy, P., Alotaibi, A. A. E., & Elgazzar, R. A. (2023). Internet of medical things and Healthcare 4.0: Trends, requirements, challenges, and research directions. *Sensors (Basel), 23*(17), 7435. Advance online publication. DOI: 10.3390/s23177435 PMID: 37687891

Omri, A., & Afi, H. (2025). Impact of Artificial Intelligence on Employment of People with Disabilities: The Moderating Role of Governance Quality. *Journal of Disability Research, 4*(2). Advance online publication. DOI: 10.57197/JDR-2025-0007

Omri, A., Omri, H., & Afi, H. (2025). Exploring the impact of AI on unemployment for people with disabilities: Do educational attainment and governance matter? *Frontiers in Public Health, 13*, 1559101. DOI: 10.3389/fpubh.2025.1559101 PMID: 40241964

OpenResearch. (2024). *Unconditional cash study: Three-year results.* https://www.openresearchlab.org/studies/unconditional-cash-study/study

Orchard, T., & Tasiemski, L. (2023). The rise of generative AI and possible effects on the economy. *Economics and Business Review, 9*(2), 5–23. DOI: 10.18559/ebr.2023.2.732

Organisation for Economic Co-operation and Development (OECD). (2025). *Algorithmic management in the workplace* (OECD Report). OECD Publishing. OECD

Organisation for Economic Co-operation and Development. (2025). *AI and work: Job quality, safety and skill development.* OECD Publishing. https://www.oecd.org/en/topics/ai-and-work.html

OXMaint. (2025). AI-powered predictive maintenance: Manufacturing's game-changer. *OXMaint Blog*. https://oxmaint.com/blog/post/ai-powered-predictive-maintenance-manufacturing-game-changer

Page, I., Reuss, K., & Zemper, Z. (2024). Changes in the U.S. labor supply. *Trendlines*. K. DeMaria (Ed.). U.S. Department of Labor Employment and Training Administration.

Pan, Y., Sun, S., & Chen, X. (2022). Adaptive learning with artificial intelligence: New frontiers in workforce education. *Computers & Education, 191*, 104629.

Park, S., & Cho, Y. (2022). Learning fatigue in digital transformation environments: Antecedents and coping mechanisms. *Human Resource Development Review, 21*(4), 413–432.

Pasmore, W. A., & Sherwood, J. J. (Eds.). (1978). *Sociotechnical systems: A sourcebook*. University Associates.

Pasupuleti, M. B., & Siddique, M. N.-E.-A. (2021). The implications of artificial intelligence for the future of the workforce markets. *Global Disclosure of Economics and Business*, *10*(2), 45–54. DOI: 10.18034/gdeb.v10i2.628

Pouliakas, K., Hippe, R., & Santangelo, G. (2025). *Skills empower workers in the AI revolution: First findings from Cedefop's AI skills survey* (Policy Brief No. 9201 EN). European Centre for the Development of Vocational Training (Cedefop).

Prosci. (2024). AI change management. *Prosci*. https://www.prosci.com/ai-change-management

Pulakos, E. D., Arad, S., Donovan, M. A., & Plamondon, K. E. (2020). Adaptability in the workplace: Development of a taxonomy of adaptive performance. *The Journal of Applied Psychology*, *105*(9), 1125–1148. PMID: 10948805

Pumplun, L., Tauchert, C., & Heidt, M. (2019). A new organizational chassis for artificial intelligence-exploring organizational readiness factors. *Proceedings of the 27th European Conference on Information Systems.*

Qian, J., Wang, B., Han, Z., & Song, B. (2017). Ethical leadership, leader-member exchange and feedback seeking: A double-moderated mediation model of emotional intelligence and work-unit structure. *Frontiers in Psychology*, *8*, 1174. DOI: 10.3389/fpsyg.2017.01174 PMID: 28744251

Qian, Y., Siau, K. L., & Nah, F. F. (2024). Societal impacts of artificial intelligence: Ethical, legal, and governance issues. *Societal Impacts*, *3*(100040), 100040. DOI: 10.1016/j.socimp.2024.100040

Qin, M., Wan, Y., Dou, J., & Su, C. W. (2024). Artificial Intelligence: Intensifying or mitigating unemployment? *Technology in Society*, *79*, 102755. DOI: 10.1016/j.techsoc.2024.102755

Qin, S., Zhang, J., & Chen, L. (2025). Artificial intelligence usage and employee innovation behavior: The mediating role of self-efficacy and the moderating role of openness to experience. *Behavioral Sciences (Basel, Switzerland)*, *15*(4), 491. DOI: 10.3390/bs15040491 PMID: 40282112

Raghavan, M., Barocas, S., Kleinberg, J., & Levy, K. (2020, January). Mitigating bias in algorithmic hiring: Evaluating claims and practices. In *Proceedings of the 2020 conference on fairness, accountability, and transparency* (pp. 469-481). DOI: 10.1145/3351095.3372828

Rahwan, I., Cebrian, M., Obradovich, N., Bongard, J., Bonnefon, J. F., Breazeal, C., Crandall, J. W., Christakis, N. A., Couzin, I. D., Jackson, M. O., Jennings, N. R., Kamar, E., Kloumann, I. M., Larochelle, H., Lazer, D., McElreath, R., Mislove, A., Parkes, D. C., Pentland, A. S., & Wellman, M. (2019). Machine behaviour. *Nature, 568*(7753), 477–486. DOI: 10.1038/s41586-019-1138-y PMID: 31019318

Rai, A. (2020). Explainable AI: From black box to glass box. *Journal of the Academy of Marketing Science, 48*(1), 137–141. DOI: 10.1007/s11747-019-00710-5

Raisch, S., & Krakowski, S. (2021). Artificial intelligence and management: The automation–augmentation paradox. *Academy of Management Review, 46*(1), 192–210. DOI: 10.5465/amr.2018.0072

Ransbotham, S., Khodabandeh, S., Fehling, R., & Kiron, D. (2021). Expanding AI's impact with organizational learning. *MIT Sloan Management Review*.

Ransbotham, S., Khodabandeh, S., Kiron, D., Candelon, F., Chu, M., & LaFountain, B. (2020). *Expanding AI's impact with organizational learning*. MIT Sloan Management Review and Boston Consulting Group.

Rao, N., O'Riordan, S., & Coulis, J. (2025). AI and labor: Captioning library audiovisual content with Whisper. *IFLA Journal, 03400352241310534*(3), 803–813. Advance online publication. DOI: 10.1177/03400352241310534

Rapid Innovation. (2024). AI-powered dynamic pricing in retail and e-commerce. *Rapid Innovation*. https://www.rapidinnovation.io/post/ai-powered-dynamic-pricing-in-e-commerce

Rashid, A. B., Kausik, A. K., Sunny, A. A. H., & Bappy, M. H. (2023). Artificial intelligence in the military: An overview of the capabilities, applications, and challenges. *International Journal of Intelligent Systems, 2023*(1), 8676366. Advance online publication. DOI: 10.1155/2023/8676366

Rathore, M. (2024). The Role of Artificial Intelligence in Social Welfare: Harnessing AI For Positive Societal Impact. In *AI in the Social and Business World: A Comprehensive Approach* (pp. 277–293). Bentham Science Publishers. DOI: 10.2174/9789815256864124010015

Reuben, J. M. (2023). Training and skills alignment for the AI generation. *GSJ, 11*(6), 1503–1518.

Rinf Technology. (2024). AI-driven optimization for sustainable manufacturing. *Rinf Technology*. https://www.rinf.tech/ai-driven-optimization-for-sustainable-manufacturing

Rodrik, D. (2018). *New technologies, global value chains, and developing economies (No. w25164)*. National Bureau of Economic Research. DOI: 10.3386/w25164

Rosenblat, A. (2018). *Uberland: How algorithms are rewriting the rules of work*. University of California Press., DOI: 10.1525/9780520970632

Rosenblat, A., & Stark, L. (2016). Algorithmic labor and information asymmetries: A case study of Uber's drivers. *International Journal of Communication, 10*, 27–27.

Rousseau, D. M., Sitkin, S. B., Burt, R. S., & Camerer, C. (1998). Not so different after all: A cross-discipline view of trust. *Academy of Management Review, 23*(3), 393–404. DOI: 10.5465/amr.1998.926617

Rowan, J., Ammanath, B., Perricos, C., Sniderman, B., & Jarvis, D. (2025). *Now decides next: Generating a new future. Deloitte's State of Generative AI in the Enterprise, Quarter four report*. Deloitte Development LLC.

Rudko, I., Bashirpour Bonab, A., Fedele, M., & Kosiba, J. P. B. (2025). New institutional theory and AI: Toward rethinking of artificial intelligence in organizations. *Journal of Management History, 31*(1), 45–67. DOI: 10.1108/JMH-09-2023-0097

Rudolph, C. W., Rauvola, R. S., Costanza, D. P., & Zacher, H. (2021). Generations and generational differences: Debunking myths in organizational science and practice and paving new paths forward. *Journal of Business and Psychology, 36*(6), 945–967. DOI: 10.1007/s10869-020-09715-2 PMID: 32901173

Ruiz-Talavera, D., Cruz-Aguero, J. E. D. L., García-Palomino, N., Calderón-Espinoza, R., & Marín-Rodriguez, W. J. (2023). Artificial intelligence and its impact on job opportunities among university students in North Lima, 2023. *ICST Transactions on Scalable Information Systems, 10*(5). Advance online publication. DOI: 10.4108/eetsis.3841

Russell, S., & Norvig, P. (2021). *Artificial intelligence: A modern approach* (4th ed.). Pearson Education.

Rysty, S., Zhanargul, S., Ainur, T., Sharbat, B., & Zhanat, Y. (2025). Wages and working conditions in the context of digitalization. *International Journal of Innovative Research and Scientific Studies, 8*(3), 1824–1835. DOI: 10.53894/ijirss.v8i3.6891

Sahoo, D. K., Kumar, A., Kanwal, P., & Rana, R. (2024). AI-Driven Market Intelligence: Enhancing Competitive Analysis and Market Positioning. In AI, Corporate Social Responsibility, and Marketing in Modern Organizations (pp. 89–108). IGI Global. https://doi.org/DOI: 10.4018/979-8-3373-0219-5.ch005

San Diego State University. (2025). CSU announces landmark public-private AI initiative, SDSU contributing to efforts. *SDSU News*. https://www.sdsu.edu/news/2025/02/csu-announces-landmark-public-private-ai-initiative-sdsu-contributing-to-efforts

Santoni De Sio, F. (2024). Artificial Intelligence and the Future of Work: Mapping the Ethical Issues. *The Journal of Ethics*, *28*(3), 407–427. DOI: 10.1007/s10892-024-09493-6

Schaeff, A., & Rother, M. (2024). *Deploying AI to the real world: How Siemens Erlangen factory is leading the AI charge*. Siemens AG.

Schwab, K. (2017). *The fourth industrial revolution*. Crown Business.

Septiandri, A. A., Constantinides, M., & Quercia, D. (2024). The potential impact of AI innovations on US occupations. *PNAS Nexus*, *3*(9), pgae320. Advance online publication. DOI: 10.1093/pnasnexus/pgae320 PMID: 39319327

Shaji George, A. (2024). Artificial intelligence and the future of work: Job shifting not job loss. PU Publications. https://doi.org/DOI: 10.5281/ZENODO.10936490

Shandler, R. (2019). Zuboff, S. (2019). The age of surveillance capitalism: The fight for a human future at the new frontier of power [Review of the book The age of surveillance capitalism]. *Journal of Cyber Policy*, *4*(2), 303–304. DOI: 10.1080/23738871.2019.1637914

Shani, A. B. (2017). William A. Pasmore: Navigating between academy and industry – Designing and leading change. In Springer eBooks (pp. 1–15). DOI: 10.1007/978-3-319-49820-1_52-2

Sharma, K., Tomar, M., & Tadimarri, A. (2023). AI-driven marketing: Transforming sales processes for success in the digital age. *Journal of Knowledge Learning and Science Technology*, *2*(2), 260–266. DOI: 10.60087/jklst.vol2.n2.p260

Sheikh, S. (Ed.). (2020). *Understanding the role of artificial intelligence and its future social impact*. IGI Global.

Shneiderman, B. (2020, May 27). *Human-centered artificial intelligence: Reliable, safe & trustworthy.* University of Maryland, Department of Computer Science. https://www.cs.umd.edu/article/2020/05/shneiderman-proposes-human-centered-artificial-intelligence-reliable-safe

Shneiderman, B. (2020). Human-centered AI: Reliable, safe & trustworthy. *International Journal of Human-Computer Interaction*, *36*(10), 919–922. DOI: 10.1080/10447318.2020.1741118

Sholler, D., & MacInnes, I. (2024). AI and income inequality: the danger of exacerbating existing trends toward polarization in the US workforce. In *Handbook of artificial intelligence at work* (pp. 338–355). Edward Elgar Publishing. DOI: 10.4337/9781800889972.00026

Simmonds, R. (2019). Eubanks, V. (2018). Automating inequality: How high-tech tools profile, police and punish the poor [Review of the book Automating inequality]. *Science & Technology Studies, 81–83*. Advance online publication. DOI: 10.23987/sts.77647

Singapore, A. I. (2025). *AI Apprenticeship Programme (AIAP)*. https://aisingapore.org/industryinnovation/aiap/

Singh, I., Salaria, D., & Bhambri, P. (2010). Comparative analysis of JAVA and AspectJ on the basis of various metrics. In Proceedings of the International Conference on Advanced Computing and Communication Technologies (IEEE Sponsored) (pp. 714-720).

Singh, P., & Bhambri, P. (2007). Alternate organizational models for ports. *Apeejay Journal of Management and Technology*, *2*(2), 9–17.

Singh, P., Bhambri, P., & Sohal, A. K. (2006, January). Security in local networks [Paper presentation]. *National Conference on Future Trends in Information Technology*, India.

Slimi, Z., & Villarejo-Carballido, B. (2023). Navigating the ethical challenges of artificial intelligence in higher education: An analysis of seven global AI ethics policies. TEM Journal, 12(2), 592–603. https://doi.org/DOI: 10.18421/TEM122-02

Slingerland, C. (2025). *90+ Cloud computing statistics: A 2025 market snapshot.* CloudZero. https://www.cloudzero.com/blog/cloud-computing-statistics/

Srivastava, S. K. (2021). Susskind, D. (2020). A world without work: Technology, automation and how we should respond [Review of the book A world without work]. *Metamorphosis*, *20*(1), 45–46. DOI: 10.1177/09726225211026818

Sukharevsky, A., Kerr, D., Hjartar, K., Hämäläinen, L., Bout, S., & Di Leo, V. (2025). *Seizing the agentic AI advantage*. McKinsey & Company.

Sydorenko, T. (2024). The impact of AI explainability on cognitive dissonance and trust in human-AI recruitment teams. *European Journal of Science, Innovation and Technology. 5(1), 154-167, 2025.*

Tarafdar, M., Beath, C. M., & Ross, J. W. (2019). Using AI to enhance business operations. *MIT Sloan Management Review*, *60*(4), 37–44.

Tarafdar, M., Cooper, C. L., & Stich, J.-F. (2019). The technostress trifecta — techno-eustress, techno-distress and design: Theoretical directions and an agenda for research. *Information Systems Journal, 29*(1), 6–42. DOI: 10.1111/isj.12169

Tetlock, P. E. (2006). *Expert political judgment: How good is it? How can we know?* Princeton University Press., DOI: 10.1515/9781400830312

Thaler, R. H., & Sunstein, C. R. (2008). *Nudge: Improving decisions about health, wealth, and happiness*. Yale University Press.

The changing nature of work. (2018). In The World Bank eBooks (pp. 17–34). DOI: 10.1596/978-1-4648-1328-3_ch1

Thomson Reuters Institute. (2024). *2024 generative AI in professional services report*. Thomson Reuters. https://www.thomsonreuters.com/en-us/posts/technology/generative-ai-in-professional-services-2024/

Tims, M., & Bakker, A. B. (2010). Job crafting: Towards a new model of individual job redesign. *SA Journal of Industrial Psychology, 36*(2), 1–9. DOI: 10.4102/sajip.v36i2.841

Tomprou, M., & Lee, M. K. (2022). Employment relationships in algorithmic management: A psychological contract perspective. [ACM Digital Library]. *Computers in Human Behavior, 126*, 106997. Advance online publication. DOI: 10.1016/j.chb.2021.106997

Topol, E. J. (2019). *Deep medicine: How artificial intelligence can make healthcare human again*. Basic Books. https://www.basicbooks.com/titles/eric-topol/deep-medicine/9781541644632

Tschang, F. T., & Almirall, E. (2021). Artificial intelligence as augmenting automation: Implications for employment. *The Academy of Management Perspectives, 35*(4), 642–659. DOI: 10.5465/amp.2019.0062

UNCTAD. (2025). Technology and innovation report 2025: Inclusive artificial intelligence for development. *United Nations Conference on Trade and Development.*

UNESCO. (2021). *AI and education: Guidance for policy-makers*. UNESCO Publishing.

UNESCO. (2024). *AI competency frameworks for students and teachers*. UNESCO Education Sector.

United Nations. (2024). *Governing AI for humanity: Report of the UN AI advisory body*. https://www.un.org/en/ai-advisory-body

US Census Bureau. (2023). Only 3.8% of businesses use AI to produce goods and services, highest use in information sector. *Census Bureau Stories*. https://www.census.gov/library/stories/2023/11/businesses-use-ai.html

Vaccaro, M., Almaatouq, A., & Malone, T. (2024). When combinations of humans and AI are useful: A systematic review and meta-analysis. *Nature Human Behaviour*, *8*(12), 2293–2303. DOI: 10.1038/s41562-024-02024-1 PMID: 39468277

Vakola, M. (2016). The reasons behind change resistance in the workplace. *Journal of Organizational Change Management*, *29*(2), 213–229.

Verma, J., Sandys, L., Matthews, A., & Goel, S. (2024). Readiness of artificial intelligence technology for managing energy demands from renewable sources. *Engineering Applications of Artificial Intelligence*, *135*(108831), 108831. DOI: 10.1016/j.engappai.2024.108831

Vicsek, L. (2021). Artificial intelligence and the future of work – lessons from the sociology of expectations. *The International Journal of Sociology and Social Policy*, *41*(7/8), 842–861. DOI: 10.1108/IJSSP-05-2020-0174

Vogel-Heuser, B., & Bengler, K. (2023). Von Industrie 4.0 zu Industrie 5.0 – Idee, Konzept und Wahrnehmung. *HMD Praxis der Wirtschaftsinformatik*, *60*(6), 1124–1142. DOI: 10.1365/s40702-023-01002-x

Voros, J. (2017). Big history and anticipation. In Springer eBooks (pp. 1–40). DOI: 10.1007/978-3-319-31737-3_95-1

Voss, A. S., Soucek, R., Moser, K., & Drexler, H. (2025). The differentiated roles of resilient behavior and job crafting in interaction with work intensity and their impact on employee health and performance. *International Journal of Environmental Research and Public Health*, *22*(3), 429. Advance online publication. DOI: 10.3390/ijerph22030429 PMID: 40238562

Waelen, R. A. (2025). The Desirability of Automizing Labor: An Overview. *Philosophy Compass*, *20*(1–2), e70023. DOI: 10.1111/phc3.70023

Wagner, G. (2021). Liability for artificial intelligence: A proposal of the European Parliament. SSRN Electronic Journal. DOI: 10.2139/ssrn.3886294

Weber, E., Zika, G., Maier, T., Mönnig, A., Kalinowski, M., Ulrich, P., Wolter, M. I., & Hummel, M. (2025). *Künstliche Intelligenz: Potenzielle Effekte für den deutschen Arbeitsmarkt* [Artificial intelligence: Potential effects for the German labour market]. Institut für Arbeitsmarkt- und Berufsforschung (IAB), Bundesinstitut für Berufsbildung (BIBB), & Gesellschaft für Wirtschaftliche Strukturforschung (GWS). https://iab.de/kuenstliche-intelligenz-potenzielle-effekte-fuer-den-deutschen-arbeitsmarkt/

Weill, P., Woerner, S. L., & Sebastian, I. M. (2024). *Building enterprise AI maturity* [Research briefing]. MIT Center for Information Systems Research.

Wei, W., & Li, L. (2022). The Impact of Artificial Intelligence on the Mental Health of Manufacturing Workers: The Mediating Role of Overtime Work and the Work Environment. *Frontiers in Public Health, 10*, 862407. DOI: 10.3389/fpubh.2022.862407 PMID: 35480579

Williams, J., Alexander, K., Wilson, T., Newton, B., McNeil, C., & Jung, C. (2021). *A better future: Transforming jobs and skills for young people post-pandemic*. Institute for Employment Studies.

Wilson, H. J. (2018). *Human + machine: Reimagining work in the age of AI*. Harvard Business Review Press.

Wilson, H. J., & Daugherty, P. R. (2018). Collaborative intelligence: Humans and AI are joining forces. *Harvard Business Review, 96*(4), 114–123.

Wilson, K., & Caliskan, A. (2024). Gender, race, and intersectional bias in resume screening via language model retrieval. In *Proceedings of the 2024 AAAI/ACM Conference on AI, Ethics, and Society* (pp. 1578–1590). Association for Computing Machinery. DOI: 10.1609/aies.v7i1.31748

Wolff, J., Pauling, J., Keck, A., & Baumbach, J. (2021). Success factors of artificial intelligence implementation in healthcare. *Frontiers in Digital Health, 3*, 594971. DOI: 10.3389/fdgth.2021.594971 PMID: 34713083

Wood, A. J., Graham, M., Lehdonvirta, V., & Hjorth, I. (2018). Good gig, bad gig: Autonomy and algorithmic control in the global gig economy. *Work, Employment and Society, 33*(1), 56–75. DOI: 10.1177/0950017018785616 PMID: 30886460

Woodward, R. (2022). OECD reform. In Routledge eBooks (pp. 122–140). DOI: 10.4324/9781351025867-7

World Bank. (2024). Accelerated by COVID and AI, global digital landscape remains uneven [Press release]. https://www.worldbank.org/en/news/press-release/2024/03/05/accelerated-by-covid-and-ai-global-digital-landscape-remains-uneven

World Economic Forum. (2023). The future of jobs report 2023. World Economic Forum.

World Economic Forum. (2023). *The future of jobs report 2023*. World Economic Forum. https://www.weforum.org/publications/the-future-of-jobs-report-2023/

World Economic Forum. (2025). *The future of jobs report 2025*. World Economic Forum. https://www.weforum.org/publications/the-future-of-jobs-report-2025/

World Economic Forum. (2026). *Four futures for jobs in the new economy: AI and talent in 2030*. World Economic Forum. https://www.weforum.org/publications/four-futures-for-jobs-in-the-new-economy-ai-and-talent-in-2030/

World Intellectual Property Organization. (2024). Patent landscape report on generative artificial intelligence. WIPO. https://www.wipo.int/en/web/patent-analytics/generative-ai

Xu, Z., Ren, F., Wang, P., Cao, J., Tan, C., Ma, D., Zhao, L., Dai, J., Ding, Y., Fang, H., Li, H., Liu, H., Luo, F., Meng, Y., Pan, P., Xiang, P., Xiao, Z., Rao, S., Satler, C., & Zhavoronkov, A. (2025). A generative AI-discovered TNIK inhibitor for idiopathic pulmonary fibrosis: A randomized phase 2a trial. *Nature Medicine*, *31*(8), 2602–2610. DOI: 10.1038/s41591-025-03743-2 PMID: 40461817

Yeung, K. (2018). Algorithmic regulation: A critical interrogation. *Regulation & Governance*, *12*(4), 505–523. DOI: 10.1111/rego.12158

Yu, X., Xu, S., & Ashton, M. (2023). Antecedents and outcomes of artificial intelligence adoption and application in the workplace: The socio-technical system theory perspective. *Information Technology & People*, *36*(7), 2584–2616. DOI: 10.1108/ITP-04-2021-0254

Zawish, M., Dharejo, F. A., Khowaja, S. A., Raza, S., Davy, S., Dev, K., & Bellavista, P. (2024). AI and 6G into the metaverse: Fundamentals, challenges and future research trends. *IEEE Open Journal of the Communications Society*, *5*, 731–758. DOI: 10.1109/OJCOMS.2024.3349465

Zeng, Z., Pantic, M., Roisman, G. I., & Huang, T. (2022). A survey of affect recognition methods: Audio, visual, and spontaneous expressions. *IEEE Transactions on Pattern Analysis and Machine Intelligence*, *44*(1), 11–38. PMID: 19029545

Zhang, A. (2018). Study on ecologicalization of electronic information industry. 2018 4th International Conference on Education, Management and Information Technology (ICEMIT 2018). DOI: 10.25236/icemit.2018.211

Zhang, L., & Leidner, D. (2023). The growth mindset and digital transformation: The human side of AI adoption. *Information Systems Journal*, *33*(2), 217–238.

Zhang, Y., Liao, Q. V., & Bellamy, R. K. E. (2020). Effect of confidence and explanation on accuracy and trust calibration in AI-assisted decision making. *Proceedings of the 2020 ACM Conference on Fairness, Accountability, and Transparency*, 295–306. https://doi.org/DOI: 10.1145/3351095.3372852

Zhang, Z. (2023). The impact of the artificial intelligence industry on the number and structure of employments in the digital economy environment. *Technological Forecasting and Social Change*, *197*, 122881. DOI: 10.1016/j.techfore.2023.122881

Zhou, G., Chu, G., Li, L., & Meng, L. (2020). The effect of artificial intelligence on China's labor market. *China Economic Journal*, *13*(1), 24–41. DOI: 10.1080/17538963.2019.1681201

Zhou, J., Müller, H., Holzinger, A., & Chen, F. (2024). Ethical ChatGPT: Concerns, challenges, and commandments. *Electronics (Basel)*, *13*(17), 3417. Advance online publication. DOI: 10.3390/electronics13173417

Zirar, A. (2023). Worker and workplace AI coexistence: Emerging themes and research agenda. *Technology in Society*, *75*, 102322. DOI: 10.1016/j.techsoc.2023.102322

Zohuri, B., & Mossavar-Rahmani, F. (2024). The symbiotic evolution: Artificial intelligence (AI) enhancing human intelligence (HI) an innovative technology collaboration and synergy. *Journal of Material Sciences and Applied Engineering*, *3*(1), 01–05. DOI: 10.63620/MKJMSAE.2024.1015

Zou, T., & Li, F. (2025). Generative artificial intelligence adoption and the future of cognitive and social skills. *arXiv preprint arXiv:2503.09212*. https://arxiv.org/abs/2503.09212

Zubaidi, H., & Elsaid, M. (2024). AI in the workplace: A systematic review of skill transformation in the industry. *Administrative Sciences*, *14*(6), 127. DOI: 10.3390/admsci14060127

About the Contributors

Agnieszka Wójcik-Czerniawska Warsaw School of Economics; Department of Management and Finance. The PhD of Economics field- Management based on the thesis" Development strategies of enterprises in the biofuel sector"; MBA in Spanish- ICEX-CECO- Madrid, DBA (Doctor of Business Administration,), LL.D (Doctor of Laws), DPH (Doctor of Public Health). Visiting Professor at many foreign Universities in Europe (Italy, Spain, France) and World (Peru, Kenya, Turkey, Georgia). The area of research are connected with: modern finance, finance technology, digital currency, financial isolation, silver generation, circular economy, innovative marketing, society in digitalization world. The participant in many international conferences in all around the world. The keynote speak in world conferences in: Milan, Turkey, Republic of South Africa, Ireland, Bahrain, London . The polyglot with more than twelve languages. The classes with the student will be about: " Finance of the changing world".

***

Burcu Arsan completed her Ph.D. in Management and Organization at Yeditepe University. Her current research focuses on digital transformation in organizations and the formation of cyber culture. She holds a Master of Business Administration (MBA) degree from Yeditepe University and a Bachelor's degree in Healthcare Management from Acıbadem University. She is currently teaching Management courses at both Yeditepe University and Boğaziçi University. Dr. Arsan's academic interests include organizational behavior, digital leadership, and the integration of technological advancements into healthcare systems.

V Arunkumar is an assistant Professor and Placement officer - School of Management in SASTRA Deemed University. He has bachelor degree in Computer Application, MBA in marketing & HR, Ph.D in Business Administration Having

14 years of teaching experience in various HRM, marketing and business subjects (HRM, Entrepreneurship, E-commerce, Advertisement, Digital Marketing and more). Guiding the Research students in the Industry5.0 area. He has intimate connections with various corporate networks, co-ordinated SASTRA - TCS CSR projects (teaching, learning center), This projects hold a net worth of 3.5 crores. Faculty co-ordinator for UGC PARAMARSH and AICTE MARGDARSHAN projects.

Tanushri Bagdi is a young researcher and management student with a keen interest in business, technology, and emerging trends in society. Her work primarily focuses on the impact of artificial intelligence, business transformation, taxation, and digital innovation. She is passionate about exploring how modern technologies influence industries, employment, and organizational growth. Along with her academic interests, she has experience in digital marketing, team coordination, and business operations, which adds practical insight to her research work. Tanushri actively engages in content development, project management, and creative business initiatives. Her article reflects her interest in combining academic knowledge with real-world business perspectives, aiming to contribute meaningful insights to contemporary research discussions.

Pankaj Bhambri is an Associate Professor in the Department of Information Technology at Guru Nanak Dev Engineering College, Ludhiana, with over twenty-one years of teaching and research experience. He holds a Ph.D. in Computer Science and Engineering from I.K.G. Punjab Technical University, Jalandhar, and is currently pursuing a Post Doctorate Fellowship at Lincoln University College, Malaysia. Recognized as a Top 2% Scientist by Stanford University and Elsevier in 2025, his research focuses on areas including machine learning, AI-driven digital twins, blockchain, and sustainable technologies. He has an extensive publication record in Scopus-indexed books and journals and has guided several Ph.D. candidates to completion.

Rupam Hazra, a passionate and determined student currently pursuing a Bachelor of Technology (BTech) in Computer Science and Engineering at Krishnanagar GIMT. I have a strong interest in the fields of Artificial Intelligence, Cybersecurity, and emerging technologies. With a dedication to academic excellence and innovation, I have authored 16 research publications in globally recognized platforms, focusing on real-world applications and technological advancement.

Herath is an Associate Professor of Accounting at Clark Atlanta University. Her academic distinction was highlighted in 2022 when she was named a Renwick Faculty Fellow at New York University Stern School of Business . She holds impressive academic credentials, including a Ph.D. and MCOM Honors in Accounting from University of Wollongong, and an MBA and BCOM (Hons) from University of Colombo. She is also a recipient of membership in Beta Gamma Sigma, the international business honor society recognizing top-performing business students. Her extensive experience includes faculty roles at numerous institutions, such as the University of Lynchburg, Georgia State University, Georgia Institute of Technology, and several universities internationally. A prolific researcher, Dr. Herath has contributed over 80 publications, including 23 book chapters, with research focused on key areas like Accounting Education, Management Control, Data Analytics, and Sustainability Accounting. Her commitment to the field is further demonstrated by her current role as Editor-In-Chief for both the Asian Journal of Economics and Business and the Global Journal of Accounting and Economy Research, and her service on other editorial boards. She also holds a TESOL Professional Certificate from Arizona State University and the Professional Certificate in Google Data Analytics. Furthermore, she is a Distinguished Toastmaster (DTM) and has held leadership positions within Toastmasters International, serving as an Area Director and as President and Treasurer for the Georgia Institute of Technology club.

Siddhi Juneja is a finance and economics student at CHRIST University with a strong interest in financial analysis, investment research, and global business studies. Her academic interests include corporate finance, economics, and international markets. Siddhi is passionate about research, analytical problem-solving, and exploring emerging trends in business and finance.

Anita Maharani is an expert in Human Resources. She currently is responsible of blended learning in master program. She published more than 20 international journal articles.

Rachna Rana is an Associate Professor in the Department of Computer Science and Engineering at Ludhiana Group of Colleges, Ludhiana with over fifteen years of teaching and research experience. Her research focuses on areas including machine learning, wireless sensor networks, and network security. She has an extensive publication record in Scopus-indexed books.

Rajveer received his Ph.D. from Bharathiar University, Tamil Nadu, India, and his MBA in finance from the Cardiff Metropolitan University, Wales, UK. He teaches in the Department of Business & Management at CHRIST University. His research interests include areas of Capital Markets, Investment Analysis, and Portfolio Management, and he has more than 25 years of experience in the above, covering the US and Indian Markets. He is the author of the popular financial blog Ahead of the Curve. He reviews for Emerald and Sage.

Göran Roos is a globally recognised expert in intellectual capital management, manufacturing competitiveness, industry policy, and innovation systems. With around 19,000 Google citations and more than 300 publications, he has established himself as a leading authority on strategic management, economic complexity, and sustainable industrial development. Academic Credentials and Appointments Professor Roos holds a PhD from the University of South Australia (2019), an MBA from INSEAD (1989), and an MSc in Engineering Physics from Chalmers University of Technology (1982). His current academic positions and fellowships include: • Adjunct Professor at the Institute for Sustainability, Energy and Resources (ISER), The University of Adelaide (2023-2025) • Fellow of the Australian Academy of Technological Sciences and Engineering (ATSE) since 2014 • Fellow of the Royal Swedish Academy of Engineering Sciences (IVA) since 2015 Areas of Expertise Intellectual Capital and Knowledge Management Professor Roos is a world-renowned expert in intellectual capital, having developed theories and implemented practical solutions that have shaped the

Sachin Sharma is currently working as a Professor at Amity School of Engineering and Technology, Amity University Punjab, Mohali, India. He also worked as Associate Dean of International Affairs and Professor, Department of Computer Science and Engineering at Graphic Era Deemed to be University, Dehradun, Uttarakhand, India. He has experience of 16+ years in industry and academia. He is also Co-founder and Chief Technology officer (CTO) of IntelliNexus LLC, Arkansas, USA based company. He also worked as a Senior Systems Engineer at Belkin International, Inc., Irvine, California, USA. He received his Philosophy of Doctorate (Ph.D.) degree in Engineering Science and Systems specialization in Systems Engineering from University of Arkansas at Little Rock, USA with 4.0 out 4.0 GPA and M.S. degree in Systems engineering from University of Arkansas at Little Rock with 4.0 out 4.0 GPA. Dr. Sharma has authored/coauthored over 300+ publications in the form of books, book chapters, patents, and papers in refereed journals and conference proceedings. He holds 100+ US, Indian and international patents in the area of IoT, wireless communication.

Jae Koo Yoo is an instructor in the Department of Decision Sciences Supply Chain Management at Clark Atlanta University. He received his MBA from Clark Atlanta University. He certified SAP Business Associated in SAP ERP 6.0 EHP5 (TERP 10), SAP Certified Business Associate – BPI with SAP S/4 HANA, and ERPSim level 2. His research interests include Business Intelligence, Data Mining, Business Warehouse, Business Objects, and Business Analysis.

Esin Yucel holds a Ph.D. in Business Administration (Management and Organization) from Yeditepe University. She is currently a Lecturer in Business Management at the University of Bedfordshire, where she teaches graduate courses on strategy, organisational behaviour, leadership, and people analytics. Her research interests include organisational behaviour, leadership, human resource management, diversity management, and the future of work, and she has published extensively in international journals, books, and edited volumes. Before her academic career, Dr. Yucel held managerial positions for many years in multinational companies both in Turkey and abroad. She also served in senior administrative roles at universities, including as Vice Dean. Beyond her teaching and academic leadership, Dr. Yucel has guided numerous graduate theses and plays an active role in the academic community as an editor, reviewer, and contributor to scholarly publications. She is also an active member of professional organisations such as CILT and WILAT Turkey.

Index

A

C

D

E

F

G

H

I

L

O

S

T

W

www.ingramcontent.com/pod-product-compliance
Lightning Source LLC
LaVergne TN
LVHW081545300926
849161LV00006B/1516